MW00856209

INTEGRATIONS

INTE

GRATIONS

*The Struggle for Racial
Equality and Civic Renewal
in Public Education*

Lawrence Blum and Zoë Burkholder

THE UNIVERSITY OF CHICAGO PRESS
Chicago and London

The University of Chicago Press, Chicago 60637
The University of Chicago Press, Ltd., London
© 2021 by The University of Chicago
All rights reserved. No part of this book may be used or reproduced in any manner
whatsoever without written permission, except in the case of brief quotations in critical
articles and reviews. For more information, contact the University of Chicago Press,
1427 E. 60th St., Chicago, IL 60637.
Published 2021
Printed in the United States of America

30 29 28 27 26 25 24 23 22 21   1 2 3 4 5

ISBN-13: 978-0-226-78598-1 (cloth)
ISBN-13: 978-0-226-78603-2 (paper)
ISBN-13: 978-0-226-78617-9 (e-book)
DOI: https://doi.org/10.7208/chicago/9780226786179.001.0001

Library of Congress Cataloging-in-Publication Data

Names: Blum, Lawrence A., author. | Burkholder, Zoë, author.
Title: Integrations : the struggle for racial equality and civic renewal in public education /
    Lawrence Blum and Zoë Burkholder.
Other titles: History and philosophy of education.
Description: Chicago ; London : The University of Chicago Press, 2021. | Series: The history
    and philosophy of education series | Includes bibliographical references and index.
Identifiers: LCCN 2020046182 | ISBN 9780226785981 (cloth) | ISBN 9780226786032
    (paperback) | ISBN 9780226786179 (ebook)
Subjects: LCSH: Educational equalization—United States. | Racism in education—
    United States. | Racism in education—United States—History. | Minorities—
    Education—United States—History. | School integration—United States. | Educational
    equalization—Philosophy.
Classification: LCC LC213.2 .B58 2021 | DDC 379.2/60973—dc23
LC record available at https://lccn.loc.gov/2020046182

♾ This paper meets the requirements of ANSI/NISO Z39.48-1992 (Permanence of Paper).

Larry Blum dedicates this book to Judy Smith.

Zoë Burkholder dedicates this book to her parents,
Christina Miesowitz Burkholder and Ervin Burkholder.

CONTENTS

INTRODUCTION

THE FAULT LINE IN PUBLIC EDUCATION

The promise of a free, high-quality public education from kindergarten through high school for all children regardless of race, socioeconomic standing, religion, geographic location, and even immigration status is an enduring component of the American creed.

Unfortunately, America's public schools have been unable to keep this promise for all, and many of the students left behind are children of color. The US Department of Education recently concluded:

> Our education system, legally desegregated more than a half century ago, is ever more segregated by wealth and income, and often again by race. Ten million students in America's poorest communities—and millions more African American, Latino, Asian American, Pacific Islander, American Indian and Alaska Native students who are not poor—are having their lives unjustly and irredeemably blighted by a system that consigns them to the lowest-performing teachers, the most run-down facilities, and academic expectations and opportunities considerably lower than what we expect of other students. These vestiges of segregation, discrimination, and inequality are unfinished business for our nation.[1]

This book examines the enduring problem of racial inequality in American public schools through a historical and philosophical analysis. Our goal is to help readers better understand racial inequality in the American public education system in order to advocate for more equitable and just forms of schooling. To do so requires a meticulous consideration of school segregation and inequality and what has often been assumed to be its most obvious cure—integration.

Today, American public schools are noticeably segregated in terms of race and, since the late 1980s, have been "resegregating"—or becoming more racially segregated—so that today Black students are more likely to attend segregated schools than they were in 1970. A massive body of scholarship finds a direct link, though not always a causal one, between racial segregation and educational inequality. Legal historian James E. Ryan contends this "boundary has been the fault line of public education for half a century, doing more than anything else to define and shape the educational opportunities of public school students. On one side stand predominantly white, middle-income, and relatively successful schools. On the other side stand predominantly minority, poor, and relatively unsuccessful schools."[2]

This fault line has a long and shameful history in America, one that is intertwined with restrictions in housing, employment, and generational wealth. As early as 1903, W. E. B. Du Bois pronounced, "The problem of the Twentieth Century is the problem of the color-line."[3] For much of the nineteenth and twentieth centuries, racially explicit policies of federal, state, and local governments defined where whites and people of color could live—and where their kids were allowed go to school. Historian Richard Rothstein confirms, "Today's residential segregation in the North, South, Midwest, and West is not the unintended consequence of individual choices and of otherwise well-meaning law or regulation but of unhidden public policy that explicitly segregated every metropolitan area in the United States. The policy was so systematic and forceful that its effects endure to the present time."[4]

High levels of school segregation and inequality create a national achievement gap between white and Asian students on one side and Black, Latinx, and Native American on the other. The average Black eighth grader is performing at the nineteenth percentile of white students, and the average Latinx student is at the twenty-sixth percentile. Native Americans as a group lag behind all other students in both reading and math.[5] Asian American students fall on both sides of the equation—many are within a subgroup that outperforms white students, but Asian American students from marginalized ethnic groups slip through the cracks.[6] These racial achievement gaps are explained not by an individual student's racial identity but by whether a student attended an under-resourced, majority-minority school or was subjected to racial discrimination in an integrated, well-resourced one.[7] Despite the tremendous success of the civil rights movement and significant gains in educational equality, the color line in public education remains both durable and devastating.

Racial inequality in American public education is not permanent, natural, fixed, or unchangeable. In fact, we believe that the time is ripe to eradicate racial inequality in our public schools once and for all. A long history of successful reforms in American public schools prove that our current system can be improved. We believe that well-informed parents, students, teachers, administrators, and citizens can bring about revolutionary changes to the way we think about and run public schools in ways that will prioritize racial and social justice. Not only can we improve educational equality and dismantle institutionalized racism, but we can also strengthen the civic function of public education in a democracy.

Our study is distinctive in our interdisciplinary approach grounded in both history and philosophy. Through a historical lens in the first half of the book, we analyze how ideas about race influenced the creation and development of public schools from their formation in the mid-nineteenth century to the present; how educational discrimination played out very differently for African American, Native American, Latinx, and Asian American communities; and how educational activists in those communities sought educational equality, the in-school promotion of their distinctive cultures and heritages, self-determination, and—ambivalently and in different ways—school integration. Prominently featured in this social history are firsthand accounts of the courageous women, men, and students who fought against racial discrimination in public education and worked tirelessly to transform schools into institutions that came closer to the democratic ideal.

In the second philosophical half of the book, readers will grapple with what an equal education based on this history should and could look like. What is equal when education is equal? Is it opportunities to compete for unequal rewards in the job market? Or is it an array of intrinsic educational goods related to moral, personal, and civic growth?

How exactly does "race" interact with questions of educational equality? How does class-based injustice (for example, in housing, health, income, and wealth) inevitably play a part in racial injustice? What constitutes fair and appropriate reparations to communities who have suffered generations of discrimination in public (including educational) institutions?

We also tackle the most exalted and controversial ideal in the struggle for racial justice in education: school integration. Decades of civil rights activism focused specifically on this objective, although with significant variations among different communities. Yet when we look more closely, we see that disagreements over the desirability of integration were often caused by competing definitions—does integration simply mean students of different races attending schools together, or does it require that they be treated respectfully and equally inside the school? Does integration mean the eventual diminishing of racial and ethnic identities through assimilation, as the early twentieth-century form of schooling often encouraged? Or does integration allow, or even require, the affirming of students' distinct racial and ethnic identities that minority educational activists sought?

In addition, many citizens have questioned whether integration (in any of its forms) is required—or even beneficial—to the larger struggle for racial justice. Throughout American history, some people of color have argued for self-determination in education, specifically the right to control school administration, teacher hiring, curriculum development, discipline policies, and educational objectives. These activists vehemently oppose state-sponsored school segregation but are cautious in their support of deliberate school integration policies and sometimes advocate separate, community-controlled schools as a vital alternative.

In this book, we propose a conception of integration closely tied to egalitarian, civic-minded schools committed to the training of future citizens for a pluralistic democracy. This conception draws inspiration from the visionary educational activism we have described.[8] But ultimately, we argue that unless and until the larger structures of race and class injustice in society as a whole are dismantled, it will be impossible to achieve both the goal of educational equality and the civic equality for which civic education aims.

UNDERSTANDING RACE

A thorough reckoning of racial inequality in American public schools necessitates a shared vocabulary for speaking about racial diversity and inequality. "Race" has traditionally referred to an intergenerational human group that differed from other such groups in visible physical features, ancestral origins in particular continents or regions (sub-Saharan Africa, Europe, East Asia), and attributes of temperament, character, and intelligence seen as inherent in their nature and thus immutable. Generally, these differing characteristics cast some groups as superior to others, resulting in a hierarchy in which every group is posited on a scale above or below one another. These false ideas have been used historically to deny basic rights, civic standing, and decent treatment to the groups regarded as inferior.[9]

But scientists today, including geneticists and physical anthropologists, agree that there are no races in this sense and that there never were. Groups that roughly contrast in visible characteristics and ancestral origins do not sufficiently differ from one another genetically for the massive distinctions in human characteristics required by this traditional understanding of race to exist.[10] The very long and continual history of human migration means that people have always been mixing up the gene pool, and even geographically isolated groups do not differ from one another genetically in substantial ways.

Many Americans at least consciously reject the idea of race and are somewhat aware that scientists have rejected it. Yet almost everyone, both believers and disbelievers in race, continues to use racial terminology such as "Black," "Latino," and "Asian" to refer to groups and individuals. Why is that? Shouldn't we drop racial terminology entirely and refer to these groups and individuals in some other way—for example, as ethnic groups—African American, Mexican American, Korean American? Or perhaps we should just drop racial language entirely without putting anything else in its place. If race implies the possession of inherent psychological characteristics, but the groups we call races do not possess those characteristics, shouldn't we stop using words that have that implication?

We think not. Racial terminology is still useful and even essential because the groups we call races were historically viewed and treated as if they did possess those characteristics. That treatment—in the case of Blacks, enslavement, segregation, and racial discrimination; of Mexicans, territorial annexation, segregation, and discrimination; of Native Americans, displacement, genocide, forced assimilation, and discrimination—was guided by a racial ideology that said these groups deserved inferior and harmful treatment because they were inferior to whites. These were false ideologies and ideas, but they had real influence on the historical experiences of Black, Mexican, Native American, Asian American, and white people. These groups were racialized by being treated as if they were races, and so we can call them not races but *racialized groups*. Therefore, we can think of "Black," "white," and "Native American" as referring to racialized groups, even though they once referred to groups thought of as actual races.[11]

People of color's historical experiences with racialization are largely negative, characterized by oppression and discrimination. But racialized experiences have not been solely negative. They have also encompassed resistance to unjust treatment and the development of alternative ideologies committed to liberation and justice. Thus, political struggle against racial mistreatment also forms a part of racialized experience; slave rebellions, anticolonial struggles, and equal rights movements for racially subordinated peoples, as well as intellectual and artistic challenges to racist ideas and representations, all contribute to the foundation of a positive sense of peoplehood within a racialized group. If the meaning of race were confined to associations of superior and inferior racial groups, it would be incomprehensible why so many people conventionally understood as "black" identify with the (now-preferred) racial term *Black*, take pride in being Black, and cherish Black identity and solidarity. This usage instead expresses a positive vision of shared identity among a group understood as racialized while rejecting the negative associations that accompany conceiving of Blacks as an actual race.[12] Similarly, "white" can name a group that, while not viewed as inherently superior, is understood as benefiting in the present from the creation of an international historical racial order, rationalized by racial ideology. This hierarchy created a sense of racial solidarity for many white citizens and mobilized them to take action to protect their privilege. Understanding racial inequality in the long history of American public schools requires us to acknowledge these racialized identities and processes.

The challenge is to think of, and talk about, Black, white, Asian American, Latinx, and Native American people in ways that avoid attributing inherent characteristics to these identities, especially any that imply inherent superiority and inferiority, while recognizing that these groups have distinctive social and historical experiences. We have to acknowledge those historical and social differences and simultaneously wholly reject the racial ideology that informed them. It is true that retaining racial language, such as "Black," "white," "Native American," and so forth, to name racialized groups has an unfortunate potentiality for reinforcing racial and racist ideas, even when the speaker disavows those conceptions. This is why scare quotes are sometimes used for terms like "Black" or "white" as a way of indicating that racialization rather than race is intended. But many people find that usage annoying and clumsy, and we will stick with the familiar terminology, reminding the reader that we use it to refer to racialized groups, not actual races.

For our book, we investigate the question of racial equality in public schools by focusing on four racialized minority groups: African Americans, Native Americans, Latinxs, and Asian Americans. Of course, white people play a prominent role in this history. We will use the term *white*, not Caucasian, to describe people of European descent, as the latter term, while more technical sounding, is a sinister holdover from the era of scientific racism. Everyone who does not identify as white will be described by the generic term *people of color*, which is distinct from the dated term *colored people*. Americans of African descent are described as Black or African American, and we often use these terms interchangeably, except when highlighting a more recent American Black ethnic group, such as Haitians or Cape Verdeans. The term *Latinx* recognizes a preferred gender-neutral form embraced by many younger Americans who are either from, or who have ancestry from, Latin America. Whenever relevant, we employ more specific ethnic identities such as Puerto Rican or Mexican American. Indigenous people in the United States often refer to themselves as American Indians or Indigenous Americans, but here we use the term *Native American*. These terms are all contemporary, but at times we will cite historical documents that use other words to describe racial difference in America. Some of these terms, such as "Negro" or "colored," were once the terms of choice for African Americans but are no longer appropriate today. Other terms of reference, needless to say, were deliberately demeaning or intended to shore up white supremacy.[13]

RACE AND AMERICAN EDUCATION

Our analysis of racial equality in public schools focuses on the experiences and activism of people of color, specifically in African American, Native American, Latinx, and Asian American communities. It is worth noting, however, that some children from groups now thought of as white have also suffered racial discrimination in American schools. During the late nineteenth and early twentieth centuries, American teachers viewed many European immigrants, including Jewish students, as racially distinct from the "native," white Anglo-Saxon Protestant "stock." These educators also frequently complained about the "racial traits" of immigrant children from Russia, Greece, Italy, and other European countries that Americans would now consider "white." One New Jersey school administrator wrote in 1916, "The influx of foreigners, with their divergent personal ideals and antagonistic racial traits, imposes upon the schools an infinitely difficult problem."[14] And yet, even though certain white ethnic and religious groups faced discrimination based on perceived racial differences, they were nevertheless regarded officially as "white" under the 1790 naturalization law confining citizenship to "free white persons."[15] Although some educators may have viewed European immigrant students as racially distinct, they were still understood to be white and eligible for American citizenship—and the full benefits of a public education.[16]

Despite the hardships experienced by some white racialized minorities, people classified as "nonwhite" or "colored" suffered more severe exclusion, segregation, and deliberate and sustained educational discrimination. But which students qualified as "colored"? Although we might imagine the color line in education to be fairly obvious, with white people of European descent on one side and everyone else on the other "colored" side, the truth is more complex when examining American history. In order to separate students based on race—either by law, as was the case in the Jim Crow South, or through social pressure, as was the case in many other parts of the country—someone was required to do the dirty work of figuring out school assignments. Some schools in California, for example, decided to segregate Chinese American students from white students, while Japanese Americans attended the "white" schools.[17] Whites in Mississippi classified Chinese Americans as "colored" and sent them to school with Black children, when just across the river in neighboring Arkansas, school administrators considered Chinese American students as "white" and segregated them from Black students.[18] In Virginia, precious resources were wasted to establish separate schools for white, Black, and Native American children—but administrators refused to allow Monacan Indians to attend any of these schools, as the racially mixed Monacans did not fit neatly into any category.[19] The city of Houston, Texas, operated separate schools for white, Black, and Mexican American students well into the modern civil rights era.[20] As this book will show, the color line in public education, while formidable, was also contradictory, ambiguous, illogical, and changed over time and across arbitrary borders. This inherent racial instability made public schools vulnerable, and educational activists used school boycotts, diplomatic pressure, petitions, and lawsuits to challenge unjust and discriminatory school segregation.[21]

Whites responded in kind, eager to maintain control over these venerable citizenship-training institutions as minority educational activism expanded in the early twentieth century. Public schools erupted as the sites of fierce culture wars over not only school segregation but also control of curriculum and pedagogy. From the common school era of the 1820s through the civil rights era of the 1960s, whites believed that proper education required the destruction of minority cultures, whether they were European, Native American, Mexican, Puerto Rican, Chinese, Japanese, or African American. Schools were not apologetic in their aggressive assimilation of children; to the contrary, Americans expected public schools to forge a common culture out of a polyglot citizenry. Teachers understood it as their professional duty to "weld the many peoples of any community into one body politic and create throughout the nation the unity and power that come from common ideals, a common language, and a uniform interpretation of citizenship."[22] When teachers floundered, lawmakers stepped in to help. For instance, southwestern states outlawed the use of any non-English language in public schools in an effort to force Mexican American students to assimilate. More tragically, official US policy required Native Americans to surrender their children to government-run boarding schools for the explicit purpose of what amounts to cultural genocide.[23]

Although whites had the power to determine educational policies and curricula, students of color did not function as blank slates, passively receiving whatever education was doled out by school authorities. Students, parents, and community leaders developed formidable responses to educational racism and fought to remake schools to suit their own purposes. Black educators quietly explained that white claims of racial superiority were false and taught Black children that the American dream was their birthright as well. "America means opportunity for the ambitious man to develop his power to the fullest extent," insisted a southern Black teacher during the height of Jim Crow.[24]

When the Black civil rights movement erupted during World War II, grassroots coalitions of Black students, parents, teachers, and leaders organized to challenge racial injustice in schools and the larger society. "The time to sing the blues and play Uncle Tom is passed," wrote an impassioned Black teacher in 1944. "Negroes, like all other real men, must win by their STRENGTH, rather than their WEAKNESS."[25] Although there were far fewer Latinx, Native American, and Asian American public school teachers during the era of school segregation, educational activists from these communities also worked to resist white oppression and remodel public education. The history of American education, therefore, reveals both how whites instituted racist practices in public schools and how people of color subverted these efforts and transformed local schools into institutions that reflected their own hopes and dreams for democratic public education.[26]

CHAPTER SUMMARIES

Integrations: The Struggle for Racial Equality and Civic Renewal in Public Education begins with a historical analysis of racialized minorities in American public schools and then turns to philosophical considerations of equality, civic purpose, racial justice, and integration.

Chapter 1, "Segregation," investigates the histories of African American, Native American, Mexican American, Chinese American, and Japanese American students from the earliest public schools through the *Brown v. Board of Education* ruling in 1954. It demonstrates that white officials intentionally discriminated against students of color first by excluding them from early public schools, then by segregating them as access to public education expanded, and finally by attempting to limit the curriculum for students of color to "manual training" and industrial work. It also highlights how minority educational activists fought back through both direct legal and political attacks on segregated schools as well as more subtle forms of accommodation and resistance. A key finding is that while it was clear to all that segregated facilities engendered unequal opportunities, many activists nevertheless questioned integration as a solution, and some saw enormous value in schools led by Black, Mexican American, or indigenous educators. World War II and the rising postwar civil rights movements centered new attention on segregated schools as a tool of white supremacy that must be abolished.

Chapter 2, "Desegregation," opens in 1954 as the nation's highest court proclaimed, "In the field of public education, the doctrine of 'separate but equal' has no place. Separate educational facilities are inherently unequal."[27] Although *Brown* is rightly celebrated as an epic civil rights milestone, its lasting influence on educational equality is less clear. Where school integration worked, especially in the South, educational inequality was significantly reduced, and the degree of positive interracial contact between students increased. But over time these gains were reversed, and many students of color never experienced the benefits of integrated schools. This chapter explores African American, Native American, Latinx, and Asian American struggles for more equitable and integrated schools after 1954. It also considers how and why people of color sometimes pursued alternatives to integration, such as community control, in hopes of attaining both educational equality as well as other goals like self-determination and community empowerment. We emphasize the tremendous educational victories in the post-*Brown* era while acknowledging that school desegregation did not achieve the intent of equalizing educational opportunities for all students of color. Chapter 2 emphasizes three key findings: first, that white citizens, often unapologetically, opposed school integration and equalization measures from 1954 to the present; second, that improvements in public education were a direct result of sustained educational activism by communities of color; and third, that over time educational activists developed multiple nuanced conceptions of school integration as one possible tactic, among many, to equalize public education. This long history of educational activism and the multiple visions of school integration that came out of it, we argue, provide crucial lessons for how to revive public education today.

Chapter 3, "Equality," examines the ideal of equal education that rests at the center of racial justice in education. US citizens often see the idea of "opportunity" as the content of this ideal, but we argue that the American ideal of equality of opportunity is focused too narrowly on marketable skills and competition for rewards, omitting the distinctly educational value of what is learned in school. It also fails to provide students with the critical perspective, and the corresponding intellectual capabilities, to recognize injustice in society and form life goals without being beholden to current cultural structures and dominant values. We argue for a conception of "educational goods" (including the development of moral and civic capacities) that are valuable in their own right, as well as to society, and that should and can be provided to every child through schooling.

We also argue that schools by themselves cannot create educational justice. Genuine educational equality can be only partially realized in a society as unjust and unequal as ours. Educational justice must ally with class- and race-focused initiatives and activism for economic, health, and housing justice. These initiatives must lift up families and students at the low end of the economic spectrum, curb the ability of advantaged families to hoard opportunities for themselves, and correct for a history of specifically racial injustices against students of color.

We ask what are the responsibilities of different constituencies—parents, students, teachers, citizens—to ensure that our public schools deliver on the promise of educational equality to all. And, finally, we confront some of the pedagogical challenges of teaching diverse students about struggles for historical and contemporary justice.

Chapters 4 and 5, "Integrations: The Capital Argument" and "Integrations: The Civic Argument," explore the ideal of school integration as it relates to educational equality and racial justice. We suggest that integration should be thought of in the plural—as "integrations"—so that we can better evaluate its various forms. Does integration involve students of different racial identities learning together in the same schools, or does it require a more "ideal" definition that requires respect, welcoming, and concern across these racial divides? Various arguments have been given for integration in one or another of its forms. We will look in detail at a prominent contemporary argument—that disadvantaged students benefit from being in schools with advantaged students (the advantages in question can be either racial or class-based) because the latter possess more social, financial, and cultural "capital." We find not only very little merit in this argument but also serious drawbacks. However, if a school takes a social justice perspective on society and education itself, capital benefits can be embraced without shaming disadvantaged families or encouraging a morally damaging sense of entitlement in advantaged families.

Ultimately, the strongest argument that we find for integration is civic in character, breathing renewed life into what has until recently been a central purpose of public education. Bringing diverse students into the same classes (which requires avoiding academic tracking) is the most secure foundation for developing students' civic knowledge and capability, which will enable them to work together to enhance and promote justice within the multiracial democracy they share. At the same time, integrated schools must be able to protect and affirm the plurality of students' racial and ethnic identities, not adopt a color-blind (much less assimilationist) form of integration. This *egalitarian civic integrationist pluralism* provides the strongest foundation for pursuing racial equality in American public schools, but it requires a substantial reduction of overall inequality and correcting for historical racial injustice outside the school.

CHAPTER 1

SEGREGATION

Established in the four decades preceding the Civil War, America's first free, tax-supported "common schools" taught reading, writing, arithmetic, and a little bit of geography and history, as well as Protestant morality, a sturdy work ethic, mastery of the English language, and patriotism. The purpose of common schools was to prepare young people to be active and engaged democratic citizens. As reformer Horace Mann wrote in 1846, the United States must provide a free education to all, "sufficient to qualify each citizen for the civil and social duties he will be called to discharge." Rich and poor, Catholic and Protestant, boy and girl—the public schools promised to forge a nation of immigrants into a united citizenry.[1]

This expansive undertaking, however, contained a major loophole. If public schools were designed to prepare democratic citizens, how would they treat people who didn't qualify for US citizenship? In the common school era, this included large numbers of African Americans, Native Americans, Chinese Americans, Japanese Americans, and Mexican Americans, as well as others understood to be nonwhite according to racial ideologies of the day. As historian James D. Anderson argues, Americans were "virtually obsessed with the ways in which race affected fundamental questions of citizenship, civil equality, and political power." By the time the question of citizenship for people of African, indigenous, Latin American, and Asian descent was mostly settled, public schools discriminated on the basis of race.[2]

It is worth noting that racial ideologies of the common school era also labeled many white ethnics as racially distinct from the Anglo-Saxon Protestant majority. Although some European immigrant students faced educational discrimination, they never experienced the deliberate, state-sponsored racism suffered by African American, Asian American, Native American, or Latin American students. As one teacher put it, students who were not of European ancestry failed the "obvious test of color" and should be treated accordingly.[3]

A growing body of scholarship investigates the dynamic educational histories of African American, American Indian, Native Alaskan, Native Hawaiian, Chinese American, Japanese American, and Mexican-origin communities. Thanks to this painstaking research we know more about both the tremendously varied and complex experiences of students of color in American public schools as well as the rich and nuanced forms of indigenous knowledge production and cultural transmission that took place outside of these institutions. We know less, however, about how racial ideologies functioned more broadly in educational history, how whites wielded state-sponsored racial discrimination as a form of power, and how people of color developed expansive, and at times contested, strategies to achieve counterhegemonic objectives that went well beyond securing equal educational opportunities.[4]

This chapter analyzes educational racism and struggles for racial equality in the histories of African Americans, Native Americans, Mexican Americans, and Chinese and Japanese Americans. It considers a small sample of the tremendously diverse experiences of students of color in the period leading up to *Brown v. Board of Education*, which outlawed (but did not end) racial segregation in the public schools. All history is contextually specific, and these few examples are not meant to depict the full range of historical encounters with education racism in the United States. We have selected a few compelling examples to illustrate the evolution of American educational racism while also emphasizing people of color as active agents of resistance and change.[5]

We argue that Americans built and reinforced state-sponsored educational racism through a three-part process involving the exclusion, segregation, and differentiation of resources and curriculum. Segregation, or dividing students on the basis of their racial identity, was essential to creating and maintaining inequality in public education. In his famous study of American race relations in 1944, Swedish economist Gunnar Myrdal observed, "One deep idea behind segregation is that of quarantining what is evil, shameful, and feared in society." In this sense, school segregation was a form of violence perpetrated by whites against students of color. Segregation is quite distinct from the project of separation, which was a voluntary strategy by people of color to establish and attend institutions dedicated to racial uplift and the affirmation of Black and indigenous identities. For instance, many African American and Native American educational activists have historically supported the option of separate, Black- and indigenous-led schools.[6]

All people of color committed to educational reform abhorred state-sponsored school segregation, however, debates over integration as a strategy for reform were persistent. The very meaning of school integration shifted depending on context—sometimes activists wanted to end the isolation of all students in a single classroom at a racially mixed school, while other times they were satisfied if a handful of Black children attended a white school.[7] In the Jim Crow South, integration posed a direct threat to Black teachers, which gave activists pause, while in other examples the preservation of teaching jobs was not a major concern. Some activists, moreover, did not target school segregation as problematic but instead attempted to manipulate the system by classifying their children as white in order to access better-resourced schools.

In other words, the ways that people of color understood the relationship between educational inequality and school segregation varied significantly based on specific barriers to equality and how they envisioned public schools as sites of community empowerment, and so it should come as no surprise that school integration took myriad complex forms. What follows is not a single history of the struggle for school integration in the United States but instead the histories of the many school integrations designed to remedy educational injustice and remake public education to secure the democratic ideal.[8]

EDUCATION AS LIBERATION

Born into enslavement in 1818, Frederick Douglass used the power of oratory and the written word to persuade Americans of the evils of human bondage. Like many nineteenth-century Black leaders, Douglass believed that "the direct pathway from slavery to freedom" was education. He campaigned for "equal school rights" for Black students, which for Douglass meant attending the new common schools on a nonsegregated basis. According to Douglass, if Black students attended school alongside white peers, common schools would reduce prejudice, improve race relations, and symbolize equal citizenship for all. Douglass prioritized public education's civic function in a democracy over more mundane concerns like preparing for a better-paying job. He believed public schooling had a singular power to help abolish enslavement and secure equal rights for African Americans during the era of slavery.[9]

Emancipation in 1863 brought about a fervent, almost missionary faith in education as a key to Black liberation. Numerous studies document the universal outcry for education among freedmen, women, and children of all ages in the South. At the end of the Civil War in 1865, there were very few free, tax-supported common schools anywhere in the region, and virtually none that were available to Black students. While sympathetic whites in the Union army, northern churches, the Freedmen's Bureau, and northern philanthropies established private schools for Black southerners, archival data reveal that freedpeople seized control of education for themselves. Literate African Americans stepped forward as teachers, community leaders, and political activists during the era of Reconstruction from 1865 to 1877, setting up schools in the South based on the model of northern common schools' academic curriculum.[10] Black families expressed a preference for Black teachers, and as many as one-third of all teachers in the new schools for freedpeople between 1861 and 1876 were Black. African American school attendance in the South grew from less than 2 percent in 1860 to 10 percent a decade later, then tripled to nearly 30 percent of school-aged children by 1880.[11]

When Reconstruction ended in 1877, southern whites reasserted their dominance by requiring literacy tests, poll taxes, and other measures to deny African Americans' enfranchisement. Stripped of their civil rights, southern Blacks were consigned to second-class citizenship on the basis of race. Many of the schools established for freedpeople were closed, as southern whites adamantly opposed education for Black youth. Southern states established a system of racial apartheid known as Jim Crow, enforced through law, the police and courts, the press, social custom, and the relentless threat of vigilante violence.[12]

By the time the US Supreme Court ruled in *Plessy v. Ferguson* that it did not violate the equal protection clause to require "separate but equal" facilities for African Americans in 1896, very few Black southerners had access to public education. A fledgling system of public schools for whites had only just been created, and the southern aristocracy and the white working class agreed it was best to deny universal education to Black youth. Neither wanted Black children to have access to schools that could lead to economic competition with whites or, worse, Black enfranchisement and political equality. Under these conditions, Black southerners had to fight for the right to pay for and build their own public schools.[13]

As James D. Anderson argues, common schools for Blacks in the South expanded between 1900 and 1935 thanks to the tireless advocacy and financial contributions of African American students, parents, and community members. Some white philanthropists, like Julius Rosenwald, supported Black common schools, but only if Black families agreed to accept a special "manual training and industrial" curriculum, a deal that many resisted. These schools were to be light on academics and focus instead on teaching manual labor skills deemed "appropriate" for Black youth, typically agricultural and manual labor for boys and domestic work for girls.[14]

Booker T. Washington and other Black leaders declared that schools

FIGURE 1. African American schoolchildren pose with their teacher outside a school, possibly in South Carolina, c. 1900–1910. Library of Congress, Prints & Photographs Division, LC-DIG-ppmsca-13304.

should teach Black children the "dignity of labor" instead of elitist and impractical academic subjects like French, chemistry, geology, mechanics, mathematics, and literature. This was a strategy to cultivate white support for Black common schools, and although it was controversial, it helped assuage white fears of an educated Black citizenry. White southerners grudgingly supplied small measures of public funding to the schools that southern Black communities had built for themselves. States agreed to provide a tiny measure of financial support if segregated schools promised to offer a manual training and industrial curriculum that greatly differed from white schools' courses.[15]

Civil rights leaders like W. E. B. Du Bois vigorously protested a manual training and industrial program for Black students. "Do Negroes oppose this because they are ashamed of having their children trained to work?" Du Bois asked. "Certainly not. But they know that if their children are compelled to cook and sew when they ought to be learning to read, write and cipher, they will not be able to enter the high school or go to college as the white children are doing." He concluded, "It is a deliberate attempt to throttle the Negro child before he knows enough to protest."[16]

Inequalities between white and so-called colored schools in the Jim Crow South were staggering by every measure through the first four decades of the twentieth century. White southern politicians openly campaigned to limit public education for Black students. "I am firmly convinced, after most careful thought and study," the South Carolina governor-elect pronounced in 1911, "that the Almighty created the Negro to be a hewer of wood and a drawer of water. I also believe that the greatest mistake the white race has ever made was in attempting to educate the free Negro."[17]

Not surprisingly, "colored" schools in the Jim Crow South had far less funding than white schools, operated in dilapidated structures with few supplies, and were open only a few months a year. Elementary schools were usually one- or two-room structures, and many lacked electricity and plumbing. Denied access to academic high schools, secondary schools for Black students were called "county training schools" and did not prepare students for the academic rigors of higher education. Schools restricted to "colored" students in the South rarely had gymnasiums, cafeterias, libraries, or science laboratories, which were increasingly common in white schools. The highest-paid Black teachers made less than the lowest-paid white teachers, and "colored" schools were few and far between in rural areas. There were exceptions, such as high-quality all-Black schools in cities like Atlanta, Washington, DC, and Baltimore, but for the most part separate schools for Black children were terribly unequal.[18]

Black teachers established professional associations to advocate for improved school funding, facilities, and teacher salaries in order to fortify southern Black communities. As the Arkansas State Teachers Association put it, "Real teachers seek rather to be of the greatest good and usefulness to those taught; seek to elevate the nature and capabilities of the human soul and tremble under the responsibility of attempting to be its educator. The real teacher strives to bring out the gem from its earthen casket, polish and make it fit to be placed in humanity's diadem." Despite vast inequalities, "colored" schools grew to become valued institutions and, in some cases, cherished sources of community pride. Over the course of the twentieth century, dedicated Black educators continued to improve the quality and curriculum of segregated schools, thereby enriching the socioeconomic prospects of their students and the quality of life for Black families and communities.[19]

The South's apartheid schools institutionalized both white privilege and discrimination against African Americans. State legislators required school administrators to assign white children to one school and African American children to another, making it a crime to permit any degree of racial mixing. These laws codified racism and signified whites' refusal to interact with Blacks on an equal basis. They implied that Black people were inferior and that even casual interaction between children of different races was inherently dangerous, effectively using the power of the state to transform the social preferences of an elite group of whites into unyielding law. Black southerners through the first half of the twentieth century fought to access public education and then struggled to equalize opportunities in a system that used race as the single most important factor to allocate public resources. As soon as it was politically feasible, Black educational activists would fight to abolish school segregation.[20]

Meanwhile, the much smaller—but growing—population of African Americans in the North faced a very different struggle for education. When common schools were created in the 1820s, 1830s, and 1840s, reformers promised they would cultivate productive, patriotic citizens. But as historian Hilary Moss explains, a rationale focused on education for citizenship was deeply problematic for African Americans. Because African Americans were not recognized as full citizens before the ratification of the Fourteenth Amendment on July 9, 1868, it was difficult to claim a place in public institutions dedicated to citizenship training, even in the North.[21]

By promoting civic inclusion rather than social justice, common school reformers justified denying African Americans, as noncitizens, equal access to public schools. For instance, Ohio legally excluded Black students from common schools until 1848. After that point, state legislators permitted communities to create segregated schools, but only if sufficient taxes could be raised from Black households. Similar practices existed throughout the North, and as a result Black children living in rural areas rarely had access to common schools before the Civil War. Towns and cities with larger Black populations, including Providence, Portsmouth, Portland, Salem, New York, Philadelphia, Trenton, New Haven, Hartford, and Boston, established segregated and unequal "African" schools.[22]

The Fourteenth Amendment, ratified in 1868, stated that all persons born or naturalized in the United States were citizens. It contained the equal protection clause, which notes, "Nor shall any State deprive any person of life, liberty, or property, without due process of law; nor deny to any person within its jurisdiction the equal protection of the laws."[23] Soon after, northern communities permitted all African American children to enroll in common schools, although the practice of segregating Black students continued. Black northerners spoke out against state-sponsored school segregation, but white school leaders found they could dampen this critique by hiring Black teachers and principals to work in all-Black or majority-Black classrooms and schools.

This created a challenge for northern Black educational activists. They recognized that Black youth suffered educational discrimination, and it was clear that school segregation led to unequal treatment, but integration threatened what few Black teaching jobs existed in the North. Some Black families, especially recent arrivals from the South, wondered aloud if it would not be better to have the option of separate, Black-controlled schools, where dedicated Black teachers could see to the emotional well-being of Black youth and teach "Negro history." Other Black northerners, especially civil rights leaders, countered that separate schools represented a threat to Black social and political equality and therefore vigorously opposed any kind of voluntary school separation.[24]

This debate raged for decades in Black communities throughout the North. For instance, in January of 1881 the town of Fair Haven, New Jersey, closed its one-room public school for "colored" children after the school's only teacher resigned. Several Black families enrolled their children in Fair Haven's white public school, where they were admitted. When other Black families indicated their willingness to enroll their children in the town's only functioning school, local whites objected. The *New York Times* reported, "When the colored boys and girls went over to the building occupied by white children," the resulting "mixing of the races created such intense indignation that the Trustees were compelled to close the schools."[25] Belatedly, the school board found a "competent teacher" for the "colored" school, but by this time Black parents objected to being excluded from the white school when they paid the same taxes as other citizens. Meanwhile, the "colored" school caught fire and burned to the ground. The white press accused Black parents of starting the fire so their children would not have to return to a segregated school.[26]

Thanks to the media frenzy over "the race warfare on the school question at Fair Haven," New Jersey state senator James Youngblood introduced a bill that outlawed racial segregation in public schools, providing "that no child, between the age of five and eighteen years of age, shall be excluded from any public school in this state on account of his or her religion, nationality or color." The bill was signed into law in 1881, officially outlawing school segregation in New Jersey.[27] As Davison M. Douglas has demonstrated, other northern states followed suit as Republican politicians found the question of state-sponsored school segregation of paramount concern to Black voters.[28]

Despite widespread antidiscrimination legislation, school segregation increased in the North through the first four decades of the twentieth century. This was in part because of the massive internal migration of hundreds of thousands of African Americans to the North, especially during the First and Second Great Migrations. School officials gerrymandered district lines and selectively assigned students on the basis of race to ensure a high degree of racial segregation in many schools.[29]

Black civil rights leaders vocally opposed this de facto school segregation, but many parents and ministers were far more concerned about the quality of education for Black youth than the degree of racial mixing in schools. Many Black northerners posited that separate, Black-controlled schools would help more Black children gain the best possible education. In Fair Haven, even though the school "race war" helped ban school segregation in New Jersey, Black citizens agreed to give up the struggle for school integration in exchange for a newly constructed "elegant and commodious colored school" with Black teachers.[30]

Before 1954, there was little consensus on whether school integration was the best strategy to improve public education for Black northerners. Many educational activists fought for integration in order to gain access to better schools and resist the encroachment of southern-style racial apartheid. According to Horace Mann Bond, "In Ohio, and Indiana, and Kansas, and Illinois, Philadelphia, and southern New Jersey, wherever the schools are separated, you will find after ten or fifteen years, the colored school is going into decline." And yet, parents, students, and Black teachers questioned whether Black students could truly achieve academically in a school run by hostile whites. At the heart of this debate was the question of Black teachers, which Black parents viewed as essential to their children's success.[31]

Most Black teachers in the North were restricted to majority-Black classrooms or schools, and high school students had virtually no chance of studying with a Black teacher unless they attended a separate school before 1940. For example, in 1930 only one Black teacher taught in New Jersey's racially mixed high schools, although thirty-two Black teachers taught at the all-Black Bordentown Manual Training and Industrial School for Colored Youth. Black principals, likewise, were restricted to separate schools or to supervising designated "colored" schools within the district, such as in Atlantic City, New Jersey. This made it very difficult for Black teachers to secure teaching jobs, which was an additional problem when teaching was one of the best jobs available for college-educated African Americans. Observing that the number of northern Black college graduates increased every year, one scholar noted, "The only hope for this new army of the unemployed is separate schools." School integration, therefore, was not an obvious or simple way to resolve the enduring problems associated with educational inequality in the North.[32]

Established in 1909, the National Association for the Advancement of Colored People (NAACP) was an interracial organization dedicated to

Black civil rights in the United States. In the 1930s, NAACP leaders decided that the most effective way to achieve equal rights was to abolish state-sponsored racial segregation, not only because it engendered inequality but more importantly because it buttressed white supremacy. Black leaders targeted the "separate but equal" doctrine established in 1896 in order to hasten the end of Jim Crow in all aspects of American life.

In the late 1930s and early 1940s, the NAACP won a series of legal victories that set the stage for *Brown v. Board of Education*.[33] A case in Maryland compelled school authorities to either equalize or integrate high schools for Black and white students in 1937, proving that the courts were willing to enforce equality in segregated public schools. The US Supreme Court ruling in *Gaines v. Canada* confirmed that if the state of Missouri offered in-state graduate legal training to white students, it must offer an equal education to Black students in a state-sponsored college. In June of 1940, the Fourth Circuit Court of Appeals ruled that Norfolk, Virginia, could not pay Black teachers lower salaries than white teachers. These cases did not overturn the separate but equal doctrine, but they chipped away at it while proving the NAACP was capable of leading a formidable legal campaign for educational equality.[34]

World War II thrust the Black civil rights movement into the national arena for the first time since Reconstruction. The war ended the Great Depression and pulled Black workers into urban areas in the North, Midwest, and West, where Black political power grew exponentially. One million Black service members served their country with honor, and although they were restricted to segregated units, military service provided education, combat training, travel, and exposure to new people and ideas that fueled a vibrant postwar civil rights movement.[35]

By 1946, the NAACP had grown to six hundred thousand members, and it coordinated the effort to achieve full economic, social, and legal justice for African Americans. The campaign against school segregation became a defining part of this activism. Thurgood Marshall reasoned, "It became increasingly apparent that the supreme test would have to be made—an attack on segregation at the elementary and high school levels. Acceptance of segregation under the 'separate but equal' doctrine had become so ingrained that overwhelming proof was sorely needed to demonstrate that equal educational opportunities for Negroes could not be provided in a segregated system."[36]

Drawing on cutting-edge social science scholarship, Marshall demonstrated that arbitrary and artificial barriers such as race or color in education had an adverse effect on the personality and social development of youth. Any experience as the despised "other" in a segregated society was bound to cause lasting harm, and in the case of schoolchildren, this would impair a child's chance to do well in school. Working with Black communities nationwide, the NAACP ushered five cases through the legal system all the way to the US Supreme Court. School desegregation cases from Virginia, Washington, DC, South Carolina, Kansas, and Delaware were consolidated under the name of the case from Kansas, *Brown v. Board of Education of Topeka*.[37]

On May 17, 1954, the US Supreme Court issued a unanimous decision in *Brown v. Board of Education* that overturned the separate but equal doctrine established by *Plessy v. Ferguson* in 1896 and outlawed racial segregation in public schools. After acknowledging public education as the very foundation of good citizenship and the principal instrument in awakening children to cultural values, Chief Justice Earl Warren declared, "We conclude that in the field of public education, the doctrine of 'separate but equal' has no place. Separate educational facilities are inherently unequal."[38]

Legally, racial segregation in the public schools was outlawed. In practice, however, the fight for integrated schools and equal educational opportunities for African Americans had only just begun.[39]

FORCED ASSIMILATION

Whereas African Americans viewed public education as an opportunity to advance struggles for equal citizenship, political equality, and economic opportunity, the nation's vast and diverse population of Native Americans experienced formal schooling very differently, primarily as a program of forced assimilation and cultural genocide. The expansion of free, tax-supported common schools depended on the appropriation of Native American lands and the displacement of indigenous people. Provisions dating back to the Northwest Ordinances in 1785 and 1787 dedicated portions of newly acquired federal lands to fund education, a model that was expanded in subsequent territorial acquisitions. In this way, schools were a tool of settler colonialism. Federal provisions for schools, generated from the sale of indigenous land, encouraged the kinds of family formation and institution building necessary to occupy and hold territory while advancing Anglo models of self-government and citizenship training.[40]

Federal treaties with individual tribes and the Civilization Fund Act of 1819 also sponsored schools for Native American youth. The results were inconsistent, but occasionally the Bureau of Indian Affairs (BIA) contracted with a church, missionary society, or individual teacher to provide a modest school on tribal lands. This kind of formal schooling was very different from indigenous self-education, and many Native American communities were ambivalent or hostile to the idea of government-sponsored schools. However, some Native Americans worked to shape these early schools to their own purposes or even develop their own system of education designed to fortify the sovereignty and political identity of Indian nations.[41]

Between the 1840s and 1890s, the Creek Nation, along with neighboring Cherokees, Choctaws, Chickasaws, and Seminoles, used schools as a tool of indigenous nation-building to enhance their capacity for self-determination within the American settler colonial state. Native Americans built a system of primary and secondary schools modeled on US common schools that were subsidized, legislated, and managed by their own national governments. These schools taught a curriculum that corresponded to elite seminaries, including geography, grammar, philosophy, US and ancient history, chemistry, algebra, geometry, trigonometry, and Latin. Because these schools trained students to move fluidly between white and indigenous worlds, they were contested by those who preferred a more isolationist approach. Some parents, like the Choctaw leader Peter Pitchlynn, encouraged their children to attend school and study hard so they would be better prepared to negotiate effectively with whites and lead their communities.[42]

Schools run by the Cherokee, Choctaw, Chickasaw, and other indigenous nations grew until they represented a threat to white hegemony, as they allowed youth to opt out of the so-called civilizing effects of white-dominated schools. State and federal governments began to dissolve indigenous-run schools, especially as Native Americans were pushed west, and the territory they inhabited was incorporated into new states. For instance, the federal government closed the Creek national school system in 1907 and required students to attend schools run by state or federal agencies. Although Native American experiences with indigenous-run schools were mixed, some families had come to value formal schooling as a way to strengthen the identity and sovereignty of Indian nations.[43]

The vast majority of Native Americans, however, did not have access to indigenous-run schools and instead encountered schools designed and run by whites. These schools expanded in the late nineteenth century nationwide. White reformers proposed to "civilize" Native Americans by requiring them to learn English, own personal property, and work toward the accumulation of personal wealth. They imagined schools would function as a more humane policy to conquer indigenous populations than the more violent options of genocide or war.[44]

The stated function of government-run schools was to transform Native Americans from "savages" into "civilized" Americans, with the understanding that any form of native culture—clothing, food, music, religious practice, or matriarchal social organization—must be eliminated.[45] Newspaper articles with titles like "Indians Becoming Civilized: Education Proving of Great Benefit to the American Aborigines" popularized this agenda for a national audience. Carl Schurz, former commissioner of Indian Affairs, typified reformers of the 1880s who insisted that Native Americans were confronted with "this stern alternative: extermination or civilization."[46]

Once government officials agreed that schools would accomplish what guns could not, they had to wrestle control of Native American education away from missionary schools scattered on reservations throughout the West. This process did not go uncontested, as missionaries' education style greatly differed from elite white reformers' vision of government-run schools. For example, at the Dakota school in Minnesota, three generations of missionaries had developed a Dakota-language curriculum designed to convert students to Christianity, assimilate them to American culture, and teach them about US civics and democracy. Missionary teachers were distraught to learn the federal government would require instruction in English and forbid Native American cultural practices. While the assimilationist goals of missionaries and the federal government overlapped, policy makers insisted that education for Native Americans required the complete rejection of all native languages and cultural practices.[47]

The US government began their education project by building day schools on Native American reservations. Largely dedicated to language instruction and cultural assimilation, these schools taught a little reading, writing, and arithmetic, as well as a good dose of manual training and industrial education: farming and manual labor for boys, and cooking, cleaning, and child-rearing for girls. There were forty-eight reservation day schools by 1870, but some reformers were frustrated when they failed to accomplish basic objectives and placed the blame on the continuing presence of students' families, who exerted a more powerful socializing influence than white teachers. As one agent complained in 1878, "To place these wild children under a teacher's care but four or five hours a day, and permit them to spend the other nineteen in the filth and degradation of the village, makes the attempt to educate and civilize them a mere farce." In other words, the Native American children were not becoming less "Indian" even after years of instruction at schools that educated children for only a few hours each day.[48]

Government officials experimented next with on-reservation boarding schools, where Native American youth lived for eight or nine months away from the supposedly corruptive influence of their families. This model gave educators far more control over the everyday lives of students, who were prohibited from speaking native languages and forced to live in institutionalized settings where eating, sleeping, washing, and playing were monitored by the BIA. But even with this extended supervision, on-reservation boarding schools failed to completely eradicate indigenous ways. A federal agent working with the Mescalero Apache fumed, noting that as soon as the Native American children returned home, "They go back at once to the savage mode of life, and a few weeks is sufficient to obliterate every vestige, so far as casual observation goes, of the teacher's long and patient labor." The most zealous reformers concluded that on-reservation boarding schools did not sufficiently remove students from their friends and families.[49]

Native Americans, in turn, fought to negotiate the explicit dangers and veiled opportunities of government-run day and boarding schools. Some, such as Shawnee chief Thomas Wildcat Alford, believed that Native Americans could reap benefits from government schools while resisting blunt attempts at cultural annihilation. He explained, "There was a feeling among our people that some of our young men should be educated so that they could read and write and understand what was written in the treaties and old documents in our possession." Others gained an education and then returned to work as teachers in BIA schools, where they helped Native American students learn while also cherishing their identities, experiences, and cultural knowledge. For the most part, however, Native Americans contested the expansion of compulsory, white-controlled schooling with its aggressive assimilationist agenda. Frustrated but hardly defeated, the most dedicated white reformers puzzled over the dilemma of how to educate a population that resisted assimilationist schools.[50]

Tellingly, it was a lieutenant in the US Army who proposed off-reservation boarding schools as a solution. Richard Henry Pratt honed his expertise supervising Native American prisoners of war at Fort Marion in St. Augustine, Florida. Pratt believed he could convert Native American captives into "good" Americans with a little education and military discipline. Cutting off first the chains that bound their feet and then the hair that hung down their backs, Pratt dressed his charges in discarded army uniforms, taught them to speak English, and worked to integrate them into the economic and social life of St. Augustine.

Word spread through philanthropic circles that a new kind of school successfully converted "savages" into "civilized people." Harriet Beecher Stowe, the white abolitionist and author of *Uncle Tom's Cabin*, visited Pratt's prison-school in 1877 and wrote, "We have tried fighting and killing the Indians, and gained little by it. . . . Suppose we try education. . . . Might not the money now constantly spent on armies, forts, and frontiers be better invested in educating young men who shall return and teach their people to live like civilized beings?"[51]

The following year Pratt received word that the US government was ready to release the Fort Marion American Indian prisoners of war. Seventeen of Pratt's younger prisoners asked to continue their education at American schools. Pratt could locate only one institution willing to accept the former warriors as scholars.

Samuel Chapman Armstrong, another military man and the son of missionary parents in Hawaii, founded the Hampton Normal and Agricultural Institute for Black students in Virginia in 1868. This boarding school offered a "manual training and industrial education" to boys and girls "of color" in the South, specifically Black students. The curriculum at Hampton Institute was light on academics and heavy on the kinds of manual skills that white southerners believed were "appropriate" for Blacks—farming and carpentry for boys, and domestic labor for girls. By making Hampton students toil in the fields, kitchens, laundry, and workshops for hours each day, Armstrong believed he was teaching students to accept their place in a racially stratified society, and he saw no reason why this approach would not work equally well for Native Americans. The federal government agreed and offered to pay for fifty indigenous students to attend Hampton Institute in 1878.[52]

Pratt visited Hampton Institute just long enough to convince himself that the model of a manual training and industrial boarding school was perfect for Native Americans. However, he fretted that if Native Americans were educated alongside African Americans, then they would be locked into the lowest caste of the American racial hierarchy. To counter this, Pratt created the first segregated, off-reservation boarding school for Native American students with the financial support of the US government. The Carlisle Indian Industrial School opened in 1879 and recruited children from the Pine Ridge and Rosebud Sioux Reservations in the Dakotas.[53]

In an effort to ensure that Native Americans would fall on the more privileged side of the color line, Pratt rejected students who showed up at the Carlisle Indian School if they had any discernible African ancestry. Thus, when a group of Shinnecock Indian boys from Long Island, New York, showed up for the start of the fall semester in 1882, Pratt took one look at them and sent them home. According to Carlisle student records, the youth were officially discharged for having "too much Negro" heritage.[54]

Whites celebrated the success of off-reservation boarding schools like Carlisle Indian School, which appeared to "civilize" Native American students at a remarkable rate. The supposed triumph of these schools was advertised through dramatic "before" and "after" photographs of students. Pratt took photos of young Native Americans when they first arrived surrounded with artifacts such as indigenous clothing, blankets, feathers, and

FIGURE 2. Native American men and a boy pose outside of Carlisle Indian School, c. 1890. Library of Congress, Prints & Photographs Division, LC-USZ62-124294.

beads. The second round of pictures depicted the same children scrubbed clean and posed with American-style haircuts and clothing. Through the use of special lighting and the application of white face powder, the "after" photographs even managed to show a distinct "whitening" of Native American students who experienced a boarding school education.[55]

By 1903, there were twenty-five off-reservation boarding schools, including Carlisle (Pennsylvania), Chilocco (Oklahoma), Genoa (Nebraska), Haskell (Kansas), Phoenix (Arizona), Salem (later known as Chemawa; Oregon), and Sherman (California).[56] David Wallace Adams notes, "Only by attending boarding school, policymakers were now convinced, could savage institutions, outlooks, and sympathies be rendered extinct. Only by attending boarding school could Indian youth, stripped bare of their tribal heritage, take to heart the inspiring lessons of white civilization."[57]

Through a combination of promises, threats, bribery, persuasion, and force, thousands of young Native Americans were shipped off to remote boarding schools. These institutions wielded almost total control over the lives of students. Upon arrival, white teachers cut off students' long hair and assigned them new English names. Students were required to speak English, wear uniforms, march in military formation, adhere to rigid schedules, and eat bland, nutritionally inadequate institutional food. Teachers and administrators punished students for speaking in their native tongue or for any minor infraction of the rules, and there is evidence of rampant physical and sexual abuse by school staff. Thousands of Native American children died from disease, neglect, overwork, abuse, and malnutrition in government-sponsored boarding schools; thousands more fought back.[58]

The most common form of Native American resistance was the endemic problem of runaways. Unhappy students executed elaborate schemes to escape from boarding schools. Navajo student Hopi-Hopi and a small group of friends practiced swimming for months in a river near the Santa Fe Indian School to become strong enough to swim across the massive Rio Grande River and make their escape. The boys successfully outran a search party, swam through the raging river, and hiked over open land for days to get home. At the Chilocco School in Oklahoma, records show that 111 boys and 18 girls ran away in a four-month period in 1927. The boarding school at Fort Mojave in Arizona lost so many students that school administrators established a campus jail as a deterrent. The administration was stunned when the kindergarten class executed a jailbreak of their fellow classmates, using a log as a battering ram to hammer down the door and make a dash for freedom.[59]

In an example from 1919 at the Haskell Institute in Kansas, students ripped down electric lines during an evening assembly and used the cover of darkness to smash light fixtures, raid the kitchen, and ring the school bell while calling out to an unpopular administrator, "Let's string him up!"[60] Other forms of resistance included setting fire to school property—which was quite widespread—as well as willful acts of disobedience, speaking secretly in native languages, refusing to participate in scheduled activities, pranks, and work slowdowns on school farms and workshops.[61] Other Native American students adopted a pragmatic acceptance of boarding school life in order to bide their time until graduation and their return home. Some were encouraged by family members or decided of their own accord that learning the white people's language and way of life did not require a wholesale abandonment of their native heritage.[62]

As a young Lakota, Charles Eastman was initially unconvinced when his father encouraged him to attend boarding school. He finally agreed to attend Santee Indian School in Nebraska, where he thrived, later graduating from Dartmouth College and then Boston University's School of Medicine. Eastman spent his life working as a doctor among Native Americans and served as a lobbyist and legal representative for the Sioux tribe in Washington, DC.[63] Accommodation did not necessarily mean surrender, and many Native American students used government schools to their advantage.[64]

Support for off-reservation boarding schools faded in the early twentieth century as Native Americans vocally protested the forced removal and assimilation of their children. The young Sioux author Zitkala-Ša (Gertrude Bonnin) published a compelling testimony in the *Atlantic Monthly* in 1900. She described how her idyllic childhood spent among the Yankton Sioux came to an abrupt end when she was sent to school. Her initial fascination with the enormous brick buildings and modern conveniences faded to desperation and terror at the hands of cruel teachers. When she learned they planned to cut her long hair, Zitkala-Ša ran and hid under a bed, only to be forcibly dragged out and tied down to a chair. "I cried aloud, shaking my head all the while until I felt the cold blade of the scissors against my neck, and heard them gnaw off one of my thick braids," she recounted for *Atlantic Monthly*. Zitkala-Ša continued: "Then I lost my spirit. Since the day I had been taken from my mother I had suffered extreme indignities. People had stared at me. I had been tossed about in the air like a wooden puppet. And now my long hair was shingled like a coward's! In my anguish I moaned for my mother, but no one came to comfort me. Not a soul reasoned quietly with me, as my mother used to do; for now I was only one of many little animals, driven by a herder."[65]

Moved by such devastating testimonies, a new generation of reformers questioned the logic of off-reservation boarding schools. They noted that schools failed to accomplish the wholesale assimilation of indigenous children promised by reformers like Pratt and worried that prolonged institutionalization would generate long-term and expensive reliance on government support. William Jones, the commissioner of Indian Affairs, stated baldly in 1902 that government-run schools actually impeded the assimilation process. Observing that at boarding schools, "the Indian youth finds himself at once, as if by magic, translated from a state of poverty to one of affluence," Jones complained such schools undermined Native Americans' independence and ambition. "The child of the wigwam becomes a modern day Aladdin, who has only to rub the Government lamp to gratify his desires," he chided. "It is not denied that under . . . the school system, there has been some progress, but it has not been commensurate with the money spent and effort made."[66] Jones's report marked the beginning of a new policy of gradualism. In 1918, an investigation of the Carlisle Indian School led government officials to close down the flagship boarding school, signaling a new approach to the unresolved "problem" of indigenous education.[67]

As off-reservation boarding schools were closed down, Native American students enrolled in traditional public schools, a process that accelerated after the Indian Citizenship Act of 1924 guaranteed US citizenship to indigenous people, and Native Americans left reservations to live in nearby towns and cities. Records show that only 246 out of 26,451 Native American children attended public schools in 1900, but by 1925 this number had risen to 34,452 out of 65,493 children.[68]

In 1928, the Institute for Government Research published *The Problem of Indian Administration*, more commonly known as the Meriam Report after the primary author, Lewis Meriam. The Meriam Report was critical of the forced assimilation of Native American children and especially suspicious of boarding schools that were found to be poorly funded, overcrowded, ill-equipped, and dangerous. The authors of the report encouraged the expansion of day schools that honored Native American culture and language, and wherever possible the report urged integration of Native American youth into local public schools.[69]

Attending public schools created new opportunities but also new challenges for Native Americans. In Phoenix, for example, Native American children found that white teachers mistook them for Mexican Americans or looked down on them for their indigenous heritage. They experienced high levels of segregation and discrimination, often alongside Mexican Americans, and failed to thrive in hostile learning environments. In some regions, Native Americans collaborated with Mexican Americans to challenge educational racism and create more equitable schools, a theme that is explored in detail in the next chapter. The educational alliance between Mexican Americans and Native Americans was a fragile one, in large part because Mexican Americans faced distinct challenges given their legal status as "white" and their racial status as "colored."[70]

WHITE BY TREATY

Mexican Americans were the largest Latin American ethnic group in US schools from the common school era through the mid-twentieth century. They were also an incredibly diverse group, hailing from different ethnic, political, cultural, religious, and socioeconomic backgrounds. Mexican Americans occupy a unique place in the history of American education because they enjoyed the legal privileges of whiteness even as they suffered explicit, race-based discrimination in public schools. This paradox was further complicated by the fact that both the legal and the social construction of Mexican Americans' racial status changed over time and across different regions, while the demographics of this group experienced tremendous growth fueled by immigration.

At the end of the Mexican-American War in 1848, over 525,000 square miles of territory, including present-day Arizona, California, western Colorado, Nevada, New Mexico, Texas, and Utah, became part of the United States. Nearly seventy-seven thousand Mexicans living in this region became American citizens overnight by the terms of the Treaty of Guadalupe Hidalgo. This treaty guaranteed Mexican nationals living in newly acquired American territory US citizenship as well as the right to own property. Later courts ruled that because the treaty guaranteed citizenship and because only white people were eligible for American citizenship at the time, Mexican Americans must be "white."[71]

This legal definition, however, did not mesh with social norms in the Southwest, where Anglos viewed people of Mexican descent as mixed race. While a small number of Mexican American elites emphasized their European heritage and passed for white, most suffered virulent discrimination in all aspects of public life. Mexican Americans labored in low-wage jobs first on railroads and later on farms, and they faced exclusion from white-dominated public schools, political associations, public accommodations, and juries in southwestern towns throughout Texas, Arizona, New Mexico, Colorado, and California. In response, Mexican Americans created their own societies and coalitions, held meetings, events, and fundraisers, and published Spanish-language newspapers that advocated for specific political and social causes, including better schools.[72]

Public schools were slow to come to the Southwest, and those that existed before the 1870s typically excluded Mexican-origin children, no matter their citizenship status. During the second half of the nineteenth century, some Mexican American children in the Southwest attended private schools run by Catholic or Protestant churches. These missionary schools offered trade training alongside a traditional academic curriculum. Like the early missionary schools for Native Americans, they developed an assimilationist curriculum that incorporated aspects of traditional Mexican language and culture in order to entice families to join the school and church.[73]

The expansion of missionary education overlapped with the growth of public schools in the Southwest, as formal schooling became increasingly important in the expanding capitalist economy in the late nineteenth and early twentieth centuries. At first, locally administered public schools for Mexican American children in the Southwest were similar to their missionary counterparts. These early public schools offered a good dose of religious instruction, community involvement, and, when useful, instruction in Spanish. Many Mexican American families sought out these schools for their children, believing an education would improve their social and economic life chances.[74]

However, some Anglo officials feared that "foreign" practices like speaking Spanish undermined the patriotic purposes and Americanizing agenda of public schools. As public education expanded, Anglo leaders pushed out Mexican American and Catholic teachers and replaced them with school workers committed to the eradication of Mexican cultural traits, including the Spanish language. Texas and California, the two states with the largest Mexican American populations, passed laws mandating the use of English and limiting the use of Spanish in public schools in 1870. New Mexico passed a similar law in 1891. These laws served no pedagogical function and made it harder for teachers to communicate with Mexican American children and their families. Teachers could legally punish students for speaking Spanish at school, even during casual conversations in the hallways and playgrounds. Such laws symbolized the power of the state to subordinate Mexican American people and their way of life, creating a hostile learning environment.[75]

As Anglo-controlled public education expanded in the Southwest, so too did the segregation of Mexican American students between 1900 and 1930. David G. García documents the elaborate ways that Oxnard, California, mayor and school superintendent Richard B. Haydock engineered segregated neighborhoods and public schools in order to satisfy white parents in the early twentieth century. These community leaders were aided by white men and women who advocated for segregated schools through labor, cultural, and educational organizations, including Parent Teacher Associations. García identifies these people as the "White architects of school segregation." He argues, "The racial hierarchy Haydock and the other White architects established in schools functioned to relegate Mexicans, with very few exceptions, to the bottom as a seemingly normal practice enforced well beyond the classroom."[76]

School segregation expanded and hardened as the Mexican-origin population grew. Scholars estimate that roughly one million Mexicans moved to America during the first three decades of the twentieth century, joining a Mexican American population of roughly five hundred thousand. Pushed out of Mexico by violence and land reform associated with the Mexican Revolution, migrants were pulled to the United States by the promise of jobs on farms, railroads, mines, and factories. This was an incredibly diverse and transnational population with direct ties to Mexico. For example, the Mexican-origin population in Chicago included working-class Mexican radicals, middle-class immigrants who promoted liberal reform projects, and conservative immigrants who stressed family values, religion, and mutual aid. Despite this robust diversity, virtually all Mexican Americans faced high levels of racial discrimination in real estate, employment, and public education.[77]

Discrimination against Mexican American students is discernible through very high levels of school segregation. Of course, this segregation was technically illegal, since Mexican Americans were legally "white." To get around this problem, school leaders proposed to segregate Mexican-origin children because of supposed cultural and linguistic needs, although in practice they simply assigned all students who either looked Mexican or had a Spanish last name to segregated facilities. School leaders isolated Mexican American children in separate classrooms, constructed new schools in racially restricted barrios, and adjusted residential enrollment boundaries to satisfy white requests for school segregation.[78]

Segregated Mexican schools had lower per pupil funding, higher class sizes, fewer school days, less-qualified teachers, and fewer resources such as indoor toilets, cafeterias, and school nurses than majority-white schools. Margarie Blackman, a white teacher at a Mexican American school in Lamar, Colorado, in the early 1920s, wrote of her facility, "You would never know it was a school. It looked like an adobe hovel. It did not have bathrooms. It had outhouses. We had a well for water. It had no playground, no equipment, no swings, no nothing. There were two teachers. We had old books and they were dirty. We had round stoves to keep the room warm. I taught first, second, and third. She [the other teacher] taught fourth, fifth, and sixth." Commenting on the academic achievement of Mexican American students in her school, Blackman concluded, "The kids didn't do too well."[79]

Anglo administrators crafted an aggressive Americanization program that prohibited the use of Spanish and omitted any mention of Mexican American history and culture, especially after World War I. This stood in stark contrast to separate schools for African Americans, which, although underfunded and housed in inferior buildings, often developed into nurturing institutions under the leadership of Black teachers and administrators. While white southerners readily agreed to hire Black teachers for separate "colored" schools, whites in the Southwest preferred Anglo teachers for Mexican Americans because they believed they would more effectively assimilate their charges. While a small number of Mexican American students managed to earn a high school diploma, the vast majority tended to drop out of school much earlier and in greater numbers than their white or African American peers. In fact, the segregation of Mexican American children usually ended around fourth grade simply because there were so few children who stayed in school beyond the age of ten or eleven.[80]

Mexican American families believed education could improve opportunities for their children and expand their communities' political and social power, and so they fought to improve the quality of public education for their children. School segregation was an obvious and terrible source of educational inequality in the Southwest, and from the beginning educational

FIGURE 3. Mexican American student at a grade school in Questa, New Mexico, 1943. Library of Congress, Prints & Photographs Division, LC-DIG-fsa-8d25964.

activists therefore demanded school integration, especially since they had the power of law on their side.[81]

The earliest recorded school integration "blowouts," or strikes, were organized by Mexican American families in the small, rural Texas town of San Angelo in 1910 and again in 1914, where strikers protested the inferior quality of the segregated Mexican American school and demanded admission to the larger and better-funded Anglo school. The school board ignored parents' requests, even after the second school boycott lasted into 1915. School segregation in San Angelo continued for many decades because Mexican American activists did not have the social or political power needed to force white authorities to equalize the public schools.[82]

More successful educational activism in the early twentieth century came from Mexican American communities in urban areas that included a small, but influential, middle class. In some cases, Mexican Americans were able to petition the Mexican government to intervene on their behalf.

For instance, on June 7, 1919, Ramón de Negri, the consul general of Mexico in San Francisco, wrote a letter to California governor William D. Stephens complaining that children in the towns of Santa Paula and El Centro were excluded from public schools for white children and assigned to schools with Black students. De Negri added that this deliberate slight to Americans of Mexican descent was part of "a systematic campaign by certain interests who seek to create for their own selfish interest ill-feeling between the people of Mexico and the United States."[83]

Governor Stephens ordered an investigation of Mexican American school segregation in California. The state superintendent of public instruction concluded that while many Mexican American students were segregated, this reflected not racial discrimination but instead pedagogical innovation. After visiting the schools that the Mexican consul had cited in his report, he wrote:

> I am clearly of the opinion that there has been no segregation of Mexican children in California upon the grounds of nationality or race. Where segregation has been ordered, and this is true only in a few instances, the segregation has been based upon the fact that the children segregated had no knowledge of the English language, and for that reason could not carry on the same work as the children of American parentage. In my judgment, such segregation in the early grades is not only perfectly legal, but eminently desirable from the standpoint of non-English speaking children themselves.[84]

The magnitude of school segregation for Mexican Americans, however, suggests that administrators paid little heed to individual children's learning needs and instead simply assigned them to segregated facilities. By the 1930s, Mexican American school segregation was well established throughout the Southwest. California, for example, reported that 85 percent of school districts segregated Mexican American students. In Texas, school administrators reported 90 percent of school districts segregated Mexican-origin students in 1930.[85]

Segregation spread into secondary schools as Mexican Americans began to stay in school longer, and administrators assigned them to special classes for children with low intelligence or vocational programs that emphasized manual training and industrial education. Many found public school to be a demeaning experience that offered little in terms of economic or social advancement. Stark institutionalized discrimination harmed academic achievement in terms of school attendance, median years of school completed, test scores, and high school graduation rates. Data from the Texas public schools reveal that in 1900, 39 percent of Anglo children attended public school, while only 17 percent of Mexican American children did so. Three decades later this gap had widened, even as the numbers of students attending school increased. By 1928, when 83 percent of Anglo children in Texas enrolled in public school, only 49 percent of Mexican American children did so. These statistics were echoed throughout the Southwest, which inspired Mexican American leaders to target public education as a key site of political reform.[86]

Organized into the League of United Latin American Citizens (LULAC), Mexican Americans launched a legal attack on segregated public schools. LULAC, the largest and most important civil rights organization for Mexican Americans, initiated its first school integration lawsuit in 1930, *Independent School District v. Salvatierra*. In the small town of Del Rio, Mexican American families led by Jesus Salvatierra filed an injunction to prevent the school district from using public funds to build an extension to the town's Mexican school. Explaining that this new construction would only exacerbate racial segregation, community members instead asked that the school district integrate Mexican American children into the existing white school.[87]

During the trial, the Del Rio superintendent argued that Mexican Americans had different educational needs than whites and therefore required segregated schooling. He testified: "There are decided peculiarities of children of Mexican or Spanish descent which can be better taken care of in those elementary grades by their being placed separately from the children of Anglo-Saxon parentage, because the average Spanish speaking children know English as a foreign tongue, and consequently when you put him in a class with English speaking children and teach him according to the method of teaching English speaking children he is greatly handicapped."

The superintendent added that Mexican Americans were especially gifted in music and art, and that they preferred "handiwork" to academic studies. Anglo school officials saw no problem claiming that Mexican American children's "peculiarities" predisposed them to a different kind of school than children of "Anglo-Saxon" heritage.

The American judicial system had to carve a path between the generally shared assumption that Mexican Americans belonged to a different race than Anglos and the fact that Mexican Americans were white by law. The solution, it would seem, was for courts to designate Mexican Americans as one of the "other white races." This allowed judges to acknowledge the legal status of Mexican Americans as white and distinguish between Anglos and Mexican Americans for public education. Accordingly, the judge agreed with the Del Rio school district that the segregation of Mexican American children was done for pedagogical reasons, not discriminatory ones. The judge paused to explain that for convenience, he would distinguish between "the Mexican race" and "all other white races."[88]

Like the Anglo school superintendent, Judge J. Smith believed that Mexicans and Anglos belonged to two distinct races and that, moreover, the two groups possessed "widely diverse racial characteristics." He concluded that the courts were loath to interfere in local school administration and that, in this case, there was no evidence that Del Rio school officials discriminated against Mexican Americans. The ruling freed up money so that Anglo officials could build an addition to the Mexican school in Del Rio, thereby preserving and expanding school segregation. The lesson that southwestern school districts took away from *Independent School District v. Salvatierra* was that it was illegal to arbitrarily segregate Mexican American students by race but permissible for a reason such as language needs.[89]

Mexican Americans refused to be relegated to second-class citizenship through segregated and unequal schools. When whites in Lemon Grove, California, built a new Mexican school that looked more like a two-room barn than a proper schoolhouse in 1931, local parents refused to send their children. Except for one household, the entire Mexican American community boycotted the facility and demanded access to the better-funded white school. With assistance from the Mexican consul, attorneys on behalf of eighty-five children filed suit against the school district. At the trial, Mexican American students demonstrated their fluency in English to prove there was no pedagogical need to segregate them from whites. The court agreed and ordered the Lemon Grove public schools to abolish segregated Mexican schools. Despite being hailed as the nation's first successful school desegregation case, *Alvarez v. Lemon Grove School District* was an isolated decision that failed to set precedent for other school desegregation cases and therefore failed to reverse educational discrimination against Mexican American students.[90]

The growing visibility of African American educational activism and the experiences of Mexican American service members in World War II fueled a more ambitious Mexican American civil rights movement in the postwar era. Like Black civil rights activists, many Mexican Americans came to view segregated schools as institutionalized discrimination that produced gross educational inequality and symbolized second-class citizenship. LULAC, like the NAACP, decided to wage a coordinated legal battle against school segregation to protect Mexican Americans' constitutional rights, denote equal citizenship, and guarantee access to a high-quality, equal education. When an Anglo teacher at Westminster Main School told Soledad Vidaurri that her two daughters could be registered at the local, majority-white neighborhood school, but that her niece and two nephews "were too dark" and had to register at the Mexican school down the road, Vidaurri along with Gonzalo and Felícitas Méndez contacted LULAC for help.[91]

In 1946, LULAC and the Méndez family won a tremendous victory when the court ruled the segregation of Mexican American students in California violated the equal protection clause of the Fourteenth Amendment. The historic *Mendez v. Westminster* case anticipated *Brown v. Board of Education* by nearly a decade and helped establish legal precedent to overturn racial segregation in public schools. The legal victory in California was matched by another in Texas in 1948, where *Delgado v. Bastrop Independent School District* signaled the court's growing impatience with school leaders' flimsy excuses for segregating students of Mexican descent.[92]

These legal victories, important as they were, were not enough to compel Anglo leaders to welcome Mexican American students into predominantly white schools. White business leaders, politicians, and school administrators conspired to maintain segregated schools that offered an inferior education to Mexican Americans. For instance, even after the Texas superintendent of public instruction required every school district in the state to immediately admit Mexican American children into white schools, segregation persisted.[93]

Given the immense power imbalance between the Anglo elite and Mexican Americans in the Southwest, the struggle for equal education remained unresolved through the 1950s, at which point a new and more ethnically diverse generation of Mexican American and Puerto Rican activists would take up the challenge to obliterate educational racism and integrate and equalize public schools for all children.

YELLOW PERIL

Unlike Mexican Americans, Asian immigrants were denied US citizenship from the moment of their arrival through the 1940s, making public education an especially contentious and complicated matter. These citizenship denials began for Chinese and Asian Indians in the mid-nineteenth century, Japanese in the late nineteenth century, and Koreans and Filipinos in the first decade of the twentieth century. Immigration laws restricted Asian American populations (a term that dates to the 1960s) to very small numbers through 1954, so that Asian immigrants and their descendants were less than 1 percent of the US population in 1940. From the time of their arrival through the 1930s, Asian Americans in the United States faced extreme discrimination in labor, housing, and education, often working in dangerous and physically demanding jobs, such as transcontinental railroad construction, salmon-canning factories on the Northwest coast, and fishing and farming in California. In Hawaii, Asian Americans labored in sugarcane fields under terrible and exploitative conditions.[94]

Immigrants from Asia were the only group to be categorically denied US citizenship based on race. The Naturalization Act of 1790 guaranteed the right of citizenship to "free, white persons." Congress later extended citizenship to people of African descent in 1868 and Native Americans in 1924, while Mexican Americans were considered "white by law," as we have seen. The children of Asian immigrants born on American soil were granted citizenship based on their place of birth, but their parents remained "aliens ineligible for citizenship." This blunt racism created a troubled and contentious relationship for Asian immigrants and their children in the public schools.[95]

Immigrants from first China and then Japan pioneered the Asian immigrant experience in the United States, and it is these groups that give us the clearest picture of the varied educational experiences of Asian Americans before 1954. California was home to large numbers of Asian immigrants in the mid- to late nineteenth century, but their children were not always welcome in public schools. In one well-known case, Mary and Joseph Tape decided to enroll their eight-year-old daughter, Mamie, in the public school closest to their house in San Francisco in 1884. Mamie's parents believed that because they paid taxes and their daughter was an American citizen, she and her younger brother had the right to attend the neighborhood public school.

Principal Jennie Hurley disagreed, citing the San Francisco Board of Education's strict policy of excluding Chinese Americans. The Tapes wrote to the Imperial Chinese Consulate in San Francisco for assistance, and on October 4, 1884, Consul General Frederick A. Bee penned an angry letter to the San Francisco Board of Education stating that the exclusion of Chinese children from American public schools represented a stark violation of international treaties and US law. When the school district still refused to admit Mamie because of her racial identity, her parents sued.[96]

On January 9, 1885, the court issued a strongly worded decision in the Tapes' favor requiring Principal Hurley to admit Mamie without further delay. Judge Maguire reasoned that according to California law, public schools were mandated to admit "all children between six and twenty-one years of age residing in the district." He concluded, "The only reason urged against her admittance is that she was born of Chinese parents. In other words, because she is descended from the Chinese branch of the Mongolian race, she is excluded by law from participating in the benefits and privileges of free public education, which are by the same law accorded to the children of all other races—white, black and copper colored."[97]

The court did not consider Mamie to be white but instead part of the

"Chinese branch of the Mongolian tree." The ruling established that the state had an obligation to educate children of all races, including "white, black and copper colored," and that it was illegal to bar Mamie just because she "was born of Chinese parents." The San Francisco Board of Education was quick to grasp the implication of this ruling. Looking at the example of segregated schools in the Jim Crow South, California lawmakers hastily passed a bill legalizing segregated schools for "Mongolians." The law was signed on March 4, 1885, one day after the California Supreme Court upheld the lower court's decision in the Mamie Tape case.[98]

On April 7, 1885, Mamie showed up for her first day at the Spring Valley School only to be informed that she did not have the correct medical records on file. While her parents were seeing to the paperwork, the San Francisco Board of Education opened a school for "Mongolian" children in a dilapidated old building in the heart of Chinatown. By the time Mamie's application was in order, the board of education had assigned her to the new school, which she was forced to attend since the court had only ruled that the city could not exclude Chinese American children from public schools. It was perfectly legal, however, to segregate them.[99]

The Tapes may have lost their legal battle, but Mary Tape had the last word. Her furious letter to the board of education was published in local newspapers, where she extolled city leaders for their vicious and anti-democratic prejudice. She wrote, "What right have you to bar my children out of the school because she is a chinese Descend. . . . Mamie Tape will never attend any of the Chinese schools of your making! Never!!"[100]

Chinese American enrollment in the California public schools grew slowly but steadily after 1885. San Francisco, Sacramento, and three small towns in the delta region of the Sacramento River assigned Chinese American students to segregated schools. In other communities, especially those with very small Asian immigrant populations, Chinese American students were admitted to majority-white schools with little fanfare. Despite the fact that Chinese American students developed a reputation for good behavior and excellent grades, San Francisco remained hostile to students of Chinese origin well into the twentieth century.[101] A judicial ruling in 1902 cited the separate but equal doctrine to rule that the San Francisco Board of Education had the right to bar a Chinese American student from his neighborhood public school and require him to attend the segregated Chinese school.[102]

Meanwhile, the West Coast Japanese immigrant community waged a parallel battle for fair and equal treatment in public schools. After the Chinese Exclusion Act of 1882, Japanese immigration swelled as young men and some women decided to take advantage of relatively well-paid work opportunities in Hawaii and California. Anti-Japanese feelings on the West Coast grew to a frenzied pitch, resulting in racist charges of an Asian "yellow peril" and demands to end Japanese immigration. The Russo-Japanese War, which erupted in 1904, shifted the context of this debate, as a series of significant military victories compelled Americans to view Japan as a military adversary and major global power. These tensions set the stage for an international showdown when the San Francisco Board of Education announced its intention to assign children of Japanese origin to the segregated school for children of the "Mongolian" race.[103]

"Japs Must Go with Chinese" announced the *San Francisco Chronicle* on September 11, 1904, noting, "It is probable that some 200 Japanese children will be excluded from the public schools and required to attend the Chinese public schools, if they wish to enjoy the advantages of the public school system." The Japanese government and the Japanese American community recognized school segregation as the hardening of racial prejudice into state-sponsored discrimination and immediately protested.[104]

The question whether San Francisco could segregate Japanese American schoolchildren drew national attention. White southerners vociferously supported San Francisco's right to segregate Chinese and Japanese American youth in public schools. As the *Daily Press* of Newport News, Virginia, wrote, "If the federal government by treaty was forced to allow Mongolians into the white schools of California, a like treaty could force the negroes of Cuba, Santo Domingo, and Hayti into the schools of Tennessee in defiance of the laws for the separation of the races."[105]

On October 11, 1906, San Francisco issued a decree requiring all students of Chinese, Japanese, and Korean descent to be removed from their neighborhood schools and reassigned to the "Mongolian" school in Chinatown. Japanese American parents refused, keeping their children home and appealing to the Japanese consulate. The consulate not only contacted the Japanese government for help but also sent telegrams to Japanese newspapers detailing the outrage. Japanese papers such as *Mainichi Shinbun*, a Tokyo daily, published scathing editorials criticizing the American government: "Stand up. Our countrymen have been HUMILIATED on the other side of the Pacific. Our boys and girls have been expelled from the public schools by the rascals of the United States, cruel and merciless like demons. . . . At this time we should be ready to give a blow to the United States. Yes, we should be ready to strike the Devil's head with an iron hammer. . . . Why do we not insist on sending ships?"[106]

What followed was an international crisis resolved by the famous "Gentlemen's Agreement" between President Theodore Roosevelt and Japanese leaders. Roosevelt persuaded the San Francisco Board of Education to rescind the segregation order for students of Japanese descent (but not

Chinese or Korean). In return, Japan agreed to end the emigration of laborers to the United States, with the notable exception of family members of Japanese nationals already living in the United States. This new policy dramatically reduced Japanese immigration and thus satisfied California's outspoken anti-Asian activists.[107]

The Gentlemen's Agreement was a remarkably successful diplomatic intervention in American public education by a foreign nation. Similar efforts by Mexico and China, as we have seen, were less successful. This compromise had important implications for all Asian American students. It halted the segregation of Japanese American students and proved that international political pressure could force the president of the United States to intervene in local school practices. As a result, except for the period of internment during World War II, Japanese American students attended public school on an integrated basis during a period when many other students of color did not.

Because Japanese American students had access to the same schools as whites, they enjoyed quality facilities, teachers, and curricula, which led to high rates of academic success. Japanese American students in the public schools set a precedent on the West Coast that would eventually pave the way for students of diverse Asian backgrounds to attend school on an integrated basis with minimal opposition from whites, especially when compared to the white backlash against Black and Mexican American school integration.

While the majority of Asian immigrants lived on the West Coast in the late nineteenth and early twentieth centuries, some occasionally pursued jobs in factories and farms up and down the East Coast. This created a special challenge for southern school administrators, who were legally required to segregate students by race.[108] For example, in 1898 white leaders in Paducah, Kentucky, could not figure out where to place the mixed-race son of Ida Sen, a white woman married to a Chinese man. City attorney E. W. Lightfoot struggled to assign the boy to a school since Kentucky law insisted "no white child shall be allowed to attend the colored school, nor shall any colored child be allowed to attend any white school."[109]

Lightfoot decided that since the boy was not "Caucasian" he must be "colored," even if he looked "white." He added, "It may be doubtless true, that the child with mixed blood may be whiter in appearance than the Caucasian, but the mixture of the races, in law, prevent such a child from being considered a white person. Therefore, the law which says that a colored child shall not go to the white school would prevent the Chinaman from attending that school." Fascinatingly, after reviewing Lightfoot's conclusion, the board voted seven to one to admit the boy to the white school "inasmuch as his mother is a white person." As this example suggests, southern racial apartheid was not designed to manage children of Asian descent, and as a result school assignments were left to the whims of local officials.[110]

School administrators in the Northeast seemed curious about, but not necessarily opposed to, the presence of pupils of Asian descent in public schools. The *New York Times* published a warm story about the "hard-working" Chinese students in New York City in 1922, noting, "most of them go to public school on Bayard street, but a few of them go to American schools in Brooklyn and other sections of the city." The reporter not only praised the Chinese American students for being studious and successful but also observed that education was of grave significance to the entire community: "Sometimes when the lessons are in progress wise men of Chinatown slip quietly into the schoolroom, where, from a corner of the room, they view the proceedings with grave, solemn faces. Some of them are fathers or relatives of the students, and not having had the educational advantages of the present generation they are eager nevertheless to have the coming race obtain the best American and Chinese education that is obtainable."[111]

Appreciation of Asian American students cooled as Chinese immigrants moved out of low-wage jobs into more lucrative positions as laundry, restaurant, and grocery store owners in the early twentieth century, and the immigrant population swelled. Tensions mounted in the Jim Crow South as more districts relegated Chinese Americans to poorly funded "colored" schools.

In 1924, Mississippi native Martha Lum registered for and was assigned to the white school in Rosedale, which she had attended along with her sister and two other Chinese American girls in town for years. But during lunch on the first day of school, Principal J. H. Nutt pulled Martha and the other Chinese American girls aside and sent them home. The girls were all colored, he told them, and therefore not welcomed at the white school. Martha Lum and her sister walked straight home, where their parents ran a small grocery store. Together, they discussed their options. Should the girls agree to attend the "colored" school in town, which would not start until November after the cotton harvest, or should they fight to continue attending the far nicer, newly constructed brick school that promised to prepare students for college? The Lum family decided to fight.[112]

The Lums filed a lawsuit against Rosedale Consolidated High School on October 28, 1924. Attorneys argued that Martha was not "colored," as that racial category referred specifically to people of African ancestry. They elaborated, "She is not a member of the colored race nor is she of mixed blood, but . . . she is pure Chinese." Since there was no school for "Mongolian" children, Martha's lawyers contended she should be allowed to use the white one. The Mississippi Circuit Court for the First Judicial District of Bolivar County ruled in Martha's favor, but the school district appealed.

The Mississippi Supreme Court overturned the lower court's ruling, insisting that the point of segregated schools was to safeguard white racial purity from any taint of outside influence, whether African or Asian. This ruling was important, as it exposed the blatant white supremacist ideology that undergirded school segregation. The justices wrote:

> To all persons acquainted with the social conditions of this state and of the Southern states generally it is well known that it is the earnest desire of the white race to preserve its racial integrity and purity, and to maintain the purity of the social relations as far as it can be done by law. . . . When the public school system was being created it was intended that the white race should be separated from all other races. It is true that the negro race was the only race of consequence so far as numbers were concerned. . . . So far as we have been able to find, the word "white," when used in describing the race, is limited strictly to the Caucasian race, while the word "colored" is not strictly limited to negroes or persons having negro blood.[113]

In other words, the purpose of separate schools was to preserve the "racial integrity and purity" of "the white race" by separating whites from "all other races." Chinese American students, according to the Mississippi Supreme Court in 1925, were not white, so they must be "colored," and their children should be assigned to schools accordingly. With support from the Mississippi Delta Chinese community, the Lums appealed the decision to the US Supreme Court, but this was to little avail. Citing *Plessy v. Ferguson*, the Supreme Court affirmed that it was perfectly legal to provide separate but equal facilities for white and "colored" citizens and that Chinese Americans could be classified as colored.[114]

Even after this ruling, southern school leaders had no clear policy for school assignments of Asian American students. In communities with significant Chinese American populations, school officials sometimes opened separate Chinese schools. "The school officials split up the children three ways in Mississippi," George S. Schuyler described in 1936 in the NAACP magazine, the *Crisis*, accompanied by photographs of the "white, black and yellow schools" in Greenville, Mississippi. Not surprisingly, the white high school was an immense brick structure with white columns so large Schuyler could not fit the entire building into a single photograph. The Black county training school, although it served more students, was a modest two-story brick building. The public school for Chinese American students was housed in a small, one-story wood-frame building with four windows on each long side and a door on the end. "Three sets of public schools supported by one set of taxpayers to accommodate what is really just one set of American children," lamented Schuyler.[115]

The Japanese attack on Pearl Harbor on December 7, 1941, marked a sharp turning point in Asian American history. Ronald Takaki writes, "The conflagration would require the immigrants and their offspring to determine more sharply than ever before their identities as Asians and as Americans. They had been viewed and treated as 'strangers from a different shore,' but now they would be asked to support their country in crisis and serve as Americans in the armed forces."[116]

On December 8, 1941, Congress declared war on Japan and allied the United States with China against the Axis forces. US officials declared that all people of Japanese ancestry living on the mainland were suspect "enemy aliens." On February 19, 1942, President Franklin D. Roosevelt authorized the secretary of war to place certain areas under military authority and remove people of Japanese descent, including men, women, and children who were US citizens.

Citing vague claims of "military necessity," the entire Japanese American population of the West Coast was forcibly removed from their homes, stripped of their personal property, and sent to concentration camps in the American interior. Eventually more than 110,000 mainland Japanese Americans, including 30,000 children, were placed in camps where they were forced to live in crowded, hastily constructed wood barracks surrounded by barbed wire, guard towers, and armed guards. Eventually, military leaders built schools for incarcerated children inside the internment camps. Japanese American students recognized the absurdity of studying American ideals, institutions, and practices in classrooms surrounded by barbed wire. "I feel like I am a dangerous enemy spy being held in prison," wrote one student in a required composition.[117]

This unfair treatment forced the US government to prove that ethnicity did not determine how an individual was treated in a democracy. In 1943, officials lifted the ban on military service by Japanese Americans and repealed the Chinese Exclusion Act, which established a small quota for annual immigration from China for the first time in decades. Jobs opened up to men and women of Asian descent that had never existed before, and thousands rushed to work in shipyards, factories, and aircraft plants. Eventually over thirty-three thousand Nisei served in the armed forces and the Military Intelligence Service during World War II, while four thousand Japanese American youth volunteered to serve as "ambassadors of goodwill" by enrolling in colleges and universities nationwide. Despite the outrageous injustice of Japanese American internment, Asian Americans successfully chipped away at the barriers to full equality during World War II.[118]

When the war ended in 1945, more than two-thirds of interned Japanese American families returned to the West Coast, but thousands of young and well-educated second-generation Japanese Americans moved to cities like Chicago, Minneapolis, Denver, and Cleveland, where their children attended school on an integrated basis. Middle-class families moved from San Francisco's Chinatown into the Richmond and Sunset districts, where their children were welcomed in public schools. But thousands of other Chinese American families, many of them very poor, remained in Chinatown, and thousands of Japanese Americans continued to live in segregated neighborhoods in Los Angeles, where anti-Japanese hostility flared anew.[119]

The growing Cold War created new opportunities for Chinese and Japanese American communities to advocate for equal civil rights. In 1948, Asian American activists secured the Japanese-American Claims Act, which authorized the settlement of property loss claims related to internment. That same year the US Supreme Court ruled that restrictive housing covenants were discriminatory and illegal, and in 1952, the Supreme Court struck down state laws denying land ownership to Asian immigrants known as "aliens ineligible to citizenship." Also in 1952, the McCarran-Walter Act nullified the racial restriction of the 1790 naturalization law that had been used to deny Asian immigrants American citizenship.[120]

America's new attitude toward citizens of Asian descent was characterized by President Harry Truman's address to the Nisei soldiers of the 442nd Regimental Combat Team on the lawn of the White House on July 15, 1946. He stated, "You are to be congratulated on what you have done for this great country of ours. I think it was my predecessor who said that Americanism is not a matter of race or creed, it is a matter of the heart." Truman continued, "You fought not only the enemy, but you fought prejudice—and you have won. Keep up that fight, and we will continue to win—to make this great Republic stand for just what the Constitution says it stands for: the welfare of all the people all the time."[121]

Despite Truman's compassionate words, the battle against prejudice was not yet won, and the welfare of all citizens was not yet secure, especially when it came to public education. The campaign for equal opportunities would blossom into expansive, multiple, and overlapping movements for civil rights and social justice following *Brown v. Board of Education* in 1954.

CONCLUSION

American public schools have functioned as tools of settler colonialism, forced assimilation, and racial oppression to consolidate power and authority among privileged whites. From the very beginning, people of color rejected educational inequality and fought to reimagine public education as something that could serve their families, communities, and nation. This work was contextually specific, and antiracist educational activism therefore looked very different depending on the community and the time and place in which it took place. Activists fine-tuned their approach to school integration and the struggle for educational equality in response to the specific discrimination they encountered, their relative economic and political power, and their unique vision for how public education could advance larger goals related to equal citizenship, racial uplift, self-determination, community empowerment, and economic equality.

These educational histories reveal three key findings that can help us design more effective strategies for contemporary educational justice. First, there is compelling historical evidence that whites excluded children of color from the earliest public schools and then, when forced to include them, assigned youth of African, indigenous, Chinese, Japanese, and Mexican origin to segregated facilities. This pattern played out across the country in educational experiences for African American students in Massachusetts and Virginia, Mexican American students in Texas and Arizona, Chinese American students in California and Mississippi, and Native American students in Oklahoma and South Dakota. This remarkable and highly durable pattern reveals how the ideology of white supremacy was literally built into US public schools and fortified over time.

Second, in virtually every region—the North, South, Midwest, and West—school segregation resulted in unequal funding, facilities, teachers, resources, and curricula. It is notable how many times whites attempted to force a "manual training and industrial" curriculum on students of color while reserving an academic curriculum for whites. Persistent disparities in standardized test scores, high school graduation rates, and college attendance rates demonstrate the pernicious effects of educational segregation and inequality before 1954.

Third, this history highlights the fierce and well-organized resistance by students, parents, teachers, and community leaders who were compelled to fight for their right to a quality public education, however they defined that ideal. Young people and women feature prominently in these stories, especially students and mothers who refused to give up their most cherished hopes and dreams for a better future. When activists came together to combat educational racism, they often targeted the primary instrument of its delivery—school segregation. Whether legally sanctioned or illegally gerrymandered, segregated facilities engendered inequality. Little surprise, then, that so many people of color targeted school segregation as a major impediment to educational equality or that these activists won their battle against the flagrant violation of the Fourteenth Amendment's equal protection clause.

Brown v. Board of Education in 1954 marked the culmination of more than a century of educational activism and signaled the start of a new era where the federal government would uphold civil rights for all. The question remained: would outlawing racial segregation be enough to create equality for all students, regardless of race, creed, or color in the public schools?

CHAPTER 2   **DESEGREGATION**

On May 17, 1954, the US Supreme Court outlawed racial segregation in American public schools in *Brown v. Board of Education of Topeka, Kansas*. A monumental victory for Black civil rights activists and the NAACP, *Brown* was a historic decision with profound implications for all students.

Reversing the "separate but equal" doctrine established by the 1896 *Plessy v. Ferguson* decision, Chief Justice Earl Warren explained that in the modern era, education was essential to the very foundation of good citizenship. He elaborated that education awakened children to the nation's cultural values, helped them adjust to their environment, and prepared them for future professional training, adding, "In these days, it is doubtful that any child may reasonably be expected to succeed in life if he is denied the opportunity of an education. Such an opportunity, where the state has undertaken to provide it, is a right which must be made available to all on equal terms." In other words, if a state taxed citizens in order to fund public schools, these schools must be equal for all.[1]

The question for the court then became whether it was possible to offer a truly equal education in segregated schools. As the previous chapter demonstrates, white Americans used school segregation to concentrate public resources in majority- or all-white schools while denying equal resources to schools that served large numbers of students of color. But what if school leaders agreed to genuinely resolve these inequalities—what if separate schools were truly equal in terms of funding, facilities, teacher quality, and other material goods?[2]

Chief Justice Warren tackled this question directly: "We come then to the question presented: Does segregation of children in public schools solely on the basis of race, even though the physical facilities and other 'tangible' factors may be equal, deprive the children of the minority group of equal educational opportunities?"

The Supreme Court answered in the affirmative, stating, "We believe that it does."

Warren cited cutting-edge social science to argue that segregated facilities conveyed a message of racial inferiority to students in segregated schools. Refusing to allow an individual to enter or participate in a specific institution, such as a public school, because of his or her racial identity implied that there was something terribly wrong with that person—something so wretched that white people could not risk even casual association among children. School segregation, therefore, was found to be illegal because it could undermine Black students' self-esteem and make it harder for them to succeed in school.

As Warren put it, "To separate them from others of similar age and qualifications solely because of their race generates a feeling of inferiority as to their status in the community that may affect their hearts and minds in a way unlikely ever to be undone." Racial segregation violated the civil rights of Black students guaranteed by the equal protection clause of the Fourteenth Amendment. Warren ruled, "We conclude that in the field of public education, the doctrine of 'separate but equal' has no place. Separate educational facilities are inherently unequal."[3]

Brown drew passionate responses, ranging from righteous fury by whites who interpreted the ruling as an assault on the "southern way of life" to unbridled enthusiasm by Black citizens who viewed it as long overdue. Today, the vast majority of Americans believe that the decision is just and that racial segregation in schools—and everywhere else—violates the equal protection clause of the US Constitution. In this context, *Brown* represents not only a legal victory but also a moral one that heralded the end of American racial apartheid and the beginning of the Second Reconstruction. However, if the goal of *Brown* was to equalize education for students of color, then it has not been entirely successful, as high levels of segregation and corresponding educational inequality continue to haunt American schools.[4]

This chapter considers examples from the diverse educational histories of African Americans, Native Americans, Latinxs, and Asian Americans from 1954 to the present. It argues that although school desegregation in the United States dramatically improved educational opportunities for many students of color, it did not equalize public education for all. In fact, many of the significant gains achieved through school desegregation efforts in the 1960s and 1970s have retreated as school segregation has increased since the mid-1980s.

This chapter highlights three important themes in the history of American education. First, whites continued to enforce segregation and inequality in public schools for many years following *Brown*. This historic ruling resulted in neither immediate school desegregation in terms of racially mixed schools nor an end to educational discrimination and inequality. Instead, *Brown* provided a strong legal basis for activists to challenge educational racism and served as notice to all citizens that the judiciary viewed equal education as a basic civil right.

Second, after 1954 grassroots struggles for school desegregation became a core component of modern civil rights movements orchestrated by African American, Native American, Latinx, and Asian American citizens and their allies. At the same time, integration was never the only goal of educational activism designed to redress educational racism, and at times it was explicitly rejected. The widespread practice of isolating Black, Native American, Latinx, and some Asian American students meant that segregated schools stood as monuments to state-sponsored racism. Little surprise, then, that so many educational activists interpreted school integration as a way to equalize resources and facilities and secure the civic function of common schools to train all children for equal citizenship in a democracy. What happened next was a remarkable uprising of not only civil rights leaders but also students, parents, and teachers who mobilized friends and neighbors in social movements to reject school segregation in all its insidious forms.

Finally, this history highlights the myriad complex and evolving ways that activists imagined desegregation as a strategy to dismantle educational racism and build better public schools. School integration was rarely neat, simple, easy, or straightforward. Often, school desegregation was not even linear—victories would be won, only to be followed by setbacks and reversals that prompted renewed rounds of protests, boycotts, and judicial actions. Many school desegregation battles, like those in New York City, are still raging. Educational activists have rarely been satisfied with school desegregation orders that simply mixed students of color together with white students in a single school.

After generations of institutionalized racism, newly desegregated schools did not typically reflect the needs of students of color in terms of a diverse faculty, an antiracist curriculum, equal access to extracurricular activities, an appropriate vocational program, fair disciplinary policies, equitable access to advanced coursework, and effective support services like counseling and English language instruction. Meaningful school integration requires a dramatic restructuring of American public education in order to affirm the unique cultures, heritages, and needs of all students and to strengthen civic bonds in a multiracial democracy.[5]

This kind of meaningful school integration has not yet been widely achieved in American public schools. According to the Civil Rights Project at the University of California, Los Angeles, the most effective period of school desegregation took place between 1964 and 1988, which represented the high point of racial mixing for Black students in majority-white schools. Since 1988, American public schools have been "resegregating" due to an increasingly conservative Supreme Court, which authorized the termination of desegregation plans, and as a result of declining political support and the rise of market-based reforms like "school choice" that can exacerbate racial and socioeconomic segregation. Educational policy in recent decades has emphasized charter schools, vouchers, high-stakes testing, and state and federal accountability measures, which propose to improve the quality of schools without addressing racial and socioeconomic segregation.

As a result, today African American and Latinx students face both the highest and fastest-growing rates of racial segregation in American public schools, as well as the inequality that almost always accompanies this segregation. In the past twenty-five years for which we have data, the number of "intensely segregated" schools with white student enrollment of 0 to 10 percent has more than tripled. A massive amount of scholarship shows that school segregation correlates with inequality, while racially diverse schools both equalize resources and opportunities and prepare all students to live and function in a multiracial, modern democracy.[6]

The fact that we have yet to achieve racially integrated classrooms or equal opportunities in American public schools makes this history a vitally important one, especially for citizens who believe that public education helps fortify the democratic ideal by providing all children, no matter the circumstances of their birth, the chance for a better life. This chapter highlights the gains Americans have made toward equalizing public education since 1954 but also lays bare disturbing evidence of persistent, pernicious racism. It prepares readers for a philosophical inquiry of the meaning of educational equality in chapter 3 and the possibilities of emancipatory school integrations as detailed in chapters 4 and 5.

NO FALSE SENSE OF SECURITY

Horace Mann Bond celebrated the *Brown* decision as a watershed moment in the long Black freedom struggle, writing, "Out of the blood and tears of the millions of Americans of African descent, this decision comes as a majestic break in the dark clouds with which the face of Man's destiny everywhere has been obscured."[7] The Black press overflowed with praise for *Brown*, interpreting it as "probably the most important single victory for the American Negro since emancipation."[8] This sentiment was shared by

Walter White, executive secretary of the NAACP, who declared the ruling to be one of eight epochal events in the three-hundred-year history of the American Negro.[9] Martin Luther King Jr. sermonized, "To all men of goodwill, this decision came as a joyous daybreak to end the long night of human captivity."[10]

This optimism, however, was soon tempered by caution, given that whites enjoyed the lion's share of political, economic, and social power in most communities. Offering a more measured response to *Brown*, Mary McLeod Bethune, president emeritus of Bethune-Cookman College, warned, "We must be ready to meet their clever devices—for they will have many. The work of the NAACP is not done. And it would be a serious and calamitous mistake for any person to relax vigilance in our struggle to build a moral state. . . . Let there be no undue rejoicing—no hysteria—no hate—no precipitant action—no false sense of security!"[11]

Historian Kevin Gaines emphasizes the critical distinction between "integration as the demise of separate black institutions" and "desegregation [as] the overthrow of the regime of racial subjugation defined by the exclusion of black people to access to power, wealth, education, status and dignity." Based on this definition, while all African Americans supported desegregation as an end to American racial apartheid, support for school integration was far more guarded, given the risks associated with merging "colored" and white schools.[12]

Separate schools in the South, although almost always unequal to white schools in terms of funding and resources, were nevertheless often revered as vital Black-controlled institutions. Parents wondered how white classmates, teachers, and administrators would treat Black students in integrated schools and how discriminatory treatment would affect their children's academic achievement. Despite these concerns, Black families volunteered their children to dismantle state-sponsored school segregation. Black girls in particular were likely to be the first students to desegregate formerly white schools in the South after 1954.[13]

In the United States, seventeen states and the District of Columbia required or permitted school segregation in 1954. *Brown* instructed school districts to eliminate dual systems with "all deliberate speed." Initial white outrage hardened into political intransigence on March 12, 1956, when Virginia representative Howard Smith, chairperson of the House Rules Committee, read a document titled "Declaration of Constitutional Principals" into the *Congressional Record*. Signed by eighty-two representatives and nineteen senators, this "Southern Manifesto" denounced *Brown* as an abuse of judicial power that trampled on states' rights. It insisted that the separate but equal doctrine in public schools "is founded on elemental humanity and commonsense, for parents should not be deprived by Government of the right to direct the lives and education of their own children." White lawmakers urged citizens to exhaust all "lawful means" to resist court-ordered school desegregation. Southern representatives rose from the House floor to applaud Smith's speech. Not a single person rose to speak against it.[14]

Massive southern white resistance in the wake of *Brown* was spectacular and, at times, appalling. Yet these same qualities served to undermine the effort altogether. The national press broadcast racist attacks on Black schoolchildren that moderate whites found distasteful, while the federal government interpreted overt anti-Black racism as problematic given the global battle between communism and democracy during the Cold War. One of the most famous episodes of massive white resistance came from Little Rock, Arkansas, a racially moderate city that took tentative steps to desegregate public schools in 1957 at the request of local NAACP leader Daisy Bates. Black high school students Minnijean Brown, Elizabeth Eckford, Ernest Green, Thelma Mothershed, Melba Patillo, Gloria Ray, Terrance Roberts, Jefferson Thomas, and Carlotta Walls volunteered to be transferred into the previously white Central High School. The school board carefully reviewed their transcripts and agreed to assign these nine Black students to Central High for the 1957–58 school year.[15]

Just two days before the start of school, Governor Orval E. Faubus mobilized the Arkansas National Guard to bar the Black students from entering Central High, a move that directly challenged the school district's pupil assignments and shocked local school leaders. Daisy Bates was able to make a last-minute plan to avoid the white mob, but she did not get a chance to notify fifteen-year-old Elizabeth Eckford of the change. When Elizabeth arrived alone on the first day of school, she was met by armed soldiers who refused to allow her to enter the school grounds. As Elizabeth struggled to figure out what to do, a furious white mob pushed closer, jeering, "Don't let her in, go back to where you came from!" She narrowly escaped with the assistance of white teacher and civil rights activist Grace Lorch, who insisted, "She's scared. She's just a little girl. . . . Six months from now you'll be ashamed at what you're doing." The entire debacle was caught on camera and broadcast on television screens worldwide, becoming one of many powerful images that would generate global sympathy and support for the Black civil rights movement.[16]

President Dwight D. Eisenhower federalized the Arkansas National Guard and called in the 101st Airborne Division of the US Army to escort the Black students safely inside Little Rock's Central High, an act that pushed school integration to the center of America's domestic political agenda. Across the nation and around the world, people were riveted by nightly news broadcasts, photographs, and spectacular scenes from Little Rock's yearlong school desegregation fiasco. Armed soldiers escorted Black students to their classes each day, but this was not enough to deter vicious harassment by whites. Central High expelled one of the Black students, Minnijean Brown, for supposedly dumping a bowl of chili on one of her tormentors in the cafeteria. Ernest Green persevered to become the first Black graduate of Central High School at the end of the year. Distraught by unflattering media attention, Little Rock closed its public high schools the following year after citizens refused to vote for a referendum that required integration to keep the schools open.[17]

School leaders throughout the region blanched at the thought of similar violent and humiliating events unfolding in their own communities. Many quietly developed more subtle means of subverting school desegregation, such as "freedom of choice" plans that ostensibly allowed children to select which school they wanted to attend but in practice exposed Black families to violent retribution if they tried to enroll in a white school. In an extreme example, Prince Edward County, Virginia, closed its public schools in the spring of 1959 to avoid desegregation, then used tuition grants to support "school choice" so white students could attend private, segregated schools, while Black pupils were denied an education for five years. Eventually moderate southern whites agreed to accept a miniscule degree of racial mixing in order to keep public schools open. This strategy came to dominate southern politics in the decade after *Brown* and resulted in only token racial mixing until the federal government intervened in 1964.[18]

Although most Americans interpreted *Brown* as applying only to segregated schools in the South and border states, many Black educational activists in the North believed the ruling applied nationwide. "School segregation and inferior education are among the biggest problems facing northern Negroes today," Robert L. Carter, general counsel of the NAACP, wrote in 1959. Residential segregation—which increased alongside suburbanization and white flight in the postwar era—was partially responsible for widespread de facto segregated schools, but it was also common for northern school boards to manipulate assignment policies and gerrymander school catchment zones to isolate Black students in certain schools.[19]

In Springfield, Massachusetts, school leaders repeatedly adjusted assignment policies so that Black students were assigned to majority-Black schools even when they lived outside of that school's attendance zone, while white students who lived within a majority-Black zone were permitted to transfer out. Similar discriminatory school assignment policies existed in Plainfield, New Jersey; Hempstead, New Rochelle, and Manhasset, New York; Gary, Indiana; Pontiac, Michigan; and Cincinnati, Ohio, through the early 1960s.[20]

Many communities in New Jersey had especially high rates of de facto school segregation by 1954. In September of that year, two mothers of Black kindergarteners in Englewood charged the local school board with deliberate segregation and discrimination. The *New York Times* observed, "The case is the first in New Jersey in which a public school board has appeared as a defendant on charges of discrimination. It is also possibly the first such case north of the Mason Dixon line since the Supreme Court outlawed racial discrimination."[21]

Citing *Brown*, Susan Anderson and Mary Walker filed a formal complaint after Englewood's all-white board of education removed Black students, including their sons, from the predominantly white Liberty School and transferred them to the majority-Black Lincoln School. The previous year, the kindergarten class at Liberty was 43 percent Black, but after the revised school assignment policy went into effect, Liberty's kindergarten class was 100 percent white, while Lincoln's was 100 percent Black. In a show of support for the *Brown* ruling, the New Jersey commissioner of education ruled in favor of the plaintiffs and ordered school authorities to redraw school catchment zones to create racially mixed schools. He also ordered the closing of Lincoln Junior High School so that Black students would be assigned to existing, predominantly white middle schools throughout the district.[22]

While this example shows that Black educational activists were able to use *Brown* to effectively challenge school segregation in the North, it is important to recognize the limitations of these victories. Dismantling school segregation in the North was a long and uneven process with dissatisfying results. For example, seven years later, Englewood's Lincoln Elementary remained 98 percent Black, while the nearby new, multimillion-dollar Donald A. Quarles School was nearly all white. Englewood school officials stubbornly insisted that all students must attend the school closest to their home, even as they refused to acknowledge that the school boundaries were drawn along conspicuously racial lines. Black citizens organized to fight this blatant racism and demand more equal and integrated schools. In 1962, hundreds of Black parents and students, joined by local rabbis, NAACP activists, and Freedom Riders fresh from battles in Mississippi, crowded into the Englewood City Council chambers where they sang protest songs and held signs aloft proclaiming, "We're for Freedom!" "Equal Education!" and "Better Housing!"[23]

Boycotting the start of the 1962–63 school year, 350 Lincoln School students marched in front of the dilapidated brick school. One placard read, "The Supreme Court Integrates—City Hall Abdicates!" Under sustained pressure from the Englewood Black community, the NAACP, the Urban League, and the Congress of Racial Equality, in 1963 the Englewood Public School District proposed to close the Lincoln School and expand Black enrollment in predominantly white schools. These were significant improvements, but Englewood continued to grapple with white flight, resegregation, and a racial achievement gap that signified the durability of educational racism and the limitations of racial mixing as a strategy to achieve educational equality.[24]

The long, slow struggle for school integration in Englewood, New Jersey, was echoed in communities throughout the North and Northeast. New York City, Boston, Chicago, Detroit, Milwaukee, Philadelphia, Buffalo, New Rochelle, New Haven, Springfield, Massachusetts, and Montclair, New Jersey, were among dozens of northern towns and cities with surges of grassroots community activism that cited *Brown* to demand an end to segregated schools.[25] Activists used integration as a strategy to equalize opportunities in districts where decades of segregation had left majority-Black schools bereft of funding, political support, and quality teachers compared to majority-white schools. Robert Carter explains, "We believed that the surest way for minority children to obtain their constitutional right to equal educational opportunity was to require removal of all racial barriers in the public school system, with black and white children attending the same schools." He continues, "Integration was viewed as the means to our ultimate objective, not the objective itself."[26]

Practically speaking, Black educational activists believed that "green follows white" in school politics or, more bluntly, that educational funding followed white students. School integration was an effective way to equalize opportunities because if Black students were dispersed throughout the district, they were less likely to find themselves isolated in schools with less money, run-down facilities, less-qualified teachers, and an inferior curriculum. School integration had a potent ideological value as well, as many people believed that if young Americans grew up learning and playing together in school, then racial prejudice would dissipate. Integrated and equal public schools would help create an integrated and equal citizenry.

Through a meticulous commitment to nonviolent protest, Black civil rights activists in the 1950s and 1960s persuaded Americans of the dangers of state-sponsored prejudice and the possibilities of a color-blind democracy. By the late 1960s, Black students regularly demanded and received Black history courses, more Black teachers, counselors, and administrations, and more equity in extracurricular programs such as school plays, athletics, student governance, and social events. In Newark, New Jersey, in 1971, students fought for the right to fly the Black liberation flag in public schools. Lawrence Hamm, a seventeen-year-old Black student elected to the Newark Board of Education, proposed to place the flag in every classroom where at least one-half of students were Black. Black high school students crammed into a school board meeting to show their support for the measure, claiming it represented pride in their cultural heritage. Thanks to Hamm's enthusiastic support, the resolution passed.[27]

Youth civil rights protests rocked not only large cities like Newark, New York, Detroit, Chicago, and Boston but also small towns and suburban villages like Waterloo, Iowa, Madison, Illinois, and Spring Valley, New York. "What are they doing out there rioting in the cornfields?" asked perplexed white observers in Waterloo, Iowa, in 1967 after Black high school students walked out of school to protest a lack of equal opportunities. "The whites have got to face it, man," said Byron Washington, a sixteen-year-old Black protestor. "This is a new generation. We aren't going to stand for the stuff our mamas and fathers stood for."[28]

Following the dramatic March on Washington in the summer of 1963, Black civil rights activists won a series of legislative victories, including the Civil Rights Act of 1964, the Voting Rights Act of 1965, and the Elementary and Secondary Education Act of 1965. Together, these laws sparked the most successful era of school integration in American history. For the next twenty years, school desegregation unfolded first in the South and then in the North, Midwest, and West as school officials (often under court order) mixed students together.[29]

A series of US Supreme Court rulings accelerated school desegregation for African American students. In 1968, *Green v. County School Board of New Kent County* struck down "freedom of choice" plans used to subvert school desegregation, declaring instead that school districts had an "affirmative duty" to eliminate segregated systems "root and branch" and that integration must be achieved in terms of facilities, staff, faculty, extracurricular activities, and transportation. *Alexander v. Holmes County (Mississippi) Board of Education* in 1969 ruled that schools had to be desegregated "at once" and "operate now and hereafter only unitary schools." In 1971, the court ruled in *Swann v. Charlotte-Mecklenburg Board of Education* that "racially neutral" school assignment policies were unacceptable if they produced segregated schools as a result of existing patterns of residential segregation. It also approved busing as an acceptable strategy to overcome residential segregation. Two years later, the court turned its attention to the northern and western United States in *Keyes v. Denver School District No. 1.* Here justices ruled that even in a district with no history of legal school segregation, school leaders were responsible for policies such as constructing schools in racially isolated neighborhoods or gerrymandering school district lines that resulted in segregated schools. This case recognized that like African Americans, Mexican Americans and Puerto Ricans had a right to attend public schools on an equal and integrated basis.[30]

Historian Charles Clotfelter explains, "The result of these developments was a breathtaking transformation of public education in many communities in the South. In the space of just a few years—principally, 1969–72—levels of interracial contact in schools shot up all over the South." In 1963, about 1 percent of Black children in the South attended school with white children. By 1970, fully 90 percent of Black children in the South attended racially mixed schools, and efforts toward school integration were shifting northward.[31]

These crucial victories came at steep political costs, and as vocal white hostility to school integration grew nationwide, political support for the reform declined precipitously. "Busing inner-city black children to suburban schools may still be a scary prospect in many parts of the country where whites believe it would lead to violence, intermarriage and other nightmares of the affluent," quipped a *New York Times* reporter in 1971.[32]

President Richard M. Nixon, elected in 1968, was an outspoken critic of school desegregation, especially the busing programs required to break down severe residential segregation. During his first term, Nixon appointed four Supreme Court justices as members of the Warren Court retired. He replaced Chief Justice Earl Warren with Warren Burger, a sixty-one-year-old Republican from Minnesota with a reputation as a staunch conservative. The Burger Court would prove to offer far less support for school desegregation than its predecessor. Meanwhile, school integration in the North remained hampered by white resistance, residential segregation, and a growing Black and Latinx population concentrated in urban areas as whites and middle-class families decamped to the suburbs.[33]

The rising Black Power movement renewed interest in the possibility of separate, Black-controlled schools as an alternative to school integration, especially in the urban North.[34] African Americans in New York City were exasperated with the board of education's abysmal track record on school integration. Despite the fact that school officials claimed to be working on school integration since 1954, school segregation had increased as Black and Latinx families moved to the city, and whites absconded to the suburbs. Although Black and Latinx communities had fought long and hard for school integration in New York City, many were ready to consider alternative strategies to improve educational opportunities. As Preston Wilcox explains, "The residents of that community decided once and for all that the educational problems of their children derived not from a *failure to integrate* but from the *success* of the New York City Board of Education in *failing to educate* their children."[35]

Black Power activists maintained that community-controlled schools would build strong Black institutions, prepare Black youth to thrive in a hostile society, and promote Black social and economic development. This strategy built on a long tradition of separate, Black-controlled schools dating to the start of the common school era in the mid-nineteenth century.[36] Instead of fighting political intransigence and white resistance in order to desegregate the schools, activists wanted to build new institutions dedicated to Black and Latinx youth. "It was generally concluded that the existing educational systems were not responsive to the wishes of the black community," notes Charles V. Hamilton. "Black people, having moved to the state of questioning the system's very legitimacy, are seeking ways to create a new system."[37]

"Action now, baby; right now!" insisted Black parents in Boston, where plans for school integration had stalled for years. Parents and community leaders made similar demands throughout the urban North. Native American educational activists supported the growing Black community-control movement, comparing it to the long struggle for cultural self-determination among indigenous peoples. Native American scholar Jack D. Forbes wrote, "Thus the integration-segregation controversy is entering a new and more complex stage brought on by the anti-integration stance of some Afro-Americans coupled with the traditional attitude of Indians."[38]

New York City's famous community-controlled school experiment led to bitter, violent clashes between Black and Puerto Rican educational activists and the New York City teachers' union, which was mostly white. Following a prolonged teacher strike in 1968, state leaders negotiated a plan to decentralize the nation's largest school district, giving marginally more control to local communities while maintaining sufficient protections to placate union leaders. In the end, this compromise did very little to redistribute educational power or resources to Black and Latinx families in New York. Black educational activists in the urban North continued to experiment with variations of both school desegregation and community control as strategies to improve public education.[39]

After 1974, a series of court rulings made it harder for Black citizens to pursue judicial remedies to school segregation and inequality. *Milliken v. Bradley*, a Supreme Court ruling that struck down an ambitious interdistrict school desegregation plan in Detroit, effectively eliminated the possibility of combining urban districts of mostly Black and Latinx students with nearby majority-white suburban ones.[40] Through the 1980s, the Ronald Reagan and George H. W. Bush administrations' Justice Departments waged a legal attack on school integration plans. By 1991, a more conservative Supreme Court made it easier for formerly segregated school districts to declare "unitary status" and dismantle court-ordered integration plans.[41] Studies have shown that as the courts released school districts from mandates to desegregate, racial segregation quickly spiked, and with it, inequality increased for minority students.[42]

This is what happened in Seattle, Washington, after the school board voted unanimously to dismantle its school desegregation plan in 1991. Launched in 1977 to improve the academic achievement of all students, the "Seattle Plan" grew out of pressure from the local NAACP, the Church Council of Greater Seattle, the local Urban League, and the American Civil Liberties Union to improve the quality of public education for Black students.[43]

Seattle was a liberal, West Coast city with public school demographics that were roughly 67 percent white, 17 percent Black, and 14 percent Asian American. According to the Seattle Plan, both minority and white students would spend part of their elementary years in a nearby neighborhood school and part of their time riding a bus to a different neighborhood. Before desegregation, four of the city's eleven high schools were "racially imbalanced," or had high levels of racial segregation. By 1980, only Cleveland High School remained out of balance, and that by a mere two students. Elementary and middle schools, likewise, were integrated by pairing majority-Black schools with majority-white ones.[44]

By 1988, Seattle's public school enrollment had fallen from about one hundred thousand to fewer than fifty thousand due to shifting demographics, white and middle-class flight, and vocal white resistance to the Seattle Plan. Some Black families began to question busing as a policy and school integration as an objective. They were especially frustrated that test scores and graduation rates remained far behind white students, even in integrated schools. Black parents called for new reforms to equalize educational opportunities, including more funding for all schools, more Black teachers, a multicultural curriculum, and Black mentors for Black children.[45]

In a calculated effort to appease white families and stem middle-class flight, city officials began to dismantle the Seattle Plan, which was eliminated in 1991 and replaced with a much smaller plan that focused only on high schools. Under the new "controlled choice" plan, students indicated their preferences for high school, and the district made assignments with an eye to increasing racial diversity in each school. The results were modestly successful, with more racial mixing than would have been achieved through traditional residential zoning.[46]

In 2000, a group of white parents sued the Seattle School Board for racial discrimination after their children did not get into their first choice high school. In 2007, the US Supreme Court ruled in *Parents Involved in Community Schools v. Seattle School District No. 1* that "racial classifications" used by the Seattle School Board violated white students' Fourteenth Amendment right to equal protection. Quoting the 1955 *Brown II* decision, Chief

Justice John G. Roberts Jr. wrote in the majority opinion, "The way to stop discrimination on the basis of race is to stop discriminating on the basis of race."[47]

Parents Involved in Community Schools made it more challenging, but not impossible, for districts to promote racial and socioeconomic integration. Importantly, the ruling preserved school leaders' ability to foster diversity in other ways, such as locating new schools between racially distinct neighborhoods, redrawing school attendance zones, and targeting recruitment of students for particular schools.

By 2008, roughly one-third of Seattle public schools had nonwhite populations that far exceeded the district's average of 58 percent. In twenty of these schools, nonwhite populations were 90 percent or more of the student body. Noting that they would "rather spend money to improve student instruction than busing students across the city," Seattle adopted a revised school assignment policy in 2009 that exacerbates segregation and educational inequality. Expressing the concerns of many Black parents, Angela McKinney told a *Seattle Times* reporter, "I think [the schools] should all be equal if we are going to be told, or restricted, as to where we can send our kids."[48]

Unfortunately, as a growing body of scholarship demonstrates, majority-Black public schools are rarely equal. As Amy Stuart Wells and Erica Frankenberg document, the problems associated with unequal opportunities that stem from concentrated poverty, teacher quality and high teacher turnover, inadequate curriculum and supplies, and limited aspirations and social networks are a major factor for this inequality. Unequal educational outcomes in "majority minority" schools, including low levels of academic achievement and graduation rates as well as instability and lack of public support, are an additional factor. They conclude, "Taken together, all of these factors demonstrate the layered, all-encompassing nature of racial inequality and its impact on separate public schools."[49] Gary Orfield and Frankenberg note, "A half century of research shows that many forms of unequal opportunity are linked to segregation. Further, research also finds that desegregated education has substantial benefits for educational and later life outcomes for students from all backgrounds."[50]

Since *Brown*, Black educational activists have used school desegregation as an especially potent and successful strategy to push back against racist school policies. History shows us that school integration can be an effective way to remedy decades of school segregation and inequality, but it also demonstrates that whites have refused to accept racially and socioeconomically mixed schools or the redistribution of public resources that they entail. Many educational activists, of all races and political affiliation, have concluded that since school integration "did not work," we should dedicate ourselves to providing more resources and demand high accountability from "majority minority" schools. Educational activist and award-winning journalist Nikole Hannah-Jones writes, "True integration, true equality, requires a surrendering of advantage, and when it comes to our own children, that can feel almost unnatural." Nevertheless, she is one of countless Black educational activists who insist that Americans cannot give up on integration as a strategy, an ideal, or an essential component of public education in a democracy.[51]

ALWAYS BE INDIANS, NO MORE, NO LESS

"Indians, Too!" hailed the *Afro-American*, a Black newspaper from Baltimore reporting on the widespread effects of *Brown*. It continued, "The May 17 decision not only struck a blow at the separation of colored and white children in schools, but also facilitated the integration of Indian youngsters in the public schools of New Mexico." In the wake of *Brown*, New Mexico superintendent of public instruction Tony Wiley took steps to integrate Black, white, and Native American students. "I can say today that there no longer is segregation in the New Mexico school system," he confirmed. Arizona responded similarly to *Brown* by closing a segregated high school for Black students in Phoenix and adopting new policies of color-blind admissions that applied to white, Black, and increasing numbers of Native American students in public schools.[52]

The question of school desegregation after 1954 was a complicated one for Native Americans, as many remained suspicious of government-sponsored education and unconvinced that integration was a desirable strategy to improve educational opportunities. "Sir, I am writing you this letter to let you know that the statement made by the NAACP, namely, 'that the Indians of the Southwest benefitted from the Supreme Court ruling on racial segregation which enables Indians to attend schools with whites' has bothered me, an Indian, no end," wrote Jeronimo Netzehualcoyti in his article entitled "Negroes Can Integrate, Indians Never!" He continued, "As you probably know, we Indians of America are genuinely proud of our race, our traditions etc. We, regardless of who our children attend school with, will always be Indians, no more, no less."[53]

Native American scholar Jack D. Forbes agreed, arguing that a "uni-ethnic" school was not necessarily academically inferior to a "multi-ethnic" school and that Native Americans viewed control over educational institutions as a key component of self-determination and political sovereignty in a hostile, white-dominated society.[54] African American writer and folklorist Zora Neale Hurston admired the way Native Americans advocated for educational equality in the wake of *Brown.* "The American Indian has never been spoken of as a minority and chiefly because there is no whine in the Indian," Hurston wrote in the summer of 1955. "Certainly he fought, and valiantly, for his lands, and rightly so, but it is inconceivable of an Indian to seek forcible association with anyone."[55]

Despite these kinds of major misgivings, many Native American educational activists experimented with school integration as a strategy to equalize educational opportunities. This was especially true in the South, where Native Americans interpreted segregated schools as detrimental to their civil rights and began demanding access to public schools on a nonracial basis in the wake of *Brown.* Just as they resisted admitting Black students to formerly white schools, white southerners fought to keep Native Americans locked into segregated and inferior facilities.

In 1955, North Carolina passed a law that permitted school administrators to assign all students to specific schools, a strategy designed to undermine *Brown.* In January of 1956, Bolton Bullard (Lumbee) attempted to enroll his three children in a Sanford, North Carolina, public school. The Bullards had recently moved from Robeson County to Lee County, but Lee County officials cited a state law that required the separation of white, Black, and Native American children and refused to admit the Bullard children to the white school. The state superintendent of public instruction told the Bullards that if they wanted to use the public schools, they would have to attend the state-sponsored "Indian" school—even though it was located in another county, and the parents would be responsible for transportation.

While the Bullards did not object to the existence of a separate Indian school, they found it costly and inconvenient to travel so far for school, especially when there was a public school just down the road. Citing *Brown,* the Bullards tried—and failed—to get their children enrolled in the local white school. After 1954, these efforts became more common throughout the region, as Native American families attempted to enroll their children in local public schools, sometimes for the sake of convenience and other times in a deliberate effort to challenge state-sponsored segregation.[56]

Displeased by this rising tide of Native American political activism, the Ku Klux Klan (KKK) burned crosses on the front lawns of two Native American families in Maxton, North Carolina, in January of 1958. A few days later, fifty robed and hooded Klansmen gathered in an empty cornfield outside of town where they preached hate against the local Lumbee Indians and raised a giant, oil-soaked cross into the night sky. When the cross was ignited, and flames roared into the air, several hundred Native Americans exploded from the cover of darkness firing a hail of bullets from pistols, rifles, shotguns, and automatic weapons at the white men.

As the Black press gleefully reported, "The Klansmen, terrified as much by Indian war whoops as by the rain of slugs, left in a such a hurry many thought it expedient to shed their robes and pillowcase hoods." Local police escorted the fleeing Klansmen to safety, while the Native Americans gathered the spoils of their battle and taunted the KKK grand wizard to "come get your cross."[57] As this example illustrates, Native Americans were occasionally able to use violence and intimidation against white supremacists, a strategy that southern Blacks eschewed for fear of terrible retribution. By the early 1960s, Native Americans in the South began to win access to racially restricted public schools by engaging in school boycotts, student sitdowns, and petitions for admission to so-called white schools.[58]

Native American educational activism in the West followed a very different trajectory. Decades of experience with schools as hostile institutions bent on forced assimilation and the annihilation of indigenous cultures left many families skeptical that public schools, whether run by the Bureau of Indian Affairs (BIA) or local whites, had anything to offer native communities. Nevertheless, a rising generation of Native Americans, including twenty-four thousand World War II veterans and forty thousand defense industry workers, found themselves on the front lines of educational reform in the postwar era.[59] For example, the McGaa family left the Pine Ridge Oglala Sioux Reservation for Rapid City, South Dakota, to pursue wartime industrial work and never returned. They preferred the local public schools of Rapid City to the reservation schools available at Pine Ridge. "I've educated my children," Mrs. McGaa acknowledged. "They've done well, and we've never asked anything of the Government. People have been telling the Indians what to do so long that they've come to expect it. We're better off that we left the Reservation."[60]

Between 1952 and 1956, more than fifteen thousand Native Americans participated in federal relocation programs to move off of reservations. Together with termination policies initiated in 1945, the goal of these federal programs was to sever the government's trust relationship over Indian lands and relocate indigenous residents to majority-white towns and cities. This practice proved devastating to Native American nations in the Southwest and West as it scattered community members, ended federal financial aid, and opened vast tracts of reservation land to white buyers. Instead of thriving in urban communities as policy experts anticipated, Native Americans faced virulent discrimination in education, housing, and employment, which resulted in heightened financial insecurity. In this context, many urban Native Americans came to view the struggle for a high-quality education as a defining component of the civil rights movement.[61]

K. Tsianina Lomawaima and Teresa McCarty found that as more Native American students pursued college and graduate degrees in the 1950s and

1960s, the majority of these degrees were in education. This shows that Native Americans were actively seeking to take control of educational theory, practice, and policy in their communities. Native American educators developed revolutionary new bicultural and bilingual curricula that expressed authentic indigenous voices and perspectives while resisting the colonizing and assimilating agendas of white-dominated educators. They successfully petitioned to access federal money for indigenous-run Head Start programs, K–12 schools, and tribal colleges. Tribal leader Stanley Smartlowit (Yakima), educators Annie Dodge Wauneka (Navajo) and Esther Burnett Horne (Shoshone), political activists Dennis Banks (Ojibwe) and Russell Means (Lakota), and scholars Vine Deloria Jr. (Lakota), Helen Scheirbeck (Lumbee), and Alfonso Ortiz (Ohkay Owingeh Pueblo) were some of the many voices advocating for tribal sovereignty based in self-government, self-determination, and self-education.[62]

Native American educational activists were deeply concerned by low levels of academic achievement in both traditional public schools and the federally run BIA schools. Pointing to 81 BIA boarding schools and 159 BIA day schools in the fall of 1966, the Association on American Indians Affairs declared that federally run schools were training a generation of "no-culture people" hopelessly lost between a Native American world they knew nothing about and a hostile, unfamiliar white society. Native American educational activists demanded that federal, state, and local governments take steps to equalize educational opportunities for indigenous youth in both BIA and traditional public schools.[63]

Under pressure from indigenous activists, Senator Robert F. Kennedy convened a subcommittee on Indian education and invited Native American leaders to come to Washington to present their concerns. Dr. Alfonso Ortiz, an anthropology professor at Princeton University originally from New Mexico, argued that those boarding schools still in existence were "very bad things" that deprived twenty-eight thousand Native American adolescents each year of the "psychic and emotional support" of their families. Senator Kennedy denounced the government's "barbarous" policy of Indian education and launched a formal investigation of all federal and public schools.[64]

The final report, *Indian Education: A National Tragedy—A National Challenge*, was published in 1969 under the direction of Senator Edward M. Kennedy, following his brother's assassination. It blasted termination and relocation programs as "coercive assimilation of American Indians," concluding, "The goals were to get rid of Indians and Indian trust land by terminating federal recognition and services and relocating Indians into cities off the reservations—a policy viewed as a major catastrophe by the Indians." Through a meticulous survey of Indian students in public and BIA schools, investigators documented profound inequality, including dropout rates that were twice the national average and approached 100 percent at some schools. The report also established that Native Americans were two to three years behind whites in reading and math, that there were too few Native American teachers, and that Native American students experienced a harsh Eurocentric curriculum that either ignored or disparaged indigenous culture and history. Finally, researchers found that 25 percent of public school teachers preferred not to have Native American students in their classroom, an astonishing statistic that revealed the depth of teachers' prejudice.[65]

Indian Education: A National Tragedy—A National Challenge embraced Native American self-determination as a crucial first step in educational reform. "It is essential," the report authors affirmed, "to involve Indian parents in the education of their children and to give them an important voice—both at the national and local levels—in setting policy at those schools in which Indian children predominate. Whenever Indian tribes express the desire, assistance and training should be provided to permit them to operate their own schools under contract." The report pointed to the example of Rough Rock Demonstration School, run by the Navajo in Chinle, Arizona, as a successful example of an indigenous-run school.

By all accounts, Rough Rock Demonstration School was an extraordinary institution. Founded in 1965 by the Navajo (Diné) Nation with $214,300 in federal grants, the school was housed in a brand-new $3.5 million building with facilities for boarding and day students located in a remote region of northeastern Arizona. Navajo community leaders demanded an active role in running the school and created the first federally chartered, indigenously run school in the nation. Navajo educators prioritized community economic development, parental involvement, and a bicultural curriculum that taught both Navajo and American language and culture. Raymond Nakai explained, "The Rough Rock Demonstration School is the nation's most unique and exciting experiment in the field of Indian education. It is proving conclusively that Navajo parents do care and are able to provide leadership and control over the education of their children. It is thrilling to witness the involvement of Navajo parents in all aspects of the school and its program. This is what we want for the Navajo People throughout the Reservation."[66]

As a school run by and for indigenous people, the Rough Rock Demonstration School looked nothing like either traditional BIA or public schools. At Rough Rock School, white and Navajo teachers supervised children in hands-on, child-centered projects that reflected the most cutting-edge progressive pedagogy. Parents and community elders participated in the school's daily operation, demonstrating weaving, telling stories, and joining the children for meals in the cafeteria. The school paid parents and local artists for their help, which supported local economic development while recognizing the value of indigenous contributions to the curriculum. Hundreds of educational scholars, politicians, and community activists came to visit Rough Rock Demonstration School to see this new kind of Native American education, and many tried to replicate the vision of indigenous-controlled schools in other communities.

While academic results at Rough Rock Demonstration School were mixed, and the institution had its fair share of critics, it nevertheless revolutionized Native American education. Born in the wake of civil rights victories including the Civil Rights Act of 1964 and the Voting Rights Act of 1965, Rough Rock Demonstration School was part of a sweeping Native American civil rights movement. Following the lead of Black Power activists, Native Americans placed self-determination, political empowerment, and cultural revitalization at the center of an ambitious agenda of social justice.

Rough Rock Demonstration School offered an exciting way to bring these goals together, which propelled public education to the forefront of indigenous civil rights activism. In 1972, the Indian Education Act put into practice reforms suggested by the *Indian Education* report, including increased funding for Native American students in public schools and financial support to expand community-controlled Native American schools. By 1973, eleven additional schools had contracted with the BIA to establish indigenous, locally controlled schools committed to the kind of bicultural and bilingual education pioneered at Rough Rock.[67]

Encouraged by grassroots indigenous reform, BIA schools in the 1970s tailored educational programs to the needs of local communities. By this time, roughly 70 percent of native students were in public schools, where indigenous educational activism became more evident.[68] For example, in Phoenix, student leaders such as Michael Hughes (Hopi) walked door-to-door to talk with Native American families about their experiences in the local public schools. They organized Native Americans with different tribal affiliations to fight for better treatment and a more supportive learning environment. Hughes described a tremendous sense of energy and enthusiasm among the many Native American families he visited. Each one asked, "What's next? Let's get in and fight!"[69]

On December 1, 1973, Hughes invited a diverse group of indigenous families to join him at a local Community Advisory Council (CAC) meeting in Phoenix. At the meeting, he made a motion to discuss the challenges for Native American students in the city's public schools. The CAC denied the request, which angered families in the audience who stood up and shouted, "You don't care about the Indian students!" Committee members abruptly canceled the meeting and walked out, but the school board agreed to hear Native American concerns at the next meeting on December 20. After parents and students presented their grievances, the Phoenix School District adopted a plan to apply for federal funds to support Native American students, include Native Americans in all policy discussions, seek out Native American teachers and guidance counselors, and create new extra-curricular programs tailored to the needs of indigenous students.[70]

This modest victory demonstrates that Native American educational activists were developing new and more sophisticated grassroots organizing and that white school boards were more willing to address these concerns. To take another example, with financial support from the Indian Education Act of 1972, the Chicago Public Schools opened the Little Big Horn High School, which emphasized indigenous history, art, and culture. Little Big Horn boasted a graduation rate of 89 percent, a remarkable feat given the citywide high school graduation rate for Native Americans was only 5 percent.[71] Similar instances of educational activism were taking place in BIA schools, a process that helped transform the relationship between the US government and Native American communities. Responding to the demands of indigenous educators and families, both BIA and public schools began to articulate a commitment to the social, emotional, and intellectual growth of Native American students.[72]

Success with indigenous-controlled schools complicated Native Americans' relationship to school integration, just as school desegregation was gaining momentum through the courts nationally. In some communities, racially diverse schools offered better educational opportunities for Native American youth. For instance, between 1968 and 1970 rural Hoke County, North Carolina, initiated a complicated three-way school desegregation plan for white, Black, and Native American children. Superintendent of schools Donald D. Abernathy testified before a Senate Committee on Equal Educational Opportunity that school desegregation was successful and that Black and Native American student achievement was improving, while the educational standards for all children remained high. "I just don't think that could have happened with compensatory programs in segregated schools," Abernathy insisted.[73]

Other Native American communities, however, believed their children would be best served in indigenous-controlled schools, including the Lumbees of North Carolina. For the first two weeks of school in 1970, five hundred Lumbee students boycotted their new school assignments and instead showed up at the Robeson County Indian school, where they sat in empty

classrooms, as the county had closed the school as part of its desegregation plan. When the sit-in failed, Lumbee parents sued the district for the
right to attend a separate school, which they envisioned as a community-
controlled institution that would emphasize Native American history, culture, and knowledge.

North Carolina governor Bob Scott praised the Lumbees when they
abandoned the boycott and sent their children to the integrated public
schools while the lawsuit progressed through the courts. He also expressed
relief that he did not have to take direct action against the group notorious
for routing the Klan in 1958. "The way the Lumbees handled the Klan situation, I'm not going to go down there and tell them what to do," he admitted.
As these examples suggest, Native Americans did not support a single plat-
form of either school integration or separation but instead tailored their
approach to the needs of indigenous families living in specific times and
places.[74]

In northeastern cities like Boston, where Native Americans were a small
minority, court-ordered school integration undermined efforts by native
families to concentrate their children in specific schools. "Prior to desegregation, Indian families, by settling near each other, had been able to ensure
that their children could attend neighborhood schools with other neighborhood children," explained Native American activist Victoria Hughes of
Dorchester, Massachusetts, in 1980. Because of school desegregation and
busing, she added, "such is no longer the case." Hughes complained that
school administrators in Boston classified Native American students as either white or Black. "Since the Indian student falls into neither category
as black or as white," she continued, "he is left isolated and further con-
fused in terms of his own sense of himself." Hughes commended the Boston Public Schools for contracting with the Boston Indian Council to provide enrichment programs on Native American heritage, but she lamented
the near total lack of Native American faculty and administrators. Hughes
asked the district to acknowledge that Native Americans had different
needs that were not being considered in the heated debates over "forced
busing" of white and Black children.[75]

By 1991, nearly 90 percent of the 383,000 Native American students nationwide were enrolled in public schools. That same year a federal study
concluded, "It is evident that the existing educational systems, whether
they be public or federal, have not effectively met the educational, cultural,
economic or social needs of Native communities." Native American students had the highest high school dropout rate of any racial or ethnic group
in the United States at 36 percent and the lowest test scores in eighth-grade
math. The report offered ten recommendations designed to equalize op-

portunities by the year 2000, such as requiring all public schools to take a multicultural approach that respected Native American languages and culture. Unfortunately, low levels of Native American academic achievement have persisted into the twenty-first century.[76]

Speaking at the Standing Rock Sioux Reservation in North Dakota on June 13, 2014, President Barack Obama reiterated the federal government's commitment to improving Native American education, echoing many of the same themes developed during the American Indian civil rights movement of the late 1960s and early 1970s: "Let's put our minds together to improve our schools—because our children deserve a world-class education, too, that prepares them for college and careers. And that means returning control of Indian education to tribal nations with additional resources and support so that you can direct your children's education and reform schools here in Indian Country." He elaborated, "And even as they prepare for a global economy, we want children, like these wonderful young children here, learning about their language, and learning about their culture, just like the boys and girls do at Lakota Language Nest here at Standing Rock."[77]

The same government that deliberately used schools to "kill the Indian and save the man" in the nineteenth century now supports programs that are bilingual, bicultural, and designed in cooperation with local Native American families. This transformation is extraordinary, yet it has not been enough to equalize educational opportunities for Native American youth, who continue to have the highest dropout rates of any minority group. Native students cite uncaring teachers and an irrelevant curriculum as the two main reasons for quitting school. Scholars note that high school can feel both overwhelming and boring to students who do not have adequate reading and math skills, suggesting that reformers need to address disparities in early childhood and elementary education in order to increase rates of high school graduation.[78]

Native American activists are also taking steps to address the legacy of boarding schools on Native American communities. According to Andrea Carmen, executive director of the International Indian Treaty Council (IITC), "The fate of many Indigenous children who never returned home after forced removal by the U.S. to Boarding Schools, including those in the many unmarked graves at former Boarding School sites, remains an ongoing human rights violation under international law."[79] Together with the National Native American Boarding School Healing Coalition, the Native American Rights Fund, and the National Congress of American Indians, the IITC is working to file a submission with the United Nations calling on the United States to provide a full accounting of American Indian and Alaska Native children who were taken into custody under US boarding school policy and whose fate and whereabouts remain unknown.[80]

In August 2017, the bodies of two boys, Little Chief and Horse, were exhumed and repatriated to the Northern Arapaho people on the Wind River Reservation in Wyoming. Following this step toward reconciliation, representatives of more than fifty native nations met to discuss the repatriation of nearly two hundred native children buried at Carlisle Indian Industrial School. "There's more that needs to be looked into about the boarding schools—the treatment and care and responsibility that they had to our children—in life and in death," noted Christine Diindiisi McCleave (Ojibwe). Indigenous activists insist the only way to heal intergenerational trauma is to break the silence surrounding the history of boarding schools, collect testimony from survivors and descendants, gain full access to government records, and repatriate the hundreds of children buried at these schools. Their motto is "Break the silence, begin the healing."[81]

The number of citizens self-reporting as Native American in the US census has increased exponentially since 1980. This number grew by 31 percent between 1980 and 1990, with a further increase of 26.4 percent by 2000 and 26.7 percent beyond that in 2010. The number of people who identify as only Native American has grown from 1,959,234 in 1990 to 2,932,248 in 2010—a noteworthy increase, especially when this is added to the number of people claiming to be partially Native American, which was 5,220,410 in 2010.[82] Instead of "vanishing," as nineteenth-century white reformers predicted, Native Americans are thriving. The challenge remains, however, to transform an educational system once used for colonization and cultural annihilation into a nurturing space of intellectual, emotional, and academic growth for Native Americans.

MEJOR EDUCACION

Jennie Caridad Diaz's feet hurt, and her arms ached. And no wonder, as the six-year-old girl was marching across the Brooklyn Bridge with four thousand others in the Puerto Rican–led Silent Prayer March of early spring 1964. Along with other protestors, Jennie had picketed city hall for more than two hours before heading on a two mile, eerily silent protest march to the New York City Board of Education headquarters in Brooklyn. "I'm tired," Jennie confessed halfway across the bridge, as her huge placard, nearly as big as she was, drooped to the ground.

Without a word Ramon Igleas scooped up the little girl and kept walking. District assembly leader Jose R. Erazo grabbed her sign and held it aloft as they continued across the bridge. "Mejor Educacion Para El Nino Puerto Riqueno!" it proclaimed, expressing the widely shared sentiment that New York City public schools must improve educational opportunities for the city's growing Puerto Rican population. For many Puerto Rican and Mexican American educational activists, this would require school integration, better treatment of Latinx students, and more Latinx teachers and school administrators. Placards in Spanish and English echoed these sentiments: "Jim Crow Is Not Teaching Democracy!" "We Demand More Respect—Now!" "200,000 Puerto Rican Children—200 Puerto Rican Teachers?" "Quality Integration—Now!"[83]

Like many big cities in the mid-1960s, New York City had failed to enact meaningful desegregation following *Brown*, and its public schools were known for a high degree of racial and socioeconomic isolation. In June of 1955, the board of education appointed a special Commission on Integration to study racial segregation and educational inequality. The commission found that segregated housing patterns combined with prejudiced school assignment policies created segregated and unequal schools for Black and Latinx students in New York City. It proposed a series of modest reforms, including raising academic standards in all schools, equalizing resources and teachers, improving parent-teacher relationships, and fostering desegregation through new school assignment policies. The board of education embraced these suggestions and created a new "open enrollment" option that allowed nine thousand Black and Puerto Rican children in 1962 to transfer to predominantly white schools.[84]

These token efforts were inadequate to stem the sharp uptick in residential and school segregation, and the number of identifiably minority schools more than doubled in New York City between 1958 and 1964. Similar patterns were visible in other cities, including Chicago, Detroit, Boston, and Los Angeles.[85] To combat school segregation and the inequality that came with it, more than 100,000 Puerto Rican students joined more than 250,000 Black students in a massive school boycott in New York City on February 3, 1964, demanding integrated and equitable public schools.[86]

Puerto Rican educational activists in New York City were part of a growing Latinx social movement that used boycotts, petitions, and grassroots campaigns to challenge racial discrimination in public schools nationwide. "The recent Negro campaign has certainly stimulated the Puerto Rican drive for more rights," observed Joseph Monserrat, director of the Migration Division of Puerto Rico's Department of Labor. "With all this concern over civil rights, people are hollering all over for us to come and help them organize," confirmed Robert P. Sánchez, vice president of the Political Association of Spanish-Speaking Organizations.[87]

Although inspired by and sometimes allied with African Americans, Latinx educational activists developed a distinct agenda shaped by the historical experiences of growing numbers of Latinx students—an ethnically and socioeconomically diverse population. Some activists prioritized school funding, curriculum reforms, and hiring more Latinx teachers and administrators over the goal of school integration. Others rejected school integration and worked instead to change the way that schools taught Latinx students, emphasizing bilingual education and curricula that celebrated Hispanic heritage. "The Mexican community is not concerned with 'integration' or 'assimilation' like the Negro people, but with the principle of biculturalism," insisted John Mendez in a letter to the *Los Angeles Times* in 1963.[88] Latinx academic achievement remained very low as measured by test scores, grades, and graduation rates—but growing numbers of Latinx parents, students, and community leaders identified public education as an essential site of civil rights reform.[89]

In March of 1968, Mexican American students at Los Angeles's Lincoln High School organized one of the largest school protests of the civil rights era. Dubbed "the beginning of a revolution," thousands of students in East Los Angeles boycotted school. The 1968 East Los Angeles blowouts represented a new and more radical youth-based activism that differed sharply from movements led by an earlier generation of older, politically moderate, middle-class Mexican Americans. Identifying as Chicanos, these young activists took pride in their brown racial identity and scorned assimilation in favor of pride in *la raza* and militant demands for social justice.

What followed was a week and a half of blowouts, speeches, arrests, demands, picketing, sympathy demonstrations, sit-ins, police tactical alerts, and emergency school board sessions that spread from school to school throughout Los Angeles. Students demanded more respectful teachers, the right to speak Spanish, courses on Mexican American history and culture, more Mexican American teachers and administrators, bilingual education, and increased student rights.

Frances Spector, a sixteen-year-old white student at Belmont High School, was arrested for joining the blowout at her school. She told reporters, "At Belmont, you look at the industrial arts classes and it's all Chicano and Black. You look at the college preparatory classes, and it's all Anglos and Asians. That can't be the way they really fit! They can't be getting the right counseling. They're just putting people where they think they belong because of what color they are."[90]

Echoing cries of "Chicano Power," school blowouts erupted in Denver, Chicago, and dozens of towns and cities in Texas in the late 1960s. These student protests attracted media attention, inspired Mexican American

youth to become active in educational politics, and alerted school authorities to the plight of Latinx students more broadly. They marked an era of
more militant educational activism that included more youth, women, and
working-class activists than Mexican American activism of an earlier era.

Although not every protest resulted in major improvements, students
reveled in their newly found power to effect change. After one thousand
students walked out of school in Crystal City, Texas, the US Civil Rights
Commission visited the district and threatened to withhold more than three
hundred thousand dollars in federal financial aid if the district did not end
discriminatory policies against Mexican American students. School leaders then capitulated to student demands, which included allowing Mexican
American students to participate as equals in the social life of the school.
Students wanted to be eligible for homecoming queen and cheerleading
squad tryouts, significant victories for adolescents tired of being excluded
because of their racial and ethnic identities.

As Gael Graham reminds us, "Seemingly trivial issues such as the selection of cheerleaders or homecoming court members sparked furious explo-
sions because many whites believed that compulsory integration required
only chilly toleration of the newcomers' presence; they did not intend to
incorporate minority students into the fabric of school life, let alone re-
weave that fabric into a new pattern."[91] By fighting for—and winning—
integration into the social life of Crystal City High School, these students
helped secure their fundamental right to an equal education.[92]

Latinx educational activism was given a boost in 1968 when President
Lyndon B. Johnson signed the Bilingual Education Act into law. This law encouraged, but did not require, schools to recognize the educational needs
of students with limited English-language proficiency and provided financial assistance to help these students succeed. Although modest in scope, it
signaled the federal government's rejection of discriminatory English-only
laws and supported school districts that developed programs to assist English language learners. Some supporters believed that bilingual education
would help reverse historic patterns of Mexican American and Puerto Rican
underachievement by incorporating non-English languages, cultures, and
communities into the education of minority youth. This version of bilingual education represented a visionary plan to remake white-dominated
institutions into schools that would recognize the unique needs of diverse
learners. Over the next decade, bilingual education was strengthened and
transformed though a series of key court rulings, executive actions, and
demands by diverse Latinx families. At the same time, this program drew
the wrath of some conservatives who suspected bilingual education under-

mined Latinx students' patriotism and hindered their assimilation into mainstream society.[93]

The growth of a new bilingual and bicultural curriculum complicated Latinx students' encounters with school desegregation in the late 1960s. This was a delicate issue for Latinx families, and there was a great variety of experiences with and responses to school desegregation nationwide. Latinx educational activists, including Puerto Ricans in New York City, Mexican Americans in Chicago, and Cuban Americans in Miami, viewed desegregation as a necessary step in equalizing educational funding and resources for all students, especially in the early 1960s. However, as bilingual education expanded, some feared that desegregation plans would disperse Latinx students throughout the district and make it harder to secure Spanish-speaking teachers, bilingual programs, and courses on Latin American history and culture. Beginning in 1966 in New York City, some Puerto Rican educational activists began to advocate not for integration but instead for community control of schools. Similar ideas were percolating among Mexican Americans on the West Coast.[94]

In 1970, more than one hundred Mexican Americans met to consider how Los Angeles's bold new school integration plan would affect their children. Some people feared that school integration would harm, instead of help, Mexican-origin children. "Our Chicano kids will be blended and melted down with black and white," cautioned teacher and educational activist Raquel Galan. Noting that only 18 percent of the public school population in Los Angeles was Mexican American, she argued that busing would undermine the effort to provide Mexican American students with teachers who understood Spanish and respected their culture. She added that bilingual programs would not work in schools with only a handful of Spanish-speaking children. Juan Gómez, a professor of history at the University of California, Los Angeles, added that the money earmarked for busing should go instead to improving the schools serving Mexican American and Black students. Alicia Sandoval, a teacher from East Los Angeles concluded, "A lot of the community doesn't realize that a lot of what we have built up will disintegrate." For these activists, school integration threatened the coalition building, community activism, and federal support for bilingual education that had generated tangible school improvements in the past decade.[95]

In other communities, Mexican Americans had to contend with plans that disingenuously used their legal status as "white" to comply with court-ordered school desegregation. This is precisely what happened in Houston, Texas, in 1970. Federal district judge Ben C. Connally ordered the Houston Independent School District to mix students from predominantly Mexican

American schools with students from predominantly Black schools for the purposes of integration, while predominantly Anglo schools were left untouched. When local Mexican Americans learned of the plan, the question of school integration quickly moved to the forefront of their educational agenda.[96]

Organized through the Mexican American Education Council (MAEC), Houston activists orchestrated a massive school boycott to draw attention to the unjust school integration plan. For two and a half weeks, more than 3,500 students participated in this action, and many attended *huelga* schools, or strike schools, organized by community members and featuring lessons on Mexican American history and culture. Meanwhile, MAEC activists initiated a legal battle to force the Houston Independent School District to recognize Mexican-origin students as an identifiable ethnic minority. Brown, Not White became the slogan of protestors who wanted recognition that Mexican Americans faced unique educational challenges related to poverty, racial discrimination, and limited English-language proficiency that required special accommodations in public schools.[97]

As the battle for school integration continued, the school board acted proactively to recognize Mexican Americans as an ethnic minority for the purposes of student transfers on September 9, 1972. The following year, the US Supreme Court ruled that Mexican Americans were an identifiable minority group for school desegregation purposes.[98] While this marked a legal victory for Mexican American educational activists, it was not enough to secure integrated and equal public schools for all. Instead, the majority of Mexican American, Puerto Rican, and other Latinx students remained trapped in majority-minority schools with high concentrations of student poverty and low levels of academic achievement. A report by the US Commission on Civil Rights in 1974 accused school officials in Arizona, California, Colorado, New Mexico, and Texas of failing to provide Mexican American students with the same quality of education offered to whites, noting that only 60 percent of Mexican Americans in these states completed high school, compared to 90 percent of whites. Another report discovered similar patterns of discrimination against Puerto Rican students in New York City in 1977, finding that many schools placed Puerto Rican students in separate classrooms within otherwise racially integrated schools and that nonnative English speakers were "barred from meaningful participation in education programs."[99]

In response, scholars and activists such as Kenneth B. Clark and Jorge Batista called for more effective plans to overcome segregation and create more equitable schools. They rejected the fallacy that racially mixed schools would impair bilingual education programs. "Only a minority of Hispanic children participate in special language programs, as the board well knows. Those programs should not account for widespread segregation throughout the school system," lambasted Clark and Batista.[100]

The debate over whether school integration, bilingual education, or both at the same time represented the best strategy to improve Latinx educational opportunities was never resolved, especially as levels of Latinx academic achievement remained low through the 1970s, and the diversity of students increased following immigration reform in 1965. Reflecting on the complexities of Chicano educational activism in this era, historian Guadalupe San Miguel Jr. explains, "Gradually, unimpressive results led to diminished support for desegregation among Mexican origin activists and support for bilingual education flagged in the face of organized opposition to the concept. Fragile coalitions that had fought together for both programs weakened once there was no longer a common programmatic goal."[101]

The 1980s and 1990s brought new challenges for Latinx educational activists, especially as immigration from Latin America continued to expand and diversify at unprecedented rates. For example, the percentage of Hispanics in New York City grew from 16.3 percent of the population in 1970 to 19.9 percent in 1980 and 24.4 percent in 1990. While in the 1970s Latinx New Yorkers were almost always Puerto Ricans, by 1990 Puerto Ricans accounted for only half of the Latinx community in New York City, as hundreds of thousands of Dominicans and Mexican Americans moved to the region. Racial and ethnic tensions further complicated Latinx educational activism, as activists sometimes disagreed over strategies and goals.[102]

President Ronald Reagan's administration eroded federal support for bilingual education and school desegregation. As a result, bilingual programs were scaled back, and the racial segregation of Latinx students increased through the 1980s and 1990s. A growing backlash against immigrants from Central and South America resulted in a series of propositions voted into law in California in the 1990s that ended affirmative action for college admissions, scaled back reduced bilingual education programs to one year of "structured immersion" in English-only courses, and even attempted to bar the children of undocumented residents from public schools.[103]

This rising tide of anti-immigrant, anti-Latinx sentiment in the United States fueled the election of President Donald Trump in 2016, who promised to build an impenetrable wall on the southern border and create deportation squads to round up and expel immigrants who lacked legal status. President Trump's explicitly anti-immigrant and anti-Latinx rhetoric spawned an enormous increase in bias incidents, including harassment, insults, and physical attacks, against Latinx students in K–12 schools in the wake of his election. On a slightly more positive note, during the same election California voters overwhelmingly repealed the 1998 mandate requiring English-only instruction and restored bilingual education in the state's public schools.[104]

Diverse immigrant communities have been at the forefront of a dramatic transformation in the racial demographics of American public education in the past four decades with a startling 495 percent increase in the number of students of Latin American heritage. Today Latinx students are the dominant racialized minority in the West and outnumber Black students in the South, and their representation has surged in all parts of the nation. Mexican Americans account for approximately two-thirds of the Latinx population in the United States, and these students presently face the highest levels of racial isolation in the public schools. The percentage of Mexican American students attending intensely racially segregated schools between 1968 and 1988 has more than doubled, and by 2011, fully 45 percent of Latinx students in the West attended schools that were 99–100 percent minority.[105]

Scholars Patricia Gándara and Frances Contreras are among those working to reverse what they describe as "the Latino education crisis." Noting that Latinxs are the largest and fastest-growing minority group, they contend that policy makers must take concrete steps to reverse decades of failed educational policy. Scholars estimate that today only 53 percent of Latinx students graduate from high school, while the graduation rate for white students is around 75 percent. Similarly, national data from the National Assessment of Educational Progress show that only 16 percent of Latinx fourth graders in 2005 scored proficient in reading, compared to 41 percent of white students. Gándara and Contreras insist, "If the high dropout rates and low educational achievement of Latinx youth are not turned around, we will have created a permanent underclass without hope of integrating into the mainstream or realizing their potential to contribute to American society." Gándara and Contreras suggest practical steps to revitalize public education, calling for Latinx families to work together with government agencies and community organizations to develop preschool intervention, elementary school support services, and college and career advisory services for secondary school students. In addition, they insist that Latinx educational reform cannot be separated from housing policies designed to integrate working-class Latinx families into more racially and economically diverse communities. Reflecting on the possibility of cultivating bilingual, multicultural Latinx students ready to thrive in the twenty-first century, they conclude, "If we find a way to educate them well, their future and ours is bright."[106]

MODEL MINORITY

Conceding that Yukiko Tamashiro was "perhaps even a little better qualified than the other" applicants for a teaching position, the Falls Church, Virginia, public schools flatly refused to hire an American citizen of Japanese descent in the summer of 1959. A graduate of Wheaton College and New York University, Tamashiro was startled to find that Jim Crow racial codes applied to her four years after the US Supreme Court had outlawed racial segregation in public schools.

Tamashiro decided not to challenge the school board's decision, adding that she hoped public reaction "will result in more responsible handling of any subsequent applications for teaching posts." The *New York Times* covered the episode, observing that before the *Brown* decision, Virginia's segregation laws were mainly directed at "Negroes," not "Orientals" and other "non-whites." The controversial ruling, however, prompted southerners to police the color line in schools with renewed vigor. In the post-*Brown* era, Americans debated how citizens of Asian descent should be integrated into the body politic—and the public schools.[107]

After World War II, thousands of Japanese Americans left the West Coast for cities like Chicago, New York, Detroit, Minneapolis, and Cleveland, where they encountered greater levels of acceptance than before the war. Chinese Americans suffered to some extent from association with Chinese communism during the Cold War, but the Chinese American population overall was becoming increasingly native-born, middle-class, and assimilated. Changes in immigration and naturalization statutes, combined with the belated admission of Hawaii to statehood, focused new attention on the question of how Americans of Asian descent, or Asian Americans as they would come to be called, would assimilate into mainstream culture. By the mid-1960s, this included how school leaders should classify and assign Asian American students for the purpose of school desegregation.[108]

First was the question whether Asian Americans should be classified as white, Black, brown, "colored," or some other racialized category. Many school districts developed a pragmatic approach to this question, such as the Falls Church school administrators who labeled Yukiko Tamashiro as "colored," then used this classification to prohibit her from teaching in an all-white school. Other school leaders considered Asian Americans as white in a blatant attempt to subvert court-ordered school desegregation.

In 1966, the Boston School Committee reclassified Chinese American students as "white" to reduce the number of "racially imbalanced" schools that had a student population of more than 50 percent students of

FIGURE 4. Miss April Lou, teacher at PS 1, Manhattan, with six Chinese children, recent arrivals from Hong Kong and Formosa, who are holding up placards giving his or her Chinese name (both in ideographs and in transliteration) and the name to be entered in the official school records in 1964. World Telegram & Sun photo by Fred Palumbo. Library of Congress, Prints & Photographs Division, LC-USZ62-112148.

color. This reclassification was designed to remove Abraham Lincoln and Quincy schools in Boston's Chinatown from the state's list of forty-six racially imbalanced schools, thus officially reducing school segregation without reassigning a single student. Boston School Committee member Louise Day Hicks disingenuously reasoned that since the state racial census forms had only two categories, white and nonwhite, the school committee "did not wish the pupils to be affected by the state racial imbalance law." Hicks would soon become one of the leading architects of massive white resistance to school integration in Boston, which exploded in violent protests in 1974.[109]

William G. Saltonstall of the Massachusetts Board of Education was not so easily fooled. "I have been brought up to believe there is a white race, a black race, a yellow race, and the Chinese are of the yellow race," he said, adding that the state would never support the classification of Chinese American pupils as white. Chinese American families in Boston expressed a range of responses to being classified as white. Ging Hung Chin, father of five children in the public schools, said he "couldn't understand why they did it. It bothers me." Others were indifferent, including a mother of three who observed, "We are proud of our race, but what the committee says doesn't change our ancestry." Chinatown resident Chuck Soo Hoo agreed, declaring, "It makes no difference; we are still Chinese."[110]

The state rejected the school committee's plan to count Chinese Americans as "white" for the purpose of school desegregation. In 1974, Judge W. Arthur Garrity Jr. created a plan that relied on busing to mix Black, white, and Asian American students together in certain schools. The plan required junior high school students at Lincoln and Quincy to be bused to the Michelangelo School, a predominantly Italian American school in the North End. Chinese American parents met to discuss how this would affect their children, wondering why Chinese American students had to bear the burden of busing and whether English language instruction would be available at the majority-white school.

Michael Chu, a fifth grader at Quincy, shook his head when a reporter asked if he would like to attend the Michelangelo School. "I want to stay at Quincy," he said. "All my friends are Chinese. I know the people here in Chinatown. I live here. I don't know what's at Michelangelo and its very scary." Michael's fears proved unfounded, however, and he discovered that he did not mind attending Michelangelo in the fall of 1974. "Most of the white kids are pretty friendly.... It's much better than I thought," he told reporters.

White school administrators, parents, and students at Michelangelo agreed that integration with Chinese American students went better than expected. Sixth grader Pat Quarato reported, "Some of them are in my classes. Some are shy, but they're mostly nice and they don't start any trouble like some of the black kids." Maryann Pepicelli, whose son was in the seventh grade at Michelangelo agreed, "We don't mind having the Chinese bused in—better them than anybody else." White Bostonians tended to view Chinese Americans in stereotypical terms as quiet, shy, and dedicated to traditional values, such as respect for authority and academic achievement. By 1966, the image of Asian Americans as a "model minority" was gaining momentum and, as this example shows, was often used to distinguish them from African Americans.[111]

The model minority myth mitigated white resistance to Asian American school integration, but it also cast Asian Americans as meek, passive, and unwilling to challenge racial injustice. In Boston, this image was shattered when the school desegregation plan was expanded to include more than two thousand Chinese American students. Chinese American educational activists organized into the Boston Chinese Parents Association (BCPA). The BCPA reported, "Schools to which a substantial number of Chinese students have been assigned still do not have Chinese teachers, Chinese transition aids, or Chinese parents represented on biracial councils." Citing concerns over the length of bus rides, the safety of Chinese American students, and the ability of schools to communicate with Chinese parents, the Chinese American community petitioned the Boston School Committee and the federal court for assistance. When the court and the school district failed to respond, parents took action. "Chinese parents are united in boycotting the schools because we feel that school and court officials, by not taking concrete action in our demands, have demonstrated an overall disregard for the rights of all Chinese parents and students," explained the BCPA in the fall of 1975.[112]

Asian American civil rights activism grew and expanded nationwide through the late 1960s and into the 1970s. As the home of a large, diverse, and well-educated Asian American population, California was a vital site of community organizing and grassroots educational activism. In the spring of 1971, Judge Stanley A. Weigel crafted an ambitious school integration plan to desegregate the San Francisco public schools.

While many assimilated, middle-class Chinese American families had been moving out of San Francisco's Chinatown in the postwar era, thousands of new Chinese immigrants, many from Hong Kong, had continued to arrive in the city since 1965. Run by a confederation of family associations known as the Chinese Six Companies, San Francisco's Chinatown retained a strong ethnic identity that encompassed the local public schools. This included the Commodore Stockton School, once known as San Francisco's "Oriental" school, where all Chinese American students were assigned to attend. By the end of World War II, Chinese American students attended schools throughout the city. Nevertheless, many families living in Chinatown preferred a school with a discernible Chinese identity that included special before- and after-school programs where students studied Mandarin and Chinese history and culture.[113]

Taking a different view of the situation, Judge Weigel interpreted the Chinatown public schools as segregated and therefore illegal. Under his plan approximately 6,500 Chinese American students would be bused away from their neighborhood schools, while Black, white, and Mexican American students would be bused in. Leaders of the Chinese Six Companies were wary of this plan, which they believed was designed to aid Black and Mexican American students, not Chinese Americans.

Community leaders asked school officials to develop a modified plan that would take into account the needs of Chinese American students. "You are using our children as guinea pigs," chided Ernest Wong, past president of the Chinese Six Companies, at a board of education meeting on June 3, 1971. The *Los Angeles Times* noted Wong's comment was accompanied "by the booing and foot stomping of 600 Chinese opposing bussing [*sic*]." On

June 18, the Chinese Six Companies filed a federal court complaint contending the integration plan would inflict "severe emotional and mental distress and will operate to weaken the family ties and responsibilities fundamental to the Chinese culture."[114] Unwilling to consider any challenges, Judge Weigel ignored these requests and instituted citywide busing in September. Angry at being snubbed, Chinese Americans organized a massive school boycott, demanding a return to neighborhood schools.[115]

"It reminds me of the lioness in the jungle," reflected Herb Chew, a member of the Chinese Parents Committee. "You know, how docile she is until you bother the cubs? That reminds me of how we are about this thing with our children." Some parents expressed frustration at being forcibly integrated, as they believed Asian Americans no longer faced discrimination. "Now we are in the process of integrating. You can see the Chinese living in all neighborhoods in San Francisco," noted Dr. Wong, a pharmacist who lived in Chinatown. These activists defended the rights of families to choose to live in an ethnic community where they could take advantage of cultural opportunities unavailable in the suburbs. They also wanted to protect recent arrivals from China, especially young children. "What happens to the child 5 or 8 years old," asked Henry Gee, "who can't speak English well enough to talk? What happens if he's lost? He can't speak English well enough to say he's lost. We're worried about these kids who've come over here and they want to ship them out there."

For Chinese American parents like Gee, school integration was designed to improve educational opportunities for Black and Mexican Americans students, but it would only interfere with the ability of Asian American parents to choose the school that was right for their child. If school authorities insisted on including Chinese American students in integration orders, they at least wanted a say about how the plan worked. "The main thing is, we have to be recognized as Chinese," Gee continued, "not as a minority to be used against another minority."[116]

Although there were vocal Chinese American supporters of school integration in San Francisco, the majority were opposed to the busing plan and boycotted the 1971–72 school year. On the first day of school, only fifteen or twenty Chinese American students showed up at the Commodore Stockton School, and six hundred students who were supposed to climb aboard buses destined for other parts of the city remained at home. A citywide coalition of antibusing parents called We All Love Kids estimated that only 2 percent of Chinese American students attended the first day of school. Financed by the Chinese Six Companies, Chinatown offered the largest and most sustained opposition to San Francisco's school integration plan. More than one thousand Chinese American students stayed out of public schools for the year, with many attending privately sponsored "freedom schools" that drew on the model of the Black civil rights movement and taught Chinese history and culture to boycotting students.[117]

Although the boycott did not persuade officials to modify San Francisco's school integration plan, it nevertheless captivated a new generation of Asian American educational activists. In San Francisco, civil rights activists questioned whether school integration could be beneficial to Asian American youth. "If you're giving better education by this busing situation, then I'm for it," stated Bertha Chan, chairperson of the Parents Committee. "But if you can't, leave my children at home." Of special concern was the question of how public schools could better support recent arrivals from Asia whose greatest barrier to academic achievement was a lack of fluency in English.[118]

In 1971, approximately 2,800 students of Asian ancestry in the San Francisco public schools did not speak English fluently, yet only 1,000 received supplementary English language instruction. Chinese American families initiated a class action suit against the San Francisco Unified School District alleging that they were not being provided with equal educational opportunities. Although the lower courts denied relief, the US Supreme Court agreed to hear the case and ruled in favor of the students in 1974. In *Lau v. Nichols*, Justice William O. Douglas affirmed, "There is no equality of treatment merely by providing students with the same facilities, textbooks, teachers, and curriculum; for students who do not understand English are effectively foreclosed from any meaningful education." Citing the Civil Rights Act of 1964, Justice Douglas argued that school districts must take "affirmative steps" to make sure that non-native English speakers could succeed in public schools.[119]

Scholars have labeled *Lau v. Nichols* as "monumental in the history of civil rights" and compared its significance to the *Brown* decision that preceded it by twenty years. *Lau* had far-reaching implications for the nation's growing and increasingly diverse immigrant population. The Asian American population grew exponentially after the *Brown* ruling in 1954. According to the US census there were 259,397 Asian American and Pacific Islanders in 1950 and 1,369,412 in 1970. Thanks to immigration reform in 1965, this population experienced unprecedented growth, reaching a population of 7,273,662 in 1990 and 18,546,051 in 2010. In 2013, the Pew Research Center identified Asian Americans as the "highest-income, best-educated and fastest-growing racial group in the United States."[120]

The educational experiences of Asian Americans after the *Lau* decision in 1974 are decidedly mixed. Many view Asian American performance in the educational system as a remarkable success story, which continues to fuel the model minority myth. Asian American students outperform white students in the public schools, earning higher grades and scores on standardized tests. They are also more likely to finish high school and attend college than white students. This is true even for many low-income Asian American students. For instance, a recent study by Amy Hsin and Yu Xie found that disadvantaged children from Vietnamese and Chinese immigrant families routinely outperform their native-born, white, middle-class peers. What is more, these findings hold true for other Asian immigrant groups, including East Asians, Filipinos, and South Asians. Hsin and Xie concluded, "Asian and Asian American youth are harder working because of cultural beliefs that emphasize the strong connection between effort and achievement. Studies show that Asian and Asian American students tend to view cognitive abilities as qualities that can be developed through effort, whereas white Americans tend to view cognitive abilities as qualities that are inborn."[121]

While cultural beliefs and parenting practices play a significant role in the story of Asian American educational achievement, it is also important to recognize that since 1965 a majority of Asian immigrants have come to the United States with higher levels of education than any other group, even native-born whites. In recent years more than six in ten (61 percent) Asian adults between the ages of twenty-five and sixty-four have come to the United States with at least a bachelor's degree, which is twice the rate among non-Asian immigrants. Scholars argue that observers have misunderstood Asian American academic achievement by failing to recognize that historically, many Asian immigrants come from privileged backgrounds. Facing discrimination or problems with academic credentials in the United States, some Asian immigrants from professional backgrounds end up working menial jobs in the United States. Meyer Weinberg states, "Former college teachers, engineers, factory managers, and lawyers stressed to their children the centrality of higher education, thus supplying indispensable academic motivation." This is important, according to Weinberg, because "outsiders might view the resulting upward mobility as a stirring of ambition in the lower ranks of society. More so, it was a continuation of a trend within the upper reaches of Chinese society. The same was also true of other Asian American groups." In other words, children of professional families, even when they live in temporary conditions of poverty, have an academic advantage over children whose parents did not go to college.[122]

This brings us back to the fact that Asian American educational achievement is high—but not for all students of Asian descent. Scholars caution that the model minority myth, or the assumption that all Asians are smart, hardworking, deferential, and academically successful, is a particularly dangerous stereotype. It can be used to claim that Asian Americans have overcome racial discrimination and achieved full equality in American society, while instead there is concrete evidence that Asians continue to face potent and destructive racism in schools, colleges, and workplaces.

The model minority myth can also be used to disparage other racialized minorities, especially Blacks and Latinxs, for failing to work hard, follow the rules, and achieve the American dream. These characterizations ignore not only differences in educational attainment and the socioeconomic background of immigrants but also the enormously varied forms of historical and institutionalized racism different people have experienced. The model minority myth additionally masks the fact that some Asian Americans do not perform well in school and lack satisfactory remedies to address this underachievement.[123]

Following the end of the Vietnam War in 1975, the United States welcomed significant numbers of Asian refugees from Southeast Asia, including Thailand, Cambodia, and Laos. Arriving in the midst of harrowing childhoods in war-torn countries and refugee camps, these children found themselves suddenly transplanted to an American community, where they attended schools with a completely unfamiliar language and set of customs. "The stories these children tell are so horrible that you obviously feel sorry for them," said Caroline Tryon, a teacher in Arlington, Virginia, in 1979. "But my job is to teach them English so they can survive here. It's not easy for many of them."[124]

A teacher from Costa Mesa, California, made similar observations after thousands of Vietnamese refugees moved to her district: "You see very little crossing of friendships. I think the Indochinese kids are leery of the Anglo-American kids. And our other kids have some real prejudices to cross over." Cordelia Gutierrez elaborated that Vietnamese American children were so overwhelmed by their circumstances that they tended to just nod their head and answer yes to everything, making it difficult for teachers to discern whether students understood lessons. Schools struggled to find teachers or even aides who could speak the native languages of refugee children.[125]

Today Vietnamese Americans have college education rates of 20 percent, which is less than half that of other Asian American ethnic groups. The rates for Cambodians, Hmong, and Laotians are even lower, at less than 10 percent. While there are encouraging signs of progress for all Asian American minorities, evidence of racial discrimination remains. For instance, following the valedictorian speech by two Vietnamese American students in Houma, Louisiana, in 2008, school leaders tried to outlaw the speaking of any language other than English at a graduation ceremony.

Officials took offense to the fact that the graduation speakers, who were cousins in the same class, said a few words in Vietnamese thanking their grandparents. "Out of the whole speech, it's one sentence dedicated to them to give thanks," Cindy Vo stated as she struggled to understand why school officials would object. "I felt if I expressed myself in Vietnamese it would be more heartfelt," added her cousin Hue Vo. Local whites like Terrebonne Parish School Board member Rickie Pitre disagreed, "I don't like them addressing in a foreign language. They should be in English." Comments like this lay bare the thinly veiled racial hostility that Asian American students— even high-achieving ones—continue to experience in majority-white public schools.[126]

CONCLUSION

On a recent fall morning, roughly 150 students from two New York City high schools staged a walkout to demand school integration and greater racial equality in the city's public schools. The students linked arms and waved homemade signs reading, "Educate, Don't Segregate!" and "We Need Equity!" The teenagers attended two small public schools in the same large building, but in a stark illustration of the present-day high rates of school segregation, the student populations at each school differed significantly. At the selective NYC iSchool, 46 percent of the enrollment was white, while Chelsea Career and Technical Education High School only had a 4 percent enrollment of white students.

"This is a systematic issue that needs a citywide solution," insisted Carla Gaveglia, an iSchool senior who helped organize the protest. "They must do better, and they must know that our voices matter." Alexander Ruiz, a senior at Chelsea Career and Technical Education High School, added that it was unfair that students at iSchool were heading to more selective colleges next year than his own classmates. He elaborated, "It's not because they're smarter than me. It's just that they've been given the supplemental tools, while I haven't." These students were part of a massive wave of student-led protests sweeping New York City, where highly organized teenage activists—a racially and ethnically diverse group—employed walkouts, lock-ins, and phone calls to Mayor Bill de Blasio's weekly radio show to demand decisive action to reverse racial segregation and inequality that plagued the nation's largest school district of 1.1 million students and 1,800 schools.[127]

This student-led activism is inspiring and heartwarming, but it is also a sobering reminder that Americans have failed to create equal educational opportunities for all children and that children of color, especially African American, Latinx, and Native American children, as well as many Asian American students, bear the brunt of this inequality.

The educational histories of African Americans, Native Americans, Latinxs, and Asian Americans since 1954 demonstrate that there is no

FIGURE 5. New York City high school students demand school integration in 2019.
Photograph by Christina Veiga, published in "New York City Students Walk Out of Class,
Pledging Weekly Strikes to Demand School Integration," *Chalkbeat*, November 18, 2019.

single or simple model of school integration that can function to solve the
complex problem of institutionalized racism in American public schools,
nor has integration always been viewed as the best path to equity, self-
determination, or challenging educational racism. Flexible school desegregation plans should respond to specific challenges found in a community
in a particular time and place, such as Little Rock in 1957, New York City in
1964, Los Angeles in 1968, Phoenix in 1973, Boston in 1991, or the Standing
Rock Sioux Reservation in 2014. What is more, racial mixing alone rarely
functions as a viable strategy to equalize historic patterns of institutionalized white supremacy in public education. Instead, school leaders and local
communities must be prepared to significantly restructure and rebuild all
aspects of school operation and governance to ensure a diverse faculty and
administration, an inclusive curriculum, and fair policies related to tracking, counseling, extracurricular activities, student discipline, access to tech-
nology, and communication and shared governance with families.

These histories also underscore the importance of cultural and political
self-determination as essential components of meaningful school desegregation. Creating integrated, inclusive, and diverse schools does not require
students of color to conform to middle-class, white cultural norms. Schools
must retain spaces for students to study and celebrate their ethnic and cul-

tural identities through special courses in Mexican American history or extracurricular organizations like Black Student Unions. To borrow a phrase from Ibram X. Kendi, it is not enough for public schools to not be racist—educators need to be actively antiracist. The Black Lives Matter at School coalition asks educators to teach about structural racism, intersectional Black identities, Black history, and antiracist movements for social justice. Schools need to take positive steps to affirm the lives and cultures of Black, Native American, Latinx, and Asian American students.[128]

This chapter additionally reveals that race and power intertwine in terrible and destructive ways in educational history and that isolating students of color has always been an effective way to hoard public resources for whites. Journalist Nikole Hannah-Jones has spent her career studying the pernicious effects of school segregation and the complex motives that Black families have had in seeking, and sometimes not seeking, integration. "No, black kids should not have to leave their neighborhoods to attend a quality school, or sit next to white students to get a quality education," she confirms. "But we cannot be naïve about how this country works. To this day, according to data collected from the Education Department, the whiter the school, the more resources it has. We cannot forget that so many school desegregation lawsuits started with attempts by black parents to simply get equal resources for black schools. Parents demanded integration only after they realized that in a country that does not value black children the same as white ones, black children will never get what white children get unless they sit where white children sit."[129]

From this perspective, school integration would seem to be an essential component of educational reform in contemporary American politics. It has often functioned effectively in the past to break down artificial barriers between students and has, in specific cases, created more equitable schools. At the same time, persistent white resistance has limited the effectiveness of school integration to enact comprehensive, meaningful, and lasting reform. Mark Winston Griffith is one of the many Black educational activists who questions integration as a strategy and a goal. He cautions, "White folks are presented as what the ideal is when the term 'integration' is used, so that's oftentimes the background that this conversation is operating in. It's hard to look at integration in a way that frees itself from all the historical baggage and assumptions that the word carries."[130]

The debate over whether school integration can effectively improve the quality of public education for students of color will continue for the foreseeable future. Is integration necessary to secure an equal education for all? If so, what would this look like in practice, and if not, should we pursue racially and ethnically diverse schools for other reasons, such as preparing young people to contribute as active and engaged citizens in a multiracial democracy? How should we understand educational activism that pursues educational goals distinct from school integration, such as community-controlled and indigenous-run schools? The following chapters turn to these questions through philosophical inquiry to shed light on the enduring dilemma of school integration and its relationship to equal education and citizenship training in American public schools.

CHAPTER 3

EQUALITY

A historical analysis of the educational trajectories of African Americans, Native Americans, Latinxs, and Asian Americans reveals a long history of educational racism in America, a privileging of the educational development of whites, an enduring struggle by racialized minorities to secure more just and equal public education, and a complex view of integration as a path to that equality.

In the next three chapters, we turn to philosophy to illuminate the ethical, social, and political issues raised by this history. We explore and examine the deeper values underlying and connecting educational equality, integration, social justice, and group affirmation with self-determination. We begin with the ideal, or principle, of *equal education*, sought by minority activists and advocates. We argue that educational equality should be understood as a specific bundle of educational goods of an academic, personal, moral, and civic character that are provided to every student. This equality cannot be realized by in-school practices alone. We argue that educational justice must be linked with a critique of racially unjust structures in the society at large and that racial injustice is itself intricately bound up with structures of class-based injustice. Teachers and schools, therefore, have a responsibility to take account of these out-of-school factors in order to make public schools more equal for all.

Competing definitions of integration affect its differential appeal to communities both historically and in the present. We focus on three distinct, but not always distinguished, historical meanings of "integration": (1) removing legal structures that require different racial groups to attend different schools (the core meaning in the *Brown* decision); (2) ensuring that those racial groups do actually attend the same schools; and (3) incorporating ideals and values into the school's functioning that build on this physical integration—such as Martin Luther King Jr.'s conception of integration as creating communities of mutual respect, care, and appreciation among the different groups in a school and affirming the identities, communities, and heritages of these groups, an ideal usually sought by varying communities of color, as we have seen.

Ultimately, we argue that the most fundamental educational goal is the guarantee that all the goods of education are made equally available to all students. Integration is secondary and can be understood as a valuable strategy if it helps bring about equality of education. It cannot generate true equality, however, if premised on the idea—very common in educational thinking today—that integration improves educational outcomes of Black, Native American, and Latinx students through their benefiting from the norms, connections, and financial advantages of white and middle-class families in an integrated school. This approach to integration leaves in place unjust white advantage that must be challenged both inside the school and in the wider society if educational and social justice is to be achieved.

At the same time, integration—in its more King-like form—is a *civic* good, in which families and students of different races and ethnicities in the same school community treat one another with respect, fostering civic attachment and a shared commitment to seeking a common good. We argue that racially integrated schools are valuable primarily because they are uniquely positioned to help prepare students for a democratic, multiracial society, and this value is distinct from equality. Without students of different racial groups attending school and classes together, it is difficult for these schools to teach the civic capacities, attachments, and understandings required for multiracial democracy.

Finally, we have seen that minority educational activists have sometimes sought goals distinct from either integration or equality. These goals do not necessarily fit under a single category. Sometimes they involve recognition of the group and its heritage, such as in school curricula or student organizations. But sometimes they have involved something more robust, like a school designed primarily for a single racial or ethnic group, as the Chinese in San Francisco or the Navajo Rough Rock Demonstration School sought. Sometimes the goal has more closely resembled group self-determination, expressed in different forms, including the community control of a school or a district. Our historical survey shows that activists and advocates have sought these goals often as part of a demand for integration and sometimes as an alternative to it. We will explore more deeply the relation between these group-focused values and the values of integration, civic good, and equality. We argue that the civic challenge in any viable integrated school must involve the affirmation of all minority racial groups and their cultures, histories, communities, and identities.

EDUCATIONAL GOODS AS EQUALITY OF EDUCATION[1]

Let us start with the idea of equal education. "Equality" is a comparative idea. Party A should be equal to party B, with regard to some specific positive good. What should that good, or goods, be in order for education to be equal?[2] For a long time, educational resources, such as qualified teachers, buildings in good repair, books and computers, and the like, seemed to constitute an equal education. Yet resources cannot be the ultimate content of an ideal of equality. They are only means to that end—students' actual learning.

Student learning is often framed in the language of "output" or "outcomes." This nomenclature does not express that educational goods are valuable for their own sake, rather than only as a means to something else, nor that learning changes students and becomes a part of their being. The oft-used term *achievement* similarly fails. Achievement is performance according to a certain standard and does not itself capture what students have themselves gained by their learning. Outputs, outcomes, and achievements are not inherent educational goods and are only imperfect indicators of them. It is difficult to engage with contemporary educational discourse without using these familiar terms, but it is also vital to recognize their limitations.

We propose that equality of education be thought of in terms of *educational goods*—that in the process of compulsory schooling and at the point of exit from schooling (say, high school),[3] all students should be in possession of certain educational goods.[4] Their possession of these goods at the exit point should be independent of their backgrounds, such as their race or family socioeconomic status. This equality is a requirement of educational justice. If all students have not been brought to the threshold of possessing the full range of educational goods, the society and school system have failed in their duty of justice to those students.

The Four Categories of Educational Good

But what are the educational goods that should be equal? A full account of educational goods is beyond the scope of our book, but we envision them falling within four broad categories.[5] The first is *intellectual* or *cognitive development*, involving subject matter mastery (math, literature, social studies, and so on) as well as more general intellectual capabilities, such as critical thinking and looking at an issue from several perspectives. This is probably the most familiar educational good and certainly the one for which assessment metrics have been by far the most developed. But there are other educational goods of great importance. A second is *personal growth* or *individual flourishing*—involving, for example, the formation of healthy friendships and the capacity to think about and try to live a meaningful life. A third category encompasses the student's *moral capabilities* or *attributes*—for example, possessing empathy, a sense of justice, and respect for others of different ethnicities and races. A fourth category is *civic*—such as a commitment to the well-being of one's polity, competent engagement with individuals of different backgrounds and experiences in seeking a common good, and a regard for fellow citizens as equals.

The four categories overlap in various ways. Personal growth, moral goods, and civic goods all involve subject matter mastery of different kinds (for example, the civic category involves historical knowledge of one's country and its evolving ideals and institutions). Moreover, both moral and civic capability are, at least in part, elements in individual flourishing, as Aristotle argued;[6] one's own life is enhanced if one is able to empathize with, manifest justice toward, and engage as equal citizens with others. And "moral" and "civic" are certainly overlapping categories (e.g., both involve respect for other persons). Nevertheless, it is useful to distinguish them in order to ensure that all four categories are in play when we conceive of equality as the parity of educational goods, especially since the latter three categories (personal flourishing, moral goods, and civic goods) tend to get sidelined in favor of intellectual goods in contemporary discussions of education.[7]

All these goods can be either intrinsic or instrumental—good in themselves or good as a means to something else. The difference is very important, but many educational goods are both. Thinking critically, for example, is valuable for all kinds of jobs and life tasks, but the ability to think critically is a fulfillment of intellectual potential that provides gratification even when not employed for some other aim. And, as another example, empathizing contributes to more fulfilling interpersonal relationships, but the capacity to empathize is also good in itself.

In relation to race, one particularly important educational good is a sense of justice—the ability to recognize injustice in one's society and care that injustice be prevented and rectified, as well as the associated cognitive abilities of being able to analyze the processes in one's society that create or sustain different forms of injustice. Because the United States remains a deeply racially unjust society, with unjust disparities among racially defined groups a persistent historical feature of our social order (though one that has undergone significant changes, often for the better, but sometimes for the worse), the development of a sense of justice is especially significant.

What's the minimum for them to be just? Adequate

Most educational goods can be possessed to different degrees—one student can analyze arguments better, be more committed to civic good, or understand chemistry better than another. Therefore, when we speak of equal possession of these goods, we must have in mind a certain threshold for each good. The equality principle will then require that every student be brought to that threshold. Sometimes the threshold level is conceptualized as "adequacy." But the threshold must be more robust than merely adequate in order to ensure that teachers will devote a substantial portion of their classroom time and effort helping all their students meet that standard. It should not be easy to attain. Otherwise schools with advantaged students may be better able to bring all their students to a given adequacy line and utilize remaining instructional time for further educational enrichment that might be denied to disadvantaged students. All students should be able to possess the threshold level of the full range of educational goods by the point of exit, and this is what educational equality consists in and educational justice requires.

The "Equal Treatment/Equal Care and Respect" Principle

The fundamental equality principle concerns "result" goods—what students should possess at the relevant exit point. But equal results are not the only appropriate form of equality in education. Students share a relationship with their teachers, and the quality of that relationship is a nonresult good of education, tied to an institutional setting and a specific period of the child's life. An "equal treatment" standard is required to govern the student-teacher relationship. If a teacher favors certain students over others and gives those students extra attention and educational enrichment, this would seem to violate an equality of treatment principle, even if all students in the class have been brought to the educational goods threshold. We suggest that the equal treatment principle should consist of teachers' *equal care and respect* for every student, which, as we have seen, has often been denied to students of color.[8]

Because of our racial focus, we distinguish between equal treatment principles that govern all students equally and an antidiscrimination form that is sensitive to particular categories of student. The latter declares it wrong for a teacher to discriminate against students based on race (or religion, language, and so on). The principle still calls for equal treatment but requires a teacher to pay particular attention to certain social identities that often render a student vulnerable to discriminatory treatment.

The "equality of educational goods" principle applies most fundamentally to the educational system as a whole. It says that that system should ensure that every student attain the threshold of educational goods. The equal treatment principle applies to individuals—teachers or school personnel more generally—and the particular students with whom they come in contact.

Equal Treatment, Not Color-Blindness

Some educators may understand equal treatment as equivalent to color-blindness—not paying attention to students' race. Teachers often express this idea with the statement, "I don't see race. I just see kids." But race is a significant axis of differential social experience, life chances, historical legacy, and identity. Color-blindness is therefore a willful denial of the importance of race in students' lives and is not an appropriate ideal for teachers.[9] The equal treatment principle does not require color-blindness but involves teachers understanding their individual students in light of their specific ethnoracial identities and correspondingly treating them with equal care and respect.

It would be beneficial if race did not have such a pervasive importance in our society and the world, if socioeconomic well-being did not correlate as strongly with race as it does at present, and if racial stereotypes did not play as great a role in people's response to racial others. If that day ever came, it might then be appropriate to affirm color-blindness as an ideal to which individual citizens should strive. But some Black thinkers disagree and see Blacks as a group that carries a heritage and culture, which it would be a loss—both to members of those groups and to the world more generally—to jettison even in a racially just world.[10] In any case, since we are nowhere near that racially just world at present, it is not appropriate to guide ourselves by color-blindness now.

WHAT'S WRONG WITH THE AMERICAN
VIEW OF "EQUALITY OF OPPORTUNITY"?

We are suggesting that the ideal of an equal education is the equality of *educational goods*. A more familiar alternative view is that what should be equal are *opportunities*. Equality of opportunity is often thought to be a particularly American principle when understood in the following way: Americans do not favor the government equalizing people's life situations, nor the rewards attached to particular occupations. What they favor is individuals' equal opportunity to employ their talents and efforts to compete with others for those unequal positions and rewards. Not everyone can, for example, work in finance, law, or medicine, but everyone should have an equal shot at trying to do so. This American ideal is *equal competitive opportunity* to attain the best position one can in an unequal system of rewards.[11]

The American version of equality of opportunity at least implicitly involves education in a particularly central way. John Rawls, the great twentieth-century American political philosopher, articulated this clearly by distinguishing between "formal" and "fair" equality of opportunity. Formal equality of opportunity means no student is prevented from attending public schools and thus striving to develop occupation-related capabilities. But the legal right to attend school does not curtail the substantial advantages and disadvantages related to family socioeconomic position among students—for example, parents' differential ability to buy educational enrichment for their offspring. Rawls regards these class-based advantages as unfair and thus unjust. His conception of fair—rather than merely formal—equality of opportunity (FEO) provides for all children to develop their own abilities and talents, without being either advantaged or disadvantaged by class background or circumstances.

John Rawls on Fair Equality of Opportunity and "Natural Assets"

Rawls does not explicitly recognize race as a distinctive type of barrier to FEO. Nevertheless, the logic of his distinction between formal and fair equality of opportunity also requires racial barriers to be removed. Although Rawls's explicit focus on schools is minimal, he does assert, "The school system, whether public or private, should be designed to even out class barriers."[12] He implies as much in his official definition of FEO: "Assuming that there is a distribution of natural assets, those who are at the same level of talent and ability, and have the same willingness to use them, should have the same prospects of success regardless of their initial place in the social system"—that is, regardless of their class background and, by implication, their racial background.[13]

FEO implicitly involves two stages in both the Rawlsian and the American conceptions. In the first, schools bring students to the same starting point, sometimes called the "level playing field" or the "starting gate," where they are not held back by a disadvantageous background nor advantaged by a favorable one. At the second stage, they go forth from that starting point to compete for positions and jobs in society with unequal rewards. This competition is fair because the earlier stage ensures that all are made ready, through an equal education, to engage in the competition; additionally, the rules of the competition are fair because the unequal positions are allocated to persons solely according to their talent, ability, and effort. A system of this sort is sometimes called a *meritocracy*.[14]

But adherents of the American conception differ from Rawls regarding whether American society currently exemplifies equality of competitive opportunity. They either tend to think that the school system actually provides an equal starting point for all students or do not clearly distinguish formal and fair equality of opportunity and believe it sufficient if a student has some opportunity even if it is not really equal to that of others. It is a common American sentiment to insist, "I got where I am by my own efforts and talents, so I deserve what I have." But if not everyone starts on a level playing field, then some portion of where individuals end up is due not to their efforts and talents but to an unequal starting place not of their own making. Unfortunately, the cultural salience of the American view serves to reconcile people to a very unjust reward system in which people's achievements are significantly determined by their background circumstances.[15]

By contrast, Rawls believes that FEO is very far from being realized in the current American educational and occupational order. Although he was writing before social science had demonstrated the myriad ways that a family's racial and class background affects students' educational fates, undermining fair equality of opportunity at the educational stage, Rawls recognized the basic phenomenon. Thus Rawls's FEO stands as a powerful condemnation of the American educational system, since class and racial background do in fact play an enormous role in determining one's initial position in society.

However, although FEO is superior to the American conception, it is not an adequate account of educational equality. First, it relies on an idea of "natural talent" that is not only educationally unsound but also strongly resonant with historical rationalizations of racial and class hierarchies in education. Second, it shares with the American conception an overly narrow and instrumental view of the purposes of education—that its main function is preparation for the labor market. The language of opportunity in both the American conception and FEO is tainted by a failure to articulate intrinsic, distinctly educational values. Finally, the American conception is deficient in one further way that Rawls avoids, in that it takes society's occupational reward structure as a noncriticized and implicitly morally acceptable given and as a framework in which the competitive opportunity is to operate. The equality of educational goods conception avoids these three deficiencies, which we will now discuss in more detail.

Rawlsian "Natural Assets"

Rawls's conception of FEO relies on the ideas that children possess certain "natural assets" (abilities and talents) independent of their class background that schooling will reveal and develop and that children's willingness to put in effort to develop these assets is, or can be made, independent of their background circumstances.

This idea of natural talents and effort does not comport with what we know about the character and development of capacities, abilities, and talents. There is no possible way to identify an ability or talent as a "natural asset" independent of and prior to environmental influences. Any actually identifiable ability is a product of genetic characteristics, intentional development, and random environmental factors. Although we can infer that a developed ability may have a genetic component, we cannot isolate a distinct genetic "bit" to it.[16] The different factors are inextricably mixed up together. We are thus unable to say what is "natural" in a child's ability, and we can identify something as an ability only in a developed form.

This is true of intelligence, both as a quality closely tied to school performance and as one for which some scholars have claimed a strong genetic component.[17] But intelligence is not a uniform quality. The intelligence involved in following an abstract argument in philosophy differs from the intelligence needed to assess interpersonal dynamics in a complex situation, and both differ from the intelligence used in artistic creation.[18] All the different types of intelligence are capable of development through various kinds of learning and may also be affected by additional environmental influences of which we do not now know the exact character. No doubt some or even all these forms of intelligence have a partially genetic component. But differentiating an environmental from a genetic bit in the overall developed intelligence(s) is impossible.

"Natural Assets" and Race and Class Hierarchies

Not only is Rawls's "natural asset" idea false, but it is both detrimental to sound educational practice and also potentially reinforcing of race- and class-based educational inequities. Recent research has established that students who think of intelligence as a trait that is always being developed, dependent on the continual effort of the individual student, outperform otherwise similar students who think of intelligence as a Rawlsian natural asset—an already-existing feature of one's mental equipment that one's school performance reflects. Teachers who operate with this "developmental" or "growth mindset" view are better able to help their students develop their cognitive capacities than those beholden to a natural asset or "fixed mindset."[19] These teachers recognize that while there are ultimate limits to the cognitive functioning any given student will be able to develop, they can never be certain that the student has reached that limit in the present, and so they should operate on the assumption that the student can always develop further. By adopting, and conveying to their students, the developmental view, teachers can better enhance student learning.

Moreover, the idea of intelligence as a fixed trait has strong associations with racial ideologies claiming that some races are more innately intelligent than others. We very much still live with the legacy of the belief in Blacks' (and, to a lesser extent, Native Americans' and Mexican Americans', and more generally Latinxs') intellectual inferiority, mentioned in earlier chapters, that has deep roots in American culture and history.[20] The natural asset view of intelligence could well function as reinforcement of this racist ideology (and vice versa). Rejecting the natural asset view in favor of a developmental view of intelligence would help reject that aspect of racist ideology, which is particularly damaging in educational contexts.[21]

The educational goods conception of equal education is not vulnerable to the "natural asset" problem. It does not posit or require consideration of individual capabilities the student possesses prior to being educated. The educational goods conception is committed only to what students should possess at a particular end point of their education and assumes only that all or almost all students are capable of attaining the educational goods in question through the learning process. This view need not deny that developed capacities are a product of both genetic and environmental factors.[22]

In this regard, the educational goods conception is in line with the contemporary standards-based educational movement in assuming that all students can achieve at relatively high levels. The difference is that our conception of the standards in question encompasses moral, civic, and personal growth goods, rather than the purely academic skills and subject matter mastery that are the heart of the standards-and-accountability movement.

Educational Goods Are Not Beholden to Society's Current Values and Reward Structures

The second major deficiency of the American conception of equal opportunity, shared by Rawls's FEO, is that it unduly narrows the scope of educational goods. Both see the primary purpose of education as preparing the student to compete for occupations and their rewards. But educational values should not be limited by and beholden to the arrangements, rewards, and dominant values of the society or culture in which they operate at any given time, nor should they concern only occupations and preparation for them. Educational values should possess their own integrity as distinctly educational, grounded in individual flourishing and moral and civic values (discussed in more detail below, chap. 5). The American conception, one might say—and this is true of Rawls's FEO as well—treats the significance of education primarily as preparation for something that comes after it, most narrowly work life.[23] But educational goods have value in their own right, along with whatever role they also play in readying the student for the competitive job market.

Finally, and relatedly, the American conception takes the occupational and reward structure at any particular time as an uncriticized given, an unexamined backdrop for the students' efforts and aspirations. This is not the same as saying that the structure is positively affirmed as a just social order, though no doubt many teachers present it that way as well. But it is to say that it is treated as "just there," implied to be an acceptable and unavoidable framework within which the student is to strive to make their way.

But educational values must serve as a critical guide for students in negotiating the society in which they do and will live. The purpose of education (in its personal growth, moral, and civic modes) is therefore to provide students with the ability to form values of their own, which they recognize may not align with dominant sociocultural values at a given time. Students should come to have the ability to assess for themselves whether, for example, prestigious and highly paid occupations would contribute to their own flourishing and whether such positions reflect values the student truly embraces. The teacher should not imply that they must embrace the given occupational and reward order, as either positively just or even merely acceptable, but should help them acquire the tools to make their own judgment on this matter. Those tools should include the lens of justice that enables students to evaluate the structures of society, including the occupational system, and the lens of personal meaning in one's life. Although it is appropriate for schools to contribute to students' acquiring skills that will enable them to gain employment, the goods of education do not derive their fundamental value and rationale from their being rewarded by the structure of society in a given moment. Thus, as a view of educational equality, the educational goods conception, properly understood, has a fundamentally different character than the American conception of equality of competitive opportunity.

A further problem with taking the current structure as an uncriticized given is that, especially from a racial vantage point, US society as currently structured (not only its occupational reward system) remains deeply unjust. This is a moral truth teachers have a responsibility to help students understand. Not only must educators help students develop their own capacities for social criticism, but they must also affirmatively teach them to recognize when a society is unjust. Certainly not everyone agrees that US society is (racially) unjust, although there has been a significant rise in that perception, especially among white people, as a result of the Black Lives Matter movement of 2013 to the present and the events that have triggered it, especially the murder of George Floyd in spring 2020. But the moral and civic educator cannot remain neutral on every moral and civic issue over which the public disagrees. To teach, or to leave students with the impression, that it is an open question whether American society today is a just social order is not intellectually or civically responsible. Instructing about this injustice is a central challenge for education and a vital step toward coming to terms with both racial injustice in education and the larger structures of social injustice to which it is linked. (More on this below, pp. 122–26.)[24]

The "Opportunity/Choice" Framework within Education and Its Deficiencies

We have preferred the term *educational goods* to *educational opportunities* as the content of equal education, because opportunity language is largely bound up with occupations and competition for them. But "opportunity" can also be employed purely within education, without any link to competition or occupation. This idea of opportunity posits that teachers and the school system in general present students with options that embody educational goods, but it is up to the student to seize these offerings.[25]

Elizabeth Anderson makes clear the deficiencies of this conception of opportunity. First, since children are not fully developed agents, it is not appropriate to hold them wholly responsible for the consequences of their choices. Second, in any case, those consequences are set by educational institutions and actors and subject to norms of fairness and appropriateness. For example, "zero tolerance" policies that suspend students for various behavioral infractions may be neither the most productive nor the most fair consequence to impose on such students.[26]

Finally, Anderson points out that education is not institutionally structured in the way the "opportunity/choice" framework seems to envision—that there is a particular moment at which the student makes a choice whether to access an educational good. Instead there are innumerable small choices whose longer-term consequences may be momentous but hard to discern for children or their parents.[27] For example, small choices about doing one's homework can over time have a large impact on whether a student is chosen for higher- or lower-track classes, a result with serious consequences for the student (see discussion of tracking below, pp. 135ff).

Such considerations call for schools to ensure that students actually access educational goods—that they learn how to think critically, to read for understanding, to analyze the social arrangements of their societies, to become respectful and considerate of others, to have a sense of justice, and so on. Accomplishing this cannot be guided by the principle, "We just give you the array of options; you have to choose among them." It is true, as mentioned earlier, that students must engage with their teacher and with the educational material, not just passively wait for something to be delivered to them. But engagement is not the same as selecting from a set of already-presented options. According to the equality of educational goods framework, students emerge from school in possession of those goods, and the school is responsible for ensuring this outcome.

However, "opportunity" is sometimes used in a third way, such as when an educator notes to a student, "This class (or job) is a wonderful opportunity for you." Here an opportunity is something provided in a manner that virtually ensures that the student avails herself of it because her ability to do so is already assured, and she is assumed to see the value of the opportunity in question.

This use of "opportunity" is often employed to reject the language of "achievement gaps" in favor of "opportunity gaps"—to shift responsibility of student learning to schools and to reject an implication of deficiency in the student. The term in this usage aligns with the educational goods conception of equality—a provision model of the student accessing the good. We saw in our historical survey that minority groups struggling for equality in education often employed the language of "equality of educational opportunity" to do so. They were implicitly drawing on this educational goods–related conception of opportunity. Unless otherwise indicated, when we use the term *opportunity* henceforth, this is the usage we will employ.

In summary, what is to be provided equally when education is equal are educational goods. It is therefore not an equality of opportunities, where that is understood as enabling all students to compete on an equal plane for post-school occupational goods, which we have designated the "American conception" of equal opportunity. Opportunity in the American sense is only an instrumental good, while educational goods are primarily intrinsic goods that are valuable to an individual in their own right (as well as, sometimes, instrumentally).

The American conception is moreover problematic because it treats the values, hierarchies, and rewards of the existing occupational order as uncriticized givens. By contrast, educational goods must provide students the wherewithal both to see beyond the values dominant in the social order of a given moment and to criticize this social order, in general and especially from a justice vantage point.

EQUALITY OF EDUCATION AND THE EFFECT
OF OUTSIDE-OF-SCHOOL FACTORS

Let us now shift from the *educational goods* aspect of "equality of educational goods" to the *equality* aspect. From the outset, there is a problem with assessing the degree and character of inequality of educational goods. While measuring educational attainment has become very sophisticated, the goods these measures are designed for are a small subset of significant educational goods. Moral growth and civic capability are seldom measured, nor is personal growth and flourishing generally.

Different educational goods are taught in partly different ways. Teaching students to be empathetic will vary from teaching them to think mathematically, and both will be distinct from teaching them to be civically engaged. Thus, the reasons for a wide gap among racially defined groups in math attainment may not apply to empathy or civic engagement.[28] So what it would take to make all children equal with respect to empathy and civic engagement will be different than with respect to math. Nevertheless, gaps among racial groups in purely academic skills, capabilities, or knowledge that have been widely measured are still very important.[29] With these as our focus, but with attention to the specificities of the broader range of educational goods, we can make some observations about equal education in general and about racial equality in education in particular.

Often, public discussion of education proceeds as if what students learn in school is fully and solely a product of activities that take place in school, perhaps supplemented by homework done after school hours. The *Brown* decision tacitly assumed that schools themselves could create equal education between Blacks and whites through integration. This assumption was understandable in context. The court thought that bringing Black students into hitherto all-white schools would solve the two barriers to equality they identified—Black students would now have the same educational resources as whites by attending the same schools, and the stigma against Black children created by segregation (which allegedly depressed Black student motivation and achievement) would be undermined once the state declared segregation as contrary to the law and Constitution. However, in 1966 James Coleman published the pathbreaking Coleman Report, *Equality of Educational Opportunity*, commissioned by the US government as part of the Civil Rights Act of 1964. The report entirely challenged this pure focus on schools.[30] Coleman and his colleagues' study of three thousand or so schools throughout the country found that the economic characteristics of students' families and classmates had a more powerful effect on differences in what students learned in school than anything contributed by teachers, school resources, or other aspects of the schooling process itself.[31] While startling at the time, Coleman's general view that factors outside of school have a large impact on students' learning in school has been repeatedly confirmed, developed, and expanded. It may be thought of as the common sense of social scientists of education in our time.

For example, children's health is influenced by their out-of-school environments, and it in turn influences school performance. Children from low socioeconomic status (SES) families have poorer health than higher-SES children, for two general reasons. One is that their environments are less healthy than middle-class environments (e.g., more exposure to lead poisoning, less access to healthy food, and more air pollution). Second, by and large they have less access to good health care than middle-class families.

Poor health affects an individual student's learning in several ways. Hunger, undiagnosed vision and hearing problems, asthma, and poor nutrition impair a student's ability to operate at top capacity in school. Greater illness also leads to more missed school days. In addition, also in line with Coleman's findings, if too many of the student's classmates attend irregularly, the resultant instability and turnover in the classroom has a negative effect on the other students.[32] Finally, subsequent research has shown that SES-related characteristics of a student's neighborhood often have an effect on school learning, independent of the student's own characteristics and those of her classmates.[33]

In addition to health, there are numerous other particular features of low-SES families that can affect student learning—homelessness and housing instability, which can cause students to move from one school to another in the middle of the school year; parental work instability and lack of income, which can heighten stress within the household environment; or parents' lower educational level, which reduces their ability to help their children with their schoolwork and with the development of verbal and other school-related capabilities.

While we have known about the deleterious effects of poverty on educational outcomes for five decades, somewhat more recently we have come to recognize inequality-generating processes at the other end of the economic spectrum. Upper-middle-class parents can improve their offspring's learning and school performance by hiring private tutors and engaging in education-enhancing activities with their children, as well as by using their class-based forms of influence and resources to get their students placed in more demanding and higher-status courses and programs and to buy their way into school districts with better schools.[34] These processes are referred to as "opportunity hoarding," a phenomenon in which advantaged groups reinforce and increase their already-existing advantages, preventing or at least making it more difficult for other groups to access those advantages.

Opportunity hoarding operates independently of the processes disadvantaging people in poverty. Purely on its own, opportunity hoarding equally disadvantages anyone below the advantaged level, such as middle-income people (say, the middle 60 percent), not only people in poverty. Nevertheless, the two processes together—opportunity hoarding at the top and poverty at the bottom—have the effect of further increasing overall inequality, and thereby racial inequality, beyond what either of those processes does alone. In this sense, people in poverty, who are already educationally disadvantaged, are further disadvantaged through wealthy people's opportunity hoarding, which makes it harder for everyone else to access educational goods.

The "Justice Framework"

The embeddedness of education in the wider field of social domains, such as health, housing, occupation, income, and wealth, needs to inform how we think about realizing educational equality, in that educational injustice is deeply bound up with forms of social injustice, of a racial and class character, in these other arenas. Let us call this larger set of interlocking systems of injustice to which educational injustice is linked the "justice framework." The justice framework highlights that injustice in each of these life domains fosters or exacerbates educational injustice and that these injustices are in turn fostered or exacerbated by educational injustice. (For example, a graduate's failure to possess equal educational goods may put her at greater risk for being unable to secure a decent job and income.)

The justice framework encompasses three ways the different interlocking systems are intertwined with regard to educational injustice. The first is *causal* or *analytical*, the point made by Coleman—health, housing, and wealth disparities help produce educational disparities. The second is *normative*. The wrongness of educational disparities—their injustice—is tied to the wrongness of disparities in the other domains. Students suffering from educational injustice due in part to their experiences of inadequate housing or parental occupational discrimination experience distinct forms of injustice simultaneously. That some people have inadequate housing is wrong in itself, apart from how it contributes to educational injustice, but it is also wrong for that reason.[35] The third way the systems are intertwined is *solutionally*. We cannot (fully) rectify educational injustice without to some degree rectifying housing, income, occupational, and health injustices. Moreover, the wider society cannot be made just through education alone.

Race and Class in the Justice Framework

The justice framework particularly emphasizes the necessary copresence of both race and class injustice. The inequality-generating processes at both ends of the socioeconomic spectrum (poverty and opportunity hoarding) are not inherently or necessarily racial in character, but in our society they generally have a strong race-related effect, referred to as a "disparate racial impact" in legal terminology. A higher percentage of Blacks, Latinxs, and Native Americans than their percentage of the population occupy the lower SES strata, and a lower percentage the upper strata.[36] Therefore, they will be disproportionately harmed educationally by, for example, the health and housing instability processes mentioned earlier and further racially disadvantaged by upper-middle-class opportunity hoarding. Thus class-based injustice contributes to racial injustice.

Conversely, class-based justice promotes racial justice. For example, raising the minimum wage would disproportionately benefit Blacks, Latinxs, and Native Americans (compared to whites). Of course historical and contemporary racial injustice and discrimination have created the disproportionate number of Blacks, Latinxs, and Native Americans in the lower and higher SES echelons (more in the lower, less in the higher) in the first place. In that sense, racism causally contributed to the socioeconomic disadvantage suffered by these groups. Nevertheless, once racial discrimination has created class-defined disparities, class-based processes in their own right perpetuate and exacerbate them.

In this book we are focusing primarily on racial educational injustice. Even if that were our sole concern, we would still have to pay attention to class-related processes. In doing so, we are following the views of Martin Luther King Jr., who, especially in the latter years of his life (but not only then), emphasized the class aspect of racial injustice, calling for a guaranteed basic income, a jobs program (the 1963 March on Washington was for *jobs and freedom*, stated in that order), and adequate housing, and criticized the funding for the War on Poverty.[37]

From analytical, normative, and solutional points of view, both class and race must be taken into consideration. Analytically, part of the reason Blacks, Latinxs, and Native Americans do not access educational goods to the degree that whites do is because they have less money than whites, and money (partly) buys educational advantage, independent of race. Economic processes thus intensify racial gaps in income.

Normatively, class is an axis of injustice distinct from race. It is wrong that Blacks, Latinxs, and Native Americans disproportionately fail to achieve (certain) educational goods to the degree that whites do. But it is also unjust that lower-income students attain these goods at a lesser rate than upper-income students do, independent of race. This means that, for example, a low-income Black student can suffer from two distinct forms of educational injustice, one related to race and one to class.[38]

The necessity of a class perspective when discussing racial injustice also affects the solutional dimension. The United States remains a profoundly unjust society with respect to wrongful inequities in health, wealth, occupational compensation, income, and general life chances by both race and class. These inequities have greatly intensified since the early 1980s, and in the past decade or so the general public has begun to pay acute attention to this increasing inequality, which has been both heightened and amplified by the COVID-19 pandemic.

Movements and initiatives aiming to reduce these disparities and help the public recognize and understand them have become an important part of the political landscape. Examples, among many others, include the Occupy movement of 2011; the Fight for $15 minimum wage campaigns around the country; Bernie Sanders's presidential campaigns of 2016 and 2020 highlighting economic inequality; the teacher protests in Kentucky, Arizona, West Virginia, Colorado, Los Angeles, Chicago, and North Carolina in 2018 and 2019 (discussed below, p. 114); proposals for increased taxes on the wealthy and corporations; and low-income communities of color organizing to control their schools and preserve schools in their communities in danger of being closed.[39] All of these have pushed back against various aspects of the United States' systemic, interlocking, and intensifying injustices. Educational justice consists in the equal possession of educational goods. The justice framework is essential for understanding how that goal can be realized. Culturally competent and antiracist pedagogy and curriculum is necessary to make progress toward bringing all students to the required threshold of educational goods, but such progress is inevitably limited by excessive inequities in life circumstances.[40] The struggle for educational justice must work in tandem with movements and policy initiatives to reduce unjust inequality in all domains of life, to lessen and ultimately end poverty, and to diminish opportunity hoarding.

The degree of race- and class-based educational disparity in the United States is by no means inevitable. International comparisons show that the United States has larger educational gaps between socioeconomically (and therefore racially) defined groups than otherwise comparable countries.[41] A major reason for this is that the United States has a greater degree of overall socioeconomic inequality and (as part of this) weaker social policies to help lower-income families.

POVERTY AND THE TEACHER'S RESPONSIBILITIES

Four Challenges to Linking Socioeconomic Disadvantage to Educational Underperformance

Nevertheless, the social science consensus that socioeconomic disadvantage is a source of educational disadvantage that should inform educational policy and practice has been challenged. The justice framework can help us see the fallacies of these challenges and clarify teachers' responsibilities in light of class-related determinants of educational inequalities. We will examine four of these predominant challenges.

1. The first challenge claims that when educators, or scholars of education, attend to the links between economic and educational disadvantage, they are "making excuses" for schools and teachers that do not put sufficient effort into trying to teach low-SES students.[42] One educator gives an example of this point of view: "I hear consistently from my coworkers and colleagues, 'I can't do anything for this child because of where they come from.' It's very easy, then, to write that child off. From personal experience, that child has just as good a chance of learning as another child, but it might take more effort on the part of the teacher."[43] Certain charter schools designate themselves as "no-excuses" schools in an effort to reject this alleged excuse-making. Such schools serve low-income and racial minority students and adhere to a demanding behavioral and academic regimen.[44]

2. A second challenge argues that "ending poverty" seems an overwhelmingly daunting goal, while focusing on in-school educational factors seems at least achievable in the present. This argument does not really deny social science findings linking socioeconomic standing to educational success but claims that nothing is gained by attending to them, or that doing so can be additionally harmful by diverting teachers' attention from what they can affect.

3. A third challenge is that dealing with poverty itself is not the professional responsibility of school-based educators. These proponents believe that teachers should not be concerned about larger political issues but should confine themselves to their responsibility to educate students.

4. A fourth challenge accepts the general causality between socioeconomic disadvantage and low educational performance but states that schools themselves, purely through their instructional regimes and school cultures, can block the causal mechanisms in play.[45] The argument points

to certain charter schools that have been successful with some low-income pupils of color, thereby claiming to demonstrate that the link between socioeconomic disadvantage and educational disadvantage can be broken. If these schools can break that link, then others can too.

These arguments are not generally framed explicitly in terms of race but rather socioeconomic disadvantage. However, they are very much meant to apply to low-income Black and Latinx students, the prime populations of urban charter schools.

Responding to the SES/Education Link inside and outside of Schools

To reply to these challenges and illustrate the need for a justice framework in thinking about education and teachers' professional responsibilities, it is helpful to group policy responses to the link between SES and educational disadvantage into three general categories:

1. Providing extra academic resources to the low-SES students (e.g., tutoring, support classes)
2. Directly improving the family's socioeconomic status
3. Buffering the student from ill effects of the family's socio-economic status through school-site efforts and initiatives not directly educational in character

All three of these approaches assume that barriers to students' learning lie in their life situations, not their educational potential, which should be assumed to be comparable to other groups. Tyrone Howard puts the implications of this point well: "Countless numbers of students who are classified as 'low achievers' by traditional standards are often some of the most talented, intellectually gifted, creative, and critical thinkers on school campuses around the country."[46]

The first category seems uncontroversial; presumably none of the arguments against attending to empirical links between SES status and educational performance denies that students from disadvantaged backgrounds may need extra help or resources, although all four noted challenges do downplay the need for greater resources. Examples of the second category include improving access to health care, raising the minimum wage, strengthening the Earned Income Tax Credit and the Child Tax Credit, providing families with and helping them to access better-paying jobs, reducing housing insecurity (through both public housing initiatives and the improvement of families' general SES standing so they can afford better housing), strengthening collective bargaining, and cash assistance for poor families.[47] These initiatives—all entirely feasible and many partially implemented—would improve low-income families' economic situation and consequentially reduce some of the educational disadvantages of low-income students. They would additionally improve attendance, reduce between-school mobility, lessen familial income- or employment-related stress on the children, and contribute to students' embracing more hopeful views of their future, by improving the life situation of individual students, their classmates, and the other families in their neighborhoods.

These proposed economic changes would serve both socioeconomic justice in its own right, by reducing poverty and unjustifiable levels of economic inequality, as well as educational justice, by making it easier for low-SES students to access educational goods equally with other students.

Ultimately, long-term and stable progress toward educational equality requires economic measures of these kinds. Reducing poverty and inequality should be viewed as educational improvement programs.

The third category of policy responses involves in-school measures, which do not focus on academics (as in the first category), that partly buffer the student against some of the effects of low SES without directly addressing the family's economic situation itself, as the second category does. An important example related to health is a school-site clinic, such as those that currently exist in many schools around the nation, which provides pediatric, optometric, mental health, and dental care to both students and parents.[48] Such clinics are components of "community schools," which have been incorporated (as one example among many other cities) into the New York City school regime: "Community Schools recognize that students who are hungry, can't see the blackboard, or are missing school regularly face critical obstacles to learning in the classroom. By providing an extra meal, connecting a parent to job training, or enrolling a student in an afterschool program, they can lower barriers to learning and help kids succeed."[49] The idea of "wraparound services" captures the idea of school-site initiatives that promote a student's overall well-being, without being directly educational in character, yet have a positive impact on student's educational engagement.[50] Community schools can also provide a foundation for parental participation and empowerment that is itself a crucial component of educational justice.[51]

The policy initiatives of categories two and three respond to arguments one ("making excuses") and two ("ending poverty is overwhelmingly daunting") (see pp. 111–12). They show that poverty is not a monolith and that when understood in its constituent, economically related disadvantages (health, housing, jobs, and income), it is subject to feasible initiatives that help families and students.[52] Category three initiatives show that recognition of poverty-related disadvantage can be addressed within the school in constructive ways that do not divert from, but rather support, the task of teaching. Of course buffering cannot do the work of removing all family-based, poverty-related disadvantages and thus cannot substitute for either the reduction of poverty itself or need-based extra resources.[53]

Some challengers say that attending to poverty-related deficits is not a teacher's responsibility. But as just mentioned, teachers' capacity to recognize the stresses and negative impacts of poverty on students is entirely compatible with, and indeed required for, doing their utmost to enhance students' learning and believing that progress is possible.

Teachers Advocating for Students outside of School: Teacher "Rebellions" of 2018–19

Acknowledging the impact of out-of-school factors on student learning also implies that it is not appropriate for teachers to regard their responsibilities as stopping at the school door (as argument three states and argument two ["teachers cannot end poverty"] implies). Teachers should view advocacy for greater overall economic equality, and more specifically a reduction of poverty, as part of their professional responsibilities as teachers. Indeed, educators have a distinctive contribution to make to political advocacy for a reduction in poverty because they see its negative impact on their students up close.[54] People in poverty in general have few advocates with political influence, and teachers are one of the few professional groups that have extended and systematic contact with them.[55] Educators must resist attempts by others to fail to credit their understanding of and concern about poverty and to shame them for it.[56]

In a remarkable development, in 2018 and 2019 teachers in several different states and large cities engaged in strikes and work stoppages that expressed in significant measure this broader conception of their professional responsibilities and identities. For example, teachers striking in the nation's second and third largest districts, Los Angeles and Chicago, in 2019 demanded more counselors and health workers in their schools.[57] More generally, the larger teacher protest wave of 2018–19 in the Republican-dominated states of West Virginia, Oklahoma, and Arizona (with smaller actions in Kentucky, North Carolina, and Colorado) generally involved demands for greater financial support for public schools and smaller class sizes, highlighting the distinctive needs of schools serving large disadvantaged populations.[58]

The Deficit Model

While poverty causes educational disadvantage, it is important that this insight is not taken in an unfortunate direction that has been called the "deficit model." The deficit model projects a conception of economically (and, by implication, racially) disadvantaged students in which a low-income or Black student becomes little more than a locus of educational deficits. The capability of these students to learn and make educational progress— their intellectual, familial, cultural, and other personal strengths and resources—virtually disappears from sight.

The "no-excuses" argument, mistaken though it is, at least avoids the deficit model. It retains a faith that students from all backgrounds can achieve. However, no-excuses schools are typically not respectful of the students' home or familial cultures or resources. They believe that students are capable of realizing their potential but think that realizing this potential requires removing students from their home and ethnic cultures. So while the individual student's capabilities are affirmed, familial and ethnocultural traditions and modalities are seen on a deficit model.[59]

Sometimes the deficit model is, however, understood much more broadly as attributing *any* deficits to a student or group of students. It would be folly to adopt a general principle of always avoiding a deficit model in this misleading sense, since doing so would require us to ignore the findings and common sense on which this section has been grounded, that class- and race-based family and environmental conditions can in fact make a student harder to educate (everything else being equal) than a student with more favorable home and neighborhood conditions. Teachers recognizing this should still be sure to avoid shaming students for their poverty-related educational deficits. The deficits are not their fault and are not a reflection of their educational potential but a feature of the injustice of their circumstances.

Degrees and Axes of Disadvantage

Although the category of "socioeconomically disadvantaged" marks an important social divide, it is nevertheless very broad. In thinking about how socioeconomic disadvantage affects learning, we must recognize significant axes and degrees of disadvantage. For example, "free and reduced lunch" is a standard criterion for children's poverty in education contexts. But "reduced lunch" is 130–85 percent of the federal poverty line for families. Families in this category are certainly disadvantaged but much less so than ones at the lower end of the "free" category (0–130 percent of the federal poverty line).[60]

Another axis of disadvantage that can encompass a wide range is how long a family has occupied the poverty category. "Persistently disadvantaged" children significantly underperform students who are currently in poverty but have been so for only a year or two, so looking only at a particular year's income level will miss important distinctions.[61] This axis has racial implications because Black families at a given level of low income are more likely to have been at that level for more years than whites at the same level.[62]

There are many other axes of disadvantage with a significant degree of spread—whether the parents have jobs (many jobs pay only a "poverty wage"), the stability of a living situation, the level of psychological stress in the family, how organized the parents are, and so on—that can have a substantial and differential impact on the child's performance in school.

Degree and axis of disadvantage are important variables in the impact of socioeconomic disadvantage on children's lives and on their learning. The overall category of "SES disadvantage" purely on its own can take us only so far in this analysis.

"No-Excuses" Charter Schools

The degree aspect of disadvantage presents a challenge to argument four, which holds up no-excuses charter schools that break the link between SES background and educational attainment by educating low-SES students at a high level (see pp. 111–12). While it is impossible to address the complex issue of charter schools more generally within the scope of this book, on this more limited issue, evidence suggests that no-excuses schools serve not a representative segment of the overall "SES disadvantaged" population (as argument four requires) but rather a significantly less disadvantaged segment of it. Chester Finn, Bruno Manno, and Brandon Wright, prominent advocates of charter schools, concede that "the no-excuses model . . . does in fact lead to self-selection and a form of creaming, whether voluntary or school-driven."[63] If so, these schools cannot demonstrate the possibility of a *general* breaking of a link between poverty and inferior school performance.

Any parent may apply to a charter school, and if oversubscribed, the school must use a lottery to admit students. It may not select students explicitly on prior grades or test scores. Nevertheless, no-excuses schools practice forms of selectivity at both the admissions and retention stages. The application process itself involves some self-selectivity in effectively excluding parents who are too stressed or dysfunctional to rise to that challenge. When parents considering application visit a school, the counseling process enables the school to discourage families who they think will not "fit" with the school's mission.

Once students are admitted to the school, the schools also have ways of weeding out (sometimes called "counseling out") students who are unsuccessful either academically or behaviorally. Parents may be told of a lack of fit with the school's strict regimen (to which they may have signed a contract) and that the student would be better off elsewhere. This may well be true, but in the larger picture this practice will contribute to selecting more advantaged families, not necessarily regarding purely economic resources but nevertheless education-related characteristics, such as the parents' ability to lend educational support to their children. This counseling out is on top of actual expulsions, which are infrequent but are still at a much higher level in charter schools than traditional public schools. A study of KIPP (Knowledge Is Power Program) schools, likely the most prominent of the no-excuses school chains, found that a "typical KIPP grade cohort shrunk by about 30% between grades 6 and 8."[64] Another study found that senior enrollment at Boston charter high schools was on average only 42 percent of freshman enrollment, compared to 82 percent at traditional public schools.[65] All of this is evidence of the significant weeding out that goes against the claim that these schools are serving a representative sample of low-income students.

Additional anecdotal evidence suggests that the average income level of students in no-excuses charter schools is higher than that in the traditional system. In a study of seventy-seven African American families choosing schools for their children in Chicago, Mary Pattillo found the average income of those ending up in a charter school to be twenty-five thousand dollars, while median income for those who selected the neighborhood school was only five thousand dollars, and the rate of parental job-holding 71 percent compared with 35 percent.[66] A study of a highly regarded Boston-based charter school showed that 44.8 percent of students fell into the "free lunch" category, compared to 74.6 percent in the Boston Public Schools.[67] And remember that the category "free lunch" is quite capacious (0–130 percent of the poverty line for a family of four), so the comparative figures given do not reveal the percentage of the persistently or extremely disadvantaged.

If a school's practices preselect and retain more advantaged among the disadvantaged group, they are no longer dealing with the random disadvantaged group required to argue that poverty is not affecting the performance of that group as a whole. So, even accepting for the sake of argument no-excuses schools' claims of success with their students would not demonstrate that schools can break the link between poverty and education.[68]

The charge of "no excuses" has been misdirected. What there is no excuse for is failing to take political action to reduce inequality and poverty, as well as the educational ill effects of poverty. The responsibility is on all of us as citizens and on our elected representatives. That political goal is achievable.[69] There is much greater wealth in US society than there has ever been, and in any case, as mentioned earlier, many less wealthy countries have achieved better educational outcomes than we have, partly through targeting poverty.[70] There are several plausible and fair "millionaire's tax" proposals, financial transaction taxes, and similar upper-income-targeted revenue sources that could raise billions of dollars for poverty reduction and school-based, poverty-buffering programs.[71] More generally, while Americans have become increasingly aware of and informed about the extreme and growing inequality in the United States, evident, for example, in the increasing proportion of low-income students in the overall student population, education thinking in the "no-excuses" mold has failed to engage with this new awareness.[72] This blindness ill serves the cause of racial educational equality, which must be tied to economic justice reform efforts.

To summarize, achieving an equality of educational goods defines a standard of educational justice a society and its school system is morally required to meet. It is impossible to meet that standard through school-based educational initiatives alone. Educational injustice is embedded within and interlinked with other systems of injustice in the broader society (health, occupation, wealth, and income), so students cannot be provided with equal educational goods without some movement toward greater justice in those other areas. Teachers are well positioned to support and advocate for those larger changes because they see the impact of social and economic inequalities on their students.

THE REPARATIVE JUSTICE FRAMEWORK

The equal educational goods standard of justice is both present and future oriented and individualistic. It says that each student must be brought to the threshold of educational goods by the exit point. If proportionally more white and Asian American, or middle-class, students emerge from schooling in possession of such goods, while proportionally fewer Black, Latinx, and Native American, or working-class and low-income, students do so, the equal educational goods standard construes this as an injustice to the individual members of the latter groups—not to the groups as groups.

However, when race is in the picture, both this purely present focus and individualism cannot express the full injustice involved in current disparities. The idea of "racial justice" or "racial equality" expresses the idea that the norm of equality applies to groups *as groups*, not merely as aggregates of individuals. African Americans', Native Americans', and Latinxs' current state of disadvantage (educational and otherwise) is a product of their historical oppression, subordination, and discrimination as specific groups. When current injustice is rooted in group-based historical wrongs that have never been rectified, that history calls for a group-focused reparative or corrective justice approach to complement the present-oriented social or distributive justice approach of the equal educational goods standard. (We will focus here only on African Americans, but a comparable case can be made for Native Americans, as suggested in our discussions of this group in earlier chapters.)[73]

African Americans as a historical collectivity were wronged by slavery and, later, Jim Crow segregation. They and their supporters have long sought reparations for enslavement. In March 1867, Representative Thaddeus Stevens of Pennsylvania introduced a "reparations bill for the [recently freed] African Slaves." It called for (among other things) "to each male person . . . who is the head of a family or not, forty acres," the land to be taken from confiscated Confederate lands, including those on which the formerly enslaved people worked, and for funds for "the erection of buildings on said homesteads." Stevens recognized that ending slavery was not enough to prevent its legacy from continuing to harm Blacks.[74] They had to be given the means, individually and collectively, to become economically self-sufficient.

In recent decades, historical scholarship has begun to converge around a general narrative that enslavement built the foundation for American wealth, not only in the South but throughout the nation; that the fruits of that wealth were largely denied to Black people for one hundred years after the end of enslavement; and that federal and state actions subsequent to slavery further contributed to the creation and sustaining of Black-white disparities.[75] The details remain a subject of ongoing research, but the broad outlines, relevant to group-based corrective justice, are clear.

Legacies of Historical Injustice

Federal and state governments in the twentieth century sustained and sometimes exacerbated the inequities of the post-slavery and segregation eras. One major thread in this narrative is federal housing policies of the 1930s–1960s that were racially discriminatory in intent and effect. The Federal Housing Administration (FHA), created in 1934 as part of President Roosevelt's New Deal, facilitated home ownership for a large number of Americans through low-interest loans and small down payments. The FHA, however, would not insure mortgages in Black neighborhoods. It subsidized the development of entire subdivisions—that is, suburbs—reserved for whites, with clauses in the deeds prohibiting resale of the homes to African Americans. FHA manuals stated that bank loans for developers were conditional on their not selling to African Americans.[76] After World War II, the Veterans Administration (established under the GI Bill of 1944) insured mortgages for returning veterans yet adopted the same racial exclusions as the FHA had done.

These forms of discrimination and their resulting inequities in home ownership, residence, and asset accumulation were largely in place before the civil rights movement and antidiscrimination legislation and judicial decisions of the late 1940s, 1950s, and 1960s.[77] Many people, especially whites, believe that this antidiscrimination legislation (for example, the Fair Housing Act of 1968) eliminated not only current and future racial discrimination but also past discrimination's effects and thus remedied the disparate effects of the historical discriminatory practices just described. However, the legislation was aimed only at *preventing* discrimination in the future. It did not take housing away from white people who had acquired it through previous discriminatory policies or inherited it from their parents. Nor should it. But this limitation means that the antidiscrimination process left in place the effects of previous discrimination, many of which therefore remained, and generally remain, unrectified.

Even this description of a post-1968 antidiscrimination regime is idealized. If government agencies do not strongly enforce antidiscrimination legislation, the discrimination it intends to prevent continues to happen. Republican administrations from the late 1960s on only weakly enforced antidiscrimination policies.[78] In fact, discrimination in the housing market and mortgage lending, by steering prospective buyers toward and away from certain neighborhoods because of the buyer's race and by charging inflated mortgage rates, has continued.[79] Disparities from the past remain and have been worsened by ongoing discrimination, both legally sanctioned and not.

In addition, recent scholarship by Keeanga-Yamahtta Taylor fills in the broader picture of why Blacks continue to be significantly disadvantaged in their living situation, homeownership, and wealth creation. She shows that housing legislation and policy in the wake of the Fair Housing Act (and the election of Nixon in 1968) turned housing for low-income Blacks over to private sector banks, real estate speculators, and developers who, following both market logic and a history of race discrimination (and not reined in by strong federal regulation), initiated what she calls "predatory inclusion." African Americans were forced into subprime mortgages, inferior and poorly maintained housing, and high expenses they often could not afford. The continuing disparities contributed to, and were exacerbated by, the Great Recession of 2008 and its housing disaster for low-income home-owners, and especially African Americans.[80]

In 2015, 72 percent of white household heads owned a home, compared with 43 percent of Black household heads. For most Americans, net worth is closely tied to home equity. In 2016, the median (not the average, which is certainly higher) net worth of households headed by non-Hispanic whites was roughly ten times that of the median Black household ($162,770 for whites, compared with $16,300 for Blacks).[81] Compared to income, net worth ("wealth") disparities are to a greater degree a legacy of prior discrimination, in large part because of the role of intergenerational transfers of wealth both during one's lifetime and through inheritance.

Reparative justice deals with injustices to a current intergenerational group (African Americans or Native Americans, in our case) that have their roots in uncorrected injustices in the past. This form of justice requires reparations to the present members of that intergenerational group.[82]

Reparative Justice and the Educational Debt

Reparations bear directly on educational injustice, in part because in the justice perspective, the various forms of racial injustice are bound up with and reinforce one another: inferior and segregated housing contributes to inferior and segregated schools, and weaker education in turn depresses occupational success, which leads to lower incomes, inferior housing, inferior health care, in a downward spiral. In this spirit, Gloria Ladson-Billings helpfully reframes the "achievement gap" as an "education debt," indicating that the nation as a whole has never delivered on the promise of racial equality in education (or equality in general) and that current educational disparities are best seen as inequities in access or opportunity, with roots in that unequal history of interlocking injustices in many domains and in our continuous failure to correct for it.[83]

We are viewing the "educational debt" framework as complementing the present-focused social justice perspective, whose moral force resides in the idea that all students deserve to leave school in possession of the fundamental educational goods. That standard of justice applies to all students equally, but it does not accord any distinctive moral force to specifically racial and therefore group forms of educational inequality. The reparative justice approach provides that group-focused moral force. That Blacks and Native Americans have not been enabled to attain equal educational goods is due to distinctively racial processes of oppression, subordination, and discrimination from our national past. If Blacks had been provided with the "40 acres" and enabled to establish economic independence, as Representative Stevens's bill attempted to do; if Jim Crow segregation had not been imposed on them; if they had had access to jobs, homes, and income equivalently to whites; if there had not been pervasive discrimination—if these things had not happened, the resulting much greater socioeconomic equality would have provided an important foundation for genuinely equal education in the present.

But this history of discriminations did happen, so *racial* equality in education as a moral principle of justice should not be regarded as of exactly the same moral character as *general* equality of education. There is an educational debt, as Ladson-Billings notes, to American Blacks (and, we would add, Native Americans) that provides a distinct moral imperative to deliver on that debt, beyond the requirement that equal education be provided for all students.[84] Racial justice (including reparative justice) should therefore be viewed as a further component of what we have called the "justice perspective" that frames educational justice and injustice.

CURRICULAR IMPLICATIONS OF THE REPARATIVE JUSTICE FRAMEWORK AND EDUCATIONAL JUSTICE

Given the centrality of the conception of US history that grounds the reparative justice framework, that history should be incorporated into the K–12 curriculum as a component of the antiracist education sought by minority group educational activists and of the justice lens on American society we discussed in relation to teachers' nurturing students' sense of justice and ability to view American society critically (see pp. 103–4). Students should learn about the failure of the American government to help formerly enslaved African Americans establish a basis for economic self-sufficiency after the Civil War ended. It is not enough to applaud emancipation. Students should be encouraged to think counterfactually about how American history, and especially relations between Blacks and whites, would have been different had Reconstruction actually lived up to its promise.

Students should learn that the programs of the New Deal, while providing great benefit to the American people, also impacted the population very unequally, significantly expanding already-existing white advantages over Blacks, Mexican Americans, and Native Americans. This disparity creation should become a standard part of the teaching of American history, just as slavery and the civil rights movement have now largely become. The historical generating of racial disparity should be taught so as to enable students to understand the racial disparities characterizing American society today. Whites are quite ignorant about this history. One study found that "64% of white Americans think the legacy of segregation is either a 'minor factor' or 'no factor at all' in today's white-black wealth gap," and 78 percent think this about enslavement.[85]

Justice Education, Racial Identities, and National Identity

Many teachers do teach these issues, but they have yet to become standard fare in American history textbooks. Nevertheless, history must be taught as a foundation of both academic and civic competence. We are not proposing a history of only one group at the expense of an overarching national history. On the contrary, injustice to African Americans and Native Americans can be understood only in the context of that national history and its distinctive aspirational ideals and institutions—equality and liberty—that such groups frequently called on their fellow Americans to live up to. Racial justice education thus does not necessarily promote Black or Native American identity in preference to or as more important than American identity, but rather regards the plurality of ethnoracial groups as a particular strength of American identity when justice among those groups is realized. Racial justice education can readily combine explicit recognition of ethnoracial groups and their distinctive experiences with an affirmation of a shared American identity.[86] Thus, racial justice education is suspicious of appeals to national identity that deny the injustice characterizing our current racial order. Ignoring group injustice in school curricula and popular discussion will not induce groups to ignore their own experience and desire to "move on."[87]

Many white people resist the idea that Black people suffer from injustice that society or the government are responsible to rectify. Some may object that they themselves did not cause slavery or segregation, and a smaller (but still large) number say that their ancestors did not create or support these oppressive structures. So why should they "foot the bill" for government programs to rectify this history?[88]

It is worth replying to this common sentiment, partly to provide support for racial justice education. Reparations are not a punishment for perpetrators of injustice, any more than a current generation's paying off a national debt incurred by previous generations is a punishment of citizens in the current generation. Someone who recently immigrated to the United States has a responsibility as a citizen to pay taxes that pay off the national debt, though she played no role in creating that debt. Reparations for racial wrongs work the same way. Your responsibility to pay for reparations flows from your status as a citizen of the state that owes the reparations. You pay taxes to fund the many undertakings of your government. You are responsible, but that does not mean you are blameworthy for the situation the undertakings are aimed to rectify.

Enhancing this civic-based responsibility is the fact that almost all white people benefited, and often continue to benefit from, the injustices Blacks and Native Americans suffered from, although many did not deliberately perpetrate those injustices. This is the implication of the emerging historical narrative about the role of slavery and subsequent discrimination in American history discussed above (119–21). Consider, for example, the millions of white people who benefited from the previously discussed housing policies by acquiring homes in the suburbs in the 1930s–1960s. They gained from what were essentially government handouts, while Blacks were excluded from those programs.[89] The same is true of the GI Bill.[90] Their descendants additionally benefited from the advantages accrued by their forebears, who thereby had more resources for bringing up their children, which they could then pass on through inheritance. Whites may have done nothing wrong by availing themselves of those suburban homes, accruing equity in them, and passing them or the equity on to their children. These benefits, however, were unjust in the sense that they were part of a system that relied on discrimination against Blacks as well as Mexican Americans and Native Americans. The argument is not that current whites are to blame for the past but that white people continue to benefit from this historical injustice, and this enhances their moral responsibility as current citizens of that society to correct for that injustice through paying taxes for revenues for reparative government action.[91]

Special Challenges of Teaching about Whites Wronging People of Color

Incorporating the history of racial injustice into secondary school curricula, especially in history and social studies as well as literature, should not be controversial. But teaching about slavery, segregation, denial of citizenship to Asians, Japanese internment, land theft from Native Americans, exploitation of Mexican Americans, and American imperialism in Latin America must be handled in a knowledgeable and sensitive way, particularly in racially mixed classes. Several pitfalls in this educational project must be either avoided or faced constructively. First, current white students might experience any historical discussion of white people treating people of color unjustly or oppressively either as a personal attack on them or as occasioning a misplaced and debilitating sense of guilt. Second, current students of color learning about these matters may be angry at or resentful of white students in their classes. Third, students of color may feel shame or stigma in discussions of their groups' historical victimization. And fourth, students of color may be demoralized by having barriers of discrimination or historical disadvantage called to their attention.

Teachers can take steps to avoid or mitigate these untoward developments in their classes. One is to emphasize that in any oppressive or unjust systems and institutions, the victimized group has always resisted and fought back. Without soft-pedaling the victimization, studying forms of resistance highlights oppressed people's agency, ingenuity, and assertion of their dignity. The study of enslaved peoples' resistance—escapes, rebellions, individual acts of subversion, contestation of pro-slavery racial ideology, and abolitionism—is a particularly historically rich source for understanding a key aspect of enslavement. Teachers can highlight ways minority communities learned to resist injustice and how they have passed those traditions on to their descendants.[92]

A second, related, guideline is to emphasize white people who did not go along with, and a smaller number who actively resisted, practices in which white people oppressed people of color. The abolitionist movement was the main vehicle for white opposition to slavery, and throughout most of American history, white and interracial organizations have arisen to ally and show solidarity with members of the oppressed groups in resistance to racial injustice. Without misleading students as to the extent of white allyship and resistance to white-caused oppression, it is important to discuss in some depth antiracist exemplars to whom white (though not only white) students can relate. (The study of resistance to racial injustice on the part of both whites and nonwhites can, and should, also include local and known persons in the present. It should not be confined to the past nor solely to figures on the national or international stage.)[93] The study of interracial movements and alliances that changed society is a particularly vital aspect of antiracist education and can enable students of all groups to come to grips with the structural character of durable inequality and to feel empowered to make a difference in reducing injustice. These approaches can also stave off students of color's shame at historical mistreatment, as they should make clear that suffering oppression is due not to deficiencies in the victimized groups but to conduct of the perpetrators or to oppressive structures that have developed historically.

Nonwhite anger at fellow white students can be muted by a strong historically based curriculum that also clearly differentiates blame for perpetration of injustice from being descended from, or being of the same racial group as, those perpetrators. Nevertheless, anger at one's ancestors' unjust sufferings is not in itself a misplaced or necessarily destructive emotion, and hopefully the community of the school and classroom can help channel it appropriately, such as into civic activism, rather than against fellow students who bear no responsibility for those sufferings.

Nor is white guilt necessarily an inappropriate reaction to a newfound recognition that purely as a member of a racial group, one has benefited from unjust and unsought advantages inherited from the past. But white students can be helped to recognize that staying in that guilty place is neither morally constructive nor conducive toward dealing with the injustice. What counts are the constructive actions that students take in the present on the basis of their recognition of unjust advantage.[94]

Regarding the downsides of knowing about unjust barriers to life success, it is better for students to be helped to understand the nature of those barriers, to see how their ancestors and peers have tried to overcome them, and to be taught that they are indeed injustices rather than personal failings than to be presented with a sanitized version of reality that will not correspond to the student's experience. This teaching about injustice is in line with our earlier insistence that students be provided with the cognitive tools to recognize and analyze injustice in society and empowered to choose values for themselves that are not dictated by the unexamined dominant values of society at a given time. Here community resources can be especially valuable in mentoring students to come to terms with unjust obstacles in the way of their success and providing role models of those who have shown the way.

Recognizing Racial Asymmetries

One significant obstacle in teaching about race is the widely held (though often unrecognized as such) assumption of "racial symmetry"—that an action or practice done by one racial group toward another, or a racialized experience undergone by one group in relation to another, has the same moral and social significance no matter which racial groups are involved. To the contrary, race is generally an asymmetric category. Actions and practices involving race largely have significantly different meanings depending on the particular racial groups involved.

Here is an example from a high school class one of us taught: A white girl in a mixed class on racism talked about having felt uncomfortable in an (otherwise) all-Black class on Black literature. A Black girl in the same mixed class said she had once been the only Black girl in an Advanced Placement class and had also felt uncomfortable. Neither girl said that the other students had done anything to try to make them uncomfortable. But the Black girl thought there was a difference between her experience and the white girl's, "a different kind of uncomfortable," as she put it. The difference, which the teacher suggested to her in the discussion, and she confirmed, was that what made the Black girl uncomfortable was a worry that the other white and non-Black students in the class would think she was not a good-enough student to be in the class. But the white student's discomfort was not caused by the same fear of judgment. Rather, she worried that some of the Black students would wish she weren't there so that they could have the classroom as an entirely Black space.[95]

The two cases of discomfort have different social, race-related meanings. The white girl's worry does not reflect doubt about her intelligence the way the Black girl felt in relation to being in the otherwise all-white class; it did not threaten her dignity the way the all-white class threatened the Black girl's. That doubt about Black intelligence has been present in the idea of race in the United States since its beginning and has far from entirely disappeared, as we have seen.[96]

Each racial group has its distinctive history and its distinctive way of having been, and still being, racialized. Although everyone has a race (in the sense of racialization), race has quite different meanings for each group. One general asymmetry among those meanings is that in the world we live in now, "white" is a favored or advantaged category. The very invention of race was intended to rationalize white superiority and dominance over various other groups. That dominance was claimed to be justified by whites' alleged inherent superiority. Even though many at least try to reject the idea that whites are inherently superior, whiteness still constitutes an all-other-things-equal advantage because the structures of white advantage remain in place even once racial ideology has been abandoned.[97] In this way race is fundamentally an asymmetric category. A recognition of this inherent asymmetry must inform teachers' understandings of their students and teachings about race, including racial history and racial justice.[98]

Asymmetry in no way implies lack of concern for white students in relation to racial demographics. If the white student in the above example had remained in the otherwise all-Black Black literature class, the teacher would have had a distinct responsibility—arising from the "equal treatment/equal care and concern" principle—to make her feel welcome and comfortable in the class and to give her special attention, if required in order to do so. More generally, an appreciation of racial asymmetry should not be taken as denying that white students can be harmed because of their race, as the familiar but misleading definition "racism = prejudice + power" might be taken to suggest.[99] White students can be unwarranted targets of racial prejudice, discrimination, and stereotyping, and the discomforts they may feel regarding racial justice education deserve to be addressed and handled with sensitivity. Every student deserves care and concern for the challenges of their educations, and that remains one overall symmetry across racial groups, among the greater and more systemic asymmetries.

The Supreme Court, Racial Asymmetries, and Systemic Racism

The Supreme Court's race jurisprudence of the past forty-five years or so has strongly contributed to the American public's failure to recognize racial asymmetry, a product, as mentioned earlier, of the conservative drift of the Supreme Court in that period. Over that time, majorities of the justices have rendered systemic racial injustice legally almost invisible. In doing so, they have made it difficult to recognize the foundation of racial asymmetry. This leaves the court saying that social policy that involves treating persons differently because of their race is wrong in itself, whether that treatment is aimed at *correcting* for historical injustice or *contributing* to it.[100] With respect to education, the nadir in this development was the 2007 *Parents Involved in Community Schools (PICS)* decision, mentioned earlier (chap. 2, 72–73). A 5–4 majority ruled that the Seattle and Louisville school districts could not make use of students' racial identities to create more racially integrated and equal school systems. Four justices stated that doing so was as constitutionally wrong as using racial identity to create a segregated school system, which was ruled unconstitutional in *Brown*.[101] The view that we cannot legally, and perhaps morally, distinguish between upholding white advantage and correcting for systemic discrimination against Blacks, Latinxs, or Native Americans contributes to symmetrizing all racial wrongs—seeing the specific racial identities of perpetrator and victim as totally irrelevant to the moral character of the wrong involved.

Particularly heartbreaking in this judicial development is that in every important race-related case in which this false racial symmetry and blindness to systemic injustice informed the majority decisions, a number of dissenting justices recognized the wrongness of this direction. They saw clearly the historical and systemic character of racial injustice, which renders the use of race to correct that history of an entirely different moral character than a morally neutral or negative use and generally justifiable. Sometimes (as in the *PICS* case or in the landmark 1978 *Bakke* affirmative action case) this recognition reflected a four-judge dissent.[102] So a single vote has frequently paved the way for the nonrecognition of racial asymmetry and institutional racism, contributing to the general public's frequent failures to see or acknowledge systemic injustice and to recognize the fundamental asymmetry involved in race.

CONCLUSION

The *Brown* decision affirmed a kind of equality of education, and educational activists from racial minority groups generally affirmed it as well. But what is equality of education? We have suggested that as an ideal of justice it consists in every student, at a given exit point (such as high school graduation), being brought to a robust threshold of the full range of educational goods (of which we have distinguished intellectual/cognitive, personal growth, moral capability, and civic capability, the latter two of which will be discussed in greater detail in chapter 5). "Educational goods" is preferable to "opportunities" as the content of equality of education because the latter is so tied to the American idea of competing on a level playing field for unequal rewards in the job market, an overly narrow conception of the value of education, which omits a justice-informed critical stance toward one's society that every student should learn.

School-based processes alone cannot bring about the equal attainment of these educational goods, an insight bequeathed by the Coleman Report. The *Brown* decision, however, implied that equality of education could be achieved solely through such school-based processes, namely school integration. In our current circumstances, inequalities among families of a class- and race-based nature powerfully affect students' learning. Unless those disparities—in housing, income, wealth, occupation, and health—are reduced, the ideal of equal education is unattainable. So any discussion of educational justice must situate it within the "justice perspective" that analyzes these larger structures, recognizes their interlocking nature, and sees them as distinct forms of injustice in their own right, apart from their impact on education. Teachers recognize the effects of poverty on their students, and it is part of teachers' professional responsibility to advocate for mitigation of the destructive effects of socioeconomic inequalities on their ability to help their students attain educational equality.

The concept of equal educational goods expresses the content of the equal educational ideal of justice. But it does not fully capture the moral urgency of creating equality between racially defined groups. The moral foundation for that distinctive character lies at least in recognizing that African Americans and Native Americans have not been provided with equal education because they have been disadvantaged by identifiable race-based historical processes (not only of a directly educational character). The resulting moral urgency of racial equality in education applies as well to teaching about those inequality-producing processes, which are by now quite well understood and documented but often not included in mainstream textbooks. We considered some of the distinctive challenges of teaching this material regarding both white students and students of color, but the challenges can be met.

CHAPTER 4

INTEGRATIONS

The Capital Argument

We now turn to racial integration in American public schools. As we have seen, school integration has been linked historically with the ideal of, and struggle for, educational equality. At the outset, however, we suggest that *integration* should really be thought of in the plural as *integrations*.[1] There are at least three ways that integration is multiple—*definitionally* (different people mean different things by "integration"), *valuationally* (different forms of integration embrace or reject distinct values, especially with respect to the discouraging, permitting, or affirming of racial group identities and community control), and *demographically* (different racial, class, and ethnic compositions of schools pose distinct challenges and opportunities to realizing the various values of integration). Whether we should seek integration requires specifying which form(s) of integration we are talking about.

DEFINITIONS OF INTEGRATION (LEGAL, DESCRIPTIVE, AND IDEAL)

Let us start with defining *integration*, which is understood in at least three distinct ways with respect to schools[2]—(1) *legal* (or "desegregation"), understood as the abolition of explicit legal barriers to children of different racial groups attending school together, (2) *descriptive*, or the copresence of different racial groups in a school without specification of the quality of interaction,[3] and (3) *ideal*, or a conception of particular values to be realized within a school (or schooling generally) by building on the copresence of racial groups.

In the 1954 *Brown* decision, "integration" meant only the first of these definitions—desegregation, or the dismantling of what is referred to in American jurisprudence as de jure (by law) segregation. Initially, this meant abolishing laws and government practices that assigned children to separate schools based on their perceived racial identities. *Brown* made it illegal for state officials to create designated "white" and "colored" schools (to run "dual" systems, in legal parlance). This meaning is vitally important historically as *Brown* was one of the first legal assaults on the entire structure of segregationist white supremacy and played a crucial role in advancing the civil rights movement (with its origins in the 1940s), leading ultimately to the destruction of this legal structure.[4] Since its *Milliken* decision in 1974, the Supreme Court has adopted this meaning of segregation as its operative conception, with its "integration" counterpart as no more than the removal of explicit legal barriers to racially different students attending the same school. The actual copresence of different racial groups—descriptive integration—in a school has over time ceased counting, in the court's decisions, as required for "integration."

In contemporary discussion of the racial composition of schools, "segregation" and "integration" are seldom used in this way. *Segregation* is more commonly used to refer to *separation*—schools that are overwhelmingly, or predominantly, of one race, irrespective of the process (either de facto, i.e., the private actions of individuals or nonstate institutions, or de jure) by which this separation was generated. Many scholars have documented increasing school segregation in this separation sense, as we mentioned earlier (chap. 1, 1–2).[5] Integration in the descriptive sense, then, is the reverse of this separation—crafting policies so that students of different races attend school together.[6]

However, the quite common contemporary usage of *segregation* to mean "separation" can be misleading, because *segregation* still carries associations with the de jure institutions of the Jim Crow apartheid era. Its use implies that current one-race-dominant schools are similarly objectionable to the way that Jim Crow–era schools were, when Black students were officially stigmatized as unfit to share a public educational space with white students. The *Brown* decision's memorable dictum "separate is inherently unequal" encourages the thinking that one-race-dominant schools, no matter which race is dominant, are thus automatically morally problematic for comparable reasons.

However, in its literal meaning, separate is certainly not inherently unequal. It is possible for two different ethnic or racialized groups to be separate from one another while still having equal resources, opportunities, and civic standing, as, for example, within a single binational state, such as Canada or Belgium. What the court meant in the *Brown* decision by this dictum was that in a society (e.g., the Jim Crow South) in which one racial group was officially seen as inferior to, and unfit to share certain spaces and institutions with, the other group, separating the inferiorized group reflects and contributes to that stigma. But talk of "inherently unequal" is not a felicitous way to make that point because, on its face, it would seem to imply that an all-Black school cannot possibly be of high quality.[7] If educational separation of racial groups is a bad thing, this needs to be demonstrated, rather than rendered true almost by definition.

Ideal Integration

The descriptive sense of integration is useful as a shared lowest common denominator among a range of varying conceptions of integration. These differences arise because both historically and currently distinct parties have seen descriptive integration as the basis for a set of differing values or ideals to be built on the existing copresence of multiple groups in the school. *Ideal* integration is, then, descriptive integration plus the values or ideals in question.

There have been key differences in the values that various groups have sought or envisioned regarding integration. We will examine three significant ones. The first value (a) is assimilationist. *Assimilationism* involves pressure on a group to abandon a distinctive group identity and culture and to adopt the norms and culture of the dominant group as the price for becoming fully accepted in a larger institution (such as a school) or polity.[8]

Through the early to mid-twentieth century, schooling was largely assimilationist in this sense, as we saw in chapter 1. New white immigrant groups, mostly from eastern and southern Europe, were pressured to weaken or abandon their distinctive original national or regional identity and culture and take on an exclusively "American" identity, which was often construed as abandoning markers enabling others to recognize them as being from those particular origins or cultures. Nonwhite racial groups cannot assimilate in this total sense since their phenotypic differences, in light of the racial history that confers so much significance on those features, mark them as distinct from the dominant white group. Nevertheless, we saw that Native Americans were subjected to an extreme form of assimilationist schooling, when they were forced to attend schools that tried to expunge their distinctive cultures and attachments to their tribal group. And, at least tacitly, integration of Blacks has often been understood to require Blacks to abandon their cultures and group identity. Indeed, some Blacks continue to see integration as requiring assimilation and reject integration for that reason. We earlier cited the historian Kevin Gaines's use of "integration" to imply "the demise of black institutions" (chap. 2, 54).[9]

Nowadays assimilationism is almost entirely rejected as a favorable ideal, but in the earlier period mentioned it was viewed as a positive aim of schooling. This is the sense in which it can be considered historically a form of ideal integration.

Dr. Martin Luther King Jr. is associated with a second influential form of ideal integration (b). According to King, "Integration is the positive acceptance of desegregation and the welcomed participation of Negroes into the total range of human activities. . . . A desegregated society that is not integrated . . . leads to 'physical proximity without spiritual affinity.' It gives us a society where men are physically desegregated and spiritually segregated, where elbows are together and hearts are apart."[10] This conception taps into an idea shared by many, which expresses that *real* integration should be understood not as the mere copresence of different racial groups but as genuine racial harmony, animated by respect, care, and appreciation among those groups.[11]

A third form of ideal integration (c) is derived from the educational activism we have discussed. Communities of color have, in different ways, sought affirmation of their distinctiveness as groups of a racial, ethnic, or cultural nature. And when supporting integration, they have sought curricula that reflected their histories and experiences, teachers from their respective groups, and often the involvement of parents and community members from their groups as part of the integrated school community. (As we saw, sometimes these goals were sought outside of an integration framework.) We can call the value involved in this third form of ideal integration *group affirmation.*

"Integration" does not have a univocal meaning in our time. Each of the three definitions (and the three variations of ideal integration) picks up on something important about the historical meaning of the term. We must simply be clear which one we mean when we talk about integration. Our focus will be on descriptive and ideal integration, although we take legal integration, the rejection of legalized white supremacy, to be a worthy goal. Within ideal integration, we recognize the assimilationist form but reject it as a commendable ideal and will give greater attention to the other two forms.

We will want to know whether the mere copresence of different racial groups in schools brings about equality, or greater equality. Descriptive integration makes no moral demands on the members of the school community about how they treat members of other groups; it would be significant if substantial benefits flowed from this form of integration alone. But we must also look at whether, as the notion of ideal integration incorporates, we must add some of the moral features in forms (b) or (c) in order to reap significant benefits from integration.

Our approach will be to examine five major arguments that have been offered, in the past or present, in favor of school integration. We will assume that the arguments are being presented as public justifications, for consideration and hoped-for agreement by both policy makers and the general public, including members of the public sending children to schools and, to some extent, the youth attending those schools. For each argument, we will look at whether it relies on descriptive or ideal integration and, if the latter, which of the three ideals it involves (although there can be more than one).

These five arguments are as follows:

1. *Resources*: Integration is the only way to ensure that nonwhite students are provided with educational resources equal to whites.
2. *Capital*: Only in integrated schools can disadvantaged minorities reap the benefits of white, middle-class financial, human, social, and cultural capital.
3. *Preparation for diverse workplace*: Integrated schools better prepare students for a diverse workplace.
4. *Intellectual benefits*: Integrated schools provide distinctive intellectual benefits (e.g., enhancing critical thinking).
5. *Civic benefits*: Integrated schools are required for or strongly facilitative of civic education for a multiracial democracy

All five arguments have merit, but, we will argue, the integrative processes the resource (1) and capital (2) arguments call for cannot possibly deliver actual *equality* of educational goods, as they sometimes claim to do, because they leave unchallenged the systemic injustices and inequalities of the outer society that, as we saw in chapter 3, inevitably produce educational disparities. In addition, the capital argument sends damaging moral and civic messages to both advantaged and disadvantaged families in the integrated school. Finally, neither argument engages with the concept of *egalitarian pluralism*, an important alternative to integration that seeks equality and group affirmation as core values and supports integration only as a possible means to equality.

The civic argument (5) is the strongest of the five, grounded in a fundamental purpose of schooling—the development of an informed, knowledgeable citizenry committed to democracy and justice—that has gotten short shrift in recent popular and social science–based thinking about educational integration. It is compatible with most of the value commitments of egalitarian pluralism and readily embraces a racial justice perspective, although it does not fully guarantee it. Though to a lesser extent, the civic argument shares a shortcoming with the other arguments in not fully embracing a challenge to the white-dominant structures of the society as a whole, as well as the extreme class-based injustices intertwined with them.

The Resource Argument for Integration

We saw that the resource argument for integration was promoted by many Black activists (chap. 2, 58). It was stated memorably by Robert Carter, a lawyer for the plaintiffs in the *Brown* case and later a judge, part of which we mentioned earlier (chap. 2, 58): "We believed that the surest way for minority children to obtain their constitutional right to equal educational opportunity was to require removal of all racial barriers in the public school system, with black and white children attending the same schools, intermingling in the same classrooms, and together exposed to the same educational offerings. . . . Integration was viewed as the means to our ultimate objective, not the objective itself."[12] If Black students were provided with the same educational resources—school buildings, qualified faculty, textbooks, services, and overall financial resources—by attending the same schools as white students, they would receive the same education.[13] The value of integration in this line of thinking, as Carter says, is purely instrumental to achieving equality. It is only because white people will not give Blacks equal resources unless they share their schools with them that integration is necessary ("green follows white" [see chap. 2, 58]). Integration, according to this logic, provides no other value.

Tracking and Integration

Carter mentions both schools and classrooms as venues of integration. But the practice of "tracking" has the effect of separating students of different racial groups within the same school into different classrooms, negating the applicability of the resource argument.

The origins of tracking lie in the early twentieth-century Progressive movement's alliance with the "intelligence testing" of that era and took root in the 1960s when school integration really started in earnest after the passage of the Civil Rights Act of 1964.[14] "Tracking" involves placing students in separate classes that operate at different levels of intellectual demand and curricular richness. The placement is officially based on some measure of students' prior achievement level. The practice is often called "ability grouping," assuming that students' previous performance is a direct reflection of their ability. As we argued earlier, this is not a valid assumption since students may have had unequal opportunities to develop their potential abilities at earlier stages (chap. 3, 99).[15] So students' achievements at any given level do not necessarily represent their full abilities. This makes *ability grouping* a misleading term for the practice of tracking.

The theory behind tracking is that students learn best when placed with students at the same prior achievement level as themselves. This view seems intuitive to many parents and teachers, but research strongly suggests it is incorrect. Students who are currently or would have been placed in a lower track learn more in "mixed" ("detracked" or "heterogeneous") classes that utilize curricula and pedagogy devised for a higher-track class than they do in lower-track classes. Derrick Darby and John Rury summarize the situation of lower-track students in the United States: "The less demanding classes where these students generally land offer scant intellectual or academic growth, doing little to prepare them for future study at the collegiate level or for skilled employment."[16]

Where a tracking system is in place, its existence makes it natural to assume that lower-track students simply would not be capable of handling the work in higher-track classes. But schools that have decided to offer the higher-track curriculum to all students in a given grade discover that with appropriate supports, the formerly lower-track students can generally master that curriculum.[17] Some research does find benefits to the high-track students in tracking systems, though this research often does not engage with whether the tracking system harms the lower-track students.[18] But most research concludes that higher-track students' achievement is not reduced by having formerly lower-track students in their classes.[19]

Tracked systems reduce learning opportunities for lower-track students in several ways. We have mentioned weaker, less challenging and engaging curricula than that in the higher tracks. In addition, lower-track classes are more likely to have less-skilled teachers (measured by lower test scores, fewer college majors in subjects taught, and other standard measures of quality).[20] Teachers also expect less of the lower-track students precisely because they are in the lower track. In a self-fulfilling prophecy, reduced teacher expectations diminish students' motivation and sense of academic efficacy, just as raised expectations have the opposite positive effects. Lower-track students recognize that they are in a lower track and feel stigmatized as inferior or deficient. Higher-track students often look down on them, and they are aware of this—constituting a "dignitary harm," in Darby and Rury's terminology.[21] At each successive grade level, the lower-track students fall farther behind the higher-track ones.[22]

The improved learning of lower-performing students in heterogeneous classes supports, and is supported by, the development of a "flexible mindset" view of intelligence, as discussed earlier (chap. 3, 101)—that intelligence is not a fixed, natural endowment but always in the process of being developed. Students' higher performance in detracked classes demonstrates that they have the capacity to do significantly better than their lower-track classes suggest and shows that the intelligence they manifest is responsive to teacher (and perhaps fellow student) expectations, more engaging curricula, and their own deliberate efforts to develop their intellectual capabilities.[23]

Thus, tracking systems deal an educational injustice to the lower-track students. They are subjected to an inferior education, less than what they are capable of, that reduces their accessing academic educational goods equal to their high-track peers.

This dynamic has no essential relationship with race or class, only previous achievement. The tracking discussed could and does take place at schools that are all white, all high income, all Latinx or Black, or all low income. Within a low-income school, a tracking system will provide inferior educational opportunities to students in the lower track, even if they are of the same SES level as those in the higher tracks.

However, when schools are also racially or class mixed, new dynamics add further layers of injustice to what is inherent in the tracking system on its own. In schools with racially diverse populations and tracked systems, white and Asian American students are virtually always found disproportionately represented in higher-track classes, and Black and Latinx students disproportionately in lower-track ones. Insofar as tracking systems deprive low-track students of equal educational opportunity and widen the already-existing gap with students in the upper tracks, adding racial disproportionality on top of this generates further racial injustice.[24]

What produces these race and class sorting disproportions in tracked systems? Several distinct processes that embody and promote injustice are involved. One mentioned earlier (107–8) is white, or upper-middle-class (of any race), opportunity hoarding—the attempt by an advantaged group to unfairly confine their advantages to their own group. White and upper-middle-class parents have the resources to be more dedicated to and proficient at securing more favorable placements for their children than Latinx and Black parents, and this development has intensified in recent decades.[25] They are more willing to challenge a school's track placement of their offspring than lower-income parents.[26] Part of this parental "capital" is whiteness itself. School personnel are more likely to heed white parents because they may be more inclined to credit white parents' than nonwhite parents' concerns.[27]

A second process producing race and class disparities is that although sorting for tracked classes is supposed to depend on objective measures such as grades and achievement levels in previous years, in fact class- and race-related biases often affect school personnel's assessment practices.[28] They perceive Black and Latinx students as having lower capabilities than they actually do and assess potential for achievement in a way that favors whites and Asian Americans.[29]

Third, independent of bias, even a genuine reliance on students' previous achievement levels already places Blacks and Latinxs at an unfair disadvantage, as their lower achievement (on average) at every stage is itself often a product of tracking in earlier schooling.[30] If a child has been previously put in a lower track, she will then be disadvantaged in subsequent selections that are based on her performance. So discrimination or unjust disparity at one point in time can have a cascading effect into the future, as we saw in our reparations discussion (117–22).[31]

Thus, racialized tracking exemplifies two importantly distinct forms of educational injustice. One is that, overall, racial minorities are thereby subjected to an inferior education compared to whites. The second is that students in lower tracks, independent of race, are subjected to an inferior education compared to students in the upper tracks. Both forms of educational injustice are present, and mutually reinforcing, in racially mixed schools with tracking systems.

This mutual reinforcement also reflects tracking ideology's dovetailing with racial ideology. The tracking ideology says students in lower tracks have lesser ability than students in upper tracks. The "ability" in question is often understood in terms like the fixed, "natural asset" way discussed earlier (chap. 3, 100–101), although it may also take the form of saying that the lower-track students are not committed to school, without necessarily casting aspersions on their innate ability.[32] Racial ideology also attributes differential abilities to different groups, and the groups in question are racial rather than track-defined groups. But when the two groups overlap— when a disproportion of the lower-track group is also Black, Latinx, or Native American—the two ideologies reinforce each other.[33] Because of this reinforcement, criticizing tracking ideology's conception of "intelligence" in favor of a more developmental or "flexible mindset" conception provides ammunition against the racist ideology that casts Blacks as innately intellectually inferior to whites. The case against racial tracking is thus strengthened by this critique of tracking itself. Until tracking is altogether dismantled, it will be very difficult to fully end racial tracking, although some minor degree of such rectification is possible without taking on the larger tracking system (e.g., training teachers to be less racially biased in track placement decisions).

The copresence of multiple racial groups in classes is itself only a necessary condition for detracked classes to work. Teachers who have not previously worked in heterogeneous classes generally need training to do so.

They have to learn how to treat their new students with respect, equal performance expectations, and appropriate individualized help. The teachers must learn to recognize insights and academic progress in these students that stereotypes may render them initially blind to. They must learn how to make the class function as a learning community and, in particular, to ensure that the formerly higher-track students come to appreciate the input offered by the new students and treat them with respect as fellow learners and members of the class.[34] While certain benefits of detracking could perhaps be obtained without the teachers adjusting their instructional methods to a new situation, the full range of detracking's educational benefits, especially when it has a racial or class aspect, clearly requires professional development and school leadership support for educators new to detracked classrooms.[35] Without this development, the students in the detracked class will receive different and unequal instructional resources and learning environments, even within the same class, and the "same resources" required by the resource argument for integration will fail to be met.

There is nevertheless one out-of-school inequity that detracking can partially mitigate—advantaged parents' using their influence and know-how to get their children into the top-track classes. If there are no higher-track classes in the school (because all classes are at the same level), this removes one major arena for such opportunity hoarding. It would not stop advantaged parents from, for example, paying for private tutors or other educational enrichment for their offspring that lower-income children cannot access. But greatly softening the in-school academic hierarchy by removing a tracking system would substantially mute the effect of educational opportunity hoarding.

Even when considering a non-tracked school, the resource argument is significantly limited by its failure to adopt the justice perspective. It accepts an overall white-dominant socioeconomic system and seeks merely to leverage that dominance to benefit racial minorities through school-attendance policies. Simply having students of color in the same schools and classes as whites is not enough to guarantee equal education, both because of the myriad ways white dominance affects the educational process itself and because the unequal racial order outside the school inevitably impacts the provision of education, as explored in the previous chapter, rendering educational equality impossible.[36]

THE CAPITAL ARGUMENT FOR
INTEGRATION AND ITS DEFICIENCIES

A second argument for integration draws on the parental capital examined briefly in the resources discussion. There, parental capital was a problem for equality because the parent used it to advantage their child over other children, resulting in a further collective hindrance to the disadvantaged children. But a very influential strand in contemporary advocacy for integration (of both a race and class nature) relies on parents using their capital to benefit the whole school, including children other than their own offspring. The argument recognizes four forms of capital—financial, human (education and skills), social (networks by which information and opportunities are transmitted), and cultural (knowledge of and facility with the often unspoken norms and codes of conduct that govern access to advantages)—that middle- and upper-middle-class white parents bring to their schools, which (according to the argument) working-class and low-income Black and Latinx parents lack or possess to a much lesser degree.[37] If disadvantaged and advantaged children attend the same schools, the advantaged children's and their parents' capital can be leveraged for the benefit of the disadvantaged children. Richard Kahlenberg, probably the most prominent exponent of the capital argument for socioeconomic integration (and thereby racial integration, though the racial form is not his primary concern), claims that the presence of a critical mass (which he sets at 50 percent) of educated middle-class parents is the best guarantee of adequate resources for and quality in schools.[38]

Compared to working-class and low-income parents, upper-middle-class parents are better able to advocate on behalf of the school and its students because they are better educated and better positioned to recognize how to go about such advocacy. They have greater connections and are more likely to know people who can help the school. They can deal more effectively with public officials, school administration, and staff. They are much better situated to raise money (including their own) for their schools. Finally, these parents generally have more time to engage in these activities and to help out at the school, compared to working-class and low-income parents.

The capital argument is primarily class-based; it depends mainly on resources. But the capital disparities themselves are racialized, in that they have a disparate racial profile (on average, people of color have disproportionately lesser capital) and are a product of a history of racism. Their exercise often also has a direct racial element, as we saw in chapter 3 (107), because, holding class constant, white school personnel and public officials are more likely to be responsive to white parents' efforts and initiatives.[39]

The parental capital argument is often complemented by a student version—that middle-class students have internalized norms of regular school attendance and homework completion, high standards for school achievement, and aspirations for college and higher-status occupations.

The working-class and low-income students' families do not imbue their offspring with these expectations to the same degree (according to the argument). Schools with a critical mass of upper-middle-class students are more likely to establish such standards in the school culture. The working-class students attending such institutions will then to a significant extent take on these norms themselves, and this will enhance their school performance.

The process envisioned here is similar to the detracking dynamic and does rely on non-tracked classrooms with different racial groups. But an important difference in the processes involved is that in the detracked classroom, it is the teacher who sets the level of expectation and helps every student to reach it. The capital argument, however, sees the advantaged students as the main source of the higher expectations.

The capital argument is largely focused on closing educational gaps with respect to academic goods, especially tested subjects. (Deployment of the argument makes extensive use of testing data to support it.) It seldom engages with moral, civic, or personal growth educational goods.

Deficiencies of the Capital Argument

Educational Benefits Only from the Advantaged

The capital argument has severe drawbacks as a foundation for integrating schools. To begin with, it recognizes and appeals only to benefits flowing from the advantaged families to the disadvantaged students. The argument fails to recognize that low-income students of color bring strengths, insights, experiences, and perspectives to the educational encounter, from which white, middle-class students can learn and benefit. This benefit is implicit in the argument for detracking and fundamental to the American common school tradition—that students can and need to learn from others of diverse backgrounds. The capital argument construes the classroom in a manner that violates the idea of a community in which each member participates, benefits from interaction with all other members, and regards everyone with respect and appreciation.

Similarly, the capital argument sees only the advantaged parents as bringing benefit to the school community. It fails to recognize ways that the disadvantaged families of color can contribute energy, experience, perspectives, commitments, and insights that enrich all members of the school.[40] These families have their own forms of social capital, often unrecognized by dominant groups, that may be nurtured through struggles against unjust systems of subjugation or exclusion. They may through action and practice have developed some degree of cultural capital, for example, in dealing effectively with school and district officials.[41] Low-income communities often have community-based advocacy organizations that can mobilize parents around educational issues.[42] The failure to recognize potential contributions of disadvantaged families and students channels deficit thinking about low-income people of color (chap. 3, 115) and thereby also undermines a sense of mutual respect and equality (including equal empowerment) within the larger school community.

Failure to Validate the Disadvantaged Group's Integrity and Community

The capital argument also fails to recognize group-related values often embraced by students of particular ethnoracial groups—for example, their attachments to each other either as residents from the neighborhood or as same-race peers in a white-dominant school even without any prior connection. The capital argument is insensitive to "critical mass" issues concerning students' desire for a sufficient number of their group to make them comfortable in a white-dominated school. We saw that both Latinx and Native American families and communities were sometimes leery of integration because it would not ensure a critical mass of students of their group in a given school (chap. 2, 77, 65–66). More generally, values of group integrity, community, and culture emphasized by educational activists from all four discussed racial minority groups are entirely absent in the capital perspective. All that matters for the argument is that each individual member of a disadvantaged ethnoracial group be placed in a school where she can individually benefit from the advantaged students' capital.

Damaging Messages to Disadvantaged Students and Families

Related to the failure to credit the strengths of disadvantaged students and families, the capital argument sends damaging messages to both the advantaged and disadvantaged groups. These messages are conveyed because the argument is assumed to be public and to express the main reason integration is regarded as desirable for the school. It is thus available to members of the school community. The messages are particularly highlighted when parents, students, or school personnel make explicit or implicit reference to capital arguments when interacting with others in the school community. But if the arguments are driving the integration policy, as we are hypothesizing in this discussion, members of the school community will be aware of them even if no one states explicitly, for example, that advantaged white families are being encouraged to send their children to the school as a way to rectify the capital deficiencies of the disadvantaged families through bringing capital-rich families in.

The central message to the disadvantaged students is that they and their families are deficient in central educational and, indeed, life resources—human, social, cultural, and financial capital. Students are then subject to messages like, "You don't have good study habits; you don't work hard; your family is unable or unwilling to give you much help; they don't have enough money or connections to help you out. Furthermore, you are a negative influence on your (working-class and low-income) peers, and they on you. To do your best learning, you need to get away from your friends and be in classes with middle-class students, though you won't be benefiting them." This message is demeaning, stigmatizing, and conveys a dignitary harm to the student.[43]

A similar belittling and shaming message is conveyed to these students' parents, who may feel that they do not have the wherewithal to help their children succeed in school and, compared to middle-class parents, lack the finances, connections, and know-how required to help the school.

Feeding Advantaged Entitlement

The capital argument conveys the reverse of this message to advantaged parents—a sense of entitlement (often experienced but not recognized as such) that the school should first and foremost serve their children, and perhaps those like them, because it is their family's presence in the school that enhances the other children's learning. Amy Stuart Wells and Irene Serna cite a middle-class parent voicing a version of this message—that because she pays higher taxes for the school than the disadvantaged families, her child should be given priority over the less advantaged children for placement in desirable classes.[44] It is not a stretch from there to imply that the advantaged are superior to the disadvantaged in an overall way, a view that, when racialized, reinforces a sense of racial superiority. This can also take the form of a "savior" mentality that casts the advantaged as charitable and good-hearted benefactors to the disadvantaged, who should be grateful for the favors bestowed through the parlaying of the advantaged's capital.[45]

Messages Resonating with Harmful Cultural Representations

These messages are particularly readily conveyed, and do more harm, because they resonate with—both drawing on and reinforcing—larger, powerful ideologies and representations in society as a whole that blame people's disadvantages in life as largely their own fault, and thus an appropriate source of shame. This is the embedded underside of the "meritocracy" idea (mentioned in chap. 3, 99); if those at the top fully deserve their positions, then those at the bottom must deserve theirs as well.

Thus the message to the advantaged can also include, by implication, that their economic success is purely a product of their own talent and effort, for which pride and entitlement are warranted and appropriate. This class-centered ideology coexists (as we saw earlier, p. 102) with representations of Native Americans, Latinxs, and, especially, Blacks as intellectually (or culturally) inferior. In Kwame Ture and Charles V. Hamilton's classic formulation, this way of thinking "reinforces, among both black and white, the idea that 'white' is automatically superior and 'black' is by definition inferior."[46] So these two ideologies, one race-based and one class-based, reinforce one another. As we argued in chapter 3, current white advantage over Blacks, Native Americans, and Latinxs is primarily a product of a history of discrimination and its uncorrected legacy into the present. Thus class and race ideologies together provide an unwarranted sense of entitlement and superiority in white, upper-middle-class people and encourage shame and diminished self-respect in low-income Blacks, Native Americans, and Latinxs, a response also supported by the capital argument.

Morally and Intellectually Damaging to White, Upper-Middle-Class Students

The capital argument's resonating with powerful strands of inegalitarian ideologies is related to a larger deficiency—that it denies, or at best fails to engage with, the structural injustices of both the educational domain and the wider world within which education is situated. It takes the capital disparities among different racial and socioeconomic populations, as well as the unjust processes that generated them, as an uncriticized given (analogous to the way the equality of competitive opportunity framework also does [chap. 3, 103]). In other words, it rejects or sidelines the justice perspective.

Its doing so works against the education for justice we began to explore in chapter 3 (122ff) and is morally and intellectually damaging to white, middle- and upper-middle-class students. The capital argument contributes to an inaccurate picture of the society they live in and their place in it. They fail to see that their own advantages are in significant measure due to a history of injustice (of both a race and class nature) that they inherit. They are thereby rendered vulnerable to the misplaced sense of entitlement mentioned above and will view resource differences between their families and their less advantaged classmates as mainly resulting from their own parents being smarter, more talented, and harder working than their peers' parents and families.[47] This entitlement can also lead to the development of morally damaging attitudes of superiority and self-satisfaction in relation to their disadvantaged peers, bolstered by stereotypic cultural tropes that attribute deficiencies to those groups. They are discouraged from any learning and enrichment that could be gained from disadvantaged students and from opening their minds to sources of enlightenment they would not encounter in their advantaged communities. Finally, and in a similar spirit, for the advantaged students, the personal goods of a relationship with disadvantaged peers in integrated classrooms, which requires a spirit of respect, genuine curiosity, and equality, are undermined by the capital perspective.

Impeding Creation of Successful School Community

The messages of the capital argument are thus likely to impede the creation of a successful school community, among both parents and students, animated by a sense of equal respect, participation, and appreciation. They discourage disadvantaged families from feeling that they have equal standing and are equally empowered and welcomed to voice their perspectives and concerns in school settings, and they conversely encourage the advantaged to regard those families as less valuable to the community. In newly gentrifying schools, low-income parents who have worked for many years to help and improve the school can sometimes feel that the newer high-income parents fail to recognize and credit their efforts.[48] Learning to interact respectfully with differently advantaged racial "others" is challenging; signing on to a justice-based way of thinking about education generally, and one's school more specifically, can help provide the perspective and motivation to do so. But if the unjust institutions and structures remain unacknowledged, as the capital argument encourages, the disadvantaged groups themselves will be viewed as the problem.[49]

Note that our argument here relies on elements of King-like and group affirmation forms of ideal integration—a sense of respect and equality among various racial groups in schools and their classrooms. The argument is that these features should be goals for any integrated school and are undermined by a capital approach to producing integration.

The justice perspective helps us recognize that some of the cultural capital that advantaged families have when interacting with school and district personnel can be more accurately considered as those personnel's unfair and inappropriate treatment of persons of different class and racial backgrounds. If they give more credence to white or middle-class parents and their concerns than to nonwhite or working-class parents, their actions are wrong and contrary to their professional responsibility to treat all families with equal attention and respect. A familiar example of a failure to meet this responsibility is the use of professional language such as "language arts skills" and "sight vocabulary," which working-class and low-income parents are less likely to be conversant with than more educated parents.[50] School personnel do not have to use that type of language in talking with parents. More generally, framing "cultural capital" as an advantage possessed by a certain group masks the unjust processes that turn it into an advantage, including unjust treatment by those who confer the advantage.[51]

Discouraging the Advantaged Families
from Recognizing Requirements of Justice

By leaving class- and race-based disparities uncriticized, the capital perspective also discourages white, upper-middle-class parents from recognizing that justice may require some diminishment of their unjust and unearned class- and race-based capital privileges. We know that in-school equality cannot be achieved without changes in the economic and racial structures within which the school is set. Some advantaged people will have to give up some of their advantages in service of the more just social order required for educational justice, just as they would have to jettison their entitlement to favored treatment within the integrated school community if that community is to become just and equal. The capital perspective implicitly defines these moral requirements as off the table.

Good Schools Should Be a Matter of Civic Entitlement

Finally, the capital argument provides an inadequate civic foundation for equal education. Good schools should be a matter of public entitlement. If schools are not adequately funded and staffed, parents should be able to demand the funding and staffing as a matter of justice due to them as citizens. Many state courts have declared that demand to be a state constitutional right.[52] Looking to the recruitment of middle-class parents to agitate for adequate funding outsources a public responsibility to private citizens and degrades the disadvantaged families as supplicants or grateful recipients rather than equal citizens who can rightfully demand adequate schooling.[53] Judge Robert Carter, whom we have cited in another context, states this point eloquently: "*Brown* altered the status of blacks before the law. No longer supplicants, seeking, pleading, to be treated as full-fledged members of the human race. . . . Now they were entitled to equal treatment as a right under the law."[54]

SCHOOLS, TEACHERS, AND DISTRICTS
ADOPTING THE JUSTICE PERSPECTIVE

Thus a fundamental problem with capital arguments for integration is their exclusion of a racial and economic justice perspective on society, education, and the capital disparities on which the argument itself rests. So it is important to see that schools, teachers, and parents can themselves adopt such a justice perspective. They can view their educational program and school mission as contributing to rectifying a history of race- and class-based injustice and can make justice-related education an explicit part of their curriculum, as suggested in the previous chapter (113–14). Schools can encourage parents in their school community, across the race and class spectrum, to buy into this perspective and to embrace a justice project as something to take pride in within their school and in the parents' own ability to contribute to it.

Districts can do this as well, and a number of districts around the country have adopted equity (the more common terminology of the moment) policies and guidelines in that spirit. These policies generally make reference to achievement or opportunity gaps that the district says it will try to reduce and may explicitly focus on resources to meet all students' needs, including pedagogy (sometimes called "culturally responsive" pedagogy) and curricula sensitive to students' different backgrounds, life situations, and cultures. According to the Boston Public Schools' (BPS) equity planning tool, the BPS's goal is "creating a District that prioritizes its capacity to give each child equitable access to opportunity and achievement, while vigilantly identifying and dismantling cultural, structural, racial, and social barriers that could hinder their access to high quality learning environments."[55]

Will Advantaged Parents Resist Programs
That Challenge Their Privileges?

Some might hold that advantaged parents will never sign on to a program that challenges their privileges and will exit any school that does so if they can. Even if that were the case, it would still be important to name the resultant situation as unjust and as abandoning, even as an aspiration, the required standard of equal education. If we are to forsake justice in the name of a lesser but possibly more realizable goal, we should at least acknowledge that abandonment and affirm justice as an appropriate standard.

But advantaged white students can actually personally benefit from integrated schools that are animated by a justice perspective, rather than the capital perspective, which focuses entirely on how disadvantaged students' alleged deficiencies can be remedied through contact with advantaged students. With a justice perspective embraced by the school and reflected in its curricula, advantaged students acquire a more accurate view of both their society and their inherited place in it. (See chap. 3, 122ff.) They are thus better informed and better positioned to determine how they want to live their own lives and engage with their society in light of this knowledge. They are less hampered by stereotypes, cultural images, and ideologies concerning lower-income students and students of color. This can improve their ability to relate to "ethnoracial others" as fellow students, as coworkers, and as friends. It enriches their understandings and their lives in these ways. Their moral, civic, and personal growth goods are enhanced by education in a justice-embracing, ideally integrated school.

Some white parents' outlook already coheres with this justice outlook, at least in part. They view what is "good for my child" in a way that takes moral and, in particular, justice concerns into account as part of that good. They do not see maximizing competitive advantage or purely academic values as defining the child's good but appreciate the broader understanding of society and the opportunity for more diverse friendships as an important part of children's flourishing. One study of a school in a gentrifying, urban neighborhood focuses in part on a group of white parents who had chosen to send their children to a school that was only 10–15 percent white. One parent says, "I felt that we could provide a lot of support for academics for our children, but one thing we could not provide was working . . . and playing with a socio-economically diverse group of kids."[56] The national organization Integrated Schools, which organizes advantaged white parents to choose more integrated schools, states as part of their mission statement, "We firmly believe that integration is not a sacrifice of our own children but rather an investment in the future of all children and building a world we want our kids to be adults in."[57]

A particularly striking example of affluent white parents supporting a social justice mission within their schools took place in Montgomery County, Maryland, where a superintendent utilized a robust understanding of equity—providing not merely equal but greater resources to lower-income schools (because of greater need) than to affluent schools—yet nevertheless gained support from affluent parents for a funding scheme in the district.[58] While ignorance about the racial situation in the country to-day afflicts the majority of white adults—highlighting the need for racial justice education—it is also true, as highlighted by a 2019 Pew Research Center study, that a substantial minority of whites say that the country has not gone far enough in "giving blacks equal rights with whites" and that Blacks are treated less fairly than whites in hiring, pay, and promotions and in applying for loans and mortgages.[59] So it seems reasonable to suppose that many whites would be open to a racial justice perspective on and in their children's schools.[60]

Justice Perspective Encourages Use of Capital for Whole Community

The parental capital argument operates on the assumption that advantaged parents will use their capital to help the school their child attends, and if dis-advantaged students are also members of that school, they will thereby ben-efit. There may be something to this, but parents may also focus their efforts on aspects of the school that particularly benefit their own children, such as particular academic (e.g., AP classes) or extracurricular (e.g., sports or the-ater) programs. It is hardly the case that every advantaged parent is generous in how they deploy their various forms of capital, and many may remain fo-cused solely on benefiting their child rather than helping the whole school.

A school's adopting a justice perspective and the King-like integration ideal would encourage advantaged parents to use their capital in a way that benefits the entire school, raise their awareness of the advantage/disadvantage dynamic in the school (and society), and help them see themselves as comembers of a larger community that should be priori-tized in their capital deployment efforts. The capital perspective does not strengthen these outcomes, despite the irony that for capital processes to fully benefit the whole school, something beyond the capital perspective must be operating.

Structural Features Encourage Focus on Own Offspring

While we decry the morally narrow focus encouraged by the capital argu-ment, we must nevertheless also recognize structural features of our cur-rent economic order that unfortunately encourage advantaged parents to hyperconcentrate on their offspring's comparative school performance (not necessarily their actual learning). Extreme inequality has increased dispar-ities of reward attached to different jobs in the occupational hierarchy and reduced the number of jobs upper-middle-class people regard as well remunerated. This situation is frequently characterized as a "winner-take-all" society, in which rewards flow increasingly to only the topmost successful persons in different domains, leaving everyone else behind.[61]

This inequality has caused understandable anxiety across the whole economic and racial spectrum of society about the next generation's prospects. It has contributed to the so-called populist revolt of the Trump era, as well as to constructive attempts to address inequality, mentioned earlier (chap. 3, 110–11). We are suggesting that it is not merely a free-floating narrow-mindedness or selfishness that prompts upper-middle-class whites' offspring-focused capital deployment but developments in the larger society that encourage and incentivize doing so.

At the same time, this intensification of inequality also heightens the urgency of a justice lens on education and society. The winner-take-all development makes the unfairness of our current economic and educational arrangements even greater, and more salient, and gives all of us more reason to sign on to a justice agenda and to link a school's educational justice mission to the larger struggle for justice in the society.[62]

We are in no way denying that advantaged families can bring distinctive benefits to an integrated school community—connections, advocacy skills, facility with academic modes of thinking, and more. We argue only that these should be welcomed as part of a justice and King-like ideal integration orientation to the school community and the world outside, which the capital argument itself works against. The idea of a community of equals both inside and outside the classroom must be embraced by advantaged families and students. They must be alive to the ways that each individual has something to contribute to the shared learning project and acknowledge that the differently advantaged bring distinctive perspectives and insights that strengthen all students' school experience and learning.[63]

PROBLEMS WITH THE EMPIRICAL
FOUNDATION OF THE CAPITAL ARGUMENT

We have considered various drawbacks of a capital approach to integration. But we have not yet engaged directly with the empirical claim on which the capital argument rests—that (descriptively) integrated schools involve educational benefits to disadvantaged students rooted in parental and student capital that are absent in minority-dominant schools (or "segregated" schools, in terminology we are wary of). Comparing the two types of schools is somewhat complex and generally not appropriately engaged with by advocates of the capital argument for integration. To do so properly, we introduce the idea of *egalitarian pluralism*.

Valuing Ethnoracial Groups, Communities, and Identities

Our discussion of integration so far has recognized multiple definitions or conceptions of the term (especially descriptive and ideal) and different arguments for integration advocating (often only implicitly) various aspects of these conceptions. We have also recognized a plurality of forms of ideal integration. One of these, the group affirmation form, centers on esteeming and affirming ethnoracial groups with respect to their identities, communities, and cultures, a value prominent in the educational activism of communities of color, as discussed earlier. We must examine this value more closely in order to provide groundwork for the concept of egalitarian pluralism. By "ethnoracial" group, we generally mean a racial group in light of its ethnic dimensions. For example, African Americans are a racial group with ethnic characteristics, and Haitian Americans are an ethnic group that is generally viewed in racial terms as well. We also sometimes mean a group that can be either racial or ethnic, without specifying which, drawing on the ways that "ethnic" and "racial" are similar. Finally, "ethnoracial group" can also refer to a *pan-ethnic* group (a collection of ethnic groups with something in common), such as Native Americans, Asian Americans, or Latinxs, that may be (but are not always) also regarded in racial terms. The context of discussion should make clear when one of these particular meanings is in play. In the historical struggles of African American, Native American, Latinx, and Asian American education advocates and activists, we frequently saw a desire for group affirmation of an ethnoracial character and recognition of various kinds inside schools, as well as sometimes community group control of schools themselves.

There is a spectrum of different positions on this affirmation/control issue, defining significantly distinct forms of integration (and, in one case, nonintegration). We distinguish four. The first is *assimilationism*, which involves pressure on a group to abandon their distinctive group identity and culture (see discussion above, p. 132).[64]

A second position on the affirmation spectrum is *neutrality* with respect to group identity. Neutrality does not require or pressure the group or its members to weaken or abandon their identity (as assimilation does), but nor does the school provide any positive affirmation or support for it.[65] Neutralism is best understood by contrast with *group or identity affirmation*, the third position (also referred to here as "pluralism," explained below). The affirmation position involves a school's changing its overall culture to confer distinct recognition and standing on particular ethnoracial groups within the community. An integrated school may allow students to form same-race or same-ethnicity student organizations that can serve several functions—a "safe space" from insensitivity, ignorance, or racial prejudice in the wider school community; a place for members of the group to analyze issues in the school together; or a venue for group cultural expression. Such organizations can also contribute in various ways to the wider school community—facilitating panels and assemblies to discuss racial issues, providing cultural expression and education for others, teaming up with other ethnoracial organizations in the school for mutual conversation and activity, or spurring civic projects with nonmembers of the organizations. Neither assimilation nor neutralism supports such organizations or groupings.[66]

Teachers can also confer positive recognition formally and informally by making use of a particular student's group-based knowledge and perspectives in service of a class's educational enrichment. More generally, students can be empowered as members of ethnoracial groups to shape the culture and practices of the school and, where necessary, to challenge a taken-for-granted white cultural dominance. So the affirmation view at least implicitly challenges the dominance in the school of the majority group's culture.[67] By contrast, the neutralist view does not involve that challenge, while assimilation positively affirms that dominance.

It is useful to think of these forms—assimilation, neutralism, and affirmation—as distinct forms of ideal integration because of their very different evaluative stances toward the constitutive groups in an integrated community. Historically, even in the period of the greatest national push toward integration (1964–85), integration leaned more to neutralism or even assimilationism. Contemporary multiculturalism as a philosophy of education has perhaps most prominently called for positively affirming ethnoracial group identities inside a multiethnic school and challenging the hegemony of whites and white cultural forms and norms in the school.[68] That affirmation brings the school closer to King-like ideal integration because it involves both welcome and respect toward the ethnoracial minority group.

However, a fourth form of ethnoracial group affirmation is *not* compatible with school integration. This is ethnoracial *group empowerment* and *group or community control* of a school, aimed primarily to serve students of one particular ethnoracial group.[69] Some version of this goal has often been sought by advocates and activists from communities of color, as an *alternative* to integration, not a form of it. The Rough Rock Demonstration School founded by the Navajo (with federal support) in 1965, involving extensive community involvement and leadership, is an example, discussed in some detail in chapter 2 (69–70).

Some Asian Americans rejected integration both because they did not regard themselves as discriminated against (and so did not require forced integration as a remedy) and because they saw the dispersing of Asian

American (usually, in this historical period, Chinese American) students into mixed schools as weakening a city's Chinese American community and undermining their culture. (It was a demand not for community control but for a school oriented around and supporting Chinese identity and culture.) Some Latinx educational activists had similar concerns, especially in the period when bilingual education was an important force in the educational world (prior to President Reagan's weakening of it in the 1980s). These activists feared that integration programs would divide Latinx students among too many different schools, diminishing the critical mass of Latinx students in schools that would make it feasible to run bilingual programs and have Spanish-speaking teachers who would respect the students' cultures.

Necessary Trade-Offs between Pluralistic Values and Integration

Some versions of group affirmation are thus compatible with integration, and some versions (especially involving group control) are not. This means that policies of both integration and separation will involve trade-offs—sacrificing some genuinely positive values for the sake of what are seen as weightier values. A school that is fully community controlled by members of a single ethnoracial group might have to jettison some distinctive values were they to transition to an (even ideally) integrated school. Most pro-integration social science literature fails to recognize such trade-offs, which is part of its failure to engage with the egalitarian pluralistic tradition and to even recognize that single-race schools with racial minority populations can exemplify distinctive positive values.[70]

But recognizing the variety and range of values in play also enables us to more readily investigate whether we have overlooked possibilities of realizing more values than we originally considered. For example, an integrated mixed school can still strongly encourage the voice of parents from particular ethnoracial groups and hire faculty of the same ethnoracial group as a significant number of students. Even an explicit school mission to foreground the welfare and educational development of disadvantaged students, implicit in a social justice school mission, is possible in an integrated school, and we have seen that some districts have embraced this. An integrated school can also advance student voices tied to ethnoracial identity and groups by supporting student-led ethnoracial organizations and pedagogy strengthening that recognition. All these pluralistic features can be incorporated into an integrated school, especially a King-like and group-affirming ideally integrated one. Integrated schools can be on the lookout for ways to implement pluralistic, group-affirming, and group-empowering values they might not have initially recognized.

More generally, recognizing the plurality of values and the possible need for trade-offs connected with educational policies enhances our understanding of what is at stake in policy choices. Such recognition has not been greatly evident in debates about integration.[71]

EGALITARIAN PLURALISM

Egalitarian pluralism is a philosophy of society and (in this context) education that embraces the affirmation of ethnoracial group identities, heritages, and experiences (thus rejecting both assimilationism and neutralism) and adds to that pluralism the principle of educational equality. It does not regard integration as a core commitment but sees it as valuable only insofar as it supports equality and/or group affirmation. Egalitarian pluralism can plausibly be regarded as expressing the central, if sometimes implicit, educational aim of the educational advocates and activists of color we discussed earlier.

W. E. B. Du Bois was a leading figure in the development of egalitarian pluralism, especially in his 1903 classic *The Souls of Black Folk.*[72] Du Bois advocated full and equal participation of Blacks in economic, social, and political life in the United States. But he did not want that egalitarianism to come at the cost of American Blacks losing their distinctive identity, sense of history and culture, or sense of community as a distinct people. This is the "pluralistic" element. Thus, egalitarian pluralism is a tradition within African American thought that affirms the possibility and potential desirability of some form of separation and distinctness and so rejects the view that separate is *inherently* unequal.[73]

Movements, advocacy, and policy initiatives of Native Americans, Latinx Americans, and Asian Americans sometimes sought forms of educational equality in institutions and programs serving the needs of their communities outside of an integration framework. Native Americans particularly strongly rejected assimilationism, in part because forced assimilationism took its most intense form toward them. They often favored separate schools that taught and affirmed Native American heritage, language, traditions, and culture. They sometimes identified the assimilationism they rejected with the goals they perceived, especially in the 1950s, to be sought by African Americans under the banner of integration (chap. 2, 64–65). At a later stage, Native Americans followed the inspiration of Black Power advocates in their drive for self-determination as community control, wedded to the concern for cultural affirmation. But some Native Americans preferred integrated public schools to separate Native American schools, though this was often primarily for the sake of convenience (chap. 2, 65).

Native Americans and African Americans were responding to very different histories and forms of racism in the ideals and goals they brought to the issue of integration. The assault by the government on Native American culture and forms of life was much more sustained and central to their treatment than that toward African Americans. The government's conception of citizenship for Native Americans was bound up with their dissociating themselves from tribal life.[74] Native American groups were separate "nations," with complex relations to the federal government which had no real parallel for African Americans. Native Americans did not all attain full US citizenship until 1924. By contrast, African Americans' identity, traditions, and political ideals were bound up with US ones. They generally sought full inclusion in American society and institutions and adopted and adapted American ideals of freedom and equality as their own in doing so, using these as tools to criticize their fellow citizens, and American institutions, for African Americans' unequal treatment. Native American political ideals, however, had indigenous roots without exact parallel in the African American case. But both groups suffered severe oppression, second-class citizenship, and racial denigration.

Notwithstanding the overall historical differences between these two groups, each group's traditions contained multiple and often competing strands within them. Du Bois's pluralism coexisted with a much more strongly assimilationist form of integrationism. At the same time, Du Bois's egalitarian pluralism represented only one form of pluralism, with Black Power and, more generally, forms of Black nationalism representing another, which much more strongly emphasized economic and political self-determination and community control.[75] The latter forms of pluralism were closer than Du Bois's to the educational self-determination strand in Native American thought.

The "equality" and the "pluralism" strands within egalitarian pluralism represent separate elements. There can be equality without pluralism and pluralism without equality, and there can also be an affirmation of both but with different emphases on each. Du Bois insisted on both, but in both Black nationalist and Native American traditions, self-determination, collective empowerment, and cultural affirmation were sometimes emphasized more than equality (though this approach was frequently coupled with the belief that it was only through communal self-determination that equality could ultimately be achieved).[76]

Egalitarian Pluralism and the Resource/Capital Arguments

Egalitarian pluralism can help us think about the resource and capital arguments for integration on both empirical and normative levels. It asks us to foreground the values of equal education and group affirmation of students of color when evaluating an argument for integration. We do not put egalitarian pluralism forward as a fixed normative point, against which every educational initiative must be assessed. Rather it is an important tradition of thought, including within education, that highlights important education-relevant values yet is almost never taken seriously by integration advocates as a point of view with which they should contend.

The Capital Argument and the Minority-Dominant School "Disaster Narrative"

Both resource and, especially, capital arguments often operate by setting up a stark empirical contrast. On one side are minority-dominant schools, populated by low-income Black and brown students and families, with underqualified teachers, high teacher turnover, and, more generally, inadequate resources in relation to student need—educational "disaster zones." On the other side are (descriptively) integrated schools with economically better-off students and families, stable and well-qualified teaching staffs, and plentiful resources. Framed this way, the integrated schools obviously provide a better education; therefore, the case for sending students away from minority-dominant schools to integrated ones seems a no-brainer, and even raising the question whether the minority-dominant schools *could* realize values of educational equality or embody group-affirming, pluralistic values worth preserving and nurturing appears absurd.

But this argument is very misleading. Let us disaggregate five characteristics of the so-described minority-dominant schools: (1) concentration of Black and brown students, (2) concentration of low-income students,[77] (3) low-quality teachers, (4) high rates of teacher turnover (presumably, partly of higher-quality teachers who are able and choose to find other jobs), and (5) inadequate resources.

An argument for integration must show that it is the mixed racial demographic itself that produces the educational equality benefits in integrated schools. Otherwise, the argument will make only the obvious point that a school with high-quality teachers, low teacher turnover, sufficient resources, and a lesser proportion of low-income students provides a superior education to one without those characteristics.[78] And if we compare two schools—one minority dominant and one descriptively integrated—with those positive educational characteristics, differing only in their racial (not economic) demographic, it is difficult to see why the integrated one is more likely to provide an equality of educational goods to its students.[79]

It is true that minority-dominant schools usually do have the other four deficiencies. But that does not mean the racial demographic itself is their cause. Rather it is the larger structures of racial and class injustice that disproportionately economically disadvantage racial minority students in the first place, concentrating that disadvantage in neighborhoods and schools and then failing to provide sufficient resources to educate those students adequately, which results in higher-quality teachers leaving those schools. For reasons we have indicated earlier (chap. 3, 118ff), our society is structured to benefit whites—one might justifiably say, to uphold white supremacy—and the extreme economic inequality of the past several decades interacts with white supremacy to place Black and brown students in this disadvantaged state.[80] Racial segregation in neighborhoods and schools may be one mechanism through which white and class supremacy operates to harm these populations, but it is not itself the *source* of the disadvantage. The well-demonstrated negative effects of these economic/racial disparities on students' educational prospects, and the associated opportunity hoarding of the wealthy, makes the ending of poverty and the reducing of inequality itself a fundamental foundation in an educational justice program (as well as a more general social justice imperative).

Until fairly recently, forthright calls for robust racial and economic justice in many life domains (health, housing, and wealth) seemed like political nonstarters, and so initiatives like integration, with little cost or threat to the fundamental structures of race and class injustice, may have seemed to be the only hope for some minor improvement in the educational fates of Black and brown students in poverty.[81]

But in the past decade, the tide has turned in the direction of King's vision of economic and racial reform mentioned earlier (chap. 3, 109) in ways few anticipated. Recognition of the fundamental and obscenely unjust disparities between rich and poor are now a mainstream concern, intensified by the COVID-19 pandemic. Raising the minimum wage, increasing taxes on wealthy individuals and corporations, free or low-cost higher education, greater funding for K–12 schools in general, and especially for schools serving low-income populations, and providing universal free health care are all on the table now, advocated in community and labor struggles, proposed by influential public figures, and, as we have seen, sometimes adopted by school districts as part of their mission statements (see p. 147). These equality initiatives could end up being given a boost by the COVID-19 pandemic, which has given greater visibility to both the horrendous damage of inequality and the need for government to deal with society-wide crises.

In the disaster narrative, and in the integration argument built on it, it is said that teachers seek to leave minority-dominant schools (thereby depriving the schools of superior teachers, according to the argument) because a critical mass of disadvantaged students makes classes more difficult to teach, including students without these SES disadvantages. It is true that working conditions inside poorly resourced schools with a significant proportion of students who bring multiple poverty-related problems through the school door every day may drive some teachers away. But it is important to recognize that many teachers actually prefer to teach students who are not from particularly advantaged backgrounds, in schools that are adequately resourced, even if they lack substantial parental capital. These educators find such an experience more gratifying than teaching in schools with a preponderance of advantaged students. Writings about Black, Native American, and Latinx students and their teachers strongly suggest that some teachers are particularly concerned and able to connect with those students; that they want to and do learn about students' cultures, families, and life situations; and that they use this knowledge to help those students learn and prefer teaching those populations.[82] The disaster narrative, and even the capital argument more broadly, fails to recognize this, implying that teachers in general would always seek to work in schools with characteristics of advantaged communities.

It is also worth remembering that the students in distressed high-poverty schools may themselves have reasons to want to remain in those schools. When the schools are in their neighborhoods, they may be attached to them for that familiarity because they have friends and acquaintances there, because the school is viewed as (and is) an important community resource, and sometimes because of the school's history and traditions.[83] They might be aware of students of color from their neighborhoods who attended white-dominant schools through an integration program and came to feel distanced from peers, like a student in one such program who told one of us that the program made her "not Black enough for my friends at home" yet viewed as "too Black" for the white kids in the integrated school.[84] Thus while these schools are poorly resourced, they might still exemplify group-affirming, pluralistic values.

The egalitarian pluralist tradition provides a vision of an educationally valuable ideal that is a distinct alternative to integrationism and that challenges and reveals some of the weaknesses of the resource and capital approaches to integration. With serious economic and racial restructuring, the educational deficits caused by poverty could be greatly mitigated, as quite a few countries have done to a significantly greater extent than the United States,[85] and the ideal of equal educational goods could be achieved in a school with students of modest economic background. Such schools could also realize the pluralist value of affirming the ethnoracial friendships, communities, cultures, and traditions of African American, Native

American, and Latinx students. The ideal of equality of education should be and can be realizable with any ethnoracial demographic, and different demographics are appealing to different students for varying and often quite legitimate reasons.

Capital processes in an integrated school can bring educational benefits to students who formerly attended poorly resourced, minority-dominant schools. But the force of that point as an argument for integration is undermined by its misidentifying the fundamental problem in those schools that the capital process aims to rectify, as separation and minority demographic dominance rather than systemic, structural race- and class-based injustice. These injustices in the broader society are left unchallenged by the capital argument and, indeed, are actually required by it. That some families possess huge amounts of capital, while others have almost none, is what allows the argument to work, by the former using that capital for the benefit of the latter. But why should there be this kind of disparity in the first place, both in the resources themselves and in the way they function more generally in the school and the educational system? The educational equality required by justice in education, and sought by egalitarian pluralism, is far out of reach of the resource and capital arguments, despite the not-infrequent invocation of equality when making these arguments. Only by seriously reducing, and ultimately ending, structural racism and systemic class domination can the foundation for educational equality, demanded by educational justice and egalitarian pluralism, be provided.

Finally, we suspect the reason ethnoracial group affirmation issue is seldom engaged by proponents of the capital integration argument is, first, that they are not tuned into it as a positive value for students and, second, that the "disaster zone" narrative makes it difficult for them to recognize any positive value realizable in such schools.[86]

CHAPTER 5

INTEGRATIONS

The Civic Argument

We have considered two historically important arguments that have been provided for school racial integration—the resource and the capital argument. While the latter has been particularly influential in the recent past, it has been found to be especially problematic. In this chapter, we discuss three more promising arguments in favor of racial integration, devoting the most attention to one in particular—the civic argument. But we begin with two more modest arguments—the diverse workplace and the cognitive benefits arguments.

PREPARATION FOR DIVERSE WORKPLACE
AND COGNITIVE BENEFITS OF DIVERSITY

The resource and parental capital arguments focus, often tacitly, primarily on the purely academic or subject matter mastery aspects of education, especially those elements included on standardized tests. We now turn to a set of arguments that concern other educational goods—the instrumental good of preparation for a diverse workplace and the academic and personal growth goods of cognitive benefits of diversity. Both have been affirmed in Supreme Court jurisprudence regarding educational diversity, which bolsters a sense that these are official arguments for diversity or descriptive integration—bringing multiple racial groups into the same educational space—although the arguments have succeeded only in cases at the higher-education level.

In several affirmative action cases in higher education, parties defending affirmative action have submitted briefs delineating various benefits of learning in ethnoracially diverse classrooms. One argument is that workplaces are increasingly diverse, regarding both coworkers and customers. Students should be prepared to function productively in this world. They can do so only if their schooling involves encountering, engaging with, and working cooperatively with people from a variety of backgrounds.[1] The value at stake in these cases is generally called "diversity," rather than "integration." In US jurisprudence, *diversity* encompasses differences of race, class, religion, ethnicity, culture, geographical region of origin, and, in theory, any other category that can contribute to differences in experience, opinion, and outlook. The court emphasizes that the sorts of diversity validated by their rulings in favor of affirmative action include this broader range, not just race. However, the policies upheld by the decisions specifically concern race preferences and thus race-related diversity.

The workplace benefits affirmed in the decisions are partially asymmetrical. People of color may learn to maneuver in, including not being intimidated by, white-dominant workplaces and their hierarchies,[2] an issue without much parallel for white workers since relatively few workplaces are dominated by people of color. This asymmetry also means that the achievement of this level of interracial comfort in the workplace benefits people of color more than whites.

Nevertheless, for all racial groups, interracial relations are both generally and in workplaces specifically too often characterized by discomfort, anxiety, strain, and a larger absence of connection. If integrated schools can help prepare people of all racial backgrounds to be more comfortable with one another in the workplace, this is a significant benefit of integration.

At the same time, in assessing the degree of benefit in light of an argument particularly at the K–12 level, one would have to know *how much* an integrated experience in primary and secondary education actually contributes down the road to interracial workplace comfort. To what degree are students of color who first attend minority-dominated secondary schools and then go on to integrated colleges significantly less likely to acquire interracial workplace comfort than those whose education has been integrated earlier? And are workplaces themselves able, through both their own formal and informal efforts, to create that comfort, even with workers who have had very separated K–16 experiences? This is not to question the workplace comfort benefit but, in the spirit of the egalitarian pluralism challenge, to assess its force as a defense of integration.[3]

A second thread in the affirmative action briefs concerns the intellectual benefit of engaging with others of different racial backgrounds, which affects the college experience itself, rather than being only instrumentally valuable in a later workplace. The increasingly sophisticated research in these briefs finds that racially diverse learning environments improve cognitive development, such as critical thinking and problem solving, foster the ability to deal with issues of greater complexity, and result in encountering a greater range of perspectives and better developing open-mindedness, including a willingness to question one's own assumptions.[4] A more integrated environment also reduces racial bias, which, especially for white students, frees up cognitive energy that might otherwise be devoted to managing unwanted negative thoughts about racial others.[5]

These arguments apply as well, and arguably even more strongly, to the K–12 context, although the Supreme Court's majority has failed to do so in any K–12 education case thus far. Integrated education in primary and secondary school can equally well contribute to this form of intellectual growth. Its benefits would also accrue in the twelve years of primary/secondary education, not only the four of undergraduate (and, for a smaller number, additional professional education), and would affect many more individuals than the subset of the K–12 population who go on to higher education.

These two arguments—workplace diversity and intellectual benefit—avoid the problems of the capital argument. They both rely on students of color being considered important educational resources for white students and, at the same time, regard each student as an educational resource for each other one. On their own terms, they thus seem to be relatively sound. As suggested above, it is not entirely clear, however, how much force they have without further research. The intellectual benefit argument in particular does not determine how much extra intellectual benefit the diversity of a classroom provides over and above other ways that educators teach critical thinking or expose students to differing experiences and points of view that do not rely on racial diversity. Still, while their weight is as of yet unclear, workplace interracial comfort and the intellectual benefits of ethnoracial diversity do appear to be reasonable arguments in favor of integrated K–12 classrooms and schools.

THE CIVIC ARGUMENT FOR INTEGRATION

Civic and Moral Goods as Educational Goods

We come now to what we regard as the most robust argument for integration—that it is a requirement for, or strongly facilitative of, civic and moral education. Civic and moral goods are two of the four forms of core educational good that the principle of educational equality requires to be provided to all students. Currently, the terminology of "social/emotional" is more familiar when referring to important nonacademic forms of learning and may be viewed as attractive partly because it seems "value neutral" and thus avoids controversy about which values should be taught. We agree that students should learn how to interact productively and be able to make friends ("social" goods) and to manage their emotions in a healthy way ("emotional" goods). But such educational goods do not remotely capture the full scope of the moral and civic dimensions of nonacademic (and not purely academic) learning, and some uses of "social/emotional" do seem to want to take into account this larger terrain with which we are concerned.

Up to this point, we have looked at educational goods primarily with respect to their value to the individual student possessing them. Civic goods such as personal civic efficacy and moral goods such as being respectful of others are indeed valuable to students themselves and contribute to a more personally flourishing life. But civic and moral goods have another equally significant aspect: their possession by citizens is good for other people and for society.[6] A democracy can function well only if citizens are knowledgeable and politically engaged, with an appreciation for democratic processes, institutions, and values. In the United States, the public school system is by tradition the institution centrally responsible for educating and creating the next generation of democratic citizens out of a diverse populace.[7] The *Brown* decision affirmed that "education . . . is the very foundation of good citizenship."[8] Americans continue to regard civic education as a core aspect of schooling.[9] And this civic value is sometimes officially tied to racial integration, as in the *Brown* decision and in 2011 guidelines issued jointly by the Obama administration's Departments of Justice and Education, which state, "Racially diverse schools provide incalculable educational and civic benefits by promoting cross-racial understanding, breaking down racial and other stereotypes, and eliminating bias and prejudice."[10]

Society itself has a deep stake in civic education, as the form of education most pertinent to preparing the next generation to run society. Schools are vital stewards of these distinctly communal values. Society's interest is different from the investment that parents have in their own children's intellectual development and personal flourishing. We cannot look primarily to parents to affirm the civic aspect of education, though their civic activism in supporting low-income schools is especially vital to sustaining healthy schools.

Despite civic education's importance, some current trends in education tend to weaken the civic function of schooling: the ascendancy of both an economic approach to schooling that sees the prime function of teaching as "career readiness"[11] and a related "consumerism" that tailors schooling to parent preferences regarding their children's education; the rise of high-stakes testing as the central measure of educational success, resulting in a shrinking of the curriculum toward the tested subjects—language arts and math—and away from civic subjects such as social studies, history, and government;[12] and privatizing the goods, function, and operation of education—so that its public purposes and public oversight are weakened or masked.[13] Policy makers and school officials, in addition, "have discouraged or even barred teachers from dealing with controversial issues."[14] In the face of all these tendencies, it is particularly vital that we recover a sense of civic goods' indispensability to education and society.

Civic Educational Goods: Knowledge, Commitment and Competence, and Attachments to Racial Others

Civic educational goods are of different types. We will highlight those with particular relevance to race. Race is seldom explicitly thought of as a source of values, yet we implicitly recognize it as such in many of the ways we think about race. Race is a vital social category, both as a locus of substantial inequalities, discrimination, stereotyping, prejudice, and interpersonal tension and anxiety and as a component of individual identity that many citizens regard as a source of personal meaning because it in part defines who they are. Civic and moral education should help students, as detailed above (chap. 3, 103–4), gain an understanding of race as a social force and social phenomenon, commit to rectifying racial injustice and other racial ills, use their learned capability to analyze racial phenomena in service of informing their civic commitments, and recognize the meaningfulness to others of their ethnoracial identities.[15]

Civic education about race must begin by acknowledging that American society has been throughout its entire history, and remains, a racially unjust society, as we argued in the last two chapters. This is not a comfortable truth, but it is educationally irresponsible for teachers to present an image of American society as one whose institutions function in a just manner. Teachers who view civic education as preparation for a society whose institutions are just and sound, not to say perfect and exemplary, risk losing students' attention, interest, and affordance of authority, and in any case such a perspective will not prepare them properly for adulthood and citizenship in their actual society.[16]

Nor is race simply one delimited social domain where injustice can be found. Racial injustices permeate virtually every major area of economic, social, and political existence—housing, education, occupation, health, political influence and empowerment, immigration, income, and wealth. So race must occupy a central place in civic education.

Civic educational goods are conventionally and usefully broken down into several categories. We will examine three below: (1) civic knowledge and understanding, (2) civic commitment, engagement, competence, and efficacy, and (3) civic attitudes and attachments.

Civic Knowledge and Understanding

Traditional civics instruction often focuses on knowledge of institutional structures, such as the three branches of government and their respective functions. Civic Mission of Schools, a prominent organization promoting civic education, expands on the understanding encouraged by civic instruction: "Have a grasp and an appreciation of history and the fundamental processes of American democracy; have an understanding and awareness of public and community issues; and have the ability to obtain information, think critically, and enter into dialogue among others with different perspectives."[17]

With race and racial justice in mind, we would add to this list the understanding that national (and international) ideals provide standards by which citizens can assess how well national (and international) institutions are functioning.[18] Plausible race-related ideals in the American context, which are not necessarily unique to the United States, are liberty, democracy, equality, and equal opportunity. These ideals can help students comprehend why and how racial injustice offends against American ideals and encourage them to attempt to correct that injustice.

In addition, civic understanding involves engaging in social analysis, which can be a component of the more general category of "critical thinking" but is particularly important for understanding race. Students need to learn to identify systems and patterns in society, such as disparities in occupation, living situation, income and wealth, and the like. They must then ask why those patterns exist and learn how to find out the answers to those questions.[19] Social analysis is distinct from, but complements, the more familiar civic study of particular events (e.g., the Trail of Tears or the Mexican-American War), political developments (e.g., immigration policy or voting patterns and shifting party loyalties of different ethnoracial groups), important prominent figures of ethnoracial groups, and social movements (e.g., the American Indian movement or the civil rights movement).

Teaching civic knowledge and understanding about race would serve "racial literacy" or "civic literacy about race"—basic knowledge every American should have about American racial history and the present.[20] While full agreement on all the elements in a racial literacy curriculum would be difficult to achieve, it is evident that widespread commitment to such a curriculum is essential. In the early and mid-2000s, Amy Stuart Wells and colleagues studied high school graduates of all racial groups from the class of 1980 who had attended integrated schools. Wells et al. found that the white graduates were less likely than their peers who had attended majority-white schools to ascribe Black poverty to laziness and a lack of responsibility. They "sensed" a more societal explanation, though they did not generally know what that explanation was.[21] Graduates of all groups reported that race was seldom discussed in their integrated school, either as part of the curriculum or more informally.[22] Some literature on teachers dealing with race shows some teachers do try, with different degrees of success, to encourage conversations about race in their classes. But a larger number either avoid them entirely, seem unable to manage students of colors' challenging contributions, or cut off incipient exchanges when they lack confidence in their ability to manage them productively.[23] Teacher training programs and continuing professional development must help teachers both achieve a robust threshold of racial literacy themselves and also learn to encourage and skillfully guide students in productive racial conversations.[24] The widespread sense that race is an emotional minefield to be avoided at all costs and the fear (mostly, though not solely, among white people) of being called or thought of as "racist" can be overcome only through normalizing informed racial conversation.

No doubt in more recent years, many teachers and schools have engaged in more in-depth racial literacy education, related to the increased move toward districts and schools adopting race-related curricula and explicit commitments to racial justice (see above, chap. 4, 147–48). But we have a long way to go, and there are new challenges, such as the rise of social media promoting new forms of disinformation and racial hate.

Civic Commitment, Engagement, Competence, and Efficacy

Civic educational goods comprise more than cognitive goods because citizens must possess not only knowledge and understanding but also a commitment to engaging in actions to promote public good and civic ideals. Civic engagement must be grounded in civic competence and efficacy (as well as knowledge and understanding). Schools must help students acquire this competence and efficacy through practice and guided reflection on such practice.

For example, students can learn about school budget processes and funding sources, then use that knowledge to engage in advocacy and protest what they may see as funding inadequacies for their school or schools in their districts.[25] Lory Janelle Dance describes a research project by her racially diverse students in which they traveled on their city's public transportation and kept track of how frequently entering passengers did and did not sit next to people of different racial groups.[26]

Students may draw on their own race-related histories, traditions, and communities for resources, support, and guidance in civic activity for racial justice. Civic education should help students recognize the possibilities and challenges of engaging in both same-race and cross-race political initiatives, in part through the study of historical and contemporary monoracial and multiracial movements.

Civic engagement has both an individual and a collective dimension. Traditional civic education tends to focus on the individual and her civic activities. But civic education informed by racial justice must also emphasize the collective character of social justice activity, which can be emphasized both in historical study of social justice movements and in the forms of civic activity the students are invited and permitted to engage in.[27]

Civic Attitudes and Attachments

Citizens in a democracy must view their fellow citizens with respect, as equal members both of the various polities they share and, in particular, of a national society, and with concern for one another's rights and welfare. They must experience a sense of linked fate and solidarity, that they are "in it together," with members of other ethnoracial groups.[28] Bonds formed in schools and classrooms provide a vital step toward the future development of such civic attachments. There are two forms of race-related civic attachments—cross-race and within-race (sometimes referred to as "bridging" and "bonding"). Both are important. Cross-race bridging requires more support and nurturance from the school because students will usually have had much less contact with other-race students in their generally segregated neighborhoods. Schools have a unique ability to bring students of different ethnoracial groups together and to use the learning process to forge ties that can provide a foundation for civic attachment among diverse groups. But same-race bonds should also be supported by the school in the spirit of ethnoracial group affirmation, as mentioned earlier (chap. 4, 151–52), and as a foundation for same-race collective civic activity. Civic attachments can be built most securely on a base of young people's day-to-day interactions with one another, of both the same and other races, in schools and classrooms envisioned as genuine communities.

The mere copresence of different racial groups in the same classrooms (descriptive integration), with at least minimal respect and care, may be a sound enough underpinning for developing commitment, competence, and knowledge. But without the greater moral demands of King-like ideal integration—care, appreciation, and robust respect—it would not be possible to develop the civic attachments and constructive cooperation on civic projects required to prepare students to help a multiracial democratic society live up to its values.

Danielle Allen employs the idea of "participatory readiness" to describe the goal of civic education. This idea nicely brings together the knowledge, commitment, and competence dimensions of that education.²⁹ Like academic goods, civic goods (and related moral and personal flourishing goods) are to be distributed equally if educational justice is to be realized. All students must possess participatory readiness and civic attachments at the relevant exit point.

Education for social justice, as well as civic engagement connected with it, more greatly involves students' racial identities than most subject matter mastery and thus highlights racial asymmetries. Students of color are much more likely than white students to have personally experienced injustice or other forms of race-related mistreatment and to have learned about these matters in their families and friendship circles, although working-class or poor white students may have also experienced class-related forms of injustice. Here race creates an asymmetry that enables students of color to be better positioned to educate white students.

The same asymmetry is likely, though perhaps to a lesser extent, in justice-related projects involved in civic education. For example, imagine a civic project where students investigate housing patterns in the metropolitan or suburban area in which their school is located. Although the overall project might bring entirely new knowledge to the students of color, many of them will likelier be able to testify to the life impact of the housing inequities and discrimination revealed in this civic research project than white students.³⁰

CIVIC EDUCATIONAL GOODS RELATED TO RACE BETTER REALIZED IN INTEGRATED SCHOOLS

All these civic educational goods are much more readily taught and realized in racially integrated schools than in separated schools (some requiring only descriptive, others elements of ideal, integration). Starting in the 1970s, in the wake of the strong national commitment to integration begun in 1964 (chap. 2, 59–60), social scientists began studying white and racial minority students' copresence in schools and classrooms and its effects on racial attitudes. The hoped-for improved racial attitudes were often viewed as a central benefit of integrated education. In this regard, some of the social, moral, and civic educational aspects of integration were highlighted from early on in the integration process.

Prejudice Reduction and the "Contact Hypothesis"

Social psychologists have often framed the desired socio-moral goal of integration as *prejudice reduction*. The foregrounding of prejudice stemmed in part from the influential 1954 work *The Nature of Prejudice* by the distinguished American social psychologist Gordon Allport. Allport developed the "contact hypothesis," which has become a research paradigm for subsequent generations of prejudice research. It proposes conditions within schools and classrooms that are particularly conducive to improving racial attitudes, such as cooperation and common goals among the students.[31]

Social psychologists recognized the complexity of altering racial attitudes. For example, people can view particular out-group members favorably (both those who are known personally to the subject or public figures and celebrities) yet still view the group itself in a negative light.[32] The contact hypothesis conditions are precisely those that make the transfer of positive attitudes from individuals to groups more likely.[33]

However, the focus on prejudice, important as it is, does not capture the full range of moral and proto-civic race-related attitudes we should want from integrated education. For example, in the current era, when many young people have become more comfortable than previous generations with people of other races and there has been (wildly premature) talk of a postracial society, troubling racial attitudes continue to surface. In a remarkable ethnography of a largely middle-class integrated school (mostly Black and white, but other groups as well), Shayla Reese Griffin found that many students, primarily but not solely white, prided the school on its racial comity, often expressed in students' ability to engage in racial joking. Griffin notes, however, "When Jefferson students said that 'everybody got along' or that they were 'beyond race,' they meant they were part of a generation in which white people had permission to say biased, bigoted, prejudiced, discriminatory and oppressive things with smiles on their faces, and people of color did not have permission to be offended by it."[34] It is not clear that the white students are themselves actually prejudiced (though some may be), but they make racially objectionable statements (without recognizing this) that should be addressed in an antiracist school, inside and outside of the curriculum.

Racial Moral/Civic Education beyond Prejudice Reduction

The complex learning necessary for students of multiple racial groups to acquire a sense of shared and equal membership in the school community is not mere prejudice reduction. It requires an awareness of ways that vulnerable or formerly excluded groups are and are not made to feel they belong. For example, students of all groups, including whites, must learn how to recognize noninclusionary messages, whether they come from administrators, teachers, or fellow students, and to challenge those messages and show support for the affected student or group of students. If a Black student insults an Asian American student in a school hallway, other members of both of those groups, as well as any others, should learn how to appropriately and constructively intervene in that situation.

Moral and civic education concerning racial attitudes and inclusionary behaviors clearly requires a plurality of racial groups in the students' world. Unless students personally encounter racial out-groups, the reduction of stereotypes, prejudices, insensitivities, and other problematic attitudes toward them will be extremely difficult to accomplish.

There is a fundamental asymmetry in racial attitude education, in that whites are still the most powerful racial group, and their prejudices and failures of racial understanding have the most power to harm other groups. Whites are much less likely to change without actual contact with people of color, yet that process can be quite stressful for the people of color subject to white ignorance, insensitivity, and prejudice, even while it is (hopefully) being reduced. This is an unfortunate feature of racial attitude change that must be accepted in the name of a greater good, as bringing white students to a more justice-informed place will ultimately benefit students of color as well. Whites can help lift this unfair burden by making clear that they recognize that they need to change and taking steps on their own to help this process along—for example, by being proactive in remedying their ignorance of the lives and histories of people of color, learning how white ignorance is produced in history and society as a part of white supremacy,[35] attempting respectful engagement with people of color, trying to stay informed about racial issues in the society, and the like. And teachers can advance this corrective work.

Although white people's attitudes were the prime concern in the first decades of integration, the increasing ethnoracial pluralization of the school population (since 2014, students of color have been a majority of school children in the United States)[36] means that all groups require education in racial understanding and respect. Latinxs, Blacks, and Native Americans are all disadvantaged and discriminated against, but this does not inoculate them against prejudice, stereotyping, or disrespect toward one another (not to speak of internalized prejudice toward their own group), although it may make them more sensitive than whites to other groups' negative experiences. The increasing number of ethnic subgroups within each racialized group can also be a source of further tensions that schools must be sensitive to. For example, Black immigrants from Nigeria, an increasing percentage of the overall Black population, are a distinctly socioeconomically and educationally advantaged population (59 percent of the offspring of Nigerians have a BA, compared to 20 percent of American-born Blacks) and constitute a proportion of Black students at elite colleges far above their proportion of the Black population.[37] Some African Americans have responded to this by arguing that affirmative action was meant to benefit Blacks who have inherited the legacy of centuries of enslavement and segregation within the United States, not recent Black immigrants who have not.[38]

The Role of Curricular Knowledge in Racial Civic Education

Civic education must emphasize curricular knowledge both of the histories and experiences of particular ethnoracial groups and of how racial processes play out in history and society. Descriptive integration by itself could facilitate such curricular learning about ethnoracial groups, but the addition of King-like and group-affirmation elements of ideal integration does so more strongly. Students' interest in their classmates makes them more engaged in learning about the groups to which their classmates belong. This effect is stronger the more the teacher is able to create a significant sense of respect and community within the class. Although no Mexican American student should be presumed (by the teacher or by other students) to be an expert on every facet of Mexican American life or history, encouragement to speak about one's experience as a member of a given group enriches class discussion. Students should be invited to make their own choices as to how they present their remarks—as "speaking for their group," "speaking just for myself," or various shades in between (e.g., "I know a lot of Mexican Americans feel this way, but I'm not saying this view is shared by all or even most Mexican Americans"). Their contributions will contribute to the kinds of race-informed conversations and learning required for racial literacy. Such civic-related curricular learning and exchange can occur only in mixed classrooms and especially in ones whose schools take on elements of ideal integration.

Recognizing the Racial Identities of Students of Color in Schools

Civic education thus draws on the strand of ideal integration that encourages recognition of ethnoracial groups and identities within a school with mixed populations (above, chap. 4, 151–52). Du Bois's egalitarian pluralism understood that ethnoracial group identities can be valuable in two different ways. One is to members of the particular ethnic or racial group themselves by providing a sense of community, familiarity, comfort, and shared pride. Second, the culture and heritage of a given group can be of value to others. Du Bois thought that Black Americans had a distinctive culture and heritage, created primarily through their experience in the United States, though with some connection to their African origins, that they were prepared, and should be prepared, to share with other Americans for the greater good of all.

In schools, both aspects of ethnoracial identity are in play. Race or ethnicity provides an important sense of personal affiliation and comfort for students, particularly (though not only) when students from minority groups are also numerical minorities in their schools. In addition, there is some evidence that the strengthening of an ethnoracial identity among disadvantaged groups can foster educational growth.[39]

Members of minority ethnoracial groups also often appropriately invoke aspects of their cultures in school, such as when bilingual students speak their home language with friends outside of class or when a student delivering a speech at a school assembly gives some of the speech in her home language so that her grandmother can understand her.[40] If second-language speakers are required or pressured by school norms to suppress use of their home language at school, students from those groups feel devalued,[41] and all students are given the message that the school community does not regard all ethnic identities equally. The Asian American and Latinx educational activists who sought bilingual education, respect for non-English languages and their use by students, and respect for their cultures were seeking these forms of identity recognition.

The students' group-based experiences, cultures, and heritages also provide educational resources for other groups (in the spirit of Du Bois's view), both in planned group activities and as a source of individual students' contributions to in-class exchange and extracurricular activities, as we mentioned above. For teachers to make the best use of those potential contributions, and to promote interracial connection and respect in their classrooms, they have to affirm those identities in appropriate ways, avoiding both under- and over-recognizing them. Doing so takes practice and a developed skill involving asking individual students what they are comfortable and uncomfortable with in relation to recognition.[42]

The ethnic pluralizing of the student population makes issues of recognition and organizational presence somewhat more complicated. Depending on numbers, there might be both an Asian American club and a Vietnamese American one, perhaps with overlapping membership and somewhat different agendas, for example, regarding the curriculum and requests for presentational time at school assemblies. The presence of this ethnic plurality does not reduce the need for a racial justice lens on curriculum and school policies. But actual student self-identities in their complex multiplicity should strongly inform the specifically recognitional dimension of school life.

Integration, especially in its group-affirming ideal form, is therefore favorable to many forms of ethnoracial group recognition and organization inside schools. But the King-like form of ideal integration is not hospitable to all of them. For example, it would detract from King-like ideal integration if student members of ethnicity-based organizations had friends *only* from these groups or only from their own ethnoracial group more generally. The ideally integrated school in its King-like form would encourage students to push beyond their social comfort zone to try to connect with students from other groups in order to both promote proto-civic bonds and understanding and simply enrich their social experience in school. Both King-like and group-affirming ideal integrations are allied with the needs of civic education in this regard.

Schools can encourage cross-racial social ties most fundamentally by ensuring that classes themselves are ethnoracially mixed, in ways we have discussed. Most fundamentally, they must avoid racial tracking. But they should also promote various extracurricular activities that attempt to draw students from a diversity of groups. For example, if the theater program or a school sport is attracting students overwhelmingly from only one racial group, that program should find ways to encourage others to join, since these extracurricular activities are vital to the social and proto-civic connections and attachments students can forge in mixed schools.

To summarize, taking civic education seriously as a core goal of K–12 education, especially with respect to racial injustice, provides a powerful argument for both descriptive and, even more so, ideal racial integration in classrooms and schools. The racial mix is either required for or strongly facilitative of civic readiness—civic knowledge and understanding, civic competencies, and core civic and moral attitudes—regarding race. These civic educational benefits are not automatically generated by the mixed demographic alone (i.e., by descriptive integration). Teachers and schools must actually utilize that demographic constructively in a civic education program.[43] Some elements of ideal integration are necessary to create respectful and caring civic attachments to racial others. As we have mentioned, civic education has taken a beating in the era of "standards and accountability" and neoliberal reform. But we have now as much of a reason as ever to revitalize civic education, and racial integration can and should be a core element in that revitalization.

Although integrated schools are the optimal setting for civic education in a multiracial society, schools with much less mixed populations can also engage in some forms of it. Civic knowledge, efficacy, and engagement can all be nurtured in majority-Black or majority-Latinx schools. Such schools have often been sites of student civic activism drawing on students' identities as disadvantaged racial minorities—for example, in the Boston student protests mentioned earlier (166; see also note 25 on pp. 256–57) against inadequate school funding. Either with or without emphasizing students' racial identities, students in non-mixed schools can acquire civic knowledge, and these schools can adopt programs for reflective civic engagement.[44]

Civic Education in White-Dominant Schools

Civic education is also possible in majority-white schools. It is indeed challenging to teach students in that setting about racial minority groups and the injustices from which they have suffered and to imbue them with an ethos of democratic and justice-informed civic engagement. Nevertheless, it can be done, and white students can be brought to understand the broader world of unjust disadvantage and advantage that might not be particularly visible to them. Educators should take into account the degree of advantage of the students. We have built a strong class-based element into the justice perspective that ought to inform the curricular approach taken. If the white students are not particularly advantaged on a class spectrum but are still advantaged on a racial spectrum, the pedagogical and curricular methods will have to reflect this.

The familiar view in many white-dominated schools that they don't need to teach about race because they have so few racial minorities is profoundly damaging to those students and prevents them from gaining an understanding both of their lived society and world in which they will become citizens and of the many nonwhite populations their lives will inevitably be intertwined with.[45]

Nevertheless, monoracial schools must be acknowledged as severely restricted in their ability to help their students get to know, respect, and work with those of other races and form the sorts of in-school attachments and civic engagement relationships that can serve as a foundation for cross-racial civic attachment and engagement among adult citizens. This limitation provides a strong civic-based argument for integrated schooling.

The civic argument for integration complements the capital, resource, intellectual/cognitive, and diverse workplace arguments. It avoids the destructive messages of the capital argument and supports King-like ideal integration's and the justice perspective's promotion of a community of equals inside the school of both families and students. It affirms that every family and student has a contribution to make and that all students can learn from all other students. In focusing on integration inside the school, the civic argument does share one limitation with the other arguments because it does not fully take on the justice perspective's highlighting of inequalities outside the school that restrict the degree of equality the school by itself is able to realize, especially in the face of poverty and upper-middle-class opportunity hoarding. The civic argument, however, partly takes on the justice perspective in that a civic consciousness produced by civic education promotes students' concern for social justice in society.

The civic perspective highlights a central educational good, which we are arguing should therefore be provided equally to all students. It is not an argument aimed at bringing about *equality* by means of integration, as, in fact, none of the other four arguments do, though the resource and capital arguments sometimes misleadingly claim to do so. The civic argument is akin to the cognitive/intellectual argument in seeing integration as facilitating one of, or an aspect of, the core educational goods—critical thinking and examining issues from multiple perspectives in the cognitive/intellectual category, and civic goods in the civic case. Both are arguments in favor of integration but not on grounds of bringing about equality. Yet the civic goods argument does engage with equality in a way that neither the cognitive/intellectual nor diverse workplace goods arguments do, because civic education prepares students to engage with unjust inequalities in their society.

DEMOGRAPHIC DIVERSITY

We have discussed two different ways integration is plural in character—*definitional* (rejecting legal segregation, descriptive, and ideal) and *valuational* (how group affirmation is dealt with). A third is *demographic*—the various racial, ethnic, and class demographics in schools and classrooms, and how these differentially lend themselves to realizing integration-related values.

Comfort in Classrooms

Recognizing that a classroom's racial and other demographic makeups affect educational goods, the Supreme Court in the important 2003 affirmative action case *Grutter v. Bollinger* utilized the idea of a "critical mass" of minority students. The justices reasoned that unless there are a certain number or percentage of racial minority students in classes, they will not be comfortable contributing to the class discussion, and neither white students nor students of color will reap the educational benefits of diversity.

Though developed for higher education, the idea of critical mass applies in the K–12 context. To see how, we must distinguish three levels of race-related comfort or belonging in mixed classes. The most minimal is when a student feels comfortable sitting in the class and occasionally participating. A second, more robust, level of comfort then is when a student feels comfortable not only sitting in the class but also challenging classmates' views, especially those that predominate in the class.[46] A third, even stronger level involves a felt, if generally only implicit, sense that the class belongs to you. Minority students in high-track classes who may feel the second level of comfort often do not feel this sense of ownership. White students often, without necessarily recognizing it, take this third level of comfort for granted, especially in Advanced Placement and other high-track classes. Being a member of a group that is a numerical majority in the class often, though not always, confers this sense of ownership, but often so does being a member of the dominant group in society.[47]

The benefits of descriptive or ideal integration are substantially affected by the level of comfort achieved by the students. If the students of color are comfortable being in the class but feel inhibited from expressing views connected to their distinctive and race-related experiences and perspectives that challenge how the majority is looking at the issues discussed, a substantial civic and academic educational benefit is absent. The white students (and, more generally, the students in racial groups other than the speaker's) must be able to hear those challenging views in order to learn about race in the way a race-related curriculum requires. Minority students must also be able to voice their views to benefit from exchange with and challenge from their classmates and, more fundamentally, to experience themselves as fully respected equals in the class.

Several factors affect whether a given student feels a particular level of comfort. Teachers can do a great deal to make students of color who are a numerical minority in the class feel valued, respected, and welcomed—or the reverse. Another factor is the critical mass—the number of students of a given student's group and the number of students of color overall.[48] When K–12 classes have fewer than this critical mass of a given group, the smaller number will make an individual vulnerable to "hypervisibility," where other students expect her to represent her group whenever she weighs in on an issue relating to that group (see discussion of this above, p. 171) or where she feels stressful expectations to counter stereotypes of her group. Every student needs to feel capable of contributing simply as an individual member of the class, while at the same time, individuals may well be happy to be valued as members of a particular group. With less than a critical mass, it will be difficult for the teacher to use the racial mix in the class to fully realize the academic, moral, personal growth, and civic educational benefits of integration.[49] Nevertheless, since many classes do not have a critical mass of every group, it is vital for teachers to establish guidelines and sensitivities for making the best of the great, and increasing, diversity of demographics.[50]

Were productive racial conversations to become much more normalized in high schools and well handled by knowledgeable teachers, they would become less of an emotional minefield, and the significance of the racial demographic in a given class would be at least somewhat reduced.

Not every integrated demographic involves whites as a majority. Whites are no longer a majority of US K–12 students, as mentioned earlier. In some integrated classrooms, they will be a numerical minority. It can indeed be a positive learning experience for them to experience being a numerical minority. It can challenge "white normativity" encouraged by being simultaneously the most privileged racial group and the numerical majority. Whites don't lose their privileged status just by no longer being the majority, but it would help them adjust to sharing their power if they were in some classes in which they had to contend with numerical minority status.[51]

Because of its history, the term *integration* tends to invoke the situation of students of color "integrating into" majority-white institutions, suggesting that integration as an issue fundamentally concerns the white/nonwhite dichotomy. We must get beyond this framework in two ways. First, many schools face integration issues in the absence of white students. Urban schools often contain a mix of African American students and immigrant students from various groups. How this complex mixture of students relates respectfully, appreciatively, and caringly with one another and adapts to learning together is an important present-day integration issue.[52] The integration challenges are also increased by the greater ethnic pluralization of Blacks, Latinxs, and Asians we mentioned earlier (170).

Second, as our historical exploration has shown, different groups of color have quite varied forms of racialized experiences and histories. In a sense, there are different forms of "racism" and "prejudice" with respect to each particular group. The term *anti-Blackness* has arisen to mark this specificity with respect to Black people, but the general concept of racism's specificity applies to all racialized groups. This also means, as we noted earlier (170), that people of color can be racist against people of color of other groups. Schools must be prepared to deal with this phenomenon in the larger area of moral and civic education around race.

The percentages of different ethnoracial groups in a given class therefore impacts types of comfort, which, in turn, affect the types and degree of educational goods realizable by integration.

Socioeconomic Class as a Demographic Characteristic

We have argued that when race is discussed in relation to education, socioeconomic class must be part of the picture. This applies to the goods involved in integration too. Part of what racially defined student groups learn about one another in racially mixed classrooms is linked to differences in their relative socioeconomic positions; this is a crucial dimension of the experience of these racialized groups, and it in turn informs the students' understanding of racial and social justice.

The class factor also affects the interpersonal dynamics among racial groups. The Civil Rights Project at UCLA increasingly refers to the dominant form of school separation (which they call "segregation") as "double segregation," of both race and class. This helpful framing highlights more clearly the challenges involved in making integration reap its potential benefits when low-income students of color are put together with white, middle-class students. Part of that challenge, which, as we have mentioned, tends to get lost in the integration debates, is that students in poverty are affected by their life situations in ways instructional approaches can only partly address. But there are also educational challenges within classrooms containing that double divide that are diminished when the divide is of *only* class *or* race. These two quite consequential divides are harder to bridge together than either one alone, producing a greater difficulty for the teacher who is seeking to garner productive conversations and student engagement with one another. This is all the more reason for having heterogeneous classes from kindergarten on. Doing so would help mute the class/race communication divide in successive grades.

Making class more explicit also calls attention to the specific challenges of integration in racially mixed schools in middle-class settings, a situation sometimes found in suburban areas and the subject of several important ethnographic studies mentioned earlier.[53] John Diamond and Amanda Lewis highlight racial tracking practices common in the middle-class school they studied, revealing that this form of racial disadvantage survives relative economic parity among racial groups (though not necessarily to the same degree as where the racial groups are also divided by class). Both Griffin and Diamond and Lewis also reveal that the conception of Blacks as a socioeconomically disadvantaged group still haunts racial interactions in middle-class schools, for example, in teachers' assumptions, often tacit, that the Black families are working class or poor,[54] or when Black students both contend with white students' stereotype of their disadvantage yet sometimes also use that stereotype to guide their own self-presentation to their fellow students.[55]

Gentrification

Gentrification—wealthy, predominantly white people moving to working-class or low-income urban areas—provides a new class-related demographic shift affecting integration. Gentrifiers as a group are more likely to desire "diversity" in their children's schools than other whites. They move to areas with schools of predominantly Black and brown students where they are, especially initially, a numerical minority. These are favorable conditions for some of the goods of integration—a welcoming of diversity on whites' part and the presence of a numerical majority of students of color, which thus reduces one source of whites' automatic dominance in the school.

But gentrification also has drawbacks in relation to integration values. People of color are often only fleetingly the numerical majority, as a school gains a reputation that attracts other white gentrifiers, over time leading to them becoming a majority, or at least a dominant force, which can diminish the families of color's voice.[56] And their self-image as progressives welcoming diversity and even committed to social justice can sometimes prove a barrier to their learning from families of color's challenges regarding their racial attitudes and sense of entitlement. A deeper level of the school demographic instability often generated by gentrification is its impact on the housing market, which essentially drives away the families of color who can no longer afford to live in the area. Thus the favorable attitudinal and demographic situation brought and sought by white gentrifiers can often be quite temporary.

The challenges of reaping integration's benefits, such as enhanced learning about the racial order and respect and appreciation across various student groups, must take account of the manifold and complex ways that class plays a role in both actual and perceived raciality. More generally, differing and changing ethnic, racial, and class dynamics in American schools constitute varied "integrations" and diverse challenges to achieving the benefits of descriptive and ideal integrations.

EGALITARIAN CIVIC
INTEGRATIONIST
PLURALISM

Pulling the pieces of our argument together then, we advocate *egalitarian civic integrationist pluralism* (ECIP). We privilege equality—ensuring that all students, independent of their backgrounds, have robust access to the full range of educational goods (of which we have delineated academic, moral, civic, and personal growth forms). Equality is the most fundamental commitment of an educational political philosophy, a demand of justice, and a fundamental goal almost always sought by Native American, Latinx, Asian American, and African American communities.[1] We are far from realizing that vision, but it is nevertheless within our reach.

Educational equality cannot be achieved within a society as racially unjust as ours. Our current regime of educational injustice is deeply intertwined with an interlocking system of racial inequality in health, housing, income, wealth, and job opportunities. This system makes low-income students as a group much more challenging to bring to the equal educational goods threshold. And, in turn, racial injustice is itself deeply entangled with class injustice, especially in its particularly extreme form at present. Movements, initiatives, and policies aimed at racial educational equality must therefore work in tandem with actions to end poverty, reduce overall socioeconomic and racial inequality, and lessen the existence and effects of opportunity hoarding by the racially and socioeconomically advantaged. The moral impetus for educational equality is further bolstered by the need for a reparations program for Native Americans and African Americans to remedy the deep, only very partially addressed, history of racial oppression and white supremacy in the United States. Educational initiatives must always be engaged with this broader racial and class justice perspective.

The justice perspective helps us understand why a traditional, and still very common, view that educational inequality is caused by "segregation"—different racial groups attending largely separate schools—is not correct and thus why the strategy of "descriptive integration"—bringing those different groups into the same schools—will not achieve an equality of educational goods. Social injustice and white supremacy are the fundamental causes of educational inequality, mediated by the larger structures of racial inequity outside the school; separation (the meaning of "segregation" in this context) is merely a mechanism by which this already-existing inequality is sustained.

White supremacy has been difficult to recognize in part because of the specific history of race and American education. The *Brown* decision dealt a severe blow to the legal structure of white supremacy in its Jim Crow segregation form, contributing to that system's ultimate demise in the 1960s. Because many Americans identify white supremacy with its Jim Crow form, however, they therefore think that with Jim Crow's destruction, white supremacy itself was overcome. But as the justice perspective spells out, US society continues to privilege whites as a group, and that privilege is still structured into our institutions in manifold ways, just not in the legally explicit manner of Jim Crow segregation.

Thus, despite the historical association of educational equality with integration, when all other variables (e.g., poverty and its concentration, teacher quality and stability, school resources, neighborhood effects, opportunity hoarding) are held constant, these two phenomena are only weakly linked empirically. What we call the "capital argument"—that disadvantaged students should be "integrated into" schools with a preponderance of advantaged parents and students with social, human, financial, and cultural capital that will benefit the disadvantaged students—is only a pipe dream as an equality-producing approach. It leaves in place, and indeed relies upon, the very structures of race and class injustice that pose an impassable barrier to educational equality. The integrationist tradition in its capital form quietly abandons the aspiration to true educational equality, retreating to an "improvement within an unequal structure" model and leaving white supremacy unchallenged. This is one reason communities of color have not wholeheartedly embraced integration as the sole route to educational equality and why, when they did support it, they often did so as only one part of a broader initiative to equalize educational goods for students of color, or simply because there seemed no better alternative.

We strongly affirm the *civic* purposes of education, a historical function of the US public school system strongly highlighted in the *Brown* decision, which is nevertheless in distinct danger of being sidelined in contemporary education.[2] Preparation for engaged and knowledgeable citizenship in a multiracial democracy benefits not only each student individually but also the society as a collective body. In light of the justice perspective, civic education must involve the nurturing of a sense of justice that will prepare students as future citizens to be able to recognize, analyze, engage with, and correct for the racial inequalities endemic in our society. This antiracist strand of civic education has been strongly supported by educational activism, including by students, within communities of color since at least the 1960s.

Regarding school integration, we view it, as both an idea and a reality, as taking distinct forms and having differing meanings, both historically and in the present, that have sometimes muddied discussion of the value of integration. We are especially concerned with the distinction between integration as the bringing of different racial populations into the same school ("descriptive integration") and as a set of ideals that can be, but often are not, built upon that demographic plurality inside the school ("ideal integration"). One such ideal, drawn from Martin Luther King Jr., is the attempt to create within classrooms and the school more generally communities of equal respect, appreciation, and care, particularly across ethnoracial lines. Another ideal, "group affirmation," involves the school's affirmative support of and respect for students' ethnoracial identities, both inside classrooms and in other school venues. This acceptance and valuing (which can take several different forms) has been a core demand of mobilized communities of color's educational activism throughout their histories, complementing their core commitment to equality.

We have provided qualified support for integration, though only in its ideal forms. Only the ideal forms retain the values of equality and affirmation of a school's racially disadvantaged populations, through which it can provide some counterweight to the racial and class injustices in the outer society. While the school cannot by itself rectify the inequities of family resources within its own community, it can, though only to some extent, mute them by implementing various poverty-buffering initiatives (as in the "community schools" idea) and by reducing occasions and structures for opportunity hoarding by the advantaged. Moreover, the school can strive to create an equality of respect, participation, and belonging in the face of (and with recognition of) those social inequities. In doing so, the school's commitment to King-like and group affirmation ideals opens it to adopting a more general justice perspective, which can then work to correct external injustices that impact the aspiration to realize equality of education inside the school. By contrast, mere descriptive integration will inevitably reproduce society's inequities inside the school.

Our affirmation of ideal integration is also grounded in the civic perspective. The primary value of having students of different ethnoracial groups attend school together derives from the importance of civic education. Though civic education should be bolstered in both minority-dominant

and majority-dominant schools, which will continue to exist even with robust (descriptive or ideal) integration efforts, the ideally integrated school
provides the most favorable setting for developing civic capabilities, knowledge, and attachments. Here skilled teachers can foster students' respectful and mutually enlightening engagement across ethnoracial lines in work
groups, civic projects, and class discussion.

The final component of ECIP is *pluralism*, in the form of recognizing and
affirming the ethnoracial groups within a given integrated school, which
is both a form or component of ideal integration and a core goal sought
by communities and students of color historically and in the present. The
forthright acknowledgment of the importance of ethnoracial groups and
identities, mindful of the increasing salience within the US student population of new ethnoracial groups, makes it much easier to craft a community of respect and care across the ethnoracial divide than a color-blind
approach that discourages attention to racial identities. Teachers can also
better accomplish racial justice education, both cognitively and emotion-
ally. By linking historical study of structural injustices among racial groups
to the diverse ethnoraciality of classmates in the integrated classes, teachers can enrich learning and preparation for civic engagement.

At the same time, the integrationist form of pluralism we favor does not
allow for stronger forms of community empowerment, such as schools devoted primarily to the betterment of a particular ethnoracial community,
usually (though not always) geographically concentrated, and "community
control" more generally, that activists of color have sometimes sought. We
have argued that multiple values are in play in deciding which educational
arrangements should be favored. Choosing some values may preclude others. A school like the Rough Rock Demonstration School (now the Rough
Rock Community School) (chap. 2, 68–69) is able to center Navajo community control and leadership and a focus on Navajo language, history, and
culture that might be very valuable to its students but would be difficult to
achieve in an ethnoracially mixed school.

The tradition of "egalitarian pluralism," particularly well-articulated
within African American social and educational thought, better reflects
the strivings of many communities of color in the past and present by foregrounding equality and group affirmation while leaving integration an open
question, to be decided by its ability, in the particular context at hand, to
serve those two goals. Different communities of color, reflecting their varied racialized histories, have then often taken divergent directions on that
integration question.

We have criticized the integrationist tradition for failing to take egalitarian pluralism, particularly its egalitarian dimension, seriously as an alter-

native approach to educational progress, especially given integration's own weaknesses in that area. Nevertheless, we believe the egalitarian pluralist tradition fails to give sufficient centrality to the civic function of schools as preparing students for public life in a multiracial democracy, and this is why we generally prefer the ECIP model. Society has a stake in the civic purposes of schooling that transcends its value to individual students. Majority- and minority-dominated schools are much less well positioned to realize this civic value.

Overall, it is impossible to teach the full range of civic educational goods outside genuinely integrated schools, with a cost to both individual students and society. But ultimately, until we dismantle the interlocking external structures of racial and class injustice, and of white supremacy and class domination more generally, genuine educational equality will remain an unattainable dream.

ACKNOWLEDGMENTS

Writing this book has been a wonderfully collaborative project, and we are grateful to acknowledge the many people who have supported our work. Randy Curren and Jon Zimmerman are at the very top of our list, as they invited us to write a book on the topic of race and education for their series on the history and philosophy of education. They urged us to think broadly and ambitiously about the topic and enthusiastically embraced our suggestion to investigate the central problem of integration as it related to educational equality. They provided terrific feedback on multiple drafts of this book, which helped us tighten the argument and reduce the page numbers significantly.

We also want to thank our fellow participants at the workshop on the history and philosophy of education organized by Jon and Randy at New York University in 2014. The workshop included many of the authors in this series, and we would like to thank all of them for their probing questions and insightful feedback during our presentation. Special thanks go to John Rury, Derrick Darby, Charles Dorn, Lisa Andersen, Rene Arcilla, Tracy Steffes, Adam Laats, Sigal Ben-Porath, Ben Justice, Michael Johanek, Colin Macleod, and Harvey Siegel.

Each of us was fortunate to be able to call on many people for help in the writing of or thinking about the ideas in this book. Larry would like to thank Christopher Lewis, who read an entire early draft of the philosophy segment of the book and offered extensive and invaluable suggestions. Tommie Shelby commented on a draft of what has become chapter 4, focusing on the capital argument for integration. Sarah Blum-Smith brought her experience and thoughtfulness as a public elementary school teacher to portions of the book concerning teacher responsibilities and how to think about students' "potential." Ben Blum-Smith talked through several issues concerning race and education, drawing partly on his work as a public school math teacher concerned with racial issues. Adam Hosein discussed affirmative action and antidiscrimination jurisprudence.

Longtime discussion groups have also helped Larry formulate and clarify his thinking on many of the issues in the book. The Neoliberalism and Education group (Winston Thompson, Quentin Wheeler-Bell, Sigal Ben-Porath, and Lily Lamboy) helped with issues of privatization and neoliberalism and their intersection with race and more generally helped shape Larry's evolving views on race and education. The Race and Philosophy group (Jorge L. A. Garcia, Sally Haslanger, Tommie Shelby, Lionel McPherson, José Mendoza, Megan Mitchell, Adam Hosein, and Elvira Basevich) has been an invaluable setting for thinking about philosophical issues concerning race and racism for two decades. The Pentimento group (Martha Minow, Mary Casey, and Richard Weissbourd) has been a context for discussing issues of moral education and politics for several decades and provided insightful feedback on a crucial section on integration in the book. The Race and Education group (Lisa Gonsalves, Nury Marcelino, Ann Ruggiero, and more recent members Lianne Hughes-Odom, Courtney Leonard, and Julie Boss) has helped keep Larry more in touch with racial issues in current educational practice. Finally, the Moral Psychology group (Sally Haslanger, Steve Nathanson, Margaret Rhodes, Chris Zurn, Adam Hosein, Naomi Scheman, Lisa Rivera, and Anat Biletzki) has been a mainstay of Larry's intellectual and political life for several decades.

Zoë would like to say a special thanks to John Rury, who offered his considerable expertise on the history of race and education in productive conversations about this book. She would also like to thank her colleagues at the NYU History of Education Writing Group for their lively conversation about earlier drafts of the history section, with a special nod to Natalia Mehlman Petrzela, Lisa Stulberg, Lauren Lefty, Judith Kafka, Nick Juravich, Dominique Jean-Louis, Talya Zemach-Bersin, and Michael Glass for lively discussions at her presentation—and others—on issues related to the history of race and education. Jonna Perrillo, David García, and Stacey Sowards schooled Zoë in the controversies and complexities surrounding the usage of *Latinx*. She hopes they will find our final choices in this book acceptable, although admittedly imperfect. Victoria Cain, James D. Anderson, Diana D'Amico Pawlewicz, Michelle Purdy, and James Fraser were kind enough to talk Zoë through some of the more challenging concepts and arguments as the book came together over coffee at various academic conferences in the past few years. Nancy Beadie and K. Tsianina Lomawaima helped Zoë fortify the sections on Native Americans through our work on a related paper on civic education. She would also like to say a special thanks to Lisa Andersen, who ended up moving to Montclair and joining Zoë on weekly brainstorming sessions while walking two poorly behaved dogs through Brookdale Park.

We both had essential support and encouragement from our academic homes. Larry has had the great good fortune of being a member of the University of Massachusetts Boston Philosophy Department for his entire career and treasures the continuing, very special collegiality and intellectual comradeship of his colleagues there. UMass Boston and its students have provided a perfect setting for philosophical scholarship that tries to stay grounded in the unjust and unequal world we actually live in, and Larry hopes this book is worthy of that demanding standard.

Zoë has benefited immensely from the support of her colleagues and friends in the Department of Educational Foundations at the College of Education and Human Services at Montclair State University. Critical conversations with Jaime Grinberg on the diverse histories of people of color, especially Latinos (his preferred term), in the United States have been especially helpful, as has his mentorship and encouragement over many years. She is grateful to have such fun and outspoken colleagues and appreciates working in a department of historians, philosophers, sociologists, and psychologists who study questions of race and social justice in American public schools. Her dean, Tamara Lucas, has been a strong and vocal supporter of Zoë's research and travel related to this book. A special thank you goes to staff at MSU's Sprague Library, especially Denise O'Shea, who tirelessly tracked down obscure sources and permitted her to check out well over the normal limit of books. A number of outstanding and dedicated graduate students at MSU assisted Zoë with research, including Arthur Schmidt, Emma Flynn, Grady Eric Anderson, David Herren, Joseph DiGiacomo, Molly Kosch, and Chae Amy Kim. She would also like to acknowledge Leslie Wilson in the History Department, who has provided feedback and encouragement for this project. And a final note of thanks to the incredibly curious and fiercely intelligent students at Montclair State University, who have shared their personal experiences about race and inequality in K–12 education along with their questions about how this happened and what we can do to solve it. Their commitment to education for social justice inspired her to write this book.

Many thanks to Elizabeth Branch Dyson for helping to create the series in the first place and for her great enthusiasm and assistance in the book's final stages. Thanks to Elizabeth Ellingboe for her excellent copyediting. Many thanks to Katherine Harper for an excellent index.

Larry would like to say a special thanks to Zoë for embracing the professional partnership we created over the many years of working together on the book. It was great working with you. Zoë returns those sentiments enthusiastically; it was a lot of fun working on this project and writing this book with you, Larry.

Finally, Larry's deepest thanks go to his life partner, Judy Smith, with whom he has discussed every facet of the book many, many times over the years. He has been incredibly fortunate to have the benefit of Judy's own deep knowledge of and powerful scholarship in US cultural history. Her particular knowledge of the culture and racial politics of the 1940–2020 period was invaluable to the philosophical arguments he was struggling to make.

Zoë would like to recognize her husband, Christopher N. Matthews, for his unending patience and tireless support over the course of many years as this book came together. His expertise in the history and anthropology of race, inequality, and struggles for racial justice in the United States proved invaluable, as did his willingness to share equally in the challenges of raising a family while working full time. She would also like to thank her teenagers, Dexter and Hollis, who ask smart and engaging questions about school integration, racial equality, and social justice based on their own experiences and what they observe in the world around them.

Finally, Zoë would like to acknowledge the extraordinary role that her parents Christina Miesowitz Burkholder and Ervin Burkholder have played in supporting her academic training and professional career, as well as her commitment to social justice and educational reform. She considers herself very fortunate to be their daughter and is honored to dedicate this book to two people who believe so deeply in the power of education to improve lives.

NOTES

INTRODUCTION

1. US Department of Education, "For Each and Every Child: A Strategy for Education Equity and Excellence" (Washington, DC: Government Printing Office, 2013), 14.
2. James E. Ryan, *Five Miles Away, a World Apart: One City, Two Schools, and the Story of Educational Opportunity in America* (New York: Oxford University Press, 2010), 3. For information on the status of segregation today versus in 1970, see Gary Orfield and Erica Frankenberg, with Jongyeon Ee and John Kuscera, "*Brown* at 60: Great Progress, a Long Retreat and an Uncertain Future" (Los Angles: Civil Rights Project at University of California, Los Angeles, 2014), 11. A sample of the scholarship documenting the connection between racial segregation and inequality in schools includes Chandi Wagner, "School Segregation Then & Now: How to Move toward a More Perfect Union" (Alexandria, VA: Center for Public Education, 2017); Grover J. Whitehurst, Nathan Joo, Richard V. Reeves, and Edward Rodrigue, "Balancing Act: Schools, Neighborhoods and Racial Imbalance" (Washington, DC: Brookings Institution, 2017); US Government Accountabilities Office, Report to Congressional Requesters, *K-12 Education: Better Use of Information Could Help Agencies Identify Disparities and Address Racial Discrimination*, GAO-16-345, April 21, 2016; Kristi L. Bowman, ed., *The Pursuit of Racial and Ethnic Equality in American Public Schools: Mendez, Brown, and Beyond* (East Lansing: Michigan State University Press, 2015); Amanda E. Lewis and John B. Diamond, *Despite the Best Intentions: How Racial Inequality Thrives in Good Schools* (New York: Oxford University Press, 2015); Orfield and Frankenberg, "*Brown* at 60"; Richard Rothstein, "Education and the Unfinished March: For Public Schools, Segregation Then, Segregation Since" (Washington, DC: Economic Policy Institute, 2013); Sean F. Reardon, Elena Tej Grewal, Demetra Kalogrides, and Erica Greenberg, "Brown Fades: The End of Court-Ordered School Desegregation and the Resegregation of American Public Schools," *Journal of Policy Analysis and Management* 31, no. 4 (2012): 876–904; Douglas N. Harris, "Lost Learning, Forgotten Promises: A National Analysis of School Racial Segregation, Student Achievement, and 'Controlled Choice' Programs" (Washington, DC: Center for American Progress, 2006); Jonathan Kozol, *The Shame of the Nation: The Restoration of Apartheid Schooling in America* (New York: Random House, 2005); Derrick Bell, *Silent Covenants: Brown v. Board of Education*

and the Unfulfilled Hopes for Racial Reform (New York: Oxford University Press, 2004); Charles T. Clotfelter, *After Brown: The Rise and Retreat of School Desegregation* (Princeton, NJ: Princeton University Press, 2004).

3. W. E. B. Du Bois, *The Souls of Black Folk* (1903; repr., New York: Dover Publications, 1994), v.

4. Richard Rothstein, *The Color of Law: A Forgotten History of How Our Government Segregated America* (New York: W. W. Norton, 2017), vii–viii.

5. US Department of Education, "For Each and Every Child," 13. Reports on Native American academic achievement reveal significant gaps for Native American eighth graders in reading and math. Steven Nelson, Richard Greenough, and Nicole Sage, *Achievement Gap Patterns of Grade 8 American Indian and Alaska Native Students in Reading and Math*, Issues & Answers Report, REL 2009-No. 073, US Department of Education (Washington, DC: Government Printing Office, 2009). See also John J. Laukaitis, *Community Self-Determination: American Indian Education in Chicago, 1952–2006* (Albany: State University of New York Press, 2015); Executive Office of President Barack Obama, "2014 Native Youth Report," December 2014, p. 3, https://eric.ed.gov/?id=ED565658; US Department of Education, Indian Nation at Risk Task Force, *Indian Nations at Risk: An Educational Strategy for Action* (Washington, DC: Government Printing Office, October 1991), http://www2.ed.gov/rschstat/research/pubs/oieresearch/research/natatrisk/report.pdf.

6. Ellen D. Wu, *The Color of Success: Asian Americans and the Origins of the Model Minority* (Princeton, NJ: Princeton University Press, 2013); Stacey J. Lee, *Unraveling the Model Minority Stereotype: Listening to Asian American Youth*, 2nd ed. (New York: Teachers College Press, 2009); Rosalind S. Chou and Joe R. Feagin, *The Myth of the Model Minority: Asian Americans Facing Racism* (Boulder, CO: Paradigm Publishers, 2008), 55–99.

7. Derrick Darby and John L. Rury, *The Color of Mind: Why the Origins of the Achievement Gap Matter for Justice* (Chicago: University of Chicago Press, 2018).

8. Elizabeth Todd-Breland, *A Political Education: Black Politics and Education Reform in Chicago since the 1960s* (Chapel Hill: University of North Carolina Press, 2018); Zoë Burkholder, "Integrated Out of Existence: African American Debates over School Integration versus Separation at the Bordentown School in New Jersey, 1886–1955," *Journal of Social History* 51, no. 1 (2017): 47–79; Leah N. Gordon, *From Power to Prejudice: The Rise of Racial Individualism in Midcentury America* (Chicago: University of Chicago Press, 2015); Sonya Douglass Horsford, *Learning in a Burning House: Educational Inequality, Ideology, and (Dis)Integration* (New York: Teachers College Press, 2011); Clarence Taylor, "Conservative and Liberal Opposition to the New York City School-Integration Campaign," in *Civil Rights in New York City: From World War II to the Giuliani Era*, ed. Clarence Taylor (New York: Fordham University Press, 2011), 95–117; Thomas J. Sugrue, *Sweet Land of Liberty: The Forgotten Struggle for Civil Rights in the North* (New York: Random House, 2008); Adam Fairclough, *A Class of Their Own: Black Teachers in the Segregated South* (Cambridge, MA: Harvard University Press, 2007); Matthew J. Countryman, *Up South: Civil Rights and Black Power in Philadelphia* (Philadelphia: University of Pennsylvania Press, 2006), 223–57; Davison M. Douglas, *Jim Crow Moves North: The Battle over Northern School Segregation,*

1865–1954 (New York: Cambridge University Press, 2005), 173–79; Jack Dougherty, *More Than One Struggle: The Evolution of Black School Reform in Milwaukee* (Chapel Hill: University of North Carolina Press, 2004), 9–33; Adam Fairclough, "The Costs of *Brown*: Black Teachers and School Integration," *Journal of American History* 91, no. 1 (2004): 43–55; Martha Biondi, *To Stand and Fight: The Struggle for Civil Rights in Postwar New York City* (Cambridge, MA: Harvard University Press, 2003), 223–49; Vivian Gunn Morris and Curtis L. Morris, *The Price They Paid: Desegregation in an African American Community* (New York: Teachers College Press, 2002); Jerald E. Podair, *The Strike That Changed New York: Blacks, Whites, and the Ocean-Hill Brownsville Crisis* (New Haven, CT: Yale University Press, 2002), 22–27; Diane Ravitch, *The Great School Wars: A History of the New York City Public Schools*, rev. ed. (Baltimore: Johns Hopkins University Press, 2000), 251–380; Derrick A. Bell Jr., "The Burden of *Brown* on Blacks: History-Based Observations on a Landmark Decision," *North Carolina Central Law Review* 7 (1975): 25–38.

9. Ibram X. Kendi, *Stamped from the Beginning: The Definitive History of Racist Ideas in America* (New York: Nation Books, 2016); Audrey Smedley and Brian D. Smedley, *Race in North America: Origin and Evolution of a Worldview*, 4th ed. (New York: Westview Press, 2012); George M. Fredrickson, *Racism: A Short History* (Princeton, NJ: Princeton University Press, 2002).

10. This rejection of race does not preclude the possibility of statistical (rather than absolute) genetic differences (for example, in susceptibility for certain diseases) among groups conventionally viewed as races. Although some scientists continue to use the terminology of "race" for groups defined by these statistical differences, many others think that doing so both misleads the public about the existence of races in the traditional sense and also misrepresents the character of the groups in question and of the attributed characteristics. See Dorothy Roberts, *Fatal Invention: How Science, Politics, and Big Business Re-create Race in the 21st Century* (New York: New Press, 2012).

11. The point about racialized groups is sometimes stated by saying that races are "social constructions" rather than real biological entities. We prefer the "racialized group" terminology because every human institution and many human groups are socially constructed. Nations and ethnicities are "constructed" in the sense that they are historical products whose character is defined by human convention and generally have somewhat undefined and permeable boundaries. But race differs from national and ethnic categories because the whole idea of race rests on a deep falsehood. This is not true of nations or ethnic groups. There really are nations and ethnic groups, even if people sometimes think about them in incorrect ways. But there are not races. In this book, we will often refer to the groups in question as "racial groups," preferring a more neutral and familiar construction, but we understand these as racialized groups.

12. Tommie Shelby, *We Who Are Dark: The Philosophical Foundations of Black Solidarity* (Cambridge, MA: Harvard University Press, 2005), explores racial solidarity among those regarding themselves as belonging to a racialized group. Linda Martín Alcoff, *Visible Identities: Race, Gender, and the Self* (New York: Oxford University Press, 2005), makes a somewhat similar argument with respect to Latinxs.

13. Ed Morales, *Latinx: The New Force in American Politics and Culture* (New York: Verso, 2018); Paul Ortiz, *An African American and Latinx History of the United States* (New York: Beacon Press, 2018); Catalina (Kathleen) M. deOnís, "What's in an 'x'?: An Exchange about the Politics of 'Latinx,'" *Chiricú Journal: Latina/o Literatures, Arts, and Cultures* 1, no. 2 (2017): 78–91; Erika Lee, *The Making of Asian America: A History* (New York: Simon & Schuster, 2015); Roxanne Dunbar-Ortiz, *An Indigenous Peoples' History of the United States* (New York: Beacon Press, 2015); John Hope Franklin and Evelyn Brooks Higginbotham, *From Slavery to Freedom: A History of African Americans*, 9th ed. (New York: McGraw-Hill, 2011); Tim Wise, *White like Me: Reflections on Race from a Privileged Son*, 3rd ed. (Berkeley, CA: Soft Skull Press, 2011).

14. M. Snyder, "Schools a Target for Critics," *New York Times*, September 24, 1916, 21; Frank Cody, "Americanization Courses in the Public Schools," *English Journal* 7, no. 10 (1918): 615. See also Alice N. Gibbons, "An International-Relations Club," *Social Education* 1, no. 6 (1937): 398–400; William T. Stone, "Education in International Affairs," *Social Education* 1, no. 4 (1937): 271–72; "International Understanding—A Symposium," *New Jersey Educational Review* 3, no. 4 (1930): 19–22.

15. Ian Haney-Lopez, *White by Law: The Legal Construction of Race* (New York: New York University Press, 1996).

16. Lawrence Blum, *High Schools, Race, and America's Future: What Students Can Teach Us about Morality, Diversity, and Community* (Cambridge, MA: Harvard Education Press, 2012); Zoë Burkholder, *Color in the Classroom: How American Schools Taught Race, 1900–1954* (New York: Oxford University Press, 2011). See also Zoë Burkholder, "Education for Citizenship in a Bi-racial Civilization: Black Teachers and the Social Construction of Race, 1929–1954," *Journal of Social History* 46, no. 2 (2012): 335–63; David R. Roediger, *Working toward Whiteness: How America's Immigrants Became White* (New York: Basic Books, 2005); Thomas A. Guglielmo, *White on Arrival: Italians, Race, Color and Power in Chicago, 1890–1940* (New York: Oxford University Press, 2003); Noel Ignatiev, *How the Irish Became White* (New York: Routledge, 1995).

17. Ronald Takaki, *Strangers from a Different Shore: A History of Asian Americans* (Boston: Little, Brown, 1989), 200–205.

18. Leslie Bow, *Partly Colored: Asian Americans and Racial Anomaly in the Segregated South* (New York: New York University Press, 2010), 96–103; James W. Loewen, *The Mississippi Chinese: Between Black and White* (Cambridge, MA: Harvard University Press, 1971), 64–68.

19. Elizabeth Gillespie McRae, *Mothers of Massive Resistance: White Women and the Politics of White Supremacy* (New York: Oxford University Press, 2018), 28–40; Melanie D. Haimes-Bartolf, "The Social Construction of Race and Monacan Education in Amherst County, Virginia, 1908–1965: Monacan Perspectives," *History of Education Quarterly* 47, no. 4 (2007): 389–415.

20. Guadalupe San Miguel Jr., *Brown Not White: School Integration and the Chicano Movement in Houston* (Houston: Texas A&M University Press, 2001).

21. Douglas, *Jim Crow Moves North*, 12–60; Horace Mann Bond, *The Education of the Negro in the American Social Order* (1934; repr., New York: Octagon Books, 1970), 367–90; US Office of Education, *History of Schools for the Colored Population* (1871; repr., New York: Arno Press, 1969), 301–400; Carter G. Woodson, *The*

Education of the Negro Prior to 1861, 2nd ed. (1919; repr., New York: Arno Press, 1968), 229–55; Leon Litwack, *North of Slavery: The Negro in the Free States, 1790–1860* (Chicago: University of Chicago Press, 1961), 113–52.

22. Cody, "Americanization Courses," 620. On the assimilationist goals of public schools, see Jeffrey Mirel, *Patriotic Pluralism: Americanization Education and European Immigrants* (Cambridge, MA: Harvard University Press, 2010); Diana Selig, *Americans All: The Cultural Gifts Movement* (Cambridge, MA: Harvard University Press, 2008). On debates over these assimilationist goals, see Natalia Mehlman Petrzela, *Classroom Wars: Language, Sex, and the Making of Modern Political Culture* (New York: Oxford University Press, 2015); Jonathan Zimmerman, *Whose America: Culture Wars in the Public Schools* (Cambridge, MA: Harvard University Press, 2002). On the complexities of educating nonwhite students in institutions dedicated to citizenship training, see Hilary J. Moss, *Schooling Citizens: The Struggle for African American Education in Antebellum America* (Chicago: University of Chicago Press, 2009); K. Tsianina Lomawaima and Teresa L. McCarty, *To Remain an Indian: Lessons in Democracy from a Century of Native American Education* (New York: Teachers College Press, 2006); James D. Anderson, *The Education of Blacks in the South, 1860–1935* (Chapel Hill: University of North Carolina Press, 1988); Carl E. Kaestle, *Pillars of the Republic: Common Schools and American Society, 1780–1860* (New York: Hill and Wang, 1983).

23. Dunbar-Ortiz, *Indigenous Peoples' History*; Richard R. Valencia, *Chicano Students and the Courts: The Mexican American Legal Struggle for Educational Equality* (New York: New York University Press, 2008); Angela Valenzuela, *Subtractive Schooling: U.S.-Mexican Youth and the Politics of Caring* (Albany: State University of New York Press, 1999); Guadalupe San Miguel Jr. and Richard R. Valencia, "From the Treaty of Guadalupe Hidalgo to *Hopwood*: The Educational Plight and Struggle of Mexican Americans in the Southwest," *Harvard Educational Review* 68, no. 3 (1998): 353–412; David Wallace Adams, *Education for Extinction: American Indians and the Boarding School Experience, 1875–1928* (Lawrence: University Press of Kansas, 1995); Robert Trennert, *The Phoenix Indian School: Forced Assimilation in Arizona, 1891–1935* (Norman: University of Oklahoma Press, 1988); Frederick Hoxie, *The Final Promise: The Campaign to Assimilate the Indians, 1880–1920* (Lincoln: University of Nebraska Press, 1984).

24. Theodora C. Williams, "Is This the Land of Opportunity?," *School Work* (Department of Principals of the Palmetto State Teachers, South Carolina) 1, no. 1 (1935): 19. See also Fairclough, *A Class of Their Own*.

25. "Interracial Cooperation at Work," *Broadcaster* 11, no. 2 (1938): 24, emphasis in original. For more on Black teachers challenging racism, see Burkholder, "Education for Citizenship."

26. Rachel Devlin, *A Girl Stands at the Door: The Generation of Young Women Who Desegregated America's Schools* (New York: Basic Books, 2018); Vanessa Siddle Walker, *The Lost Education of Horace Tate: Uncovering the Hidden Heroes Who Fought for Justice in Schools* (New York: New Press, 2018); Adrienne Berard, *Water Tossing Boulders: How a Family of Chinese Immigrants Led the First Fight to Desegregate in the Jim Crow South* (Boston: Beacon Press, 2016); Jon Hale, *The Freedom Schools: Student Activists in the Mississippi Civil Rights Movement* (New

York: Columbia University Press, 2016); Dionne Danns, Michelle A. Purdy, and Christopher M. Span, eds., *Using Past as Prologue: Contemporary Perspectives on African American Educational History* (Charlotte, NC: Information Age Publishing, 2015); Mario T. Garcia and Sal Castro, *Blowout! Sal Castro and the Chicano Struggle for Educational Justice* (Chapel Hill: University of North Carolina Press, 2011); Guadalupe San Miguel, *Chicana/o Struggles for Education: Activism in the Community* (Houston: Texas A&M University Press, 2013); Lomawaima and McCarty, *To Remain an Indian*; Brenda J. Child, *Boarding School Seasons: American Indian Families, 1900–1940* (Lincoln: University of Nebraska Press, 2000); Adams, *Education for Extinction*.

27. Brown v. Board of Education of Topeka, 347 U.S. 483 (1954).

CHAPTER ONE

1. Horace Mann, "Tenth Annual Report to the Massachusetts Board of Education, 1846," reproduced in *The School in the United States: A Documentary History*, ed. James W. Fraser, 4th ed. (New York: Routledge, 2019), 38–42. See also Carl F. Kaestle, *Pillars of the Republic: Common Schools and American Society, 1780–1860* (New York: Hill and Wang, 1983); David B. Tyack, *The One Best System: A History of American Urban Education* (Cambridge, MA: Harvard University Press, 1974).

2. For quote, see James D. Anderson, "Race-Conscious Educational Policies versus a 'Color-Blind Constitution': A Historical Perspective," *Educational Researcher* 36, no. 5 (2007): 250. See also Hilary J. Moss, *Schooling Citizens: The Struggle for African American Education in Antebellum America* (Chicago: University of Chicago Press, 2009); Edmund S. Morgan, *American Slavery, American Freedom: The Ordeal of Colonial Virginia* (1975; repr., New York: W. W. Norton, 1995), 4; Gunnar Myrdal, *An American Dilemma: The Negro Problem and Modern Democracy* (1944; repr., New York: Harper and Row, 1962), lxix.

3. Zoë Burkholder, *Color in the Classroom: How American Schools Taught Race, 1900–1954* (New York: Oxford University Press, 2011); Vernon J. Williams Jr., *The Social Sciences and Theories of Race* (Urbana: University of Illinois Press, 2006), 16–47; William Fairley, "Ancient History in the Secondary School," *History Teacher's Magazine* 1, no. 1 (1909): 7–8.

4. Zevi Gutfreund, *Speaking American: Language Education and Citizenship in Twentieth-Century Los Angeles* (Norman: University of Oklahoma Press, 2019); David G. García, *Strategies of Segregation: Race, Residence, and the Struggle for Educational Equality* (Oakland: University of California Press, 2018); Linda Tuhiwai Smith, Eve Tuck, and K. Wayne Yang, *Indigenous and Decolonizing Studies in Education* (New York: Routledge, 2018); Vanessa Siddle Walker, *The Lost Education of Horace Tate: Uncovering the Hidden Heroes Who Fought for Justice in Schools* (New York: New Press, 2018); Wayne Au, Anthony L. Brown, and Delores Calderón, *The Multicultural Roots of U.S. Curriculum: Communities of Color and Official Knowledge in Education* (New York: Teachers College Press, 2016); Dionne Danns, Michelle A. Purdy, and Christopher M. Span, *Using the Past as Prologue: Contemporary Perspectives on African American Educational History* (Charlotte: Information Age Publishing, 2015); KuuNUx TeeRIt Kroupa, "Educa-

tion as Arikara Spiritual Renewal and Cultural Evolution," *History of Education Quarterly* 54, no. 3 (2014): 303–22; Zeus Leonardo and W. Norton Grubb, *Education and Racism: A Primer on Issues and Dilemmas* (New York: Routledge, 2014), 75–102; Donald Warren, "American Indian Histories as Education History," *History of Education Quarterly* 54, no. 3 (2014): 255–85; Sonya Douglass Horsford, *Learning in a Burning House: Educational Inequality, Ideology, and (Dis)Integration* (New York: Teachers College Press, 2011); K. Tsianina Lomawaima and Teresa L. McCarty, *To Remain an Indian: Lessons in Democracy from a Century of Native American Education* (New York: Teachers College Press, 2006), 16–42; William H. Watkins, *The White Architects of Black Education: Ideology and Power in America, 1865–1954* (New York: Teachers College Press, 2001), 24–42; Steven Selden, *Inheriting Shame: The Story of Eugenics and Racism in America* (New York: Teachers College Press, 1999); James D. Anderson, *The Education of Blacks in the South, 1860–1935* (Chapel Hill: University of North Carolina Press, 1988); Horace Mann Bond, *The Education of the Negro in the American Social Order* (1934; repr., New York: Octagon Books, 1970), 316–36.

5. Burkholder, *Color in the Classroom*. See also Ibram X. Kendi, *Stamped from the Beginning: The Definitive History of Racist Ideas in America* (New York: Nation Books, 2016), 161–262; George M. Fredrickson, *Racism: A Short History*, rev. ed. (2002; repr., Princeton, NJ: Princeton University Press, 2015), 49–96; Audrey Smedley and Brian D. Smedley, *Race in North America: Origin and Evolution of a Worldview*, 4th ed. (Boulder, CO: Westview Press, 2012), 189–250; Ann Gibson Winfield, *Eugenics and Education in America: Institutionalized Racism and the Implications of History, Ideology, and Memory* (New York: Peter Lang, 2007), 45–62; John P. Jackson Jr. and Nadine M. Weidman, *Race, Racism, and Science: Social Impact and Interaction* (New Brunswick, NJ: Rutgers University Press, 2006), 29–60; Thomas F. Gossett, *Race: The History of an Idea in America*, new ed. (New York: Oxford University Press, 1997), 54–83, 253–386.

6. Kevin Gaines, "Whose Integration Was It?," *Journal of American History* 91, no. 1 (2004): 19–20; Myrdal, *An American Dilemma*, 100. See also Mark Newman, *Black Nationalism in American History: From the Nineteenth Century to the Million Man March* (Edinburgh: Edinburgh University Press, 2018); Ashley D. Farmer, *Remaking Black Power: How Black Women Transformed an Era* (Chapel Hill: University of North Carolina Press, 2017); Charles W. Mills, *Black Rights/White Wrongs: The Critique of Racial Liberalism* (New York: Oxford University Press, 2017); Tommie Shelby, *Dark Ghettos: Injustice, Dissent, and Reform* (Cambridge, MA: Harvard University Press, 2016); Manning Marable, *Race, Reform, and Rebellion: The Second Reconstruction and Beyond in Black America, 1945–2006*, 3rd ed. (Jackson: University Press of Mississippi, 2007); Derrick Bell, *Silent Covenants: Brown v. Board of Education and the Unfulfilled Hopes for Racial Reform* (New York: Oxford University Press, 2004); Roy L. Brooks, *Integration or Separation: A Strategy for Racial Equality* (Cambridge, MA: Harvard University Press, 1996); Kevin K. Gaines, *Uplifting the Race: Black Leadership, Politics, and Culture in the Twentieth Century* (Chapel Hill: University of North Carolina Press, 1996); Evelyn Brooks Higginbotham, *Righteous Discontent: The Women's Movement in the Black Baptist Church, 1880–1920*, rev. ed. (Cambridge, MA: Harvard University Press, 1994).

7. Jelani M. Favors, *Shelter in a Time of Storm: How Black Colleges Fostered Generations of Leadership and Activism* (Chapel Hill: University of North Carolina Press, 2019); Joy Ann Williamson, *Jim Crow Campus: Higher Education and the Struggle for a New Southern Social Order* (New York: Teachers College Press, 2018); Joel Spring, *Deculturalization and the Struggle for Equality: A Brief History of the Education of Dominated Cultures in the United States,* 8th ed. (New York: Routledge, 2016); Au, Brown, and Calderón, *Multicultural Roots of U.S. Curriculum,* 1–17.

8. Public schools were not the only US institution designed to perpetuate racism. As historians have long noted, the founding and development of the United States is based on a particular concept of freedom that was racialized from the very beginning. Morgan, *American Slavery, American Freedom,* 4; Myrdal, *An American Dilemma,* lxix.

9. Frederick Douglass, *My Bondage, My Freedom* (1855; repr., Mineola, NY: Dover Publications, 1969), 79–80; Frederick Douglass, "Equal Suffrage or Equal School Rights?," *Douglass' Monthly,* March 1859, 37. See also David W. Blight, *Frederick Douglass: Prophet of Freedom* (New York: Simon & Schuster, 2018); Nichols Buccola, *The Political Thought of Frederick Douglass: In Pursuit of American Liberty* (New York: New York University Press, 2012); James Oakes, *The Radical and the Republican: Frederick Douglass, Abraham Lincoln, and the Triumph of Antislavery Politics* (New York: W. W. Norton, 2008); Margaret Kohn, "Frederick Douglass's Master-Slave Dialectic," *Journal of Politics* 67, no. 2 (May 2005): 497–514; Scott C. Williamson, *The Narrative Life: The Moral and Religious Life of Frederick Douglass* (Macon, GA: Mercer University Press, 2002), 136–37; William S. McFeely, *Frederick Douglass,* reprint ed. (New York: W. W. Norton, 1995).

10. Adam Fairclough, *Teaching Equality: Black Schools in the Age of Jim Crow* (Athens: University of Georgia Press, 2001), 3. See also Manisha Sinha, *The Slave's Cause: A History of Abolition* (New Haven, CT: Yale University Press, 2016), 65–96; Ira Berlin, *The Long Emancipation: The Demise of Slavery in the United States* (Cambridge, MA: Harvard University Press, 2015); Patrick Rael, *Eighty-Eight Years: The Long Death of Slavery in the United States, 1777–1865* (Athens: University of Georgia Press, 2015), 163–97; David Brion Davis, *The Problem of Slavery in the Age of Emancipation* (New York: Alfred A. Knopf, 2014), xi–13; Hugh Davis, *We Shall Be Satisfied with Nothing Less: The African American Struggle for Equal Rights in the North during Reconstruction* (Ithaca, NY: Cornell University Press, 2011), 72–96; Patrick Rael, *Black Identity and Black Protest in the Antebellum North* (Chapel Hill: University of North Carolina Press, 2002), 1–5; Carleton Mabee, *Black Freedom: The Nonviolent Abolitionists from 1830 through the Civil War* (New York: Macmillan, 1970), 139–84; Leon Litwack, *North of Slavery: The Negro in the Free States, 1790–1860* (Chicago: University of Chicago Press, 1961), 113–52.

11. Adam Fairclough, *A Class of Their Own: Black Teachers in the Segregated South* (Cambridge, MA: Harvard University Press, 2007), 99–131; Ronald E. Butchart, *Schooling the Freed People: Teaching, Learning, and the Struggle for Black Freedom, 1861–1876* (Chapel Hill: University of North Carolina Press, 2010), 1–16. See also Christopher M. Span, *From Cotton Field to Schoolhouse: African American Education in Mississippi, 1862–1975* (Chapel Hill: University of North Carolina

Press, 2009); Heather Andrea Williams, *Self-Taught: African American Education in Slavery and Freedom* (Chapel Hill: University of North Carolina Press, 2005); Fairclough, *Teaching Equality*; Anderson, *Education of Blacks in the South*; Leon F. Litwack, *Been in the Storm So Long: The Aftermath of Slavery* (New York: Vintage Books, 1980).

12. Fredrickson, *Racism*; C. Vann Woodward, *The Strange Career of Jim Crow*, commemorative ed. (1955; repr., New York: Oxford University Press, 2002).

13. Anderson, *Education of Blacks in the South*.

14. Anderson, *Education of Blacks in the South*.

15. Booker T. Washington, *The Future of the American Negro* (Boston: Small, Maynard, 1902), 27–30. For a critique of industrial education for Black students, see W. E. B. Du Bois, *The Souls of Black Folk* (1903; repr., New York: Dover Publications, 1994), 33–46. See also Watkins, *White Architects of Black Education*; Anderson, *Education of Blacks in the South*.

16. W. E. B. Du Bois, "Editorial," *Crisis* 10, no. 3 (1915): 132.

17. "Education," *Crisis* 1, no. 3 (1911): 7.

18. Stephanie Deutsch, *You Need a Schoolhouse: Booker T. Washington, Julius Rosenwald, and the Building of Schools for the Segregated South* (Evanston, IL: Northwestern University Press, 2011); Butchart, *Schooling the Freed People*; Mary S. Hoffschwelle, *The Rosenwald Schools of the American South* (Gainesville: University of Florida Press, 2006); Peter M. Ascoli, *Julius Rosenwald: The Man Who Built Sears, Roebuck and Advanced the Cause of Black Education in the South* (Bloomington: Indiana University Press, 2006); Fairclough, *A Class of Their Own*; Watkins, *White Architects of Black Education*; Anderson, *Education of Blacks in the South*; Bond, *Education of the Negro*.

19. Walker, *Lost Education of Horace Tate*; Fairclough, *A Class of Their Own*; Vanessa Siddle Walker, *To Their Highest Potential: An African American School Community in the Segregated South* (Chapel Hill: University of North Carolina Press, 1996); David S. Cecelski, *Along Freedom Road: Hyde County, North Carolina, and the Fate of Black Schools in the South* (Chapel Hill: University of North Carolina Press, 1994); "The Spirit of the Teacher," *Arkansas State Teachers' Association Journal* 2, no. 1 (1929): 3–4.

20. Kristina DuRocher, *Raising Racists: The Socialization of White Children in the Jim Crow South* (Lexington: University Press of Kentucky, 2011), 35–92; Jennifer Ritterhouse, *Growing Up Jim Crow: How Black and White Southern Children Learned Race* (Chapel Hill: University of North Carolina Press, 2006), 55–107; Fredrickson, *Racism*; Mark V. Tushnet, *The NAACP's Legal Strategy against Segregated Education, 1925–1950* (Chapel Hill: University of North Carolina Press, 1987); Woodward, *Strange Career of Jim Crow*.

21. Moss, *Schooling Citizens*, 4; Edmund Fuller, *Prudence Crandall: An Incident of Racism in Nineteenth-Century Connecticut* (Middletown, CT: Wesleyan University Press, 1971).

22. The history of separate schools for Blacks in the North is well documented in Davison M. Douglas, *Jim Crow Moves North: The Battle over Northern School Segregation, 1865–1941* (New York: Cambridge University Press, 2005), 20–31; See also Paul J. Polgar, "'To Raise Them to an Equal Participation': Early National Abolitionism, Gradual Emancipation, and the Promise of African American Cit-

izenship," *Journal of the Early Republic* 31, no. 2 (Summer 2011): 229–58; Moss, *Schooling Citizens*, 10–11; James Brewer Stewart, "The Emergence of Racial Modernity and the Rise of the White North, 1790–1840," in *African American Activism before the Civil War: The Freedom Struggle in the Antebellum North*, ed. Patrick Rael (New York: Routledge, 2008), 220–49; David Brion Davis, *The Problem of Slavery in the Age of Revolution, 1770–1823*, 2nd ed. (1975; repr., New York: Oxford University Press, 1999), 15–21; William M. Banks, *Black Intellectuals: Race and Responsibility in American Life* (New York: W. W. Norton, 1997), 25–28; John L. Rury, "The New York African Free School, 1827–1836: Conflict over Community Control of Black Education," *Phylon* 44, no. 3 (1983): 187–97.

23. U.S. Const. amend. XIV, § 1.

24. Judy Jolley Mohraz, *The Separate Problem: Case Studies of Black Education in the North, 1900–1930* (Westport, CT: Greenwood Press, 1979); Vincent P. Franklin, *The Education of Black Philadelphia: The Social and Educational History of a Minority Community, 1900–1950* (Philadelphia: University of Pennsylvania Press, 1979); Marion M. Thompson Wright, *The Education of Negroes in New Jersey* (1941; repr., New York: Arno Press and the New York Times, 1971); Bond, *Education of the Negro*, 316–36; US Office of Education, *History of Schools for the Colored Population* (1871; repr., New York: Arno Press, 1969), 301–400; Carter G. Woodson, *The Education of the Negro Prior to 1861*, 2nd ed. (1919; repr., New York: Arno Press, 1968); W. E. B. Du Bois, *The Philadelphia Negro: A Social Study* (1899; repr., New York: Benjamin Blom, 1967); Augustus Granville Dill, "The Report of the Chicago Commission on Race Relations," *Crisis* 25, no. 3 (1923): 111–12; Chicago Commission on Race Relations, *The Negro in Chicago* (Chicago: University of Chicago Press, 1922), 241–42; "A Segregation of Public Schools," *Chicago Defender*, February 3, 1912, 5; "Negro Fighting Color Line," *Los Angeles Times*, June 17, 1911, I12.

25. "Burning a School House," *New York Times*, February 26, 1881, 2. See also "A Race War in New Jersey," *Atlanta Daily Constitution*, March 5, 1881, 4.

26. Wright, *Education of Negroes in New Jersey*, 160–71.

27. For the first quote see "The Fair Haven School Trouble," *New York Times*, March 31, 1881, 5. See also Wright, *Education of Negroes in New Jersey*, 163–71, which documents the local New Jersey media coverage of this event. For the second quote, see Laws of New Jersey, 1881, 186, as cited in Wright, *Education of Negroes in New Jersey*, 167. See also "New-Jersey Law Making: The Fair Haven School Bill," *New York Times*, March 18, 1881, 5.

28. Douglas, *Jim Crow Moves North*, 123–218.

29. Ira Berlin, *The Making of African America: The Four Great Migrations* (New York: Penguin, 2010), 152–85; Isabel Wilkerson, *The Warmth of Other Suns: The Epic Story of America's Great Migration* (New York: Vintage Books, 2010); Douglas, *Jim Crow Moves North*; David M. Ment, "Racial Segregation in the Schools of New England and New York, 1840–1940" (PhD diss., Columbia University, 1975), 201–33; Franklin, *Education of Black Philadelphia*, 12–24; August Meier and Elliott M. Rudwick, "Early Boycotts of Segregated Schools: The Case of Springfield, Ohio, 1922–23," *American Quarterly* 20, no. 4 (Winter 1968): 774–58; August Meier and Elliott M. Rudwick, "Early Boycotts of Segregated Schools: The East Orange, New Jersey, Experience, 1899–1906," *History of Education Quarterly* 7,

no. 1 (Spring 1967): 22–35; August Meier and Elliott M. Rudwick, "Early Boycotts of Segregated Schools: The Alton, Illinois, Case, 1897–1908," *Journal of Negro Education* 36, no. 4 (Autumn 1967): 394–402; William R. Ming Jr., "The Elimination of Segregation in the Public Schools of the North and West," *Journal of Negro Education* 21, no. 3 (Summer 1952): 265–75; W. E. B. Du Bois, "The Migration of Negroes," *Crisis* 14, no. 2 (1917): 63–66.

30. For quote, see *Annual Report of the State Superintendent, 1880–1881*, 70, as cited in Wright, *Education of Negroes in New Jersey*, 170. See also "Fair Haven's Colored School," *New York Times*, November 19, 1881, 5; "Fair Haven School Troubles Over," *New York Times*, November 17, 1881, 5; "The Fair Haven School Trouble: The Excitement between the White and Colored People Still Kept Up," *New York Times*, March 31, 1881, 5; "New-Jersey Law-Making: The Fair Haven School Bill," *New York Times*, March 18, 1881, 5; "The Fair Haven Colored People," *New York Times*, March 18, 1881, 5; "Notes on Education," *Christian Recorder*, March 17, 1881; "The Fair Haven School Trouble: Stormy Meeting of White and Colored People: Negroes Obstinate," *New York Times*, March 16, 1881, 5; "A Race War in New Jersey: Endeavoring to Force Colored Scholars into Schools with White Children," *Daily Constitution*, March 5, 1881, 4; "The Following Relates to Fair Haven, NJ," *Christian Recorder*, March 3, 1881; "Race Trouble in New Jersey: The Antagonism on the School Question," *New York Times*, March 1, 1881, 5; "Fair Haven's Colored School," *New York Times*, February 27, 1881, 2; "School House Burned at Fair Haven," *New York Tribune*, February 26, 1881, 2; "Color Foolishness," *Hartford Daily Courant*, February 26, 1881, 3; "Burning a School-House: Discontented Colored People in a New-Jersey Town," *New York Times*, February 26, 1881, 2.

31. Charles S. Johnson, *Backgrounds to Patterns of Negro Segregation* (1934; repr., New York: Thomas Y. Crowell, 1970), 185; W. E. B. DuBois, "Does the Negro Need Separate Schools?," *Journal of Negro Education* 4, no. 3 (Jul. 1935): 328–35; Charles H. Thompson, "The Negro Separate School," *Crisis* 42, no. 8 (1935): 230–32, 242; Horace Mann Bond, "The Only Way to Keep Public Schools Equal Is to Keep Them Mixed," *Afro-American*, March 5, 1932, 18; Lester B. Granger, "Race Relations and the School System," *Opportunity* 3, no. 35 (1925): 327–29. This debate is covered in Douglas, *Jim Crow Moves North*, 167–218.

32. Christina Collins, *Ethnically Qualified: Race, Merit, and the Selection of Urban Teachers, 1920–1980* (New York: Teachers College Press, 2011), 13–21; Douglas, *Jim Crow Moves North*, 174–77; Jack Dougherty, *More Than One Struggle: The Evolution of Black School Reform in Milwaukee* (Chapel Hill: University of North Carolina Press, 2004), 9–33; Jeffrey Mirel, *The Rise and Fall of an Urban School System: Detroit, 1907–81*, 2nd ed. (Ann Arbor: University of Michigan Press, 1999), 62–63, 186–88; David M. Katzman, *Before the Ghetto: Black Detroit in the Nineteenth Century* (Urbana: University of Illinois Press, 1933), 84–90; Ambrose Caliver, "Some Problems in the Education and Placement of Negro Teachers," *Journal of Negro Education* 4, no. 1 (1935): 99–112; "From the Press of the Nation," *Crisis* 42, no. 4 (1935): 115; "Along the NAACP Battlefront," *Crisis* 42, no. 2 (1935): 55–56; George Streator, "On to Asbury Park!," *Crisis* 41, no. 5 (1934): 133–34; Rayford W. Logan, "Educational Segregation in the North," *Journal of Negro Education* 2, no. 1 (1933): 65–67; "The Results of Barring Negro Teachers," *Crisis*

40, no. 9 (1933): 208; Report of a Survey by the Interracial Committee of the New Jersey Conference of Social Work, *The Negro in New Jersey* (Trenton: New Jersey State Department of Institutions and Agencies, 1932), 38–40. Official records were not kept by the school district, but one observer estimates there were between fifteen and twenty Black teachers working in the Chicago Public Schools in 1911, where, "as a rule, they are in schools where the majority of the children are Negroes." See "Employment of Colored Women in Chicago," *Crisis* 1, no. 3 (1911): 24–25. A noteworthy exception comes from New York City in 1918, where a Black man served as principal of P.S. 79 on the East Side, where the teachers and students were mostly white. See John Purroy Mitchel, "The Public Schools of New York," *Crisis* 14, no. 3 (1917): 132.

33. Patricia Sullivan, *Lift Every Voice: The NAACP and the Making of the Civil Rights Movement* (New York: New Press, 2009), 333–83; Richard Kluger, *Simple Justice: The History of Brown v. Board of Education and Black America's Struggle for Equality* (1976; repr., New York: Vintage Books, 2004); James T. Patterson, *Brown v. Board of Education: A Civil Rights Milestone and Its Troubled Legacy* (New York: Oxford University Press, 2001), 21–45; Tushnet, *NAACP's Legal Strategy.*

34. J. Harvie Wilkinson, *From Brown to Bakke: The Supreme Court and School Integration, 1954–1978* (New York: Oxford University Press, 1975), 1–60.

35. Charles S. Johnson and Associates, *To Stem This Tide: A Survey of Racial Tension Areas in the United States* (1943; repr., New York: AMS Press, 1969), 106–7. See also Linda Hervieux, *Forgotten: The Untold Story of D-Day's Black Heroes, at Home and at War* (New York: Harper Collins, 2015); William P. Jones, *The March on Washington: Jobs, Freedom, and the Forgotten History of Civil Rights* (New York: W. W. Norton, 2013); Cheryl Mullenback, *Double Victory: How African American Women Broke Race and Gender Barriers to Help Win World War II* (Chicago: Chicago Review Press, 2013); Kevin M. Kruse and Stephen Tuck, eds., *Fog of War: The Second World War and the Civil Rights Movement* (New York: Oxford University Press, 2012); Neil A. Wynn, *The African American Experience during World War II* (New York: Rowman & Littlefield, 2010); Lauren Rebecca Sklaroff, *Black Culture and the New Deal: The Quest for Civil Rights in the Roosevelt Era* (Chapel Hill: University of North Carolina, 2009); Adam Fairclough, *Better Day Coming: Blacks and Equality, 1890–2000* (New York: Viking Press, 2001), 181–201; Thomas Borstelmann, *The Cold War and the Color Line: American Race Relations in the Global Arena* (Cambridge, MA: Harvard University Press, 2001), 27–53; Ronald Takaki, *Double Victory: A Multicultural History of America in World War II* (New York: Little, Brown, 2000).

36. Thurgood Marshall, "An Evaluation of Recent Efforts to Achieve Racial Integration in Education through Resort to the Courts," *Journal of Negro Education* 21 (Summer 1952): 322.

37. Kluger, *Simple Justice*; Patterson, *Brown v. Board of Education*; Marshall, "Evaluation of Recent Efforts," 326.

38. Brown v. Board of Education of Topeka, 347 U.S. 483 (1954).

39. *Brown,* 347 U.S. 483.

40. Claudio Saunt, *Unworthy Republic: The Dispossession of Native Americans and the Road to Indian Territory* (New York: W. W. Norton, 2020), 3–26; Margaret A. Nash, "Entangled Pasts: Land-Grant Colleges and American Indian Disposses-

sion," *History of Education Quarterly* 59, no. 4 (2019): 437–67; Khalil Anthony Johnson Jr., "Recruited to Teach the Indians: An African American Genealogy of Navajo Nation Boarding Schools," *Journal of American Indian Education* 57, no. 1 (2018): 154–76; David E. Wilkins and Heidi Kiiwetinepinesiik Stark, *American Indian Politics and the American Political System*, 4th ed. (New York: Rowman & Littlefield, 2018), 9–21; Jaskiran K. Dhillon, *Prairie Rising: Indigenous Youth, Decolonization, and the Politics of Intervention* (Toronto: University of Toronto Press, 2017), 93; Nancy Beadie, Joy Williamson-Lott, Michael Bowman, Teresa Frizell, Gonzalo Guzman, Jisoo Hyun, Joanna Johnson, Kathryn Nicholas, Lani Phillips, Rebecca Wellington, and La'akea Yoshida, "Gateways to the West, Part I: Education in the Shaping of the West," *History of Education Quarterly* 56, no. 3 (2016): 418–44; Patrick Wolfe, "Settler Colonialism and the Elimination of the Native," *Journal of Genocide Research* 8, no. 4 (2006): 387–409; David Tyack, Thomas James, and Aaron Benavot, *Law and the Shaping of Public Education, 1785–1954* (Madison: University of Wisconsin Press, 1987), 20–42.

41. On the term *indigenous self-education*, see K. Tsianina Lomawaima, "History without Silos, Ignorance Versus Knowledge, Education beyond Schools," *History of Education Quarterly* 54, no. 3 (2014): 349–55. See also Christina Snyder, "The Rise and Fall and Rise of Civilizations: Indian Intellectual Culture during the Removal Era," *Journal of American History* 104, no. 2 (2017): 386–409; Christina Snyder, *Great Crossings: Indians, Settlers, and Slaves in the Age of Jackson* (Oxford: Oxford University Press, 2017), 18–40, 70–98; Rowan Faye Steineker, "'Fully Equal to That of Any Children': Experimental Creek Education in the Antebellum Era," *History of Education Quarterly* 56, no. 2 (2016): 273–300; Rowan Faye Steineker, "The Struggle for Schools: Education, Race, and Sovereignty in the Creek Nation, 1820–1907" (PhD diss., University of Oklahoma, 2016); Andrea Lawrence, "Epic Learning in an Indian Pueblo: A Framework for Studying Multigenerational Learning in the History of Education," *History of Education Quarterly* 54, no. 3 (2014): 286–302; Teri L. Castelow, "'Creating an Educational Interest': Sophia Sawyer, Teacher of the Cherokee," in *Chartered Schools: Two Hundred Years of Independent Academies In the United States, 1727–1925*, ed. Nancy Beadie and Kim Tolley (New York: RoutledgeFalmer, 2002), 186–210; Devon A. Mihesuah, *Cultivating the Rosebuds: The Education of Women at the Cherokee Female Seminary, 1851–1909* (Urbana: University of Illinois Press, 1993); Robert F. Berkhofer Jr., *Salvation and the Savage: An Analysis of Protestant Missions and American Indian Response, 1787–1862* (Lexington: University of Kentucky Press, 1965), 16–43.

42. Snyder, *Great Crossings*, 272–96; Natalie Panther, "'To Make Us Independent': The Education of Young Men at the Cherokee Male Seminary, 1851–1910" (PhD diss., Oklahoma State University, 2013); Lomawaima and McCarty, *To Remain an Indian*, 114–15; Amanda J. Cobb, *Listening to Our Grandmothers' Stories: The Bloomfield Academy for Chicasaw Females, 1852–1949* (Lincoln: University of Nebraska Press, 2000), 40–42; Mihesuah, *Cultivating the Rosebuds*, 1–17.

43. Steineker, "The Struggle for Schools"; James Parins, *Literacy and Intellectual Life in the Cherokee Nation, 1820–1906* (Norman: University of Oklahoma Press, 2013); Ismael Abu-Saad and Duane Champagne, eds., *Indigenous Education and Empowerment: International Perspectives* (Lanham, MD: AltaMira Press, 2006).

44. Andrés Reséndez, *The Other Slavery: The Uncovered Story of Indian Enslavement in America* (New York: Houghton Mifflin, 2016); Benjamin Madley, *An American Genocide: The United States and the California Indian Catastrophe* (New Haven, CT: Yale University Press, 2016); Andrea Smith, *Conquest: Sexual Violence and American Indian Genocide* (Durham, NC: Duke University Press, 2015), 35–54; Roxanne Dunbar-Ortiz, *An Indigenous People's History of the United States* (Boston: Beacon Press, 2014); Ward Churchill, *Kill the Indian, Save the Man: The Genocidal Impact of American Indian Residential Schools* (San Francisco: City Lights Publisher, 2004); Ward Churchill, *A Little Matter of Genocide: Holocaust and Denial in the Americas, 1492–Present* (San Francisco: City Lights Publisher, 2001); Frederick Hoxie, *The Final Promise: The Campaign to Assimilate the Indians, 1880–1920* (Lincoln: University of Nebraska Press, 2001); Margaret Jacobs, *White Mother to a Dark Race: Settler Colonialism, Maternalism, and the Removal of Indigenous Children in the American West and Australia, 1880–1940* (Lincoln: University of Nebraska Press, 2011); David E. Stannard, *American Holocaust: The Conquest of the New World* (New York: Oxford University Press, 1992).

45. Dunbar-Ortiz, *Indigenous Peoples' History*, 133–61; Lomawaima and McCarty, *To Remain an Indian*, 1–15; David Wallace Adams, *Education for Extinction: American Indians and the Boarding School Experience, 1875–1928* (Lawrence: University Press of Kansas, 1995), 5–16; Robert Trennert, *The Phoenix Indian School: Forced Assimilation in Arizona, 1891–1935* (Norman: University of Oklahoma Press, 1988); Hoxie, *The Final Promise*. This kind of forced assimilation through formal schooling was by no means limited to Native Americans but was instead part of global American imperialism through the mid-twentieth century. See Clif Stratton, *Education for Empire: American Schools, Race, and the Paths of Good Citizenship* (Berkeley: University of California Press, 2016); John R. Gram, *Education at the Edge of Empire: Negotiating Pueblo Identity in New Mexico's Indian Boarding Schools* (Seattle: University of Washington Press, 2015); Jonathan Zimmerman, *Innocents Abroad: American Teachers in the American Century* (Cambridge, MA: Harvard University Press, 2006).

46. "Indians Becoming Civilized," *New York Times*, April 30, 1894, 5; Carl Schurz, "Present Aspects of the Indian Problem," *North American Review* 133, no. 296 (Jul. 1881): 7, quoted in Adams, *Education for Extinction*, 15.

47. Jacqueline Fear-Segal, *White Man's Club: Schools, Race, and the Struggle of Indian Acculturation* (Lincoln: University of Nebraska Press, 2009), 76–100. See also Sarah M. Bennison, "'Education for Civilization': Denominational Consensus and Missionary Education on the Rosebud Reservation, 1870–1920" (PhD diss., New York University, 2006); Ross Alexander Enochs, *The Jesuit Mission to the Lakota Sioux: Pastoral Theology and Ministry, 1886–1945* (Kansas City: Sheed & Ward, 1996); Carol Devens, "'If We Get the Girls, We Get the Race': Missionary Education of Native American Girls," *Journal of World History* 3, no. 2 (1992): 219–37; Francis Paul Prucha, "Two Roads to Conversion: Protestant and Catholic Missionaries in the Pacific Northwest," *Pacific Northwest Quarterly* 79, no. 4 (1988): 130–37; Berkhofer, *Salvation and the Savage*.

48. *Annual Report of the Commissioner of Indian Affairs*, 1878, 649, as cited in Adams, *Education for Extinction*, 29. See also Lomawaima and McCarty, *To Remain an Indian*, 45–48; Hoxie, *The Final Promise*.

49. *Annual Report of the Commissioner of Indian Affairs*, 1881, 144, as cited in Adams, *Education for Extinction*, 31. See also Lomawaima and McCarty, *To Remain an Indian*, 47–48; Brenda J. Child, *Boarding School Seasons: American Indian Families, 1900 1940* (Lincoln: University of Nebraska Press, 2000), 9–42.

50. Thomas Wildcat Alford, *Civilization, as Told to Florence Drake* (1936; repr., Norman: University of Oklahoma Press, 1979), 79. See also Cathleen D. Cahill, *Federal Fathers and Mothers: A Social History of the United States Indian Service, 1869–1933* (Chapel Hill: University of North Carolina Press, 2011), 110; Lomawaima and McCarty, *To Remain an Indian*, 77–81; Michael C. Coleman, *American Indian Children at School, 1850–1930* (Jackson: University Press of Mississippi, 1993), 29–30.

51. Harriet Beecher Stowe, "The Indians at St. Augustine," *Christian Union*, April 18, 1877, reprinted in Henry Richard Pratt, *Battlefield and Classroom: Four Decades with the American Indian* (1964; repr., New Haven, CT: Yale University Press, 2003), 162. See also Donald A. Grinde Jr., "Taking the Indian Out of the Indian: U.S. Policies of Ethnocide through Education," *Wicazo Sa Review* 19, no. 2 (2004): 25–32.

52. Adams, *Education for Extinction*, 44–49; Pratt, *Battlefield and Classroom*, 154–204; Donal F. Lindsey, *Indians at Hampton Institute, 1877–1923* (Urbana: University of Illinois Press, 1994).

53. Jaqueline Fear-Segal and Susan D. Rose, *Carlisle Indian Industrial School: Indigenous Histories, Memories, and Reclamations* (Lincoln: University of Nebraska Press, 2016); Adams, *Education for Extinction*, 44–49.

54. Records of the Carlisle Indian School, student record cards, box 35, Bureau of Indian Affairs, RG 75, National Archives, as cited in Fear-Segal, *White Man's Club*, 163. See also James F. Brooks, ed., *Confounding the Color Line: The Indian-Black Experience in North America* (Lincoln: University of Nebraska Press, 2002); Jack D. Forbes, *Africans and Native Americans: The Language of Race and the Evolution of Red-Black Peoples*, 2nd ed. (Urbana: University of Illinois Press, 1993).

55. Fear-Segal, *White Man's Club*, 163–64. See also Robert A. Trennert, "Educating Indian Girls at Nonreservation Boarding Schools, 1878–1920," *Western Historical Quarterly* 13, no. 3 (1982): 271–90.

56. Lomawaima and McCarty, *To Remain an Indian*, 47–48; Adams, *Education for Extinction*, 55–57.

57. Adams, *Education for Extinction*, 59.

58. Denise K. Lajimodiere, *Stringing Rosaries: The History, the Unforgivable, and the Healing of Northern Plains American Indian Boarding School Survivors* (Fargo: North Dakota State University Press, 2019); Jacqueline Emery, *Recovering Native American Writings in the Boarding School Press* (Lincoln: University of Nebraska Press, 2017); Fear-Segal, *White Man's Club*, 255–98; Child, *Boarding School Seasons*, 87–95; Adams, *Education for Extinction*, 209–38; Clyde Ellis, *To Change Them Forever: Indian Education at the Rainy Mountain Boarding School, 1893–1920* (Norman: University of Oklahoma Press, 1996). See also David H. Dejong, "'Unless They Are Kept Alive': Federal Indian Schools and Student Health, 1878–1918," *American Indian Quarterly* 31, no. 2 (2007): 256–82.

59. Farina King, *The Earth Memory Compass: Diné Landscapes and Education in the Twentieth Century* (Lawrence: University Press of Kansas, 2018), 4–11; Minnie Braithwaite Jenkins, *Girl from Williamsburg* (Richmond, VA: Dietz Press, 1951),

283. See also Jessica Enoch, "Resisting the Script of Indian Education: Zitkala Ša and the Carlisle Indian School," *College English* 65, no. 2 (2002): 117–41; K. Tsianina Lomawaima, *They Called It Prairie Light: The Story of Chilocco Indian School* (Lincoln: University of Nebraska Press, 1994), 121.

60. Kim Cary Warren, *The Quest for Citizenship: African American and Native American Education in Kansas, 1880–1935* (Chapel Hill: University of North Carolina Press, 2010), 73–74.

61. Myriam Vuckovic, *Voices from Haskell: Indian Students between Two Worlds, 1884–1928* (Lawrence: University Press of Kansas, 2008), 211–46; Cobb, *Listening to Our Grandmothers' Stories*, 66–118; Scott Riney, *The Rapid City Indian School, 1888–1933* (Norman: University of Oklahoma Press, 1999), 138–66; Child, *Boarding School Seasons*, 87–95; Adams, *Education for Extinction*, 209–38; Coleman, *American Indian Children at School*, 146–61.

62. Gram, *Education at the Edge of Empire*.

63. Michael O. Fitzgerald, ed., *The Essential Charles Eastman (Ohiyesa): Light on the Indian World* (Bloomington, IN: World Wisdom, 2007), 207–14; Charles A. Eastman, "My People: The Indians' Contribution to the Art of America," *The Red Man* 7, no. 4 (1914): 133–40, in the Carlisle Indian School Digital Resource Center, Archives and Special Collections, Waidner-Spahr Library, Dickinson College, Carlisle, PA, http://carlisleindian.dickinson.edu/. See also Drew Lopenzina, "'Good Indian': Charles Eastman and the Warrior as Civil Servant," *American Indian Quarterly* 27, nos. 3/4 (2003): 727–57.

64. Charles Alexander Eastman, *From the Deep Woods to Civilization* (Boston: Little, Brown, 1923), 24–28, 46–47, as quoted in Adams, *Education for Extinction*, 239–40. See also Ester Burnett Horne and Sally McBeth, *Essie's Story: The Life and Legacy of a Shoshone Teacher* (Lincoln: University of Nebraska Press, 1998); Polingayski Qöyawayma and Vada F. Carlson, *No Turning Back: A True Account of a Hopi's Woman's Struggle to Live in Two Worlds*, 2nd ed. (Albuquerque: University of New Mexico Press, 1992).

65. Zitkala Ša, "School Days of an Indian Girl," *Atlantic Monthly* 85 (Feb. 1900): 187. See also Tadeusz Lewandowski, *Red Bird, Red Power: The Life and Legacy of Zitkala Ša* (Norman: University of Oklahoma Press, 2016), 17–44; Zitkala Ša, "An Indian Teacher among Indians," *Atlantic Monthly* 85 (Mar. 1900): 381–86; Zitkala Ša, "Impressions of an Indian Childhood," *Atlantic Monthly* 85 (Jan. 1900): 37–46.

66. "Indian Commissioner Jones on Indian Self-Support: Extract from the Annual Report of the Commissioner of Indian Affairs, October 15, 1901," in *Documents of United States Indian Policy*, ed. Francis Paul Prucha, 3rd ed. (Lincoln: University of Nebraska Press, 2000), 128–201.

67. Hayes Peter, *The Art of Americanization at the Carlisle Indian School* (Albuquerque: University of New Mexico Press, 2011); Adams, *Education for Extinction*, 307–28; Graham D. Taylor, *The New Deal and American Indian Tribalism: The Administration of the Indian Reorganization Act, 1934–1945* (Lincoln: University of Nebraska Press, 1980); Kenneth R. Philp, *John Collier's Crusade for Indian Reform, 1920–1954* (Tucson: University of Arizona Press, 1977), 126–29.

68. Adams, *Education for Extinction*, table 10.1, 320.

69. Lewis Meriam et al., *The Problem of Indian Administration: Summary of Findings and Recommendations* (Washington, DC: Brookings Institution, 1928).

70. Stephen Kent Amerman, *Urban Indians in Phoenix Schools, 1940–2000* (Lincoln: University of Nebraska Press, 2010); David H. Dejong, *Promises of the Past: A History of Indian Education* (Golden, CO: Fulcrum Publishing, 1993), 133–94.

71. Manuel G. Gonzales, *Mexicanos: A History of Mexicans in the United States*, 3rd ed. (Bloomington: Indiana University Press, 2019), 95–128; Natalia Molina, *How Race Is Made in America: Immigration, Citizenship, and the Historical Power of Racial Scripts* (Berkeley: University of California Press, 2014), 1–18, 43–67; Zaragosa Vargas, *Crucible of Struggle: A History of Mexican Americans from the Colonial Period to the Present Era* (New York: Oxford University Press, 2011), 79–111; Ariela J. Gross, *What Blood Won't Tell: A History of Race on Trial in America* (Cambridge, MA: Harvard University Press, 2008), 253–93; Arnoldo De León, *The Tejano Community, 1836–1900* (Dallas: Southern Methodist University Press, 1997); Matt S. Meier and Feliciano Ribera, *Mexican Americans/American Mexicans: From Conquistadors to Chicanos*, rev. ed. (New York: Hill and Wang, 1993), 53–69.

72. John H. Flores, *The Mexican Revolution in Chicago: Immigration Politics from the Early Twentieth Century to the Cold War* (Urbana: University of Illinois Press, 2018), 3–5; García, *Strategies of Segregation*, 6–7; Molina, *How Race Is Made in America*, 43–67; Rubén Donato and Jarrod S. Hanson, "Legally White, Socially 'Mexican': The Politics of De Jure and De Facto Segregation in the American Southwest," *Harvard Educational Review* 82, no. 2 (2012): 202–25; Ariela J. Gross, "'The Caucasian Cloak': Mexican Americans and the Politics of Whiteness in the Twentieth-Century Southwest," *Georgetown Law Journal* 95, no. 2 (2007): 337–92; Martha Menchaca, *Recovering History, Constructing Race: The Indian, Black, and White Roots of Mexican Americans* (Austin: University of Texas Press, 2001), 215–76; David G. Gutiérrez, *Walls and Mirrors: Mexican Americans, Mexican Immigrants, and the Politics of Ethnicity* (Berkeley: University of California Press, 1995), 13–38.

73. Guadalupe San Miguel Jr. and Richard R. Valencia, "From the Treaty of Guadalupe Hidalgo to *Hopwood*: The Educational Plight and Struggle of Mexican American in the Southwest," *Harvard Educational Review* 68, no. 3 (1998): 353–412. See also Moises Sandoval, *On the Move: A History of the Hispanic Church in the United States*, 2nd ed. (New York: Orbis Press, 2006), 37–54.

74. Rosina Lozano, *An American Language: The History of Spanish in the United States* (Berkeley: University of California Press, 2018), 89–110; Lynne Marie Getz, *Schools of Their Own: The Education of Hispanos in New Mexico, 1850–1940* (Albuquerque: University of New Mexico Press, 1997).

75. Carlos Kevin Blanton, *The Strange Career of Bilingual Education in Texas, 1836–1981* (College Station: Texas A&M University Press, 2004), 42–58; San Miguel and Valencia, "Treaty of Guadalupe Hidalgo to *Hopwood*," 360–63; Guadalupe San Miguel Jr., "Status of the Historiography of Chicano Education: A Preliminary Analysis," *History of Education Quarterly* 26, no. 4 (1986): 523–36; Arnold Liebowitz, *Educational Policy and Political Acceptance: The Imposition of English as the Language of Instruction in American Schools* (Washington, DC: Center for Applied Linguistics, 1971).

76. García, *Strategies of Segregation*, 10; capitalization of "white" racial identity in original.

77. Flores, *The Mexican Revolution in Chicago*, 3–5; Gonzales, *Mexicanos*, 129–62.

78. García, *Strategies of Segregation*, 12–78; San Miguel and Valencia, "Treaty of Guadalupe Hidalgo to *Hopwood*," 360–68; Gonzales, *Mexicanos*, 152–53; George J. Sánchez, *Becoming Mexican American: Ethnicity, Culture and Identity in Chicano Los Angeles, 1900–1945* (New York: Oxford University Press, 1993), 10–12; Arnoldo de León, *Ethnicity in the Sunbelt: A History of Mexican Americans in Houston* (Houston: Mexican American Studies Program, 1989), 98–99.

79. Rubén Donato, personal interview with Margarie Blackman, Lamar, June 3, 1999. As quoted in Rubén Donato, *Mexicans and Hispanos in Colorado Schools and Communities, 1920–1960* (Albany: State University of New York Press, 2007), 73–74; Blanton, *Strange Career of Bilingual Education*, 59–73.

80. Donato, *Mexicans and Hispanos in Colorado Schools*, 65–88; Blanton, *Strange Career of Bilingual Education*, 59–73; Richard R. Valencia, "The Plight of Chicano Students: An Overview of Schooling Conditions and Outcomes," in *Chicano School Failure and Success: Past, Present, and Future*, ed. Richard R. Valencia, 2nd ed. (New York: RoutledgeFalmer, 2002), 3–51; San Miguel and Valencia, "Treaty of Guadalupe Hidalgo to *Hopwood*," 353–412; Sánchez, *Becoming Mexican American*, 87–107.

81. García, *Strategies of Segregation*; San Miguel, "Status of the Historiography of Chicano Education," 530; Richard Griswold del Castillo, *The Los Angeles Barrio, 1850–1890* (Berkeley: University of California Press, 1982), 88–89; de León, *The Tejano Community*, 187–94.

82. Arnoldo de León, "Blowout 1910 Style: A Chicano School Boycott in West Texas," *Texana* 12, no. 2 (1974): 124–20.

83. "Schools Seek to Bar Mexican Pupils Charge," *San Francisco Chronicle*, June 8, 1919, B8.

84. "Mexican Segregation Story Found Untrue," *Los Angeles Times*, June 28, 1919, 14.

85. San Miguel and Valencia, "Treaty of Guadalupe Hidalgo to *Hopwood*," 364–70; Francisco E. Balderrama, *In Defense of La Raza: The Los Angeles Mexican Consulate and the Mexican Community, 1929–1936* (Tucson: University of Arizona Press, 1982), 55–72.

86. García, *Strategies of Segregation*; Carlos Kevin Blanton, *George I. Sánchez: The Long Fight for Mexican American Integration* (New Haven, CT: Yale University Press, 2004), 163–81; San Miguel and Valencia, "Treaty of Guadalupe Hidalgo to *Hopwood*," 364–70; Gilbert G. Gonzalez, *Chicano Education in the Era of Segregation* (Philadelphia: Blach Institute Press, 1990), 20–21. See also David Montejano, *Anglos and Mexicans in the Making of Texas, 1836–1986* (Austin: University of Texas Press, 1987), 160; Herschel T. Manuel, *The Education of Spanish-Speaking Children in Texas* (Austin: University of Texas Press, 1930). For an account of Mexican American student dissatisfaction with public schools, see Beatrice Griffith, *American Me* (New York: Houghton Mifflin, 1948).

87. Anne Waters Yarsinke, *All for One, and One for All: A Celebration of 75 Years of the League of United Latin American Citizens* (Virginia Beach: Donning, 2004), 7–8; Guadalupe San Miguel Jr., *Brown Not White: School Integration and the Chicano Movement in Houston* (College Station: Texas A&M University Press, 2001), 7–9.

88. Independent School Dist. et al. v. Salvatierra et al., 33 S.W.2d 790 (Tex. Civ. App. 1930) See also Blanton, *George I. Sánchez*, 182–206.

89. *Independent School Dist. v. Salvatierra*, 33 S.W.2d 790. See also Richard R. Valencia, *Chicano Students and the Courts: The Mexican American Legal Struggle for Educational Equality* (New York: New York University Press, 2008), 15–19.

90. Robert R. Alvarez, "The Lemon Grove Incident. The Nation's First Successful Desegregation Court Case," *Journal of San Diego History* 32, no. 2 (1986): 116–35. See also Philippa Strum, *Mendez v. Westminster: School Desegregation and Mexican American Rights* (Lawrence: University Press of Kansas, 2010), 22–34; Vicki L. Ruiz, "South by Southwest: Mexican Americans and Segregated Schooling, 1900–1950," *OAH Magazine of History* 15, no. 2 (2001): 23–27; Gilbert G. Gonzalez, "Chicano Educational History: A Legacy of Inequality," *Humboldt Journal of Social Relations* 22, no. 1 (1996): 43–56.

91. Maribel Santiago, "Mendez v. Westminster, 1947: Teaching a New Chapter of History," *Phi Delta Kappan* 94, no. 6 (2013): 35–38; Strum, *Mendez v. Westminster*, 1–3; Valencia, *Chicano Students and the Courts*, 49–52; Charles Wollenberg, "*Mendez v. Westminster*: Race, Nationality, and Segregation in California Schools," *California Historical Quarterly* 53, no. 4 (1974): 317–32.

92. Strum, *Mendez v. Westminster*; Jeanne M. Powers and Lirio Patton, "Between Mendez and Brown: 'Gonzales v. Sheely' (1951) and the Legal Campaign against Segregation," *Law and Social Inquiry* 33, no. 1 (2008): 127–71.

93. Valencia, *Chicano Students and the Courts*, 49–52.

94. Eileen H. Tamura, "Asian Americans in the History of Education: An Historiographical Essay," *History of Education Quarterly* 41, no. 4 (2001): 58–71.

95. Martha S. Jones, *Birthright Citizens: A History of Race and Rights in Antebellum America* (New York: Cambridge University Press, 2018); Mae M. Ngai, *Impossible Subjects: Illegal Aliens and the Making of Modern America* (Princeton, NJ: Princeton University Press, 2004), 21–55; Roger Daniels, *Guarding the Golden Door: American Immigration Policy and Immigrants Since 1882* (New York: Hill and Wang, 2004), 1–58; Eileen H. Tamura, "Introduction: Asian Americans and Educational History," *History of Education Quarterly* 43, no. 1 (2003): 1–9; Eileen H. Tamura, *Americanization, Acculturation, and Ethnic Identity: The Nisei Generation in Hawaii* (Urbana: University of Illinois Press, 1994), 91–164; Ronald Takaki, *Strangers from a Different Shore: A History of Asian Americans* (New York: Little, Brown, 1989), 132–78; Roger Daniels, *Asian America: Chinese and Japanese in the United States since 1850* (Seattle: University of Washington Press, 1988), 9–10; Meyer Weinberg, *Asian-American Education: Historical Background and Current Realities* (Mahwah, NJ: Lawrence Erlbaum Associates, 1997), 13–73.

96. Wendy Rouse Jorae, *The Children of Chinatown: Growing Up Chinese American in San Francisco, 1850–1920* (Chapel Hill: University of North Carolina Press, 2009), 15–116; Charles M. Wollenberg, "Yellow Peril in the Schools (I)," in *The Asian American Educational Experience: A Source Book for Teachers and Students*, ed. Don T. Nakanishi and Tina Yamano Nishida (New York: Routledge, 1995), 3–30.

97. Mamie Tape, an Infant, by her Guardian Ad Litem, Joseph Tape, Respondent, v. Jennie M. A. Hurley et al., Appellants, 66 Cal. 473 (1885). See also "Chinese in the Schools: Their Right to Admissions Judicially Declared," *San Francisco Chronicle*, January 10, 1885, 2; "Chinese in Public Schools," *Los Angeles Times*, January 10, 1885, 1.

98. Wollenberg, "Yellow Peril in the Schools," 8–9. See also "Chinese Children: Immediate Admission to the Schools Demanded," *San Francisco Chronicle*, April 8, 1885, 4.
99. Iris Chang, *The Chinese in America: A Narrative History* (New York: Viking Press, 2003), 174–78.
100. Letter from Mary Tape, *Alta*, April 8, 1885, 1, as reprinted in Franklin Odo, ed., *The Columbia Documentary History of the Asian American Experience* (New York: Columbia University Press, 2002), 72–73. Grammar, punctuation, and spelling are reproduced from the original.
101. "Americans Versus Chinese Pupils in Our Public Schools," *San Francisco Call*, August 13, 1899, 23. See also "Smart Chinese Boy: Beats All Grades in 'Frisco Schools," *North Platte Semi-Weekly Tribune*, September 8, 1899, 7.
102. Wollenberg, "Yellow Peril in the Schools," 9. See also "Chinese Ask for Justice," *San Francisco Call*, May 15, 1903; "Chinese Pupils Demand Rights," *San Francisco Call*, June 19, 1902; "Chinese in the Schools," *San Francisco Chronicle*, March 6, 1902, 5.
103. John Kuo and Wei Tchen, *Yellow Peril: An Archive of Anti-Asian Fear* (New York: Verso, 2014); Denis Warner and Peggy Warner, *The Tide at Sunrise: A History of the Russo-Japanese War, 1904–5* (New York: Routledge, 2004); Geoffrey Jukes, *The Russo-Japanese War, 1904–5* (Oxford: Osprey, 2002); Daniels, *Asian America*, 103.
104. "Japs Must Go with Chinese," *San Francisco Chronicle*, September 11, 1904, 31. See also "Board Cannot Bar Japanese," *San Francisco Call*, September 11, 1904, 36.
105. "California Should Not Be Dictated To," *Daily Press* (Newport News, VA), February 9, 1907, 1. See also "Formal Steps Taken by Government to Compel City to Admit Japanese to Public Schools," *San Francisco Call*, January 18, 1907, 16; "Not a New Question," *Evening Star* (Washington, DC), November 16, 1906, 9.
106. Luke Wright, the ambassador to Tokyo, translated the *Mainichi Shinbun*'s article into English and sent it to Washington on October 22, 1906. See Thomas Andrew Bailey, *Theodore Roosevelt and the Japanese-American Crises: An Account of the International Complications Arising from the Race Problem on the Pacific Coast* (Paolo Alto: Stanford University Press, 1934), 50. See also Masuda Hajimu, "Rumors of War: Immigration Disputes and the Social Construction of American-Japanese Relations, 1905–1913," *Diplomatic History* 33, no. 1 (2009): 1–37.
107. "Jap Order Rescinded: 'Frisco School Board Keeps Agreement with Roosevelt," *New York Tribune*, March 14, 1907, 1. See also Catherine Lee, "'Where the Danger Lies': Race, Gender, and Chinese and Japanese Exclusion in the United States, 1870–1924," *Sociological Forum* 25, no. 2 (2010): 248–71; Jordan Sand, "Gentlemen's Agreement, 1908: Fragments of a Pacific History," *Representations* 107, no. 1 (2009): 91–127.
108. James W. Loewen, *The Mississippi Chinese: Between Black and White* (Cambridge, MA: Harvard University Press, 1971), 58–64. See also Leslie Bow, *Partly Colored: Asian Americans and Racial Anomaly in the Segregated South* (New York: New York University Press, 2010).
109. "Meeting of School Board," *Paducah Daily Sun* (Paducah, KY), October 5, 1898, 2.
110. "Meeting of School Board." See also "Complaint against Lin Hing," *Times* (Washington, DC), October 4, 1900, 3.

111. "Chinese Have Their Own School Here," *New York Times*, May 29, 1922, 17.
112. Adrienne Berard, *Water Tossing Boulders: How a Family of Chinese Immigrants Led the First Fight to Desegregate Schools in the Jim Crow South* (Boston: Beacon Press, 2016), 1–6; Loewen, *The Mississippi Chinese*, 64–66.
113. Rice et al. v. Gong Lum et al., 139 Miss. 760, 104 So. 105, 1925 Miss. LEXIS 146.
114. Berard, *Water Tossing Boulders*, 65–139; "Court Order Bars Chinese Children," *Atlanta Constitution*, May 12, 1925, 10.
115. Gong Lum at al. v Rice et al., 275 U.S. 78 (1927). See also George S. Schuyler, "White, Black and Yellow Schools," *Crisis* 43, no. 4 (1936): 107; "Upholds Segregation of Chinese in Schools," *New York Times*, November 22, 1927, 14; "Bar Chinese from White School," *Chicago Defender*, May 16, 1925, 1.
116. Takaki, *Strangers from a Different Shore*, 357–58. See also Daniels, *Asian America*, 186–282.
117. Quotation from "Disadvantages of Camp Life," student essay by Y. K., ninth grade, 1942–43, in the Tule Lake Documentary Files, box 88, RG 210, National Archives, as quoted in Thomas James, *Exile Within: The Education of Japanese Americans* (Cambridge, MA: Harvard University Press, 1987), 4. See also Richard Reeves, *Infamy: The Shocking Story of Japanese American Internment in World War II* (New York: Henry Holt, 2015); Eileen H. Tamura, *In Defense of Justice: Joseph Kurihara and the Japanese American Struggle for Equality* (Urbana: University of Illinois Press, 2013); Roger Daniels, *Prisoners without Trial: Japanese Americans in World War II*, rev. ed. (New York: Hill and Wang, 2004); Greg Robinson, *By Order of the President: FDR and the Internment of Japanese Americans* (Cambridge, MA: Harvard University Press, 2003); Yoon K. Pak, *Wherever I Go I Will Always Be a Loyal American: Seattle's Japanese American Schoolchildren during World War II* (New York: RoutledgeFalmer, 2002); Lawson Fudao Inada, *Only What We Could Carry: The Japanese American Internment Experience* (Berkeley: Heyday Books, 2000); Takaki, *Strangers from a Different Shore*, 379–86.
118. *Nisei* refers to American-born children of Japanese immigrants. Jason Morgan Ward, "'No Jap Crow': Japanese Americans Encounter the World War II South," *Journal of Southern History* 73, no. 1 (2007): 75–104; Allan W. Austin, *From Concentration Camp to Campus: Japanese American Students and World War II* (Urbana: University of Illinois Press, 2003); Takaki, *Double Victory*, 137–87; Takaki, *Strangers from a Different Shore*, 398–400; James, *Exile Within*. See also Edith W. Derrick, "Effects of Evacuation on Japanese-American Youth," *School Review* 55, no. 6 (1947): 356–62.
119. Scott Kurashige, *The Shifting Grounds of Race: Black and Japanese Americans in the Making of a Multiethnic Los Angeles* (Princeton, NJ: Princeton University Press, 2008), 158–85; Wollenberg, "'Yellow Peril' in the Schools," 9–11; James, *Exile Within*, 163–64; Takaki, *Strangers from a Different Shore*, 403–13; Daniels, *Asian America*, 283–93.
120. Takaki, *Strangers from a Different Shore*, 403–13; Daniels, *Asian America*, 283–93.
121. Harry S. Truman, "Remarks upon Presenting a Citation to a Nisei Regiment," July 15, 1946, Public Papers, Harry S. Truman Library and Museum, Independence, MO, https://www.trumanlibrary.gov/library/public-papers/170/remarks-upon-presenting-citation-nisei-regiment.

CHAPTER TWO

1. Brown v. Board of Education of Topeka, 347 U.S. 483 (1954); Plessy v. Ferguson, 163 U.S. 537 (1896). See also Charles J. Ogletree Jr., *All Deliberate Speed: Reflections on the First Half-Century of Brown v. Board of Education* (New York: W. W. Norton, 2004); James T. Patterson, *Brown v. Board of Education: A Civil Rights Milestone and Its Troubled Legacy* (New York: Oxford University Press, 2001); Derrick A. Bell Jr., *Shades of Brown: New Perspectives on School Integration* (New York: Teachers College Press, 1980).

2. Clayborne Carson, "Two Cheers for Brown v. Board of Education!," *Journal of American History* 91, no. 1 (2004): 26–31; Patterson, *Brown v. Board of Education*, xvii. Some southern states continued the strategy of equalizing Black schools after the *Brown* ruling, hoping that if Black schools were equal to white schools, then Black families would not demand integration. See Max. K. Gilstrap, "Desegregation Calm . . . Through the South," *Christian Science Monitor*, February 5, 1955, 9; "Negro Teachers Face Cut in Jobs," *New York Times*, October 23, 1955, 80.

3. *Brown*, 347 U.S. 483. See also Richard Kluger, *Simple Justice: The History of Brown v. Board of Education and Black America's Struggle for Equality* (New York: Alfred A. Knopf, 1976), 700–709; James A. Banks, "Quality Education for Black Students," in *The Integration of American Schools: Problems, Experiences, Solutions*, ed. Norene Harris, Nathaniel Jackson, and Carl E. Rydingswood (Boston: Allyn and Bacon, 1975), 165–75.

4. Martha Minow, *In Brown's Wake: Legacies of America's Educational Landmark* (New York: Oxford University Press, 2010); Michael J. Klarman, *Brown v. Board of Education and the Civil Rights Movement* (New York: Oxford University Press, 2007); Manning Marable, *Race, Reform, and Rebellion: The Second Reconstruction and Beyond in Black America, 1945–2006*, 3rd ed. (Jackson: University Press of Mississippi, 2007); Derrick Bell, *Silent Covenants: Brown v. Board of Education and the Unfulfilled Hopes for Racial Reform* (New York: Oxford University Press, 2004); Richard Kluger, *Brown v. Board of Education and Black America's Struggle for Equality* (1975; repr., New York: Vintage Books, 2004); Robert J. Cottrol, Raymond T. Diamond, and Leland B. Ware, *Brown v. Board of Education: Caste, Culture, and the Constitution* (Lawrence: University Press of Kansas, 2003); Robert L. Carter, "A Reassessment of Brown v. Board of Education," in Bell, *Shades of Brown*, 27–28. See also the roundtable "*Brown v. Board of Education*, Fifty Years Later," *Journal of American History* 91, no. 1 (2004): 19–173.

5. Elizabeth Todd-Breland, *A Political Education: Black Politics and Education Reform in Chicago since the 1960s* (Chapel Hill: University of North Carolina Press, 2018); Lani Guinier, "From Racial Liberalism to Racial Literacy: *Brown v. Board of Education* and the Interest-Divergence Dilemma," *Journal of American History* 91, no. 1 (2004): 92–118; Gloria Ladson-Billings, "Landing on the Wrong Note: The Price We Paid for *Brown*," *Educational Researcher* 33, no. 7 (2004): 3–13, Derrick A. Bell Jr., "*Brown v. Board of Education* and the Interest-Convergence Dilemma," *Harvard Law Review* 93 (1980): 518–33; Derrick A. Bell Jr., "Serving Two Masters: Integration Ideals and Client Interests in School Desegregation," *Yale Law Journal* 85 (1976): 470–516; Banks, "Quality Education for Black Students."

6. This data comes from the period 1991–2007. Gary Orfield and Erica Frankenberg, with Jongyeon Ee and John Kuscera, "*Brown* at 60: School Segregation by Race, Poverty and State," Civil Rights Project/Proyecto Derechoes Civiles, University of California, Los Angeles, May 16, 2016, https://www.civilrightsproject.ucla.edu/research/k-12-education/integration-and-diversity/brown-at-62-school-segregation-by-race-poverty-and-state. See also Paul L. Trachtenberg and Ryan W. Coughlan, *The New Promise of School Integration and the Old Problem of Extreme Segregation: An Action Plan for New Jersey to Address Both* (Newark: Center for Diversity and Equality in Education, 2018), http://www.centerfordiversityandequalityineducation.com/related-links; Janelle Scott and Rand Quinn, "The Politics of Education in the Post-*Brown* Era: Race, Markets, and the Struggle for Equitable Schooling," *Educational Administration Quarterly* 50, no. 5 (2014): 749–63; Roslyn A. Mickelson, "Twenty-First Century Social Science on School Racial Diversity and Educational Outcomes," *Ohio State Law Journal* 69, no. 6 (2008): 1173–1227; Robert L. Linn and Kevin G. Welner, eds., *Race-Conscious Policies for Assigning Students to Schools: Social Science Research and the Supreme Court Cases* (Washington, DC: National Academy of Education, 2007); Susan E. Eaton, *The Other Boston Busing Story: What's Won and Lost across the Boundary Line* (New Haven, CT: Yale University Press, 2001). On the rise of market-based reforms and their effects on educational equality, see David W. Hursh, *The End of Public Schools: The Corporate Reform Agenda to Privatize Education* (New York: Routledge, 2016); Kristen L. Buras, *Charter Schools, Race, and Urban Space: Where the Market Meets Grassroots Resistance* (New York: Routledge, 2015); Diane Ravitch, *Reign of Error: The Hoax of the Privatization Movement and the Danger to America's Public Schools* (New York: Vintage Books, 2014); Michael W. Apple, *Educating the "Right" Way: Markets, Standards, God and Inequality*, 2nd ed. (New York: Routledge, 2006).

7. "Educators Comment on Schools Decision," *Chicago Defender*, May 22, 1954, 5.

8. "Outlaws School Bias," *New York Amsterdam News*, May 22, 1954, 1.

9. "NAACP Calls High Court Decision the Civil Rights Peak for 1954," *Arkansas State Press*, January 7, 1955, 1, 4.

10. Martin Luther King Jr., "Desegregation and the Future" (address delivered at the Annual Luncheon of the National Committee for Rural Schools, New York, NY, December 15, 1956), published in in Clayborne Carson, Stewart Burns, Susan Carson, Dana L. H. Powell, and Peter Holloran, eds., *The Papers of Martin Luther King, Jr.*, vol. 3, *Birth of a New Age, December 1955–December 1956* (Berkeley: University of California Press, 1997), 471–79.

11. Mary McLeod Bethune, "Mrs. Bethune Sees School Ruling as a Milestone in U.S. History," *Chicago Defender*, May 29, 1954, 11. See also Patricia Sullivan, *Lift Every Voice: The NAACP and the Making of the Civil Rights Movement* (New York: New Press, 2009), 68–80; Dara N. Byrne, ed., *Brown v. Board of Education: Its Impact on Public Education* (New York: Word for Word, 2005); Joyce Ann Hanson, *Mary McLeod Bethune and Black Women's Political Activism* (Columbia: University of Missouri Press, 2003); Mark Whitman, ed., *Removing a Badge of Slavery: The Record of Brown v. Board of Education* (Princeton, NJ: Markus Wiener Publishers, 1993); Mark V. Tushnet, *The NAACP's Legal Strategy against Segregated Education, 1925–1950* (Chapel Hill: University of North Carolina Press, 1987); Daniel M.

Berman, *It Is So Ordered: The Supreme Court Rules on School Segregation* (New York: W. W. Norton, 1966).

12. Kevin Gaines, "Whose Integration Was It? An Introduction," *Journal of American History* 91, no. 1 (2004): 19–20. See also Sonya Douglass Horsford, *Learning in a Burning House: Educational Inequality, Ideology and (Dis)Integration* (New York: Teachers College Press, 2011); Michael J. Dumas, "Sitting Next to White Children: School Desegregation in the Black Educational Imagination" (PhD diss., City University of New York, 2007).

13. As Rachel Devlin shows, Black girls were far more likely than boys to be the first to desegregate a white school. See Rachel Devlin, *A Girl Stands at the Door: The Generation of Young Women Who Desegregated America's Schools* (New York: Basic Books, 2018). See also Barbara J. Shircliffe, *Desegregating Teachers: Contesting the Meaning of Equality of Educational Opportunity in the South Post Brown* (New York: Peter Lang, 2012); Davison M. Douglas, *Jim Crow Moves North: The Battle over Northern School Segregation, 1865–1954* (New York: Cambridge University Press, 2005), 173–79; Jack Dougherty, *More Than One Struggle: The Evolution of Black School Reform in Milwaukee* (Chapel Hill: University of North Carolina Press, 2004), 9–33; Adam Fairclough, "The Costs of *Brown*: Black Teachers and School Integration," *Journal of American History* 91, no. 1 (2004): 43–55; Vivian Gunn Morris and Curtis L. Morris, *The Price They Paid: Desegregation in an African American Community* (New York: Teachers College Press, 2002); Vanessa Siddle Walker, *Their Highest Potential: An African American School Community in the Segregated South* (Chapel Hill: University of North Carolina Press, 1996); Derrick A. Bell Jr., "The Burden of *Brown* on Blacks: History-Based Observations on a Landmark Decision," *North Carolina Central Law Review* 7 (1975): 25–38.

14. "Declaration of Constitutional Principals," 84th Cong. Rec. 4515–16 (1956). See also Elizabeth Gillespie McRae, *Mothers of Massive Resistance: White Women and the Politics of White Supremacy* (New York: Oxford University Press, 2018); Matthew F. Delmont, *Why Busing Failed: Race, Media, and the National Resistance to School Desegregation* (Oakland: University of California Press, 2016); Jason Morgan Ward, *Defending White Democracy: The Making of a Segregationist Movement and the Remaking of Racial Politics, 1936–1965* (Chapel Hill: University of North Carolina Press, 2014), 142–61; Jason Sokol, *There Goes My Everything: White Southerners in the Age of Civil Rights, 1945–1965* (New York: Vintage Books, 2007), 43–52.

15. Mary L. Dudziak, *Cold War, Civil Rights: Race and the Image of American Democracy*, rev. ed. (Princeton, NJ: Princeton University Press, 2011); James E. Ryan, *Five Miles Away, a World Apart: One City, Two Schools, and the Story of Educational Opportunity in America* (New York: Oxford University Press, 2010), 21–62.

16. Benjamin Fine, "Arkansas Troops Bar Negro Pupils," *New York Times*, September 5, 1957, 1, 20. See also Daisy Bates, *The Long Shadow of Little Rock: A Memoir* (Little Rock: University of Arkansas Press, 1986). For details on Grace Lorch during this incident, see "Grace K. Lorch FBI Statement Regarding Elizabeth Eckford Incident," September 8, 1957, Little Rock Central High Integration Crisis, Federal Bureau of Investigation Records, 1957 (MC 1027, box 1, series 933), University of Arkansas Libraries, https://digitalcollections.uark.edu/digital/collection/Civilrights/id/1255.

17. Carlotta Walls LaNier, *A Mighty Long Way: My Journey to Justice at Little Rock Central High School* (New York: Random House, 2009); Karen Anderson, "The Little Rock School Desegregation Crisis: Moderation and Social Conflict," *Journal of Southern History* 70, no. 3 (2004): 603–36; Melba Pattillo Beals, *Warriors Don't Cry: A Searing Memoir of the Battle to Integrate Little Rock's Central High* (New York: Simon & Schuster, 1994); Bates, *The Long Shadow of Little Rock*; Elizabeth Huckaby, *Crisis at Central High, Little Rock, 1957–1958* (Baton Rouge: Louisiana State University Press, 1980).

18. Christopher Bonastia, *Southern Stalemate: Five Years without Public Education in Prince Edward County, Virginia* (Chicago: University of Chicago Press, 2012); Dudziak, *Cold War, Civil Rights*, 115–51; Ryan, *Five Miles Away*, 21–120; George R. Metcalf, *From Little Rock to Boston: The History of School Desegregation* (Westport, CT: Greenwood Press, 1983), 1–34.

19. Memorandum from Robert L. Carter to Roy Wilkins, June 26, 1959, folder 001516-003-0001: De facto segregation and desegregation efforts in Northern and Western states, Papers of the NAACP, Part 3: The Campaign for Educational Equality, Series D: Central Office Records, 1956–1965, Proquest History Vault, http://congressional.proquest.com/histvault?q=001516-003-0001.

20. Richard Rothstein, *The Color of Law: A Forgotten History of How Our Government Segregated America* (New York: W. W. Norton, 2017); Douglas, *Jim Crow Moves North*, 219–73. Jason Sokol argues that Springfield, Massachusetts, school leaders disingenuously used a "color-blind" defense of school segregation during the same era. See Jason Sokol, *All Eyes Are upon Us: Race and Politics from Boston to Brooklyn—The Conflicted Soul of the Northeast* (New York: Basic Books, 2014), 71–102. See also Robert L. Herbst, "The Legal Struggle to Integrate Schools in the North," *Annals of the American Academy of Political and Social Science* 407 (1973): 43–62; Robert A. Dentler, "Barriers to Northern School Desegregation," *Daedalus* 95, no. 1 (1966): 45–63; Robert L. Carter, "De Facto School Segregation: An Examination of the Legal and Constitutional Questions Presented," *Case Western Reserve Law Review* 16 (1965): 502, 516; Doxey A. Wilkerson, "School Integration, Compensatory Education and the Civil Rights Movement in the North," *Journal of Negro Education* 34, no. 3 (1965): 300–309; "Along the NAACP Battlefront: New York School Ruling," *Crisis* 71, no. 3 (1964): 178; "Along the NAACP Battlefront: De Facto School Segregation," *Crisis* 70, no. 8 (1963): 482–83; June Shagaloff, "Public Desegregation—North & West," *Crisis* 70, no. 2 (1963): 92–95, 103; "Along the NAACP Battlefront: Northern and Western Cities Slated to End School Segregation," *Crisis* 69, no. 8 (1962): 481–84; "Along the NAACP Battlefront: Plainfield Schools," *Crisis* 69, no. 7 (1962): 414; "Along the NAACP Battlefront: School Bias," *Crisis* 69, no. 6 (1962): 347–50; "Editorial: NAACP Leads Northern School Program," *Crisis* 69, no. 4 (1962): 230–31.

21. "School Bias Case Heard in New Jersey," *New York Times*, October 21, 1954, 30. See also "Hearings on Bias in School Ended," *New York Times*, November 2, 1954, 29; "Englewood Parents Decry School Bias," *New York Amsterdam News*, October 30, 1954, 38.

22. On the Englewood, New Jersey, struggle, see "Englewood Shows Slight Integration," *New York Amsterdam News*, October 8, 1955, 20; "The Englewood Pattern," *Pittsburgh Courier*, June 4, 1955, 6; "Discrimination Charged in Suit at Englewood," *Philadelphia Tribune*, February 8, 1955, 8; "Englewood City Board Denies

Bias," *Afro-American*, November 6, 1954, 6; "Englewood Parents Decry School Bias," *New York Amsterdam News*, October 30, 1954, 38; "School Bias Case Heard in Jersey," *New York Times*, October 21, 1954, 30; "School Bias Probed in Englewood, NJ," *Philadelphia Tribune*, September 11, 1954, 12; "Englewood Faces School Bias Case," *New York Times*, September 4, 1954, 13.

23. John W. Slocum, "100 at Jersey Sit-In Charge School Bias," *New York Times*, February 2, 1962, 1; John W. Slocum, "School in Bergen Held Segregated," *New York Times*, January 18, 1961, 46; "Bomb Two Homes in Englewood," *Daily Defender*, October 15, 1958, 1, 3.

24. John W. Slocum, "Jersey Pupils to Win Entry to School," *New York Times*, May 8, 1963, 29; John W. Slocum, "Englewood Acts on Bias Problems," *New York Times*, December 3, 1962, 157; Frank Johnson, "How N.J. Town Became a Racial Battleground," *Chicago Defender*, September 12, 1962, 13; "Many Negro Pupils Boycott School in Segregation Protest," *New York Times*, Sept 6, 1962, 1. See also Emily Joy Jones McGowan, "A Case Study of Dwight Morrow High School and the Academies at Englewood: An Examination of School Desegregation Policy from a Critical Race Perspective" (PhD diss., Rutgers University, 2011); Charles Anthony Cobb, "Segregation, Desegregation, and Race: A Case Study of the Englewood, New Jersey Public School District, 1962–2000" (PhD diss., Fordham University, 2007).

25. Todd-Breland, *A Political Education*; Dionne Danns, *Desegregating Chicago's Public Schools: Policy, Implementation, Politics and Protest, 1965–1985* (New York: Palgrave Macmillan, 2014); Sokol, *All Eyes Are upon Us*; Dougherty, *More Than One Struggle*; Ronald P. Formisano, *Boston against Busing: Race, Class, and Ethnicity in the 1960s and 1970s*, rev. ed. (Chapel Hill: University of North Carolina Press, 2004); Dionne Danns, *Something Better for Our Children: Black Organizing in Chicago's Public Schools, 1963–1971* (New York: Routledge, 2003); Bernadette Anand, Michelle Fine, and David S. Surrey, *Keeping the Struggle Alive: Studying School Desegregation in Our Town* (New York: Teachers College Press, 2002); Steven J. L. Taylor, *Desegregation in Boston and Buffalo: The Influence of Local Leaders* (Albany: State University of New York Press, 1998), Clarence Taylor, *Knocking at Our Own Door: Milton A. Galamison and the Struggle to Integrate New York City's Schools* (New York: Columbia University Press, 1997); J. Anthony Lukas, *Common Ground: A Turbulent Decade in the Lives of Three American Families* (New York: Random House, 1986). See also "Negro Progress in 1961," *Ebony* 17 (January 1962): 21–28; "Danger in Sudden Integration of Teachers Staffs," *Philadelphia Tribune*, May 31, 1958, 2; "Chicago Wants More School Integration," *Afro-American*, November 9, 1957, 19; Leo Shapiro, "Boston Integration Problem Serious, Says Negro Leader," *Boston Globe*, October 21, 1957, 6; Everett G. Martin, "Detroit's Orderly Integration Tied to Firm Policy," *Christian Science Monitor*, October 10, 1957, 3; Robert E. Baker, "Integration Difficulties Embarrass New York," *Washington Post*, August 25, 1957, E1; Frank Johnson, "Bar White Girl's Shift from 7-1 Negro School," *Newsday*, August 16, 1957, 7; "New York Tension High over School Integration," *Hartford Courant*, April 30, 1957, 22E; Paul Sampson, "Segregation Troublesome to N.Y. City," *Washington Post*, February 25, 1957, B1; "New York Moves Tan Pupils by Bus to Mixed School," *Afro-American*, February 16, 1957, 17; "Would You Believe It, School Integration Trouble in New York?,"

Pittsburgh Courier, November 10, 1956, 15; "New York Launches Master Plan of Integration," *New Journal and Guide*, August 4, 1956, 3; "School Segregation Here?," *New York Times*, November 8, 1955, 30; "Deny Aid to Segregated School, Teachers Urge," *Philadelphia Tribune*, October 11, 1955, 3; "School Board Asked to Redistrict for Full Integration," *Philadelphia Tribune*, March 8, 1955, 3.

26. Robert L. Carter, "The Unending Struggle for Equal Educational Opportunity," *Teachers College Record* 96, no. 4 (1995): 621.

27. Although the Newark Board of Education passed the resolution requiring every classroom in the city to fly the Black liberation flag, whites in the city strongly objected and took the issue to court, where Superior Court Judge James T. Owens banned the school district from implementing the plan. Daniel Hays, "Newark's Black Flag Hassle Reaches Legislature," *Washington Post*, December 4, 1971, A25; "Schools in Newark Restricted from Putting Up Black Flags," *New York Times*, December 4, 1971, 24. See also Kevin Mumford, *Newark: A History of Race, Rights, and Riots in America* (New York: New York University Press, 2007); Steve Golin, *The Newark Teacher Strike: Hopes on the Line* (New Brunswick, NJ: Rutgers University Press, 2002). On Black educational activism, see Thomas J. Sugrue, *Sweet Land of Liberty: The Forgotten Struggle for Civil Rights in the North* (New York: Random House, 2008), 163–99, 449–92; Gael Graham, *Young Activists: American High School Students in the Age of Protest* (DeKalb: Northern Illinois University Press, 2006), 51–81; Douglas, *Jim Crow Moves North*, 219–73; Jonathan Zimmerman, *Whose America: Culture Wars in the Public Schools* (Cambridge, MA: Harvard University Press, 2002), 107–34.

28. For quotes, see Gene Roberts, "Waterloo, Iowa Puzzled by Riots," *New York Times*, July 14, 1967, 30. See also Charles S. Isaacs, "A J.H.S. 271 Teacher Tells It like He Sees It," *New York Times*, November 24, 1968, SM52; "Students Angry in Philadelphia," *New York Times*, November 16, 1969, 74; C. Gerard Fraser, "Boycotting White Plains Pupils Return, with Demands Met," *New York Times*, April 5, 1968, 18; "School Is Reopened as Racial Tensions Let Up in Westbury," *New York Times*, April 4, 1968, 30; "Negroes Boycott Suburban School," *New York Times*, March 27, 1968, 35; "Schools Closed in White Plains," *New York Times*, April 4, 1968, 30; "Racial Fights Close Trenton High School," *New York Times*, February 29, 1968, 45; Ralph Blumenthal, "Negroes Protest Mt Vernon Buses," *New York Times*, February 17, 1968, 30; William Borders, "Negro Students Disrupt School," *New York Times*, December 16, 1967, 37; "Cheerleader Dispute Is Settled," *New York Times*, November 20, 1967, 35; "Negro Students March," *New York Times*, August 31, 1967, 24; Dan Sullivan, "Teachers Consider Problem of Integrating Plays," *New York Times*, August 21, 1967, 39; Earl Caldwell, "Negroes Astir in Spring Valley and Black Power Cry Is Heard," *New York Times*, August 11, 1967, 35; Thomas A. Johnson, "3 Groups Claim Victory, Drop PS 175 Boycott," *New York Times*, September 3, 1966, 10.

29. Clay Risen, *The Bill of the Century: The Epic Battle for the Civil Rights Act* (New York: Bloomsbury Press, 2014), 249–51; Charles T. Clotfelter, *After Brown: The Rise and Retreat of School Desegregation* (Princeton, NJ: Princeton University Press, 2004), 25–30; Frank Brown, "The First Serious Implementation of *Brown*: The 1964 Civil Rights Act and Beyond," *Journal of Negro Education* 73, no. 3 (2004): 182–90; Patterson, *Brown v. Board of Education*, 123–28; Gary Orfield and

Susan E. Eaton, *Dismantling Desegregation: The Quiet Reversal of Brown v. Board of Education* (New York: New Press, 1996), 7–9.

30. Green v. County School Board of New Kent County, 391 U.S. 430 (1968); Alexander v. Holmes County Board of Education, 396 U.S. 19 (1969); Swann v. Charlotte-Mecklenburg Board of Education, 402 U.S. 1 (1971); Keyes v. Denver School District No. 1, 413 U.S. 189 (1973). See also David J. Armor, *Forced Justice: School Desegregation and the Law* (New York: Oxford University Press, 1995).

31. Clotfelter, *After Brown*, 26–30. See also Nikole Hannah-Jones, "Lack of Order: The Erosion of a Once-Great Force for Integration," *ProPublica*, May 1, 2014, http://www.propublica.org/article/lack-of-order-the-erosion-of-a-once-great -force-for-integration.

32. For quote, see Richard J. Margolis, "Education: Busing, You Got Some Nice Things Here, Too," *New York Times*, October 24, 1971, E10. See also John Herbers, "Integration Gains but Storm Signs Grow across U.S.," *New York Times*, January 11, 1967, 27; Robert Coles, "The White Northerner: Pride and Prejudice," *Newsday*, October 8, 1966, 8W; "Riots Engender Pessimism," *Philadelphia Tribune*, October 8, 1966, 24; Dick Zander, "Nassau Dems Spurn Busing," *Newsday*, September 30, 1966, 5.

33. President Nixon released two official statements detailing his policy on busing: Richard Nixon, "Statement about the Busing of Schoolchildren," August 3, 1971, online by Gerhard Peters and John T. Woolley, *The American Presidency Project*, https://www.presidency.ucsb.edu/documents/statement-about-the -busing-schoolchildren; Richard Nixon, "Statement about Desegregation of Primary and Secondary Schools," March 24, 1970, online by Gerhard Peters and John T. Woolley, *The American Presidency Project*, https://www.presidency .ucsb.edu/documents/statement-about-desegregation-elementary-and -secondary-schools. This stance ostensibly supported Supreme Court rulings on school integration while in reality signaled his opposition to the most effective measure—transporting students to schools—available to overcome school segregation. It also definitively established his opposition to efforts to overcome northern de facto school segregation. See also Ansley Erickson, *Making the Unequal Metropolis: School Desegregation and Its Limits* (Chicago: University of Chicago Press, 2016); Orfield and Eaton, *Dismantling Desegregation*, 4–32, 311– 39; Metcalf, *From Little Rock to Boston*, 7–229.

34. Ashley D. Farmer, *Remaking Black Power: How Black Women Transformed an Era* (Chapel Hill: University of North Carolina Press, 2017), 50–92; Marable, *Race, Reform, and Rebellion*, 112–45; Peniel E. Joseph, *Waiting 'Til the Midnight Hour: A Narrative History of Black Power in America* (New York: Henry Holt, 2006), 146–50; August Meier and Elliott Rudwick, *CORE: A Study of the Civil Rights Movement, 1942–1968* (New York: Oxford University Press, 1973), 412–15; Nathan Wright Jr., *Let's Work Together* (New York: Hawthorne Books, 1968). On the tremendous diversity of grassroots Black Power campaigns, see the collection of essays in Peniel E. Joseph, ed., *Neighborhood Rebels: Black Power at the Local Level* (New York: Palgrave Macmillan, 2010).

35. Preston Wilcox, "The Kids Will Decide—And More Power to Them," *Ebony* 25, no. 10 (1970): 134–37. For statistics on school segregation, see Mario Fantini, Marilyn Gittell, and Richard Magat, *Community Control and the Urban School*

(New York: Praeger, 1970), 6–7; Board of Education of the City of New York, "Action toward Quality Integrated Education," May 28, 1964, 25–26, TAM 1853, Tamiment Pamphlet Collection, Tamiment Library & Robert F. Wagner Labor Archives, New York, NY. On residential segregation in New York City, see Nathan Kantrowitz, "Ethnic and Racial Segregation in the New York Metropolis, 1960," *American Journal of Sociology* 74, no. 6 (1969): 685–95. See also Clarence Taylor, "Conservative and Liberal Opposition to the New York City School-Integration Campaign," in *Civil Rights in New York City: From World War II to the Giuliani Era*, ed. Clarence Taylor (New York: Fordham University Press, 2011), 95–117; Martha Biondi, *To Stand and Fight: The Struggle for Civil Rights in Postwar New York City* (Cambridge, MA: Harvard University Press, 2003), 223–49; Jerald E. Podair, *The Strike That Changed New York: Blacks, Whites, and the Ocean-Hill Brownsville Crisis* (New Haven, CT: Yale University Press, 2002), 22–27; Diane Ravitch, *The Great School Wars: A History of the New York City Public Schools*, rev. ed. (Baltimore: Johns Hopkins University Press, 2000), 251–380; Wilkerson, "School Integration, Compensatory Education"; Board of Education of the City of New York, "The Open Enrollment Program in the New York City Public Schools: Progress Report," September 1960–September 1963, TAM 1854, Tamiment Pamphlet Collection.

36. Patterson, *Brown v. Board of Education*, 147–50. See also Andrew R. Highsmith, *Demolition Means Progress: Flint, Michigan, and the Fate of the American Metropolis* (Chicago: University of Chicago Press, 2015); Thomas J. Sugrue, *The Origins of the Urban Crisis: Race and Inequality in Postwar Detroit*, rev. ed. (Princeton, NJ: Princeton University Press, 2014); Danns, *Desegregating Chicago's Public Schools*; Heather Lewis, *New York City Public Schools from Brownsville to Bloomberg: Community Control and Its Legacy* (New York: Teachers College Press, 2013); Matthew J. Countryman, *Up South: Civil Rights and Black Power in Philadelphia* (Philadelphia: University of Pennsylvania Press, 2006), 223–57.

37. Charles V. Hamilton, "Race and Education: A Search for Legitimacy," *Harvard Educational Review* 38, no. 4 (1968): 669–84.

38. Jack D. Forbes, "Segregation and Integration: The Multi-Ethnic or Uni-Ethnic School," *Phylon* 30, no. 1 (1969): 35.

39. Jon Shelton, *Teacher Strike: Public Education and the Making of a New American Political Order* (Urbana: University of Illinois Press, 2017), 34–37; Jonna Perrillo, *Uncivil Rights: Teachers, Unions, and Race in the Battle for School Equity* (Chicago: University of Chicago Press, 2012), 116–47; Michael B. Katz, "Why Don't American Cities Burn Very Often," *Journal of Urban History* 34, no. 2 (2008): 185–208; Daniel Perlstein, *Justice, Justice: School Politics and the Eclipse of Liberalism* (New York: Peter Lang, 2004), 81–96; Ravitch, *The Great School Wars*, 381–87; Taylor, *Knocking at Our Own Door*, 176–207; Ira Katznelson, *City Trenches: Urban Politics and the Patterning of Class in the United States* (Chicago: University of Chicago Press, 1981), 179, 187; Sydney H. Schanberg, "City School Bill Voted in Albany," *New York Times*, May 1, 1969, 1; Nathan Glazer, "For White and Black, Community Control Is the Issue," *New York Times*, April 27, 1969, SM36.

40. Milliken v. Bradley, 418 U.S. 717 (1974). See also Orfield and Frankenberg, "*Brown* at 60," 9–10.

41. Missouri v. Jenkins, 115 S. Ct. 2038 (1995); Freeman v. Pitts, 503 U.S. 467 (1992); Board of Education of Oklahoma v. Dowell, 498 U.S. 237 (1991); Orfield and Frankenberg, "*Brown* at 60," 9–10.

42. Orfield and Frankenberg, "*Brown* at 60," 27–31; Hannah-Jones, "Lack of Order." See also Erickson, *Making the Unequal Metropolis*.

43. Linda Shaw, "The Resegregation of Seattle's Schools," *Seattle Times*, June 1, 2008, http://www.seattletimes.com/seattle-news/education/the-resegregation-of -seattles-schools. For a skeptical interpretation of Seattle's "voluntary" school integration plan, see Michael J. Dumas, "A Cultural Political Economy of School Desegregation in Seattle," *Teachers College Record* 113, no. 4 (2011): 703–34.

44. Goodwin Liu, "Seattle and Louisville," *California Law Review* 95, no. 1 (2007): 277–317; Quintard Taylor, "The Civil Rights Movement in the American West: Black Political Protest in Seattle, 1960–1970," *Journal of Negro History* 80, no. 1 (1995): 1–14; Richard Weatherly, Betty Jane Narver, and Richard Elmore, "Managing the Politics of Decline: School Closures in Seattle," *Peabody Journal of Education* 60, no. 2 (1983): 10–24.

45. Parents Involved in Community Schools v. Seattle School District No. 1, 551 U.S. 701 (2007). For the purpose of racial balance, school administrators identified the Seattle public school population as 41 percent white and 59 percent nonwhite (all other racial groups). See also Dick Lilly, "Stanford Pushes Cluster System," *Seattle Times*, October 9, 1997, B1; Ruth Teichroeb, "Stanford Pitches His Plan for City Schools Primary Focus Now Academic Achievement," *Seattle Post-Intelligencer*, October 9, 1997, B1; Paul Shepard, "NAACP Head: Integration Always Was, Is Group's Goal," *Seattle Times*, July 3, 1997, A5; Dick Lilly, "Seattle to End Busing," *Seattle Times*, November 21, 1996, A1; Kathy George, "School Board Abolishes Controversial Forced Busing Plan," *Seattle Post-Intelligencer*, November 21, 1996, A1; Jerry Large, "Making Integration Work," *Seattle Times*, November 8, 1996, B1.

46. Shaw, "Resegregation of Seattle's Schools"; Sanjay Bhatt, "Decades of Effort Fail to Close Gap in Student Achievement," *Seattle Times*, May 9, 2004, http://community.seattletimes.nwsource.com/archive/?date=20040509&slug= brown09m; Les Ledbetter, "Seattle, without Federal Pressure, Will Begin to Desegregate Schools," *New York Times*, January 3, 1978, 1. On Black critiques in the mid-1980s, see Dumas, "Cultural Political Economy," 716.

47. *PICS v. Seattle School District*, 551 U.S. 701. This case was tried together with a school desegregation case from Louisville, Kentucky, *Meredith v. Jefferson County Board of Education*.

48. Linda Shaw, "Seattle Schools Return to Neighborhood-Based System," *Seattle Times*, November 18, 2009, http://www.seattletimes.com/seattle-news/seattle -schools-return-to-neighborhood-based-system.

49. Amy Stuart Wells and Erica Frankenberg, "The Public Schools and the Challenge of the Supreme Court's Integration Decision," *Phi Delta Kappan* 89, no. 3 (2007): 180.

50. Orfield and Frankenberg, "*Brown* at 60," 2. See also, Brief of 533 Social Scientists as Presented as *Amici Curiae* in Support of Respondents, *Parents Involved in Community Schools v. Seattle School District, et al.* and *Crystal D. Meredith v. Jef-*

ferson County Board of Education, et al. (Nos. 05-908 and 05-915), US Supreme Court (2006).

51. Nikole Hannah-Jones, "Choosing a School for My Daughter in a Segregated City," *New York Times,* June 9, 2016, https://www.nytimes.com/2016/06/12/magazine /choosing-a-school-for-my-daughter-in-a-segregated-city.html.

52. "Indians, Too," *Afro-American,* May 14, 1955, 22; Alan D. Resch, "N.C. Tribes Want to Be Left Alone," *Chicago Defender,* September 10, 1960, 11; "Indians against Negro Pupils," *Daily Defender,* April 7, 1959, 11.

53. Jeronimo Netzethualcoyti, "Negroes Can Integrate, Indians Never!," *New York Amsterdam News,* August 27, 1955, 8. (Note that the author's name is spelled differently in the text of the article as Jeronimo Netzehualcoyti.)

54. Forbes, "Segregation and Integration."

55. Zora Neale Hurston, "Letter to the Editor," *Orlando Sentinel,* August 11, 1955.

56. "Spreading Protest: Negroes Push Spurs Other Minority Drives against Discrimination," *Wall Street Journal,* July 25, 1963, 1; "Indians Have School Troubles, Too," *Afro-American,* January 16, 1960, 6; "Indians Seek Entry in N.C. Schools," *Afro-American,* January 7, 1956, 19.

57. Christopher Arris Oakley, "'When Carolina Indians Went on the Warpath': The Media, the Klan, and the Lumbees of North Carolina," *Southern Cultures* 14, no. 4 (2008): 55–84. See also "Klan Leader Admits Guilt in North Carolina," *Atlanta Daily World,* May 16, 1959, 1; Alice A. Dunnigan, "Nothing New about Klan-Indian Clashes," *Pittsburg Courier,* March 22, 1958, B4; "Lumbee Indians Biggest Tribe in Eastern U.S.," *Atlanta Daily World,* January 26, 1958, 1; James L. Hicks, "Indian Mayor Dares KKK To 'Come Get Your Cross,'" *New York Amsterdam News,* January 25, 1958, 1; "Indians 'Scalp' Klan," *Afro-American,* January 25, 1958, 1. African Americans did not miss the fact that Native Americans had more leeway for armed resistance to violent white supremacists than did African Americans; see "Klan Burns Crosses—Indians Hit Warpath; Klan Burns Crosses—Negroes Murdered?," *Pittsburgh Courier,* January 25, 1958, 8.

58. "Integration or Bankruptcy, Indians Tell Schools," *Afro-American,* October 4, 1969, 13; "Order Indians to Integrate Schools," *Afro-American,* January 18, 1964, 17; "Spreading Protest," *Wall Street Journal,* July 25, 1963, 1; "Bar Indians from White Schools," *Chicago Defender,* July 16, 1962, 4; "Indians May Enter North Carolina School," *Afro-American,* October 29, 1960, 8; "Indians Plan Suit for Mixed Schools," *Afro-American,* October 22, 1960, 7; "Indian Style School Sit-down," *Afro-American,* September 17, 1960, 5; Joseph H. Brewington, "Indians Have School Troubles, Too," *Afro-American,* June 16, 1960, 6.

59. Donald L. Fixico, *Termination and Relocation: Federal Indian Policy, 1945–1960* (Albuquerque: University of New Mexico Press, 1986), 3–5. See also Ronald Takaki, *A Different Mirror: A History of Multicultural America,* rev. ed. (New York: Back Bay Books, 2008), 240–41; John Allen Reyhner and Jeanne M. Oyawin Eder, *American Indian Education: A History* (Norman: University of Oklahoma Press, 2006), 232–51; Guy B. Senese, *Self-Determination and the Social Education of Native Americans* (New York: Praeger, 1991), 3–14.

60. "Indian Finds It Hard to Live like White but He Is Trying," *Christian Science Monitor,* May 17, 1948, 11. See also Tekarihoken, "Reservation Indians," *Washing-*

ton Post, December 23, 1947, 20; Kuma Goshal, "As an Indian Sees It," *Pittsburg Courier,* November 23, 1946, 6.

61. Margaret Connell Szasz, *Education and the American Indian: The Road to Self-Determination since 1928,* 3rd ed. (Albuquerque: University of New Mexico Press, 1999), 106–15; Fixico, *Termination and Relocation,* 3–5. See also Takaki, *A Different Mirror,* 240–41; "Indians Thrive in Large Cities," *New York Times,* December 15, 1956: 75; John A. Menaugh, "The Indian Today," *Chicago Tribune,* June 22, 1947, G6.

62. K. Tsianina Lomawaima and Teresa L. McCarty, *To Remain an Indian: Lessons in Democracy from a Century of Native American Education* (New York: Teachers College Press, 2006), 114–49. See also Dennis Banks with Richard Erdoes, *Ojibwa Warrior: Dennis Banks and the Rise of the American Indian Movement* (Norman: University of Oklahoma Press, 2004); Carolyn Niethammer, *I'll Go and Do More: Annie Dodge Wauneka, Navajo Leader and Activist* (Lincoln: University of Nebraska Press, 2004); Vine Deloria Jr. and Daniel R. Wildcat, *Power and Place: Indian Education in America* (Golden, CO: Fulcrum Publishing, 2001); Esther Burnett Horne and Sally McBeth, *Essie's Story: The Life and Legacy of a Shoshone Teacher* (Lincoln: University of Nebraska Press, 1998); Russell Means with Marvin J. Wolf, *Where White Men Fear to Tread: The Autobiography of Russell Means* (New York: St. Martin's Griffin, 1996). Note that the Ohkay Owingeh Pueblo was previously known as the San Juan Pueblo.

63. "Education of Indian Children by U.S. Assailed at Parley Here," *New York Times,* November 21, 1966, 38.

64. Homer Bigart, "Tribal Leaders Assail Schools," *New York Times,* December 15, 1967, 11.

65. Subcommittee on Indian Education of the Senate Committee on Labor and Public Welfare, *Indian Education: A National Tragedy—A National Challenge* (Washington, DC: Government Printing Office, 1969), ix, 14. See also Edward C. Burks, "Indian Home Life Causes Concern," *New York Times,* March 8, 1969, 16.

66. John Collier Jr., "Survival at Rough Rock: A Historical Overview of Rough Rock Demonstration School," *Anthropology and Education Quarterly* 19, no. 3 (1988): 259.

67. Teresa L. McCarty, *A Place to Be Navajo: Rough Rock and the Struggle for Self-Determination in Indigenous Schooling* (New York: Routledge, 2010); Szasz, *Education and the American Indian,* 170–80; Senese, *Self-Determination,* 105–19; Collier, "Survival at Rough Rock"; Evan Jenkins, "Indians Seek to Allot School Aid," *New York Times,* June 25, 1973, 14.

68. D. Drummond Ayres, "White Man's Town Bows to Angry Indians," *New York Times,* March 20, 1972, 42.

69. Stephen Kent Amerman, *Urban Indians in Phoenix Schools, 1940–2000* (Lincoln: University of Nebraska Press, 2010), 105.

70. Amerman, *Urban Indians in Phoenix Schools,* 105–40.

71. "School in Chicago Caters to Indians," *New York Times,* June 16, 1976, 40. See also "Lumbee Indians File Suit against Desegregation," *Norfolk Journal and Guide,* September 19, 1970, 11; Gene I. Maeroff, "Indian Schools Turn to Pride and Culture," *New York Times,* August 9, 1976, 1; Gary Hickok, "Iowa Indians Fight Integration to Keep Own Schools," *Washington Post,* December 15, 1968, E4.

72. John J. Laukaitis, *Community Self-Determination: American Indian Education in Chicago, 1952–2006* (Albany: State University Press of New York, 2015), 61–102; Amerman, *Urban Indians in Phoenix Schools*, 105–40. Reforms were also taking place in BIA boarding schools; see Daryl E. Lembke, "Indian Bureau Reverses Policy on State Tribes," *Los Angeles Times*, June 30, 1968, B1; Howard Taubman, "Indians in Santa Fe," *New York Times*, May 16, 1967, 42; John Allan Long, "U.S. Schools Fill Gap for Indians," *Christian Science Monitor*, June 13, 1966.

73. Jack Rosenthal, "Senators Hear How Carolina Schools Integrate Whites, Blacks and Indians," *New York Times*, June 18, 1970, 30.

74. "Lumbee Indians File Suit against Desegregation," *Norfolk Journal and Guide*, September 19, 1970, 11.

75. Muriel Cohen, "Indians Fear U.S. Could Deprive Them of Educational Rights," *Boston Globe*, March 2, 1980, E69. See also "Barring Indian Students from School Stirs Row," *Hartford Courant*, July 23, 1965, 25.

76. US Department of Education, Indian Nation at Risk Task Force, *Indian Nations at Risk: An Educational Strategy for Action* (Washington, DC: Government Printing Office, October 1991), http://www2.ed.gov/rschstat/research/pubs/oieresearch/research/natatrisk/report.pdf. "Panel Urges Schools to Stress Native American Culture," *Salt Lake Tribune*, December 28, 1991, A2; Kenneth J. Cooper, "Multicultural Focus Recommended for Education of Native Americans," *Washington Post*, December 27, 1991, A19; Dirk Johnson, "Indian Rootlessness," *New York Times*, November 4, 1990, EDUC27.

77. Executive Office of President Barack Obama, "2014 Native Youth Report," December 2014, p. 3, https://eric.ed.gov/?id=ED565658.

78. Reyhner and Eder, *American Indian Education*, 9–11.

79. Quote from the National Native American Boarding School Healing Coalition website, https://boardingschoolhealing.org.

80. National Native American Boarding School Healing Coalition, "UN Filing on Missing Children," https://boardingschoolhealing.org/advocacy/un-filing-on-missing-children; National Congress of American Indians, Resolution MOH-17-014, "Call to Collect Testimony about American Indian and Alaska Native Children Who Went Missing Under U.S Boarding School Policy," June 15, 2017, http://www.ncai.org/resources/resolutions/call-to-collect-testimony-about-the-american-indian-and-alaska-native-children-who-went-missing-under-u-s-boarding-school-policy.

81. Jeff Gammage, "Indian Tribes to Meet on Retrieving More Children's Remains from Carlisle," *Philadelphia Inquirer*, October 16, 2017, https://www.inquirer.com/philly/news/indian-tribes-to-meet-on-retrieving-more-childrens-remains-from-carlisle-20171016.html; Jeff Gammage, "At Last, the Indian Children Have Come Home," *Philadelphia Inquirer*, August 18, 2017, https://www.inquirer.com/philly/news/at-last-the-indian-children-have-come-home-20170818.html.

82. Charles Glenn, *American Indian/First Nations Schooling: From the Colonial Period to the Present* (New York: Palgrave Macmillan, 2011), 5–9.

83. Sara Slack, "Puerto Rican March Marked a New Era," *New York Amsterdam News*, March 7, 1964, 33.

84. This number was up from only 284 Black and Puerto Rican students who used

the transfer policies after the open enrollment plan was introduced in 1960. See Leonard Buder, "Integration Lags in City's Schools," *New York Times*, June 25, 1962, 1; "Few Negroes or Puerto Ricans Use Right to Change Schools," *New York Times*, October 13, 1960, 39; Farnsworth Fowle, "School Date Set for Assimilating," *New York Times*, October 17, 1958, 23; Benjamin Fine, "School Gets Plan to Wipe Out Bias," *New York Times*, May 17, 1956, 33. Some Puerto Rican parents liked the idea of open enrollment but still expressed preference for sending their children to neighborhood schools; see "Puerto Rican Mothers Fight Pupil Shifting," *Chicago Tribune*, March 18, 1964, A7. On the history of school integration in New York City, see Lewis, *New York City Public Schools*; Jonna Perillo, *Uncivil Rights: Teachers, Unions, and Race in the Battle for School Equity* (Chicago: University of Chicago Press, 2012); Podair, *The Strike That Changed New York*; Ravitch, *The Great School Wars*.

85. Leonard Buder, "Negro and Puerto Rican Schools Have Doubled in City in 6 Years," *New York Times*, January 6, 1964, 1; Leonard Buder, "Ethnic Balance in Schools Shift," *New York Times*, January 1, 1964, 16.

86. Leonard Buder, "Boycott Cripples City Schools," *New York Times*, February 4, 1964, 1. See also Sonia Song-Ha Lee, *Building a Latino Civil Rights Movement: Puerto Ricans, African Americans, and the Pursuit of Racial Justice in New York City* (Chapel Hill: University of North Carolina Press, 2014), 165–71.

87. "'Negroes' Push Spurts Other Minority Drives against Discrimination," *Wall Street Journal*, July 25, 1963, 1.

88. John F. Mendez, "Mexican-American Wants Best of Two Cultures, Reader States," *Los Angeles Times*, September 20, 1963, A4. See also Lila Fernández, *Brown in the Windy City: Mexicans and Puerto Ricans in Postwar Chicago* (Chicago: University of Chicago Press, 2014); Victoria-Maria MacDonald, *Latino Education in the United States: A Narrated History from 1513–2000* (New York: Palgrave MacMillan, 2004); Rubén Donato, *The Other Struggle for Equal Schools: Mexican Americans during the Civil Rights Era* (Albany: State University of New York Press, 1997).

89. Guadalupe San Miguel Jr., *Chicana/o Struggles for Education: Activism in the Community* (College Station: Texas A&M University Press, 2013), 7–42; Richard R. Valencia, *Chicano Students and the Courts: The Mexican American Legal Struggle for Educational Equality* (New York: New York University Press, 2008), 7–78; Angela Valenzuela, *Subtractive Schooling: U.S.-Mexican Youth and the Politics of Caring* (Albany: State University of New York Press, 1999), 161–226; Guadalupe San Miguel Jr. and Richard R. Valencia, "From the Treaty of Guadalupe Hidalgo to *Hopwood*: The Educational Plight and Struggle of Mexican Americans in the Southwest," *Harvard Educational Review* 68, no. 3 (1998): 353–412.

90. Dial Torgerson, "Start of a Revolution?," *Los Angeles Times*, March 17, 1968, B1. On the East Los Angeles blowouts, see Natalia Mehlman Petrzela, *Classroom Wars: Language, Sex, and the Making of Modern Political Culture* (New York: Oxford University Press, 2015), 39–68; San Miguel, *Chicana/o Struggles for Education*, 24–32; Mario T. Garcia and Sal Castro, *Blowout! Sal Castro and the Chicano Struggle for Educational Justice* (Chapel Hill: University of North Carolina Press, 2011); Dolores Delgado Bernal, "Chicana School Resistance and Grassroots Leadership: Providing an Alternative History of the 1968 East Los Angeles Blowouts"

(PhD diss., University of California, Los Angeles, 1997); Francisco A. Rosales, *Chicano: The History of the Mexican American Civil Rights Movement* (Houston: Arte Publico Press, 1997), 175–95; Kaye Briegel, "Chicano Student Militancy: The Los Angeles High School Strike of 1968," in *An Awakened Minority: The Mexican Americans*, ed. Manuel P. Servin (New York: Macmillan, 1974), 215–25.

91. Graham, *Young Activists*, 5.
92. Mario T. Garcia, *The Chicano Generation: Testimonies of the Movement* (Berkeley: University of California Press, 2015); San Miguel, *Chicana/o Struggles for Education*, 25–27; Armando Navarro, *The Cristal Experiment: A Chicano Struggle for Community Control* (Madison: University of Wisconsin Press, 1998); Guadalupe San Miguel Jr., *Brown Not White: School Integration and the Chicano Movement* (College Station: Texas A&M University Press, 2001). See also Martin Waldren, "Texas Mexicans Win New Rights," *New York Times*, January 11, 1970, 44; "U.S. to Investigate High School Boycott in Texas," *New York Times*, December 19, 1969, 32.
93. Petrzela, *Classroom Wars*, 19–38; Guadalupe San Miguel Jr., *Contested Policy: The Rise and Fall of Federal Bilingual Education in the United States, 1960–2001* (Denton: University of North Texas Press, 2004), 5–46.
94. Lee, *Building a Latino Civil Rights Movement*, 165–210; Orfield and Frankenberg, "*Brown* at 60," 23; San Miguel, *Chicana/o Struggles for Education*, 103–4; Gordon K. Mantier, *Power to the Poor: Black-Brown Coalition and the Fight for Economic Justice* (Chapel Hill: University of North Carolina Press, 2013); William Mackey and Von Nieda Beebe, *Bilingual Schools for a Bicultural Community: Miami's Adaptation to the Cuban Refugees* (Rawley, MA: Newbury House, 1977).
95. Bill Boyarksy, "Mexican-Americans Hit School Integration Rule," *Los Angeles Times*, February 15, 1970, 2. School integration failed to substantially alter the racial isolation of Latinx students in Los Angeles; see Orfield and Frankenberg, "*Brown* at 60," 23; Henry Joseph Gutierrez, "The Chicano Educational Rights Movement and School Desegregation: Los Angeles, 1962–1970 (PhD diss., University of California, Irvine, 1990).
96. San Miguel, *Brown Not White*, 133–65.
97. San Miguel, *Brown Not White*, 97–118; Martin Waldron, "Houston Huelga Schools Open in a Mexican American Protest," *New York Times*, September 6, 1970, 36.
98. Keyes v. School District No. 1 of Denver, Colorado, 413 U.S. 189 (1973). See also Valencia, *Chicano Students and the Courts*, 66–67. Like Houston, Miami, Florida, attempted to institute school desegregation by pairing together Black and Latinx schools while leaving white schools untouched. See Orfield and Frankenberg, "*Brown* at 60," 23.
99. Leonard Buder, "New York City's Schools Accused of U.S. Civil-Rights Violations," *New York Times*, January 19, 1977, 12; US Commission on Civil Rights, "Reviewing a Decade of School Desegregation, 1966–1975" (Washington, DC: Government Printing Office, 1977); US Commission on Civil Rights, "Fulfilling the Letter and the Spirit of the Law: Desegregation of the Nation's Public Schools" (Washington, DC: Government Printing Office, 1976); US Commission on Civil Rights, "Toward Quality Education for Mexican Americans" (Washington, DC: Government Printing Office, 1974). See also US Commission on Civil Rights,

"Para Los Ninos (For the Children): Improving Education for Mexican Americans" (Washington, DC: Government Printing Office, 1974).

100. US Commission on Civil Rights, "Toward Quality Education for Mexican Americans." See also Kenneth B. Clark and Jorge Batista, "Hispanic and Unequal," *New York Times*, December 13, 1977, 43; Lena Williams, "Bilingual Education an Issue in New York," *New York Times*, November 25, 1977, 65; Leonard Buder, "New York City's Schools Accused of U.S. Civil Rights Violations," *New York Times*, January 19, 1977, 12; Paul Delaney, "Panel Says Five States Deny Rights of Chicano Students," *New York Times*, February 5, 1974, 46.

101. San Miguel, *Chicana/o Struggles for Education*, 104.

102. David Gonzalez, "Dominican Immigration Alters Spanish New York," *New York Times*, September 1, 1992, A1.

103. San Miguel, *Chicana/o Struggles for Education*, 104–14; Jorge Duany, *Blurred Borders: Transnational Migration between the Hispanic Caribbean and the United States* (Chapel Hill: University of North Carolina Press, 2011); San Miguel, *Contested Policy*, 54–92; San Miguel and Valencia, "From the Treaty of Guadalupe Hidalgo to *Hopwood*," 390–94; Sonia Nieto, ed., *Puerto Rican Students in U.S. Schools: A Brief History* (New York: Routledge, 2000).

104. Jazmine Ulloa, "Fighting for Multilingual Learning," *Los Angeles Times*, November 27, 2016, 2; Corey Mitchell, "Bilingual Education Set to Return to California Schools," *Education Week*, November 15, 2016, 20. See also Southern Poverty Law Center, "Hate at School," May 2, 2019, https://www.splcenter.org/20190502/hate-school.

105. Orfield and Frankenberg, "*Brown* at 60," 22–27.

106. Patricia Gándara and Frances Contreras, *The Latino Educational Crisis: The Consequences of Failed Social Policy* (Cambridge, MA: Harvard University Press, 2009), 13–14, 18–26, 250–333. See also Joe R. Feagin and José A. Cobas, *Latinos Facing Racism: Discrimination, Resistance, and Endurance* (Boulder, CO: Paradigm Publishers, 2014); Gary Orfield, ed., *Dropouts in America: Confronting the Graduation Rate Crisis* (Cambridge, MA: Harvard Education Press, 2004).

107. "Virginians Draw New Color Line," *New York Times*, July 29, 1959, 30. In another example from North Carolina, a racially segregated private school established to avoid school desegregation barred African American students but "regularly admitted Orientals"; see "North Carolina's School's Racial Policy Follows a Rather Uneven Color Line," *New York Times*, January 18, 1982, 12.

108. Ronald Takaki, *Strangers from a Different Shore: A History of Asian Americans* (New York: Little, Brown, 1989), 357–405; Roger Daniels, *Asian America: Chinese and Japanese in the United States since 1850* (Seattle: University of Washington Press, 1988), 283–316. See also Gladwin Hill, "Japanese Gaining in U.S. Equality," *New York Times*, August 12, 1956, 38.

109. "Mrs. Hicks Explains 'White' Chinese," *Boston Globe*, November 3, 1966, 40; "Boston Board Labels Chinese Pupils as White," *Washington Post*, October 20, 1966, A2. See also Formisano, *Boston against Busing*, 47, 128; Jeanne F. Theoharis, "'We Saved the City': Black Struggles for Educational Equality in Boston, 1960–1976," *Radical History Review* 81 (Fall 2001): 61–93; Lukas, *Common Ground*.

110. "671 Chinese Pupils Listed as White," *Hartford Courant*, October 20, 1966, 4; "Chinese 'Whites,' Boston Declares," *New York Times*, October 20, 1966, 21; "Reclassify Chinese in Integration Fight," *Chicago Tribune*, October 20, 1966, 8.

111. Manli Ho, "Bused Chinese Kids Well Received in North End," *Boston Globe,* September 14, 1974, 5; Manli Ho, "Chinese-Americans Ask Effect of Busing," *Boston Globe,* April 1, 1974, 15; "Boston Is Ordered: Chinese Stay Chinese," *New York Times,* October 27, 1966, 40; "State Rebuffs City on Chinese Pupils," *Boston Globe,* October 26, 1966, 2. See also Scott Kurashige, *The Shifting Grounds of Race: Black and Japanese Americans in the Making of a Multiethnic Los Angeles* (Princeton, NJ: Princeton University Press, 2008), 186–204.

112. David Nyhan, "In Peking, the Talk Was of Boston," *Boston Globe,* December 3, 1975, 36; "Chinese Parents Group Class for School Boycott," *Chicago Tribune,* September 9, 1975, 2; Stephen Curwood, "Chinese Parents Vote to Keep Children Home," *Boston Globe,* September 8, 1975, 13. See also Kaoru Oguri Kendis and Randall Jay Kendis, "The Street Boy Identity: An Alternate Strategy of Boston's Chinese-Americans," *Urban Anthropology* 5, no. 1 (1976): 1–17.

113. David L. Kirp, "Race, Politics, and the Courts: School Desegregation in San Francisco," *Harvard Educational Review* 46, no. 4 (1976): 572–611.

114. Daryl Lembke, "S.F. Integration Plan Evokes Chinese Wrath," *Los Angeles Times,* June 27, 1971, A5.

115. "Chinese Parents Fighting School Busing," *Hartford Courant,* August 31, 1971, 11; "Chinese Appeal School Transfer," *Harford Courant,* August 18, 1971, 7.

116. Douglas E. Kneeland, "San Francisco's Chinese Resist School Busing," *New York Times,* September 1, 1971, 25.

117. Darly Lembke, "'Freedom School' Problems Multiply, Chinatown Divided," *Los Angeles Times,* October 17, 1971, 1; Wallace Turner, "Many Shun Buses in San Francisco," *New York Times,* September 14, 1971, 18; "Hundreds Play Hooky as San Francisco Opens School Busing," *Wall Street Journal,* September 14, 1971, 22. See also Kirp, "Race, Politics, and the Courts," 599.

118. Kneeland, "San Francisco's Chinese Resist School Busing," 25.

119. Lau v. Nichols, 414 U.S. 563 (1974). See also Patricia Gándara, Rachel Moran, and Eugene Garcia, "Legacy of *Brown: Lau* and Language Policy in the United States," *Review of Research in Education* 28 (2004): 27–46.

120. Pew Research Center, Social & Demographic Trends, "The Rise of Asian Americans," April 4, 2013, http://www.pewsocialtrends.org/2012/06/19/the-rise-of-asian-americans/. For the census data, see Karen R. Humes, Nicolas A. Jones, and Roberto R. Ramirez, "Overview of Race and Hispanic Origin 2010," 2010 Census Briefs, US Census Bureau (Washington, DC: US Department of Commerce, March 2011), http://www.census.gov/prod/cen2010/briefs/c2010br-02 .pdf; Frank Hobbs and Nicole Stoops, "Demographic Trends in the Twentieth Century," Census 2000 Special Report, US Census Bureau (Washington, DC: US Department of Commerce, November 2002), https://www.census.gov/prod /2002pubs/censr-4.pdf. Note that the numbers in 2010 include individuals who identify as all or partially Asian and/or Pacific Islander.

121. Amy Hsin and Yu Xie, "Explaining Asian Americans' Academic Advantage over Whites," *Proceedings of the National Academy of Sciences of the United States of America* 11, no. 23 (2014): 8416–21, http://www.pnas.org/content/111/23/8416; Orfield and Frankenberg, "*Brown* at 60."

122. Meyer Weinberg, *Asian-American Education: Historical Background and Current Realities* (Mahwah, NJ: Lawrence Erlbaum Associates, 1997), 36; Pew Research Center, "The Rise of Asian Americans."

123. Madeline Y. Hsu, *The Good Immigrants: How the Yellow Peril Became the Model Minority* (Princeton, NJ: Princeton University Press, 2015); Ellen D. Wu, *The Color of Success: Asian Americans and the Origins of the Model Minority* (Princeton, NJ: Princeton University Press, 2013); Stacey J. Lee, *Unraveling the Model Minority Stereotype: Listening to Asian American Youth*, 2nd ed. (New York: Teachers College Press, 2009); Rosalind S. Chou and Joe R. Feagin, *The Myth of the Model Minority: Asian Americans Facing Racism* (Boulder, CO: Paradigm Publishers, 2008); Frank H. Wu, *Yellow: Race in America beyond Black and White* (New York: Basic Books, 2002), 1–78.

124. Lawrence Feinberg, "'They Killed Me, but I'm Alive': Youthful Cambodian Refugees Take to Classrooms," *Washington Post*, October 29, 1979, C1.

125. Jackie Hyman, "Isolation Still Plagues Vietnamese Students," *Los Angeles Times*, May 11, 1980, 3. See also Pamela Constable, "Newly Arrived Vietnamese Learn to Adapt," *Washington Post*, February 9, 1997, B1; Tony Marcano, "School Daze," *Los Angeles Times*, October 4, 1990, 79; Daniel R. Poster, "A Clash of Cultures, Cambodian Style," *Los Angeles Times*, September 20, 1990, 15A; Marshall Ingwerson, "Southeast Asian Refugees," *Christian Science Monitor*, January 28, 1982, B1; Ted Vollmer, "Plight of the Refugee Children," *Los Angeles Times*, April 5, 1981, A1.

126. C. N. Lee, "The Model Minority Image," *Asian-Nation*, August 13, 2015, http://www.asian-nation.org/model-minority.shtml; "Calls in Louisiana to Require English at Commencement," *New York Times*, June 30, 2008, A17. See also Chou and Feagin, *Myth of the Model Minority*, 55–99.

127. Christina Veiga, "New York City Students Walk Out of Class, Pledging Weekly Strikes to Demand School Integration," *Chalkbeat*, November 18, 2019, https://www.chalkbeat.org/posts/ny/2019/11/18/new-york-city-students-walk-out-of-class-pledging-weekly-strikes-to-demand-school-integration; Eliza Shapiro, "Lock-Ins and Walkouts: The Students Changing City Schools from the Inside," *New York Times*, September 5, 2019, https://www.nytimes.com/2019/09/05/nyregion/student-activists-nyc-schools.html; Sara Mosle, "Mr. Mayor, We Cannot Afford to Wait," *Chalkbeat*, February 15, 2019, https://www.chalkbeat.org/posts/ny/2019/02/15/mr-mayor-we-cannot-afford-to-wait-teen-group-says-new-york-city-diversity-plan-doesnt-move-fast-enough.

128. Black Lives Matter at School website, accessed May 11, 2020, https://blacklivesmatteratschool.com/about; Ibram X. Kendi, *How to Be an Antiracist* (New York: Random House, 2019).

129. Nikole Hannah-Jones, "It Was Never about Busing," *New York Times*, July 12, 2019, https://www.nytimes.com/2019/07/12/opinion/sunday/it-was-never-about-busing.html.

130. Larissa Karr, "Re-emerging Demand Seen for City's Afrocentric Schools," *City Limits*, February 18, 2020, https://citylimits.org/2020/02/18/re-emerging-seen-for-citys-afrocentric-schools/.

CHAPTER THREE

1. We utilize the historical and traditional idea of "equality" for the ideal in question, as used in the *Brown* decision. In recent educational contexts, the term *equity* has often come to replace *equality*, and the latter is often criticized as in-

volving "sameness of treatment," when different students have differing needs, and "equity" is seen as a preferable expression for responsiveness to need. (See, e.g., Boston Public Schools Racial Equity planning tool, p. 4, http://bit.ly/BPSREPT.) But as a political ideal, "equality" invokes a deeper sense of equal worth, humanity, and dignity, as well as responsiveness to differential need in the service of these deeper commonalities. So we will generally stick with that term but also recognize "equity."

2. The comparative conception of equality is vulnerable to what has been called the "leveling down objection." Comparative equality could be created by bringing those who have more down to the level of those who have less, instead of bringing those with less up to the level of those with more. Equality as a positive ideal must therefore level up—all should have equivalent access to positive educational goods.

3. The exit point is not necessarily determined by age. For example, if we think of the end of high school as the exit point, we must include the GED, which students can attain at different ages. Of course, the exit point could be extended beyond high school to include community college, an idea floated during the Obama administration.

    Helen Ladd and Susanna Loeb also caution that it is not always possible to determine either at a given point (such as an "exit point") whether students have acquired particular educational goods or the degree to which their schooling has contributed to their acquiring them. This is particularly true of moral, personal growth, and civic goods, whose manifestation may not show up in the immediate wake of learning. But this does not make those goods less central to an appropriate conception of educational value. Helen Ladd and Susanna Loeb, "The Challenges of Measuring School Quality: Implications for Educational Equity," in *Education, Justice, and Democracy*, ed. Danielle Allen and Rob Reich (Chicago: University of Chicago Press, 2013).

4. The terminology of students' "possessing" these educational goods can be misleading. The goods become part of a student's being, not a separable "thing" possessed by the student. David Labaree emphasizes that successful teaching—that is, the conveying of educational goods—requires students themselves to engage. It is not like a surgeon who can operate on and thereby convey a good to a passive patient. David Labaree, *Someone Has to Fail: The Zero-Sum Game of Public Schooling* (Cambridge, MA: Harvard University Press, 2012). We cannot think of a different single term that expresses the envisioned relation between the student and the goods in question, so will reluctantly use "possession."

5. Harry Brighouse, Helen F. Ladd, Susanna Loeb, and Adam Swift, "Educational Goods and Values: A Framework for Decision Makers," *Theory and Research in Education* 14, no. 1 (2016), introduce the idea of educational goods that we are employing (elaborated in their 2018 book *Educational Goods: Values, Evidence, and Decision-Making* [Chicago: University of Chicago Press, 2018]), but we somewhat differ with them regarding the specific educational goods.

6. Aristotle, *Nicomachean Ethics*, trans. Terence Irwin (Cambridge, MA: Hackett, 1999).

7. Brighouse et al. say that "flourishing" can encompass all educational goods. Brighouse et al., *Educational Goods*, 21. While partly a semantic issue, we would

want to emphasize that people are often referred to as flourishing without being either morally good or civically responsible and engaged. Being morally good, civically engaged, and personally flourishing seem to us three distinct, if overlapping, human goods served by education.

8. In an influential article, Christopher Jencks shows the difficulty of coming up with a coherent and acceptable equal treatment principle for a teacher in relation to her students in a single classroom. Christopher Jencks, "What Must Be Equal for Opportunity to Be Equal?," in *Philosophy of Education: An Anthology*, ed. R. Curren (Oxford: Blackwell, 2007). But the principle of "equal care and respect" survives his criticisms.

9. In an important study of graduates of racially integrated schools, Amy Stuart Wells, Jennifer Jellison Holme, Anita Tijerina Revilla, and Awo Korantemaa Atanda, *Both Sides Now: The Story of School Desegregation's Graduates* (Berkeley: University of California Press, 2009), while agreeing with this criticism of color-blindness, found a certain number of white respondents who said that the school's official stance of color-blindness sometimes helped them to get beyond stereotypes, fears, and hostilities toward Black and Latinx students. But there are other ways of accomplishing this goal that do not rely on the problematic stance of color-blindness.

10. Chike Jeffers, "The Ethics and Politics of Cultural Preservation," *Journal of Value Inquiry* 49 (March 2015): 205–20. Jeffers's argument could easily apply to Native Americans both in general and with respect to particular groups, and more generally to Latinx and Asian American ethnic groups. His argument is in the spirit of what we have historically seen to be the desire of particular ethnic and ethnoracial groups to sustain their group identities and heritages with respect to schooling (chap. 2). We will discuss the idea of ethnoracial group retention and identity recognition further below (151–52, 154–55).

11. The American conception is sometimes framed as "equality of opportunity rather than equality of results."

12. John Rawls, *A Theory of Justice*, rev. ed. (Cambridge, MA: Harvard University Press, 1999), 63.

13. Rawls restates this view of FEO almost word for word in *Justice as Fairness: A Restatement* (Cambridge, MA: Harvard University Press, 1999), 44. This is a different work from the classic *Theory of Justice* (in previous note), which, despite its publication date, was essentially completed in 1975.

14. Rawls actually rejects meritocracy as an ideal, though for reasons not relevant to our concerns here.

15. Evidence shows that in recent years, upward mobility in the United States has slowed and is now lower than in Western European countries. Edward Luce, *The Retreat of Western Liberalism* (London: Little, Brown, 2017), 43. Popular opinion has begun to recognize this and is thus somewhat less wedded to the meritocratic ideology than in the past. But some studies show that Americans still overestimate the degree to which people advance out of the income bracket into which they were born. Eric Jaffe, "Americans Think Upward Mobility Is Far More Common than It Really Is," *Citylab*, February 2, 2015, https://www.citylab.com /life/2015/02/americans-think-upward-mobility-is-far-more-common-than-it

-really-is/385086/ (summarizing study in the *Journal of Experimental Social Psychology*).

16. Joseph Fishkin illustrates the impossibility of pinpointing the genetic component of any complex human trait that also has an environmental or developmental dimension with the following visual image: We may think of the contributions of genetics (G) and environment (E) to an ability on the model of G holding a bucket with forty liters, and E holding one with sixty, then both of them pouring their buckets into a larger one-hundred-liter bucket. In this scenario, we can say what the percentage contribution of each of G and E is. But Fishkin argues that the actual situation is more like this: G turns on a spigot, and E holds the hose attached to the spigot over a one-hundred-liter bucket. G and E both stop what they are doing when the bucket is filled. Here it is impossible to attach anything like percentages to the "contributions" of G and E. Joseph Fishkin, *Bottlenecks: A New Theory of Equality of Opportunity* (New York: Oxford University Press, 2014), 95, 96.

17. Fishkin develops his critique of the natural asset view with respect to intelligence (*Bottlenecks*, 83–108). In addition, the existence of a genetic component is often taken to imply that the aspect of the trait in question that is controlled by the genetic part is fixed and unchangeable (only the environmental part is changeable). But genetic does not mean unchangeable. For example, vision problems are genetic in character, but we can correct for their trait form with glasses and operations.

    We focus here on intelligence both because of its perceived relationship to school performance and because of its role in racist ideologies. We are not engaging with the substantive issue of what qualities actually make for school success; recent research suggests that noncognitive factors play a greater role than traditional meritocratic conceptions assume. Jennifer Morton, "Molding Conscientious, Hard-Working, and Perseverant Students," *Social Philosophy and Policy* 31, no. 2 (2014): 60–80.

18. Howard Gardner has developed an influential theory of "multiple intelligences." Howard Gardner, *Frames of Mind: The Theory of Multiple Intelligences*, 3rd ed. (1983; repr., New York: Basic Books, 2011).

19. The distinction between the "natural asset" and the "developmental" view is most associated with the work of Carol Dweck. She uses the terminology of "fixed mindset" and "growth mindset." Dweck and several other researchers have established that students with the growth mindset outperform otherwise similar students who adhere to a fixed mindset. Carol Dweck, *Mindset: The New Psychology of Success* (New York: Ballantine Books, 2007). Greg Walton, "The Myth of Intelligence: Intelligence Isn't Like Height," in Allen and Reich, *Education, Justice, and Democracy*.

20. For a comprehensive history of the ideology of Black intellectual inferiority in the United States, see Derrick Darby and John L. Rury, *The Color of Mind: Why the Origins of the Achievement Gap Matter for Justice* (Chicago: University of Chicago Press, 2018). John Ogbu shows that Blacks are often acutely aware that whites regard them as less intelligent and provides suggestive evidence that some Blacks have themselves internalized this ideology. John Ogbu, *Black Amer-*

ican Students in an Affluent Suburb: A Study in Academic Disengagement (New York: Routledge, 2003), 77–80.

21. For the past several decades, education observers (and others) have been much more likely to cite an allegedly culturally based deficient work ethic or disengagement from school, rather than a genetic deficiency in intelligence, for the continued underperformance of Black and Latinx students. Lawrence Bobo and Camille Z. Charles, "Race in the American Mind: From the Moynihan Report to the Obama Candidacy," *Annals of the American Academy of Political and Social Science* 621 (January 2009): 246. This discursive shift does not represent a wholesale rejection of the ideology of Black genetic inferiority. Rather it signifies, at least in part, a change in what is regarded as socially acceptable to say (and even to think) about the source of differences in educational attainment among racialized groups. For discussion of whether this general shift toward "culturalism" and away from biologistic racism betokens a significant rejection of racialist thinking, see Darby and Rury, *Color of Mind*; Thomas McCarthy, *Race, Empire, and the Idea of Human Development* (New York: Cambridge University Press, 2009); George M. Frederickson, *Racism: A Short History* (Princeton, NJ: Princeton University Press, 2002); Lawrence Blum, "'Cultural Racism': Biology and Culture in Racist Thought," *Journal of Social Philosophy* (Spring 2020): 1–20.

    A lesser version of this point applies in the case of class. Working-class and poor students are also thought of as less intelligent than those of wealthier classes. The ideology is similar to that regarding race but lacks the historical embeddedness of an officially articulated ideology, such as existed in the race case. Indeed, Charles Murray and Richard Herrnstein's best seller *The Bell Curve: Intelligence and Class Structure in American Life* (New York: Simon & Schuster, 1994) argues, as its title suggests, that wealthier people have, on average, an increasingly greater degree of a substantially genetically based trait the authors call "general intelligence" than poorer and working-class people. The Rawlsian view of natural assets, and of intelligence as a natural asset, can be used to support this view. (However, at one point Rawls himself appears to reject, at least by implication, the idea of class-based differences in intelligence as a natural asset. He says that "in all sectors of society" there should be equal prospects of culture and achievement for everyone similarly motivated and endowed. Rawls, *Theory of Justice*, 63).

22. Richard Rothstein notes that we generally think that students' reading capability has a genetic component, but we hold schools responsible for teaching all students to read. Richard Rothstein, "Why Children from Lower Socioeconomic Classes, on Average, Have Lower Academic Achievement than Middle Class Children," in *Closing the Opportunity Gap: What America Must Do to Give Every Child an Even Chance*, ed. Prudence Carter and Kevin Welner (New York: Oxford University Press, 2013). We are taking a similar view of the capability for educational goods more broadly.

23. Rawls's FEO is not an education-focused idea. Like the American conception, FEO regards "opportunity" as a way that education provides the groundwork for occupational aspiration. It is not so much opportunity *for* education as opportunity *through* or *by means of* education. Hugh Lazenby, "What Is Equality of

Opportunity in Education?," *Theory and Research in Education* 14, no. 1 (2016): 65–76.

24. In *Theory of Justice*, Rawls does not expound explicitly on whether the American occupational order and its (then current) reward system is just, but his theory would clearly condemn it as unjust, though not along a distinctly racial axis. (The injustice is made clearer in *Justice as Fairness*.)

    We want to register a further problem with the American conception and, at least implicitly, Rawls's FEO view, highlighted by Fishkin. This is that people's opportunities for a flourishing life should not be so dependent on attainment at one specific point in time—e.g., how well they do by the end of high school. There should be "second chances" for people who fall short or mess up at one point to recover at a later one. This insight is part of what Fishkin means by his "bottleneck" idea that is central to his argument in the book (*Bottlenecks*).

25. James Coleman expresses this view: "The school provides the opportunity; but it is on the child or family to use it." James Coleman, "The Concept of Equality of Educational Opportunity," in *Equality and Achievement in Education* (Boulder, CO: Westview Press, 1989), 21. See also H. Brighouse and G. Schouten, "Understanding the Context for Existing Reform," in *Whither Opportunity? Rising Inequality, Schools, and Children's Life Chances*, ed. G. Duncan and R. Murnane (New York: Russell Sage Foundation, 2011), 509.

26. Elizabeth Anderson, "Race, Culture, and Educational Opportunity," *Theory and Research in Education* 10, no. 2 (2012): 105–29. See also R. Curren, "Equal Opportunity and Outcomes Assessment," in *Philosophy of Education 2008*, ed. Ron Glass (Urbana, IL: Philosophy of Education Society, 2009), 345–53.

27. Anderson, "Race, Culture, and Educational Opportunity."

28. Meira Levinson, *No Citizen Left Behind* (Cambridge, MA: Harvard University Press, 2012). Michael Rebell, *Flunking Democracy: Schools, Courts, and Civic Participation* (Chicago: University of Chicago Press, 2018). Both authors argue, however, that in fact there are substantial racial gaps in civic education and resultant civic competence.

29. Tyrone C. Howard, *Why Race and Culture Matter in Schools: Closing the Achievement Gap in America's Classrooms*, 2nd ed. (New York: Teachers College Press, 2020), 15.

30. Coleman's report was used to support racial integration in schools, but not on the *Brown* decision's grounds (that dismantling the structure of segregation would create equal education), but rather because race correlated with socioeconomic characteristics, and the report found that student outcomes are improved by having middle-class classmates. (This is a version of the "capital" argument for integration discussed in chapter 4.)

31. Although Coleman et al. were focused on the educational fates of race-defined groups of students, the data available to them employed only class-related characteristics of those groups—such as the educational levels of the parents. So they were unable to, or chose not to, devise a way to assess racism-related factors in their subjects' school performance—such as racial stigma (the issue central in the *Brown* decision) or discriminatory treatment of the students of color by white school personnel or fellow students.

32. Helen F. Ladd, "Education and Poverty: Confronting the Evidence," *Journal of Policy Analysis and Management* 31, no. 2 (2012): 203–27.

33. Rothstein, "Children from Lower Socioeconomic Classes," 65. Julia Burdick-Will et al., "Converging Evidence for Neighborhood Effects on Children's Test Scores: An Experimental, Quasi-experimental, and Observational Comparison," in Duncan and Murnane, *Whither Opportunity?*, 255–76.

34. Annette Lareau, *Unequal Childhoods: Class, Race, and Family Life*, 2nd ed. (Berkeley: University of California Press, 2011); Sean Reardon, "The Widening Academic Achievement Gap between the Rich and the Poor," in Duncan and Murnane, *Whither Opportunity?*; Richard Reeves, *The Dream Hoarders: How the American Upper Middle Class Is Leaving Everyone Else in the Dust, Why That Is a Problem, and What to Do About It* (New York: Brookings Institution, 2017). We should distinguish between actual educational enhancements provided by parent resources (tutoring, educational travel) and college admission enhancements, like counselors that improve the offspring's admissions application but not the educational substance of the offspring's qualifications.

35. As a social scientist, Coleman recognized the analytical dimension of the justice perspective but not the normative one. Nevertheless, he implied that the class structure of the society was in itself just, or at least not unjust, but that it gave rise to injustice in its impact on educational opportunities. Although he approached the issue of educational opportunities as an empirical matter— something to be measured—he clearly regarded "educational opportunity" as a good for society and believed that if there were unequal opportunities (as his research project demonstrated), policy should be directed to rectifying this.

36. According to the 2018 census, the poverty rates by race: Black 20.8 percent (children 32 percent), Latinx 17.6 percent (children 26 percent), Asian/Pacific Islander 10.1 percent (children 11 percent), non-Latinx white 8.1 percent (children 11 percent), and Native American children 31 percent. https://www.census.gov/library/publications/2019/demo/p60-266.html.

37. See Tommie Shelby, "Prisons of the Forgotten: Ghettos and Economic Injustice," in *To Shape a New World: Essays on the Political Philosophy of Martin Luther King, Jr.*, ed. T. Shelby and B. Terry (Cambridge, MA: Belknap, 2018). Shelby points out that as early as 1958, King said that "the poor white was exploited just as much as the Negro" (*Stride toward Freedom* [1958; repr., Boston: Beacon Press, 2010], 194) (not that we fully agree with this statement). See also Michael Honey, *To the Promised Land: Martin Luther King and the Fight for Economic Justice* (New York: W. W. Norton, 2019). It should not, but perhaps does, need saying that in claiming that racial injustice and oppression is bound up with class injustice, neither we nor King is "reducing" race to class, nor are we saying that every form or instance of race injustice is no more than class injustice. Race and class must be thought about in a "both/and" rather than an "either/or" way.

38. In *Rac(e)ing to Class: Confronting Poverty and Race in Schools and Classrooms* (Cambridge, MA: Harvard Education Press, 2015), the educational theorist H. Richard Milner IV, known for his work on race, emphasizes the class aspect of racial inequality, which he thinks has not been given sufficient attention in education writing about race and racial disparities.

39. Mark R. Warren and David Goodman, eds., *Lift Us Up, Don't Push Us Out! Voices*

from the Front Lines of the Educational Justice Movement (Boston: Beacon Press, 2018). Mark. R. Warren and Karen Mapp, eds., *A Match on Dry Grass: Community Organizing as a Catalyst for School Reform* (Oxford: Oxford University Press, 2011). Eric Blanc, *Red State Revolt: The Teachers' Strike Wave and Working Class Politics* (New York: Verso, 2019).

40. See Milner, *Rac(e)ing to Class*.

41. Measuring poverty as less than 50 percent of a country's median income, in 2018 the United States had an 18 percent child poverty rate (Kids Count Data Center, The Annie E. Casey Foundation, "Children in Poverty by Race and Ethnicity in the United States," copyright 2020, https://datacenter.kidscount.org/data /tables/44-children-in-poverty-by-race-and-ethnicity#detailed/1/any/false/37 ,871,870,573,869,36,868,867,133,38/10,11,9,12,1,185,13/324,323), compared to 14+ percent in Canada, 11 percent in the Netherlands, and 4 percent in Finland. Ladd, "Education and Poverty," 210. In 2013, the percentage of "low-income" children (150 percent of the poverty line) went over 50 percent for the first time (Columbia University Mailman School of Public Health, "America's Child Poverty Rate Remains Stubbornly High despite Important Progress," February 5, 2018, https:// www.mailman.columbia.edu/public-health-now/news/america%E2%80%99s -child-poverty-rate-remains-stubbornly-high-despite-important-progress). Cognitive skills gaps at school entry are higher in the United States than in Australia, Canada, and the United Kingdom, as are gaps in family resources. The gaps are higher both between the low and middle SES and between the middle and high SES. B. Bradbury, M. Corak, J. Waldfogel, and E. Washbrook, *Too Many Children Left Behind: The U.S. Achievement Gap in Comparative Perspective* (New York: Russell Sage Foundation, 2015), 10–11. According to data from the Organization for Economic Cooperation and Development, the United States' child-poverty rate is significantly higher than that in thirty other industrialized economies, including Poland, Mexico, and Estonia, as well as countries like Japan, Germany, and France. Annie Lowrey, "America's Poverty Rate Has Hit a Record Low," *Atlantic*, October 5, 2017. The article also makes the point that low unemployment is not having the effect of reducing poverty; government programs have to do so.

42. The title of Stephan and Abigail Thernstrom's influential work *No Excuses: Closing the Racial Gap in Learning* (New York: Simon & Schuster, 2004), a book touting charter schools in criticism of the traditional public system, expresses this point of view. See also Brighouse and Schouten, "Understanding the Context," 510.

43. Erin Quackenbush, a teacher and member of the Teach for America organization, in *One Day—Alumni Magazine: Teach for America* (ca. 2012).

44. Brian Lack, "Anti-Democratic Militaristic Education," in *Assault on Kids*, ed. R. Ahlquist, P. Gorski, and T. Montano (New York: Peter Lang, 2011), 68. Lily Lamboy and Amanda Lu, "The Pursuit of College for All: Ends and Means in 'No Excuses' Charter Schools," *Theory and Research in Education* 15, no. 2 (2017): 202–29.

45. Ladd claims that the No Child Left Behind Act, and policies that it put in place, makes this assumption—that a strict accountability regime applied to all would result in equal educational attainment by all income groups. Ladd, "Education and Poverty," 213.

46. Howard, *Why Race and Culture Matter*, 13.
47. Ladd, "Education and Poverty"; Milner, *Rac(e)ing to Class*, 39–40; Brighouse and Schouten, "Understanding the Context"; the Broader, Bolder Approach to Education (www.boldapproach.org), a research-based advocacy organization emphasizing reducing poverty and its impact on education.
48. Ladd, "Education and Poverty," 221; Milner, *Rac(e)ing to Class*, 40. The Health Resources and Services Administration reports that as of May 2017, there were two thousand such clinics functioning in schools, many of them a product of the Affordable Care Act (Health Resources and Services Administration, "School-Based Health Centers," last reviewed May 2017, https://www.hrsa.gov/our -stories/school-health-centers/index.html).
49. New York City Department of Education, "NYC Community Schools," http:// www1.nyc.gov/site/communityschools/index.page. As of fall 2018, there were 247 community schools in the NYC school system (New York City Community Schools, https://sites.google.com/mynycschool.org/newyorkcitycommunity schools/).

    The health dimension emphasized in our argument is only one component of the broader community schools idea, as suggested in the quote, which involves partnering with community organizations, family engagement and family support, after-school activities, and the use of the school as a neighborhood hub. All assume that out-of-classroom factors affect students' learning and that schools can work with their communities to help mitigate the negative effects of some of those factors. (See Jeannie Oakes, Anna Maier, and Julia Daniel, "Community Schools: An Evidence-Based Strategy for Equitable School Improvement"[Boulder, CO: National Education Policy Center, June 2017].) Oakland, CA, is in the process of becoming an all community schools district. M. McLaughlin, K. Fehrer, and J. Leos-Urbel, *The Way We Do School: The Making of Oakland's Full-Service Community School District* (Cambridge, MA: Harvard Education Press, 2020).

    New York State is a leader in the community schools idea, but several other states and, as of 2011, the federal government, also support it. Reuben Jacobson, "States Lead the Way on Community Schools Innovation," Brown Center Chalkboard, *Brookings Institution*, July 1, 2019, https://www.brookings.edu/blog /brown-center-chalkboard/2019/08/01/states-lead-the-way-on-community -school-innovation/.
50. Ladd reports that Finnish schools provide a rich range of social services, for example, social welfare teams composed of school nurses, social welfare counselors, and teachers "meet on a regular basis to discuss and address the challenges of individual children" (Ladd, "Education and Poverty," 220). But it should also be noted that when students have these needs, but the school or the system is not meeting them, many teachers feel compelled to expand their roles to include social worker, counselor, psychologist, health provider, mentor, and so forth, leading to an inability to engage in their primary function as teachers.
51. Natasha Capers, "The School Is the Heart of the Community: Building Community Schools across New York City," in Warren and Goodman, *Lift Us Up*.
52. Recognizing the constituent elements in socioeconomic disadvantage is not meant to deny that holistic approaches to dealing with the full range of such

disadvantages in a coordinated way is more effective than taking them on separately.

53. Targeting child (rather than whole family) poverty (as the Children's Defense
Fund does) is a category in-between but somewhat overlapping with both categories two and three.

54. "Educators . . . and their professional organizations have to publicly insist that
social and economic reforms are needed to create an environment in which the
most effective teaching can take place": Rothstein "Children from Lower Socioeconomic Classes," 70.

55. Gary Orfield and Erica Frankenberg, with Jongyeon Ee and John Kuscera, "*Brown
at 60: Great Progress, a Long Retreat and an Uncertain Future*" (Los Angles: Civil
Rights Project at University of California, Los Angeles, 2014), 35, 36.

56. James Forman Jr. replies to the Teach for America teacher Erin Quackenbush's
defense of the "no excuses" approach, quoting from a teacher reporting on a
teachers' discussion group on a book about the educational effects of poverty:

> They agreed that the book helped them to articulate what teachers al-
> ready know: that teaching lower-class kids is tougher than teaching
> middle-class kids. The book didn't lessen their commitment to closing the
> achievement gap. It did lead them to want to personally take new steps:
> walking tours of their school community, [getting] to know their students
> and families better, political activism to fight for the expansion of Head
> Start and other pre-school programs, etc. Most importantly they talked
> about the weight it lifted from their shoulders, allowing them to celebrate
> human-scale improvement rather than perpetually feeling bad about
> their work.

James Forman Jr., *One Day—Alumni Magazine: Teach for America*, 217n52. As
Forman implies, advocates of attention to poverty-related disadvantages are
not saying that poverty must be alleviated before any teaching and learning can
go on. Eric Hanushek, a prominent education researcher, mischaracterizes the
dispute in this way when he states, "Some argue that since poverty is strongly
related to achievement, we must alleviate poverty before we can hope to have
an effect of schools on achievement." Eric Hanushek, "What Matters for Student Achievement," *Education Next* (Spring 2016): 23. But it is a matter of "both/
and" not "one then the other," with respect to in-class teaching and attending to
poverty-related obstacles.

57. Dana Goldstein, "It's More than Pay: Striking Teachers Demand Counselors and
Nurses," *New York Times*, October 24, 2019. Goldstein notes, "In this climate
teachers' unions have renewed a centuries-old call for schools to provide health
and social services on site that can free classroom teachers to focus on academics."

58. See Blanc, *Red State Revolt*. The assertion of teachers' professional identity and
dignity, including its encompassing a recognition of the importance of outside-
of-school socioeconomic factors, has been highlighted by Doris Santoro. Santoro
argues that teachers' professional (including ethical) concerns have been overlooked or diminished in much discussion of teachers, for example, by naming

as "burnout" the phenomenon of teachers leaving the profession because their conditions of work do not allow them to practice their profession in the ethical fashion they understand to be required of them. Doris Santoro, *Demoralized: Why Teachers Leave the Profession They Love and How They Can Stay* (Cambridge, MA: Harvard Education Press, 2018).

We are focusing here on teacher responsibilities, as they have most prominently figured in the arguments about the connection between poverty and education. But Milner reminds us that school districts are a vital agent in addressing that connection. Milner, *Rac(e)ing to Class*, 29–65.

59. See Abigail and Stephan Thernstrom's characterization of KIPP schools: "If the expectations of the school conflict with their culture, students 'must leave their culture at the door'" (Thernstrom and Thernstrom, *No Excuses*, 69). Lamboy and Lu, "Pursuit of College," 209.

60. In 2020, the poverty line was twenty-six thousand dollars for a family of four. Kimberley Amadeo and Gordon Scott, "Federal Poverty Guidelines and Chart: Are You Eligible for Federal Benefits in 2020?," *The Balance*, updated February 7, 2020, https://www.thebalance.com/federal-poverty-level-definition -guidelines-chart-3305843#2020federal-poverty-guidelines-chart.

61. Susan Dynarski, "Why American Schools Are Even More Unequal Than We Thought," *New York Times*, August 12, 2016.

62. Dynarski, "Why American Schools."

63. Chester Finn Jr., Bruno Manno, and Brandon Wright, *Charter Schools at the Crossroads* (Cambridge, MA: Harvard Education Press, 2016), 163.

64. Richard Kahlenberg and Halley Potter, *A Smarter Charter: Finding What Works for Charter Schools and Public Education* (New York: Teachers College Press, 2014), 79, citing G. Miron, J. Urschel, and N. Saxton, "What Makes KIPP Work? A Study of Student Characteristics, Attrition, and School Finance," National Center for the Study of Privatization in Education, March 2011.

65. Kahlenberg and Potter, *A Smarter Charter*, 76, citing MTA's Center for Education Policy and Practice. An NAACP charter school report mentions a study in Chicago that found charter school expulsion rates to be 1000 percent higher than the Chicago Public Schools. Office of College and Career Success, Chicago Public Schools, "CPS Suspension and Expulsions Reduction Plan and Data Highlights," February 26, 2014, https://www.cpsboe.org/content/documents /student_suspension_and_expulsion_reduction_plan.pdf. According to this report, it was found that charters expelled sixty-one of every ten thousand students in comparison to traditional public schools that expelled five of every ten thousand students.

A classic in the literature on charter school selectivity is Kevin Welner, "The Dirty Dozen: How Charter Schools Influence Student Enrollment," *Teachers College Record*, April 2013, http://www.tcrecord.org, ID no. 17104.

66. Mary Pattillo, "Everyday Politics of School Choice in the Black Community," *Du Bois Review* 12, no. 1 (2015): 49.

67. Meira Levinson, "How, if at All, Should Charters Be Compared to Local Districts," in *Dilemmas of Educational Ethics: Cases and Commentaries*, ed. Meira Levinson and Jacob Fay (Cambridge, MA: Harvard Education Press, 2016), 182.

68. We are not able to address several other important criticisms that have been

made of no-excuses charter schools, or of the charter sector more generally. To mention some of them briefly: (1) The "creaming" in these schools has the effect of leaving a higher concentration of harder-to-educate students in the traditional public schools (TPS), thus harming their education. The effect is in some ways analogous to the harms caused by tracking, discussed below, pp. 135ff. (2) Charters divert resources from the traditional sector beyond their proportion of students served and thus harm TPS students. (3) The most prominent charter chains have access to huge sums of money from philanthropists, especially those (like the Walton, Broad, and Gates Foundations) favoring the infusion of markets into education. These extra funds account for some of what charter schools are able to accomplish and make comparison with TPS less viable. (4) The huge sums of private money going into charter schools and advocacy organizations weaken the democratic character of public schooling. Teachers in the West Virginia and Los Angeles protests mentioned above, p, 114, sought a weakening of pro-charter legislation and the charter sector more generally, citing arguments (2), (3), and (4). (5) Charter schools weaken public support for public schools as a whole. Though (largely) publicly funded, they are often not seen as part of the public system. (6) The market approach to public education, favored by almost all charter schools and their advocates, is contrary to a civic approach to education, in terms of both public responsibility for and oversight of schools and a commitment to civic education (see discussion of latter below, chap. 5). (7) The curricula and pedagogy in these schools is too rigid and does not teach intellectual flexibility and critical thinking required for college-level demands. (8) These schools teach students to devalue their home and community, ethnoracially-linked, cultures. (9) Charter schools serve a significantly lower percentage of special needs students than TPS. (10) Charter schools exacerbate racial segregation in the public school system. For resources on these various arguments, see H. F. Ladd, "How Charter Schools Threaten the Public Interest," *Journal of Policy Analysis and Management* 38 (2019): 1063–71, https://doi.org/10.1002/pam.22163; Sarah Stitzlein, *American Public Education and the Responsibility of Its Citizens: Supporting Democracy in the Age of Accountability* (Oxford: Oxford University Press, 2017); Mercedes Schneider, *School Choice: The End of Public Education* (New York: Teachers College Press, 2016); Gary Orfield and Erica Frankenberg, *Educational Delusions? Why Choice Can Deepen Inequality and How to Make Schools Fair* (Berkeley: University of California Press, 2013); Kahlenberg and Potter, *A Smarter Charter*; Diane Ravitch, *Reign of Error: The Hoax of the Privatization Movement and the Danger to America's Public Schools* (New York: Vintage Books, 2014); Valerie Strauss, "NAACP Sticks by Its Call for Charter School Moratorium, Says 'They Are Not a Substitute' for Traditional Public Schools," *Washington Post*, July 26, 2017; S. Ben-Porath, "Deferring Virtue: The New Management of Students and the Civic Role of Schools," *Theory and Research in Education* 11, no. 2 (July 2013): 111–28; Lawrence Blum, "Race and Class Categories and Subcategories in Educational Research and Practice," *Theory and Research in Education* 13, no. 1 (March 2015): 1–18.

69. The Broader, Bolder Approach to Education is an education advocacy organization that proposes evidence-based initiatives to mitigate effects of poverty-related disadvantages on learning. Children's Defense Fund (CDF) advocates for

children in poverty. Both groups propose many economically viable policies to achieve these goals, and CDF proposes reasonable funding sources for them. See also Rothstein, "Children from Lower Socioeconomic Classes."

70. Bradbury et al., *Too Many Children Left Behind.*

71. New Jersey adopted a millionaire's tax, primarily to help deal with revenue shortfalls caused by the COVID-19 pandemic, which has both drawn on and boosted the salience of that policy direction. Tracey Tully, "New Jersey Adds Millionaires Tax to Ease a Crunch," *New York Times*, September 18, 2020, 1, 5.

72. Orfield and Frankenberg, "*Brown* at 60," 36–37.

73. As our historical discussion also suggests, the forms of injustice and oppression involved in the histories of these two groups are very different from one another, so the forms of justice involved would have to be very different as well. Reparations for Native Americans, for example, would have to take on the issue of the policy of "Indian Removal" of Native American groups from the their ancestral homelands, as well as that of forced assimilation and what would now be regarded as cultural genocide—two issues without exact parallel in the African American case.

74. Quote from Ronald P. Sulzberger and Mary C. Turck, eds., *Reparations for Slavery: A Reader* (Lanham, MD: Rowman & Littlefield, 2004), 64–65. In defending the bill, Stevens said enslaved people had been left without education and not taught higher-skilled jobs, a situation that rendered them vulnerable to being preyed on by whites, and he feared they would be forced into a form of servitude unless Congress provided some means for their independent living. His bill was not passed, and his prediction was largely borne out, in the sharecropper system that came to replace slavery for many formerly enslaved people.

75. Some of the important works contributing to or expressing this historical consensus are Gary Nash, *Red, White, and Black: The Peoples of Early North America*, 7th ed. (London: Pearson, 2014); Edward Baptist, *The Half Has Never Been Told: Slavery and the Making of American Capitalism* (New York: Basic Books, 2016); S. Beckert, *Empire of Cotton: A Global History* (New York: Vintage Books, 2014); I. Katznelson, *When Affirmative Action Was White: An Untold History of Racial Inequality in America* (New York: W. W. Norton, 2006). M. Oliver and T. Shapiro, *Black Wealth/White Wealth: A New Perspective on Racial Inequality*, 2nd ed. (New York: Routledge, 2006); Keeanga-Yamahtta Taylor, *Race for Profit: How Banks and the Real Estate Industry Undermined Black Homeownership* (Chapel Hill: University of North Carolina Press, 2019); and R. Rothstein, *The Color of Law: A Forgotten History of How Our Government Segregated America* (New York: W. W. Norton, 2018). Some of these works make explicit reference to the class-based processes that solidify and expand race-based disparities, and more recent work, for example Beckert and Baptist, explicitly relates racial processes to the origins of American capitalism, leading to a formulation of "racial capitalism" as a way to conceptualize the overall system in which racial inequalities have been and are generated and sustained.

In August 2019, the *New York Times* devoted an entire issue of its Sunday magazine to articles very much in the spirit of this new consensus (https://www.nytimes.com/interactive/2019/08/14/magazine/1619-america-slavery.html). The issue is part of the larger *1619 Project* of the *New York Times*, which includes periodic articles, podcasts, and curricular materials (https://pulitzercenter.org

/lesson-plan-grouping/1619-project-curriculum), all relating to the legacy of slavery in American history and the present.

76. Oliver and Shapiro, *Black Wealth/White Wealth*; Katznelson, *When Affirmative Action Was White*; Rothstein, *Color of Law*.

77. For example, *Shelley v. Kraemer*, 334 U.S. 1 (1948), ruled that restrictive covenants were not legally enforceable.

78. J. Brian Charles, "As Fair Housing Act Turns 50, Landmark Law Faces Uncertain Future," *Governing*, April 11, 2018, https://www.governing.com/topics/urban/gov-fair-housing-lyndon-johnson-lc.html. The article traces the history of different administrations' treatment of and funding for the Fair Housing Act and other antidiscrimination legislation through early 2018.

79. Peter G. Peterson Foundation, "Income and Wealth in the United States: An Overview of Recent Data," October 4, 2019, https://www.pgpf.org/blog/2018/01/income-and-wealth-in-the-united-states-an-overview-of-data-released-in-2017. See Andrea Flynn, Dorian Warren, Felicia Wong, and Susan Holmberg, *Rewrite the Racial Rules: Building an Inclusive American Economy* (Roosevelt Institute, June 6, 2016), 29–30, https://rooseveltinstitute.org/rewrite-racial-rules-building-inclusive-american-economy/, which summarizes studies and scholarship of the 1980s and 1990s. The report emphasizes predatory lending that contributed to the 2008 financial crisis in which low-income Blacks and Latinxs disproportionately lost homes.

80. Keeanga-Yamahtta Taylor, "How Real Estate Segregated America," *Dissent*, Fall 2018. (Taylor's argument is further developed in *Race for Profit*.) Taylor's analysis is particularly valuable in highlighting the market and economic features of the structures perpetuating racial injustice in housing, not only the intentional racial discrimination aspects.

81. Tracy Jan, "White Families Have Nearly 10 Times the Net Worth of Black Families," *Washington Post*, September 28, 2017, https://www.washingtonpost.com/news/wonk/wp/2017/09/28/black-and-hispanic-families-are-making-more-money-but-they-still-lag-far-behind-whites/?noredirect=on. The "ten times" figure was affirmed in September 2020 by the Atlanta Federal Reserve chairman. See Reuters, *New York Post*, September 18, 2020, https://nypost.com/2020/09/18/atlanta-fed-chief-us-racial-wealth-gap-is-stuck-in-last-century/.

82. We are not engaging with the complex and much debated issue of who should be thought of as the agent(s) responsible for funding reparations programs—for example should it be the US and state governments as continuous entities responsible for causing or enabling much, but not all, of the inequality-generating processes; current citizens of the United States; descendants of enslavers or white people who lived in the United States at the time of slavery; corporations that existed (or whose predecessors existed) since the time of slavery or segregation and profited from the exploitation of Blacks; or all white people, on the grounds that they all benefited from programs and processes that advantaged them at the expense of Blacks (and Native Americans)? We are making the more minimal point that injustices in the present that have a clear source in injustices in the past have a distinct reparative justice claim to be rectified, which goes beyond the present-centric social or distributive justice claim of equality (including equality of educational goods).

It is noteworthy that the issue of reparations has recently gained a public

airing absent for many years. Representative John Conyers of Michigan introduced a bill, HR 40, in Congress every year between 1989 and 2018 (Rep. Sheila
Jackson Lee took over that role in 2019, after Conyers's retirement) to study the
general feasibility of a reparations program; until 2019 the House of Representatives leadership generally kept it tied up in committee. In the presidential
race for the 2020 election, several Democratic candidates (Kamala Harris, Cory
Booker, Elizabeth Warren, and Bernie Sanders) expressed support for reparations in general, and specifically of the Conyers approach, and it has also been
supported by conservative *New York Times* columnist David Brooks ("The Case
for Reparations," *New York Times*, March 18, 2019). In June 2019, a House of
Representatives subcommittee held the first hearings on reparations in over a
decade. Associated Press, "House Panel Holds Hearing on Slavery Reparations,
the First for Congress in over a Decade," *KTLA*, June 19, 2019, https://ktla.com
/2019/06/19/house-panel-holds-hearing-on-slavery-reparations-the-first-for
-congress-in-over-a-decade/.

83. Gloria Ladson-Billings, "From the Achievement Gap to the Education Debt: Understanding Achievement in U.S. Schools," *Educational Researcher* 35, no 7 (2006):
3–12. Ladson-Billings argues that "achievement" language misdirects our attention, implying that there is something wrong with the "non-achieving" students
themselves, denying or diverting attention from society's responsibility to them,
rooted in corrective justice. She uses "opportunity" not in the problematic American sense discussed earlier but essentially to mean access to educational goods.

84. The use we are making of the corrective justice approach is limited to the extra
moral force it supplies for achieving racial equality in education. We are not taking up the larger issue of what a full reparations program for African Americans
or Native Americans might look like. As generally understood, such a program
goes beyond achieving equality of goods in crucial life domains such as education, health, and occupation. It is generally taken also to involve symbolic and
educational measures, such as public monuments and school curricula, that
help to enhance recognition and civic standing for the groups in question. More
generally, we are by no means assuming that reparations necessarily or solely
involves direct cash payments to individual members of the target group. But it
should be kept in mind that many programs envisioned by proponents of reparations, such as community-based and -controlled cultural or economic advancement would require public funds. For a discussion of many aspects of the complexity of reparations, see Roy Brooks, *When Sorry Isn't Enough: The Controversy
Over Apologies and Reparation for Human Injustice* (New York: New York University Press, 1999).

85. Ta-Nehisi Coates, "The Case for Considering Reparations," *Atlantic*, January 27,
2016, https://www.theatlantic.com/politics/archive/2016/01/tanehisi-coates
-reparations/427041/.

86. Some strands within influential Black nationalist thought do reject a US national
identity for American Blacks. E. U. Essien-Udom, *Black Nationalism* (New York:
Dell, 1962).

87. Jonathan Zimmerman traces the history of debates about national and ethno-
centric history and criticisms about particular popular textbooks' portrayals of
national history from the 1940s to the 1980s in *Whose America? Culture Wars*

in the Public Schools (Cambridge, MA: Harvard University Press, 2002), chap. 5. This analysis shows how history texts have often presented a completely distorted picture of the racial aspect of American history that has been challenged by various racial minority groups. Our advocacy of the "consensus (racial) narrative" discussed above (119–20) is part of the ongoing struggle to "get it right," and Zimmerman shows the folly of abandoning the task of working accurate history into widely used textbooks in favor of histories that focus only on the accounts of particular ethnoracial groups. (Nevertheless, we do think there is a place for courses that focus on single groups, but seen as complementary to national history.)

88. Responding to the 2019 hearings on reparations mentioned in chapter 3, note 82, Senate majority leader Mitch McConnell stated that he doesn't think "reparations for something that happened 150 years ago, for whom none of us currently living are responsible, is a good idea" (Associated Press, "House Panel Holds Hearing on Slavery Reparations"). We are here putting aside another familiar argument, though one perfectly compatible with the one in the text, that Blacks may be disadvantaged not because of injustice but because of deficiencies in their cultures or attitudes, and hence government has no responsibility to do more than to provide opportunities to Blacks, which, according to this argument, they have already done and Blacks have simply not availed themselves of these opportunities. (See chapter 3, note 21, on culturalism.)

89. Social Security also discriminated against Mexican Americans.

90. Douglas Massey summarizes the racial disparity–increasing effects of New Deal legislation generally and elaborates: "Traditional black occupations were not covered by the Social Security Act; labor legislation was written to allow segregated unions; states were delegated authority to exclude African Americans from receiving veterans benefits; and bureaucratic rules were written to prohibit black families and black neighborhoods from receiving Federal Housing Association and Veterans Administration loans." Douglas Massey, "The Past and Future of American Civil Rights," *Daedalus* 2 (Spring 2011): 41.

91. For an excellent account of the forward-looking responsibility of those living in the present, in the absence of their direct blame for the past, see Iris Marion Young, *Responsibility for Justice* (New York: Oxford University Press, 2013).

92. T. J. Yosso refers to this community-based knowledge as "resistant capital"— knowledge and skills used to challenge inequality and oppression. T. J. Yosso, "Whose Culture Has Capital? A Critical Race Theory Discussion of Community Cultural Wealth," *Race Ethnicity and Education* 8, no. 1 (2005): 69–91. Cited in Howard, *Why Race and Culture Matter*, 55.

93. Levinson emphasizes the importance of "contemporary local heroes" for civic education in *No Citizen Left Behind*, chap. 4.

94. In this discussion of teaching, we are not assuming that the guidelines suggested would work out exactly the same for white teachers and teachers of color (nor for each specific group under that rubric), but we do want to affirm that white teachers are capable of teaching racial material to students of color, though doing so requires skill and sensitivity, an awareness of racial dynamics, and building relationships with individual students, a point forcefully emphasized by Howard, *Why Race and Culture Matter*, 74.

95. Example from Lawrence Blum, *High Schools, Race, and America's Future: What Students Can Teach Us about Morality, Diversity, and Community* (Cambridge, MA: Harvard Education Press, 2012), 177–78.

96. Above, p. 102, citing Darby and Rury's *Color of Mind.* Darby and Rury insightfully emphasize the assault on Black students' dignity implicit in the ideology of Black intellectual inferiority.

97. The discussions here and elsewhere of unjust white advantage, white privilege, and white supremacy and their significance for understanding the structure of US society are very much indebted to the work of Charles Mills. See, for example, the essays in *Black Rights/White Wrongs: The Critique of Racial Liberalism* (New York: Oxford University Press, 2017).

98. Margaret Hagerman provides a quite common example of a young student's failure to recognize asymmetry, when a middle schooler who did not understand the point of Black and Asian Student Unions in the high school stated, "I mean, there's not like the White Student Union!" Margaret Hagerman, *White Kids: Growing Up with Privilege in a Racially Divided America* (New York: New York University Press, 2018), 189.

99. For a sympathetic critique of the "racism = prejudice + power" definition, see Lawrence Blum, "Can Blacks Be Racist?," chap. 2 of *"I'm Not a Racist, But . . .": The Moral Quandary of Race* (Ithaca, NY: Cornell University Press, 2002).

100. Some of the cases ignoring or undermining racial asymmetry: *City of Richmond v. J. A. Croson Co.*, 488 U.S. 468 (1989); *Washington v. Davis*, 426 U.S. 229 (1976); and *Missouri v. Jenkins*, 515 U.S. 70 (1995).

101. The fifth justice, Kennedy, came close to this position but also recognized that the nation still had obligations to create equality of educational opportunity, though his siding with the position of the four conservative justices makes it extremely difficult to do so. See Blum, *High Schools*, 193.

102. There were 5–4 majorities in *Milliken v. Bradley, Parents Involved in Community Schools (PICS) v. Seattle School District No. 1,* and in *Bakke* and *Grutter.* (Although the latter decision went in a asymmetry-recognizing direction, by 5–4, the decisions in *Bakke* and *Grutter* rejected using racial preferences in college admission to correct for a history of racial discrimination, and the *PICS* decision most especially reflected and contributed to judicial blindness to systemic racial injustice.)

CHAPTER FOUR

1. We focus on race, but there are of course other axes of integration—linguistic, class, religious, ethnic, gender, and geographical origin. Later we argue that both class and ethnic integration are related to racial integration.

2. Integration can refer to society in general or to other domains such as neighborhoods or workplaces in particular. These each raise somewhat distinctive issues, and in this book we are discussing integration only in relation to schools.

3. This formulation is taken from Michael S. Merry, *Equality, Citizenship, and Segregation: A Defense of Separation* (London: Palgrave MacMillan, 2014), 8.

4. The familiar narrative of *Brown* as spurring the formation of the civil rights movement omits the important civil rights initiatives in the 1940s, which give

rise to a newer conception of the "long civil rights movement." See Jacquelyn Dowd Hall, "The Long Civil Rights Movement and the Political Uses of the Past," *Journal of American History* 91, no. 4 (March 2005): 1233–63. The 1944 *Smith v. Allwright* case, declaring "white primaries" unconstitutional, was an additional important assault on Jim Crow segregation that predated *Brown*.

5. See chap. 2, 53.

6. To add to the complexity, sometimes "desegregation" is used to mean "integration" in sense 2—bringing racially distinct populations together in schools—in addition to its historic meaning in sense 1 (dismantling white supremacy). See, for example, the February 2019 mission and vision statement for the RIDES (Reimagining Integration: Diverse and Equitable Schools) Project at Harvard Graduate School of Education, https://docs.google.com/document/d/1MLxAVUhMykaRoLT06QrwK9nEMjv1qWmG3lseDhMq9sc/edit.

7. Benjamin Mays, an African American minister and civil rights leader, made this point in the wake of the *Brown* decision: "Black people must not resign themselves to the pessimistic view that a nonintegrated school cannot provide black children with an excellent educational setting." Quoted in Derrick Bell, *Silent Covenants: Brown v. Board of Education and the Unfulfilled Hopes for Racial Reform* (New York: Oxford University Press, 2004), 115.

8. See Elizabeth Anderson's nuanced discussion of assimilation in *The Imperative of Integration* (Princeton, NJ: Princeton University Press, 2010), 114–15.

9. An influential text in the Black rejection of integration as undermining Black institutions and the Black community more generally is Kwame Ture and Charles V. Hamilton's *Black Power: The Politics of Liberation* (1967; repr., New York: Vintage Books, 1992). Mark Griffith (chap. 2, 91) expressed a related criticism of integration as inherently negative, in implying that whites are the ideal.

10. Martin Luther King Jr., "The Ethical Demands for Integration," in *A Testament of Hope: The Essential Writings and Speeches of Martin Luther King, Jr.*, ed. James. M. Washington (San Francisco: Harper Collins, 1986), 118. Note that by "desegregation," King means what we are calling *descriptive integration*, rather than "the dismantling of the legal structure of white supremacy," which is our meaning of *desegregation* and the first of the three meanings of *integration*. (So King is using "desegregation" in the same sense as the Harvard RIDES Project; see chapter 4, note 6, above.)

11. King's focus is on whites welcoming Blacks into white-dominated domains, but, for our time, we should understand his vision to include racial and ethnic groups other than just whites and Blacks (e.g., Asian Americans, Latinxs, and Native Americans), so that the welcoming is done by all groups toward all other groups. King's ideal was also for society in general, but we can use it in the school context in particular, envisioning each school as a community of multiple racial groups exemplifying something like the "spiritual affinity" he mentions.

12. Robert Carter, "The Unending Struggle for Equal Educational Opportunity," *Teachers College Record* 96, no. 4 (Summer 1995): 621.

13. Martha Minow points out that in many of the southern districts whose school systems were ruled unconstitutional in *Brown*, Black children had to walk past white schools to get to their assigned school, so if this system were dismantled and students attended schools in their neighborhoods, those neighborhood

schools would often be mixed/desegregated. Martha Minow, *In Brown's Wake: Legacies of America's Educational Landmark* (New York: Oxford University Press, 2010), chap. 1.

As mentioned in chapter 2, desegregation did not officially include integrating the teaching staffs of the envisioned mixed schools, and many Black teachers lost their jobs as a result. Whether staff, as well as student, integration should count as part of what "integration" means is another aspect of the plurality of integrations.

14. David Labaree, *Someone Has to Fail: The Zero-Sum Game of Public Schooling* (Cambridge, MA: Harvard University Press, 2012), 98, 117, 166, 171–72. Derrick Darby and John L. Rury, *The Color of Mind: Why the Origins of the Achievement Gap Matter for Justice* (Chicago: University of Chicago Press, 2018), 111.

15. While we do not think the idea of ability itself is problematic, its use in the rationale of tracking—as something directly reflected in performance—is problematic. We mention this because some discussions of tracking go so far as to reject the whole idea of ability itself. We do not share this view but do insist that ability be seen in the developmental way that informs our earlier discussion of intelligence (see p. 101). One can speak of particular students having certain abilities and having the potential to develop others, but in both cases "ability" is a developed capability and always in process of further development.

16. Darby and Rury, *Color of Mind*, 115–16.

17. In a detailed study of a detracking program in Rockville Centre, New York, the whole district abolished lower-track math and gave the formerly "accelerated" curriculum to all students. This resulted in an increase of the Black and Latinx students passing the New York State Regents exam from 23 percent to 75 percent, and white and Asian students from 54 percent to 98 percent. Carol Burris and Kevin Welner, "Classroom Integration and Accelerated Learning Through Detracking," in *Lessons in Integration: Realizing the Promise of Racial Diversity in American Schools*, ed. Erica Frankenberg and Gary Orfield (Charlottesville: University of Virginia Press, 2007), 213. B. Bradbury, M. Corak, J. Waldfogel, and E. Washbrook, *Too Many Children Left Behind: The U.S. Achievement Gap in Comparative Perspective* (New York: Russell Sage Foundation, 2015), 149–50, report that the nation of Finland, which has been much studied by education scholars partly because of its consistently high performance on international standardized tests, has a fully untracked system, with every student given the same curriculum and held to the same high standards, and 50 percent of them receiving special help. See also K. Tyson, "Tracking, Segregation, and the Opportunity Gap: What We Know and Why It Matters," in *Closing the Opportunity Gap: What America Must Do to Give Every Child and Even Chance*, ed. Prudence Carter and Kevin Welner (New York: Oxford University Press, 2013). Jeannie Oakes, *Keeping Track: How Schools Structure Inequality*, 2nd ed. (New Haven, CT: Yale University Press, 2005). Carol Burris, *On the Same Track: How Schools Can Join the 21st Century Struggle against Resegregation* (Boston: Beacon Press, 2014).

18. Marshall Jean, *Review of 2016 Brown Center Report on American Education, Part II—Tracking and Advanced Placement* (Boulder, CO: National Education Policy Center, April 2016).

19. Harry Brighouse, Helen F. Ladd, Susanna Loeb, and Adam Swift, *Educational*

Goods: Values, Evidence, and Decision-Making (Chicago: University of Chicago Press, 2018), 12.

20. Oakes, *Keeping Track*, 226–29; Burris, *On the Same Track*.

21. Darby and Rury, *Color of Mind*. See also John Diamond and Amanda Lewis, *Despite the Best Intentions: Why Racial Inequality Persists in Good Schools* (New York: Oxford University Press, 2015), 113.

22. As mentioned earlier (chap. 3, 110, and note 41 on p. 233), Bradbury et al. report in *Too Many Children Left Behind* that the gap between tracks is greater in the United States than in the other countries studied.

23. In educational thinking, "high expectations" are sometimes accorded an almost magical power to overcome almost any SES-related disadvantage. So it is worth recalling here our argument from chapter 3 (112ff) that some of those disadvantages can be dealt with only by school-based bufferings of these disadvantages and larger egalitarian and poverty-reducing reforms, not higher expectations.

24. We omit Asians from the injustice schema because it is not clear that the gap between Asian and Latinx/Black success in the tracking placement system is an injustice, as the gap between the latter groups and whites is. Because whites have a history of being both perpetrators and beneficiaries of systems that disadvantage Blacks and Latinxs, racial gaps in which whites are advantaged are plausibly regarded as unjust. But Asians were not the perpetrators of injustice against Blacks and Latinxs, nor were they historical beneficiaries of such systems. It is true, however, that in the present Asian Americans do benefit from the continuing subordination of Blacks and Latinxs, and that should figure into a justice framework in some way. At the same time, this is true of only some Asian ethnic groups. Others are as or more disadvantaged as Blacks and Latinxs. See chapter 2, 88–89.

25. Karolyn Tyson, *Integration Interrupted: Tracking, Black Students, and Acting White after* Brown (Oxford: Oxford University Press, 2011), 152. In a study of white, middle-class school advantage, Ellen Brantlinger finds that the mothers she interviewed "believe that advocating for school advantage for their children is integral to being a good parent." Ellen Brantlinger, *Dividing Classes: How the Middle Class Negotiates and Rationalizes School Advantage* (New York: Routledge, 2003), 41. Amy Stuart Wells and Irene Serna note, "In all of the schools we studied, the most interesting aspect of elite's opposition to detracking is that they based their resistance on the symbolic mixing of high 'deserving' and low 'undeserving' students, rather than on information about what actually happens in detracked classrooms." Amy Stuart Wells and Irene Serna, "The Politics of Culture: Understanding Local Political Resistance to Detracking in Racially Mixed Schools," in *Facing Racism in Education*, ed. S. Anderson, P. Attwood, and L. Howard, 3rd. ed. (Cambridge, MA: Harvard Education Press, 2004), 155.

26. Diamond and Lewis, *Despite the Best Intentions*, 91.

27. Diamond and Lewis find that part of the capital value in whiteness derives from school personnel generally associating whiteness with the middle and upper middle class, and Black and Latinx with the working or lower class, independent of the family's actual class status. So the racial capital operates partly by way of class stereotypes. Diamond and Lewis, *Despite the Best Intentions*.

28. Tyson, *Integration Interrupted*, 13–14.

29. Elizabeth Anderson, "Race, Culture, and Educational Opportunity," *Theory and Research in Education* 10, no. 2 (July 2012): 105–29.
30. The gap is not solely a product of how the students are treated in school; there is a race/class skills level gap among students prior to entering school. Greg J. Duncan and Katherine Magnuson, "The Nature and Impact of Early Achievement Skills, Attention Skills, and Behavior Problems," in *Whither Opportunity? Rising Inequality, Schools, and Children's Life Chances*, ed. G. Duncan and R. Murnane (New York: Russell Sage Foundation, 2011), 47–70.
31. Many schools have now incorporated student choice as part of the track placement process, as a response to criticism of tracking. But this development has had little impact on the demographics of the tracks. Latinx and Black students disproportionately place themselves in lower tracks compared to whites and Asian Americans. There are several plausible explanations for this. If students of color perceive that few of their peers end up in the higher-track classes, they are more likely to feel discouraged from choosing those placements, partly because it is uncomfortable to be a hypervisible underrepresented minority in a class of whites and Asians. They may also feel their white fellow students will not be welcoming to them because they do not think that Black or Latinx students belong there. This is a form of "stereotype threat," in which racial minority students are concerned about confirming the stereotypes that others hold about them. Claude Steele, *Whistling Vivaldi: How Stereotypes Affect Us and What We Can Do* (New York: W. W. Norton, 2011). Some students may also worry they will lose touch with friends clustered in the lower-track classes or that they will be perceived as "acting white" by taking advanced courses. (The phenomenon of Black students using "acting white" as a criticism of high-achieving Black students has been greatly exaggerated in popular discussion, but it does take place. See A. Harris, *Kids Don't Want to Fail* [Cambridge, MA: Harvard University Press, 2011].) Karolyn Tyson argues in *Integration Interrupted* that when Blacks criticize other Blacks for "acting white," this occurs largely as a by-product of racial tracking itself, rather than a contributor to it. Finally, some students may have themselves internalized a racial ideology that says that they are less capable than whites (and perhaps Asians). Tyson says it is in the tracked schools themselves that the lower-track students develop the sense of inferiority.
32. This is a form of *culturalism*, discussed in chapter 3, note 21.
33. Diamond and Lewis, *Despite the Best Intentions*, 115. The ideology of inferiority is stronger and more historically embedded for Blacks than for Native Americans and Latinxs. See Theresa Perry, "Up from Parched Earth," in *Young Gifted, and Black*, ed. T. Perry, A. Hilliard, and C. Steele (Boston: Beacon Press, 2004).
34. Of course if a school is detracked from the beginning, this will not be an issue, as there will not be a distinction between the formerly low-track and the formerly high-track students.
35. Processes involved in some successful initiatives of schools and districts moving from tracked to detracked systems are described in Burris, *On the Same Track*, and more briefly in Darby and Rury, *Color of Mind*, 151–55.
36. Notice that if we take into account the expenses of "buffering poverty" (chap. 3, 113–14), this will require extra resources for low-income students (and their schools), as the Elementary and Secondary Education Act provided. Because of

this, the "equality" required for equal education would not be in expenditures; the "educational goods" version of equality would better capture the form of equality in question.

37. The term *middle class* requires some comment. We have seen this defined as anyone above the bottom 30 percent of income, above the cutoff for reduced price lunch (185 percent of the poverty line), or in the middle 60 percent of the income spectrum. If self-designation is used as the criterion, some studies find that 90 percent of Americans self-identify as "middle class." It seems to us that frequently the group to whom "middle-class capital" is being attributed is really more like the educated professional/managerial class. It is they who are better positioned to advocate with district officials and politicians, drawing on social networks for such influence. It is conventional in the capital literature to use "middle class," the terminology used by Richard Kahlenberg. But we will sometimes use "middle/upper middle" or "affluent" when the context seems to render that preferable or we seek to remind the reader of the terminology's unclarity.

38. Richard D. Kahlenberg, *All Together Now: Creating Middle-Class Schools through Public School Choice* (Washington, DC: Brookings Institution, 2001), 1, 62.

39. Diamond and Lewis, *Despite the Best Intention*, 103.

40. We say "families of color" rather than "parents of color" because the relevant family unit for a given student might comprise adult figures other than their parents, a point emphasized by Ann M. Ishimaru, *Just Schools: Building Equitable Collaboration with Families and Communities* (New York: Teachers College Press, 2020), 7.

41. Andres Alonso, "Pandering in a Context of Limited Choices and Costs," in *Dilemmas of Educational Ethics: Cases and Commentaries*, ed. Meira Levinson and Jacob Fay (Cambridge, MA: Harvard Education Press, 2016), 168. See discussion of forms of "capital" specific to disadvantaged or nondominant groups in Ishimaru, *Just Schools*, and Tyrone C. Howard, *Why Race and Culture Matter in Schools: Closing the Achievement Gap in America's Classrooms* (New York: Teachers College Press, 2020), 55. For "resistant capital," see chapter 3, note 94.

42. For examples of low-income community organizing to save and improve local schools, see Mark. R. Warren and Karen Mapp, eds., *A Match on Dry Grass: Community Organizing as a Catalyst for School Reform* (Oxford: Oxford University Press, 2011); Barbara Ferman, ed., *The Fight for America's Schools: Grassroots Organizing in Education* (Cambridge, MA: Harvard Education Press, 2017); and Eve Ewing, *Ghosts in the Schoolyard: Racism and School Closings on Chicago's South Side* (Chicago: University of Chicago Press, 2018).

43. Kahlenberg, the advocate for the capital argument, recognizes the stigma problem but argues that the message of deficiency is stigmatizing only in its racial form. He says that the argument puts down Blacks' culture but that people in poverty do not have a culture that forms part of their identity in this way, and so are not insulted by the attributions of deficiency. ("The poor generally do not wish to preserve a culture of poverty.") So, he argues, the capital argument avoids stigmatization when used to support socioeconomic, but not racial, integration. Kahlenberg, *All Together Now*, 197. However, the culture issue is a red herring. It is the student in an educational setting with others who is vulnerable to stigma if she is declared or implied (by the capital argument) to be deficient in

exactly the qualities required for success in that venue. The disadvantaged students are members of a group with an identity as such within the school, even if not a culture in the ethnic sense.

44. Wells and Serna, "Politics of Culture."

45. It is also worth noting that the capital argument paints an overly rosy picture of the norms conveyed by the advantaged to the disadvantaged students. Studies of upper-middle-class students find that they are often overly entitled, disrespectful toward adults, overly competitive, materialistic, and uncaring toward others. Kahlenberg, *All Together Now*, 194. Anderson, "Race, Culture, and Educational Opportunity," 117 (". . . in a word, spoiled.") If the upper-middle-class students pass norms about school engagement to the students of color, might they not pass on these negative norms as well?

46. Ture and Hamilton, *Black Power*, 54.

47. Andrew Sayer systematically dismembers the ideology that upholds extreme socioeconomic equality as necessary, appropriate, or desirable, in *Why We Can't Afford the Rich* (Clifton, UK: Policy Press, 2016). There is a vast literature supporting this critique.

48. Linn Posey-Maddox, *When Middle-Class Parents Choose Urban Schools* (Chicago: University of Chicago Press, 2014). The New York City school system has a position for "parent coordinator" in every school, whose job is outreach to parents, with a view to bringing parents, across the class and race spectrum, into contributing to the school. (Reported by Kamar Samuels, a Community School District superintendent in the system, in a personal communication with one of the book's authors.)

49. Norton Grubb and Zeus Leonardo, *Racism and Education* (New York: Routledge, 2013), 16. The way disadvantaged families are regarded as the problem, in the absence of an acknowledgment of a justice perspective, is explored in great depth in Ishimaru, *Just Schools*.

50. Example from Annette Lareau, *Unequal Childhoods: Class, Race, and Family Life*, 2nd ed. (Berkeley: University of California Press, 2011), 210. See also Ishimaru, *Just Schools*.

51. Only some capital advantages can be traced to such unequal treatment by direct school personnel. Financial and social capital, for example, do not generally operate that way.

52. Michael Rebell details the struggles, most of them successful, to get state courts to recognize a right to an adequate education under their state constitutions. Litigation regarding school funding has been brought to forty-five of the fifty states. Michael Rebell, *Flunking Democracy: Schools, Courts, and Civic Participation* (Chicago: University of Chicago Press, 2018), 9. In a 1973 decision, the Supreme Court, by a mere 5–4 margin, explicitly rejected a constitutionally based right to equal educational opportunity, strongly suggested but not quite affirmed in the *Brown* decision. San Antonio School District v. Rodriguez, 411 U.S. 1 (1973). This unfortunate ruling spurred the state-based litigation mentioned.

53. Tommie Shelby emphasizes the importance to one's self-respect of being able to demand one's civic entitlements as a matter of justice, rather than being seen as mere beneficiaries of public, or private, largesse, in *Dark Ghettos: Injustice, Dis-*

sent, and Reform (Cambridge, MA: Harvard University Press, 2016). An argument
for the public responsibility of citizens for their public schools in a democratic
society is well made by Sarah Stitzlein, *American Public Education and the Responsibility of Its Citizens: Supporting Democracy in the Age of Accountability*
(New York: Oxford University Press, 2017).

54. Quoted in Bell, *Silent Covenants*, 96.

55. Boston Public School Racial Equity planning tool, updated April/May 2020,
p. 5, http://bit.ly/BPSREPT. A Calvert County, Maryland, school district says it
will "identify and address structural and institutional barriers that could prevent
students from equitably accessing educational opportunities in all schools."
From "Equity Policies in Maryland," a report for the Teachers Democracy
Project, an advocacy and resource organization for educational justice in Baltimore (http://www.tdpbaltimore.org/), describing six different Maryland counties that have adopted such policies. The quote is from Calvert County Public
Schools, Policy Statement no. 1015, http://www.calvertnet.k12.md.us/UserFiles
/Servers/Server_123339/File/Calvertnet/District%20Info/CCPS%20Policies
%20and%20Procedures/Administration/1015.pdf.

56. Posey-Maddox, *When Middle-Class Parents*, 69. Another similar study cited a
parent saying "I chose public education because I'd rather choose what's good
for lots of people over what's necessarily the very best for my kid." Posey-Maddox, *When Middle-Class Parents*, 53.

57. Integrated Schools, https://integratedschools.org.

58. James Ryan, "Means and Ends: Practical Considerations for Equitable School
Reform," in Levinson and Fay, *Dilemmas of Educational Ethics*, 172–73. Of course
white parents embracing a racial justice mission does not guarantee that they
will have adopted the habits of listening to and treating racial others with respect, nor that they are free of bias, conscious and unconscious. Hopefully their
schools' justice mission will make them more open to learning from racial others
and remedying their areas of ignorance and insensitivity.

59. Anna Brown, "Key Findings on American's Views of Race in 2019," Pew Research Center, April 2019, https://www.pewresearch.org/fact-tank/2019/04
/09/key-findings-on-americans-views-of-race-in-2019/. A majority of whites
say that Blacks are not treated fairly in dealing with the police (63 percent) and
in the criminal justice system (61 percent). We might expect, and hope, that the
widespread support among whites for the Black Lives Matter protests in spring/
summer 2020 will result in a further shift among whites toward openness to
justice-informed education and school missions.

60. The Making Caring Common project emphasizes the importance of morality
and moral development in the way parents should think about their children's
educations, particularly with respect to integrated schools. See Eric Torres and
Richard Weissbourd, "Do Parents Really Want School Integration?," Making Caring Common, January 2020, https://mcc.gse.harvard.edu/reports/do-parents
-really-want-school-integration.

61. See Robert H. Frank and Philip Cook, *The Winner-Take-All Society: Why the Few
at the Top Get So Much More Than the Rest of Us* (London: Penguin, 1996); Jacob S. Hacker and Paul Pierson, *Winner-Take-All Politics: How Washington Made*

the Rich Richer—and Turned Its Back on the Middle Class (New York: Simon & Schuster, 2011); Anand Giridharadas, *Winners Take All: The Elite Charade of Changing the World* (New York: Alfred A. Knopf, 2018).

62. We don't mean to imply that justice missions are appropriate only for racially and socioeconomically integrated schools. All schools need them, including predominantly white, advantaged ones. Systematic attempts to work out a curricular approach to racial justice and white advantage in all-white advantaged schools can be found in Quentin Wheeler-Bell, "Educating the Elite: A Social Justice Education for the Privileged Class," *Philosophical Inquiry in Education* 24, no. 4 (2017): 379–99, and Brandon Buck, "Realizing Wokeness: White Schools, White Ignorance: Toward a Racially Responsive Pedagogy" (PhD diss., Teachers College, Columbia University, 2020).

63. The Boston Public School Racial Equity planning tool (see chap. 4, note 55) speaks of creating "a District that views students and families [many of whom are disadvantaged in the way we are using this term] as incalculable assets," p. 5.

64. The no-excuses charter schools discussed last chapter (116) are perhaps a good contemporary example of assimilationism, in the sense that they see their students' home (family and community) ethnoracial cultures as deficient and require students to "leave them at the door." The school has its own culture, which is understood as exemplifying a middle-class, implicitly white-inflected, culture of success, and students are essentially required as part of their participation in the school to adopt this culture. H. Brighouse and G. Schouten, "Understanding the Context for Existing Reform," in Duncan and Murnane, *Whither Opportunity?*, 513. Lily Lamboy and Amanda Lu, "The Pursuit of College for All: Ends and Means in 'No Excuses' Charter Schools," *Theory and Research in Education* 15, no. 2 (2017): 209.

65. Anderson articulates, and advocates for, neutralism, as opposed to both assimilationism and group identity affirmation. Anderson, *Imperative of Integration*, chap. 6 and 9.

66. Group affirmation is neither an educational good nor a distributive good like equality. It is a good related to enhancing the students' flourishing in an institution (school) in which a person is embedded for a particular period of their life. But we argue below that it can also have salutary effects on a student's ability to access educational goods. In these respects, it is like the good of a positive teacher-student relationship (see chap. 3, 97).

67. When we speak of "affirming" a student's racial or ethnic group identity, heritage, and culture, this is not equivalent to saying that every aspect of that culture must be seen in a positive light, nor is it to deny the potential occurrence of conflict between values appropriately propounded in the school and ones the student identifies with her culture or family. Some cultures, for example, may have patriarchal or homophobic aspects that should not be affirmed. Further discussion of the basis on which elements of culture can reasonably be criticized or rejected is beyond the scope of this book but has attracted some scholarly attention. See, for example, A. Eisenberg and J. Spinner-Halev, eds., *Minorities within Minorities: Equality, Rights, and Diversity* (New York: Cambridge University Press, 2005).

68. But the philosophy of cultural pluralism more generally has older origins, such

as in the "cultural gifts" movement and "intercultural education" built on it, beginning in the 1920s, after the Immigration Act of 1924, and in philosophers such as Horace Kallen in the same period. On the educational movements, see Zoë Burkholder, *Color in the Classroom: How American Schools Taught Race, 1900–1954* (New York: Oxford University Press, 2011).

It should be noted that some contemporary indigenous scholars have rejected multiculturalism and the idea of recognition attached to it as masking the violence against indigenous peoples on which the polity engaged in the recognition was built. See Glen Sean Coulthard, *Red Skin, White Masks: Rejecting the Colonial Politics of Recognition* (Minneapolis: University of Minnesota Press, 2014), and Roxanne Dunbar-Ortiz, *An Indigenous People's History of the United States* (Boston: Beacon Press, 2014), 5.

69. Andrew Valls provides a helpful discussion of different things that can be meant by a "black school"—e.g., a school mission focused on the well-being of Black people or a school with primarily Black staff, primarily Black students, or a curriculum devoted centrally to Black people. Andrew Valls, *Rethinking Racial Justice* (Oxford: Oxford University Press, 2018), 190–95. Some of these are entirely consistent with the school having some non-Black students, who support the Black-centric focus of the school's mission.

70. For an examination of the important recent work of historians of Black education during segregation in showing the distinctive values of Black affirmation, racial uplift, and care for Black students often realized in segregated schools, see chap. 1, 16, 18.

71. Brighouse et al., *Educational Goods*, is particularly useful in recognizing the value plurality and need for value trade-offs in educational policy.

72. W. E. B. Du Bois, *The Souls of Black Folk* (1903; repr., New York: Dover Publications, 2016). In addition to Du Bois, significant defenses of some version of egalitarian racial pluralism (some explicitly in relation to education, some not) in the past thirty years are Harold Cruse, *Plural But Equal* (New York: William Morrow, 1988); Roy Brooks, *Integration or Separation? A Strategy for Racial Equality* (Cambridge, MA: Harvard University Press, 1999); Iris Young, *Inclusion and Democracy* (New York: Oxford University Press, 2002); Tommie Shelby, *We Who Are Dark: The Philosophical Foundations of Black Solidarity* (Cambridge, MA: Harvard University Press, 2005); Shelby, *Dark Ghettos*, esp. 67–76; Merry, *Equality, Citizenship, and Segregation*; and Valls, *Rethinking Racial Justice*.

73. Du Bois clearly recognized the distinction between separation and inequality with respect to schools in a 1935 essay, "Does the Negro Need Separate Schools?" (reprinted in *Du Bois on Education*, ed. Eugene Provenzo Jr. [Lanham, MD: AltaMira Press, 2002]). He said Blacks should seek schools that were equal to those of whites; whether they were racially separated was a different and, for him at that point in his (and US Blacks') history, a secondary matter.

Because of the stigma attached to the phrase "separate but equal" stemming from its use in the *Plessy* decision to uphold a system that was decidedly separate and unequal, we avoid that phrase in expressing the idea of egalitarian pluralism.

74. Rogers Smith, *Civic Ideals: Conflicting Visions of Citizenship in US History* (New Haven, CT: Yale University Press, 1997), 320, 392.

75. Black nationalism differs strongly from Du Bois's pluralism by frequently (not always) advocating forms of separation—cultural, social, economic, and political—from whites and rejecting the view that whites would ever permit US Blacks to live on a plane of equality with them. Michael Dawson, *Black Visions: The Roots of Contemporary African-American Political Ideologies* (Chicago: University of Chicago Press, 2001), 87–90. But the two views do share an affirmation of group value, tradition, and some degree of self-determination, and so are both "pluralistic," in our definition.

An important general difference, which largely but not entirely maps onto the Du Bois/nationalist difference, concerns whether the subordinated group in question is seeking some sort of recognition from the dominant group, or other groups with which it is sharing a social, educational, or political space. Generally, the nationalist tradition eschews such recognition, wanting only to not be prevented from determining their own destiny. By contrast, particularly in education contexts, but sometimes more broadly, the subordinated group is seeking recognition of its existence and value from the dominant group or other groups. Some instances of pluralism combine aspects of both, as, for example, when a Black student group seeks official recognition as a worthy enterprise within the school but also just wants to engage in its own activities without interference or monitoring.

Du Bois's version of pluralism was universalistic, in that he thought every race had its own distinctive culture and values that were of equal worth to every other. (In developing this view, Du Bois was strongly influenced by the German philosopher Johann Gottfried von Herder [1744–1803]. See K. A. Appiah, *Lines of Descent: W. E. B. Du Bois and the Emergence of Identity* [Cambridge, MA: Harvard University Press, 2014].) The more common version, as in most Black nationalist and Native American self-determination forms, affirms the particular group in question but does not say anything explicitly about other groups.

76. Shelby points to a distinctive tradition of left-wing Black nationalism in which equality was a central principle. Shelby, *Dark Ghettos*, 292n25.

77. Remember that, as the Coleman Report recognized back in 1966, individual students in poverty are educationally disadvantaged in two different ways—by their own hunger, poorer nutrition, inadequate health care, housing instability, family stress from inadequate income, and other features of poverty; and, independently, by their classmates also possessing these characteristics. (See chap. 3, 106–7.)

78. Of course, it is not a deficiency in the school itself to have low-income students, in the way that inadequate resources or high teacher turnover are. It is a deficiency in society and in the educational system that low-income students are more difficult and costly to educate and that their concentration makes doing so even more difficult and costly. More generally, it is a deficiency in society to disadvantage any students in such a way as to make their education overly demanding. It is the capital argument that tends, at least implicitly, to cast low-income students themselves as the problem.

79. In chapter 5, we will argue that, holding every other factor constant, integrated schools are superior to separated ones in their ability to provide robust civic education, a different educational good from equality.

80. Although the term *white supremacy* began to be used widely in the era of the Black Lives Matter protests following George Floyd's murder in May 2020, many still associate it only with either the Jim Crow segregation system or with overtly and extreme white supremacist movements, such as the Ku Klux Klan or other white nationalist movements that came to greater prominence in the Trump era. Neither of these associations captures the meaning intended in the text (and in its Black Lives Matter meaning): a system in which whites disproportionately hold political and economic power, the possession of which is wrongful and rests on a history of oppression and discrimination but which is no longer codified in law as it was in the Jim Crow era. White supremacy in this sense is structured into society's institutions and does not require an explicit embrace of white dominance—or even a recognition that such white dominance exists—such as is found in white nationalist and supremacist movements. Within philosophy, this conception of white supremacy has been developed and defended most fully and compellingly by Charles W. Mills, for example in *Black Rights/White Wrongs: The Critique of Racial Liberalism* (New York: Oxford University Press, 2017).

81. School choice and standards/accountability are other relatively low-cost forms of school reform besides integration.

82. Four classics of this genre are Gloria Ladson-Billings, *The Dreamkeepers: Successful Teachers of African American Children* (San Francisco: Jossey-Bass, 1994); Lisa Delpit, *Other People's Children: Cultural Conflict in the Classroom* (New York: New Press, 1995), which deals with Native American as well as African American students; Michele Foster, *Black Teachers on Teaching* (New York: New Press, 1998); and Angela Valenzuela, *Subtractive Schooling: US-Mexican Youth and the Politics of Caring* (Albany: Sate University of New York Press, 1999). Some more recent works are H. Richard Milner IV, *Start Where You Are But Don't Stay There: Understanding Diversity, Opportunity Gaps, and Teaching in Today's Classrooms*, 2nd ed. (Cambridge, MA: Harvard Education Press, 2020); Christopher Emdin, *For White Folks Who Teach in the Hood . . . and the Rest of Y'All Too: Reality Pedagogy and Urban Education* (Boston: Beacon Press, 2017); and Howard, *Why Race and Culture Matter*. These authors also make clear that some white teachers are among those who desire to and are able to be successful teachers of these students of color.

83. Some parents, sometimes allied with teachers, have opposed closing down low-performing schools in their communities because they see the schools as a community resource, without denying that they are low performing according to reasonable standards. Ewing, *Ghosts in the Schoolyard.* (Ewing's is an in-depth study of parents' and teachers' struggle to keep their district from shutting an "underperforming" school with a long and proud history in a famous Black neighborhood in Chicago.) See also R. Sanders, D. Stovall, and T. White, *Twenty-First Century Jim Crow Schools: The Impact of Charters on Public Education* (Boston: Beacon Press, 2018); Warren and Mapp, *Match on Dry Grass*; and Ferman, *Fight for America's Schools.*

84. The student reported this in a class discussion. She did not cite her negative experience as an all-things-considered reason against attending an integrated school. She recognized the educational benefits of the school. The point of the

example is that there are disadvantages to the forms of integration sought by the resource- and capital-based integration arguments, quite often left unremarked in contemporary discussions. Wells et al., in *Both Sides Now*, interview many students of color of the class of 1980 who attended integrated schools, who speak to not only the complex recognition of the benefits of these schools but also the difficulties and downsides of their experiences there. But keep in mind that many of those benefits stemmed not from the mixed demographic but from the superior resources granted to the integrated school. Amy Stuart Wells, Jennifer Jellison Holme, Anita Tijerina Revilla, and Awo Korantemaa Atanda, *Both Sides Now: The Story of School Desegregation's Graduates* (Berkeley: University of California Press, 2009).

85. On other countries doing a better job that the United States in mitigating the negative educational effects of poverty (as well as reducing poverty itself), see chapter 3, notes 43 and 52.

86. The capital argument does not require the disaster narrative as a context for it, only schools without, or with much less, parental capital than the envisioned integrated school. Our arguments against the capital approach in the earlier sections rely only on that context. But the capital argument does often operate in a disaster narrative context and appears to have greater force the more distressed and dysfunctional the minority-dominant school is.

CHAPTER FIVE

1. Amy Stuart Wells, Lauren Fox, and Diana Cordova-Cobo, "How Racially Diverse Schools and Classrooms Can Benefit All Students," *Century Foundation*, February 9, 2016. Gary Orfield and Erica Frankenberg, with Jongyeon Ee and John Kuscera, *"Brown at 60: Great Progress, a Long Retreat and an Uncertain Future"* (Los Angles: Civil Rights Project at University of California, Los Angeles, 2014).

2. Wells et al. found people of color reporting this particular positive effect of their experience in mixed schools. Amy Stuart Wells, Jennifer Jellison Holme, Anita Tijerina Revilla, and Awo Korantemaa Atanda, *Both Sides Now: The Story of School Desegregation's Graduates* (Berkeley: University of California Press, 2009), 228.

3. Historically Black colleges and universities are an entirely accepted and familiar type of institution that embodies the egalitarian pluralism challenge at the higher-education level. They are Black-centric institutions (though they no longer have entirely Black student populations) that do not count as "diverse" as it is understood in these affirmative action cases. Presumably the workplace preparation argument would claim that such institutions prepare their students less well for diverse workplaces than white-dominated but affirmative action–practicing ones. Even if that were true (and we are not familiar with studies on this matter), they might promote other sorts of egalitarian pluralistic values not equally achievable in the institutions being defended in the court cases in question.

4. Wells, Fox, and Cordova-Cobo, "How Racially Diverse Schools," 8–9, summarizes the research in the briefs in question.

5. Some of these cognitive benefits bleed into civic ones, such as reduction in prejudice, that we discuss below, pp. 168–69.

6. From here on we will focus primarily on civic rather than moral goods, but, as noted earlier (chap. 3, 96), no sharp line can be drawn between them, and some of what is said about civic goods can apply to moral ones as well.

7. David Tyack, *Seeking Common Ground: Public Schools in a Diverse Society* (Cambridge, MA: Harvard University Press). K. Bischoff, "The Civic Effects of Schools: Theory and Empirics," *Theory and Research in Education* 14, no. 1 (2016): 91.

8. Brown v. Board of Education of Topeka, 347 U.S. 483 (1954), 493.

9. Richard Rothstein, *Class and Schools: Using Social, Economic, and Educational Reform to Close the Black-White Achievement Gap* (New York: Teachers College Press, 2004), 95 (2000 poll). Sarah Stitzlein, *American Public Education and the Responsibility of Its Citizens: Supporting Democracy in the Age of Accountability* (New York: Oxford University Press, 2017), 163.

10. From Lawrence Blum, *High Schools, Race, and America's Future: What Students Can Teach Us about Morality, Diversity, and Community* (Cambridge, MA: Harvard Education Press, 2012), 191–92. This guideline was rescinded by the Trump administration and no longer appears on the Department of Education or Department of Justice websites.

11. Danielle Allen, *Education and Equality* (Chicago: University of Chicago Press, 2016). Rob Reich, "Equality, Adequacy, and K-12 Education," in *Education, Justice, and Democracy*, ed. Danielle Allen and Rob Reich (Chicago: University of Chicago Press, 2013), 58.

12. Michael Rebell, *Flunking Democracy: Schools, Courts, and Civic Participation* (Chicago: University of Chicago Press, 2018), 77, 100 (reporting College, Career, and Civic Life Framework for Social Studies State Standards). Bischoff, "Civic Effects of Schools," 92. The rise of high-stakes testing has led some proponents of civic education to advocate for the development of such tests in civics, while others say that civic understanding and commitment could not be tested for by such tests and that their existence would result in degrading civics teaching. For a cautionary take on testing for moral/civic virtue, see R. Curren and B. Kotzee, "Can Virtue be Measured?," *Theory and Research in Education* 12, no. 3 (2014): 266–82.

13. Allen, *Education and Equality*; Stitzlein, *American Public Education*; David Labaree, *Someone Has to Fail: The Zero-Sum Game of Public Schooling* (Cambridge, MA: Harvard University Press, 2012); Rebell, *Flunking Democracy*; Christopher Newfield, *The Great Mistake: How We Wrecked Public Universities and How We Can Fix Them* (Baltimore: Johns Hopkins University Press, 2018). Each of these trends bears much greater discussion than we can provide in this book.

    In 2012–13, twenty-one states required students to take a state-designed social studies test. In 2001, that number was thirty-four. Rebell, *Flunking Democracy*, 99.

14. Rebell, *Flunking Democracy*, 6.

15. There is a significant asymmetry, as well as a pedagogical challenge, in that many fewer whites (15 percent) report that they see their racial identity as very

or extremely important to how they think about themselves, compared to Blacks (75 percent). Anna Brown, "Key Findings on American's Views of Race in 2019," Pew Research Center, April 2019, https://www.pewresearch.org/fact-tank/2019/04/09/key-findings-on-americans-views-of-race-in-2019/.

16. Both Meira Levinson, *No Citizen Left Behind* (Cambridge, MA: Harvard University Press, 2012), 53, and Rebell, *Flunking Democracy*, 101, make this point. T. Epstein, *Interpreting National History: Race, Identity, and Pedagogy in Classrooms and Communities* (New York: Routledge, 2009), shows ways that history teachers, even some who have a good grasp of aspects of US racial history, often fail to provide the requisite framework for their students to understand racial injustice.

17. Civic Mission of Schools quoted in Levinson, *No Citizen Left Behind*, 43.

18. Kentucky has developed one of the most advanced sets of high school social studies standards in the country, possibly in response to its state supreme court ruling in an adequacy/equity funding case, and articulates the point in the text as follows: "Examine ways that democratic governments do or do not protect the rights and liberties of their constituents (e.g. UN Charter, Declaration of the Rights of Man, U.N. Declaration of Human Rights, U.S. Constitution)." Rebell, *Flunking Democracy*, 102.

19. Westheimer emphasizes this set of capabilities. J. Westheimer, *What Kind of Citizen: Educating Our Children for the Common Good* (New York: Teachers College Press, 2015).

20. The *New York Times's 1619 Project*, mentioned earlier, is an attempt at such racial literacy (chap. 3, note 75, on pp. 238–39).

21. Wells et al., *Both Sides Now*, chap. 5, 35, 124. The authors picked the class of 1980 because that year was a high-water mark of integration efforts, despite the Supreme Court's steady retreat from integration.

22. A white graduate said, "Race was everywhere but it was never discussed." Wells et al., *Both Sides Now*, 134–35.

23. Epstein, *Interpreting National History*; Blum, *High Schools*; Jane Bolgatz, *Talking Race in the Classroom* (New York: Teachers College Press, 2005); Shayla Griffin, *Those Kids, Our Schools: Race and Reform in an American High School* (Cambridge, MA: Harvard Education Press, 2015).

24. Gloria Ladson-Billings reports that when asked to explain contemporary Black disadvantage, some white teacher candidates cited "slavery." This is an improvement over providing no explanation at all, but by itself it implies that it was the mere fact of enslavement itself, not the manifold complex processes in the intervening years after slavery (discussed briefly in chap. 3, 119ff), that explains present-day racial disparity. Gloria Ladson-Billings, *The Dreamkeepers: Successful Teachers of African American Children* (San Francisco: Jossey-Bass, 1994), 32. Epstein, *Interpreting National History*, nicely delineates different ways that well-intentioned teachers fail to engage students in race-related classroom discussion. (See also earlier discussion of "white ignorance" in relation to the capital argument in chap. 4, 144.)

25. See examples of civic engagement from Mark R. Warren and Karen Mapp, eds., *A Match on Dry Grass: Community Organizing as a Catalyst for School Reform* (Oxford: Oxford University Press, 2011); and Ben Kirshner, *Youth Activism in an Era of Education Inequality* (New York: New York University Press, 2015). Bar-

bara Ferman has a brief discussion of a student funding protest in Boston in *The Fight for America's Schools: Grassroots Organizing in Education* (Cambridge, MA: Harvard Education Press, 2017), 2.

26. Lori Janelle Dance, "Helping Students See Each Other's Humanity," in *Everyday Antiracism: Getting Real about Race in School*, ed. M. Pollock (New York: New Press, 2008), 58.

27. Sometimes students take it upon themselves to organize and engage politically and civically outside the context of a particular school-sponsored activity, and this is to be welcomed. Kirshner, *Youth Activism*. But schools can also sometimes appropriately support such activity and use it as touchstone for in-class civic reflection.

28. Sigal Ben-Porath, "Education for Shared Fate," in Allen and Reich, *Education, Justice, and Democracy.*

29. Allen, *Education and Equality*, 27–50. Although the civic area is Allen's main focus, she extends the participatory readiness idea to other domains of life. Allen also notes that the term *civic* is safer than *political* in the context of education (33). The latter more clearly highlights that the terrain in which the civic agent operates involves power and the challenging of power, in a context of injustice. For this reason we would accept referring to the educational goal we are describing as "political education" or "civic and political education." Nevertheless, the term *political* has a second association that complicates its use. It is often taken to mean "partisan," that is, aligned with a particular political party. Civic education should *not* be political in that sense. We will retain the "civic" terminology to avoid this semantic complexity, but we desire to make clear that our use of "civic" is very much engaged with social/racial injustice, by no means limited to action within conventional channels, and recognizes the importance of power.

30. Some literature has found a racial "civic empowerment gap" that favors advantaged students over disadvantaged ones—most famously Levinson, *No Citizen Left Behind.* We are not engaging with that overall finding but only pointing out that there are forms of civic knowledge (and perhaps practice as well) in which the gap goes in the other direction.

31. Gordon Allport, *The Nature of Prejudice* (New York: Basic Books, 1954). For a more recent comprehensive summary of studies in the contact hypothesis tradition, see Thomas Pettigrew and Linda Tropp, "A Meta-analytic Test of Intergroup Contact Theory," *Journal of Personality and Social Psychology* 90, no. 5 (2006): 751–83.

32. Our usage of "out-group" is the social science meaning of "a group other than a particular reference group, such as that of the subject," rather than the more colloquial "a marginalized or stigmatized group." In our use (the former meaning), it is a term of scholarly convenience and has no moral charge.

33. Although prejudice researchers recognized that prejudice could take semi-aware and unconscious forms, a more recent development toward an understanding of unconscious, or implicit, bias has deepened the prejudice paradigm and its importance in school settings. See Tracey A. Benson and Sarah E. Fiarman, *Unconscious Bias in Schools: A Developmental Approach to Exploring Race and Racism* (Cambridge, MA: Harvard Education Press, 2019).

34. Griffin, *Those Kids, Our Schools*, xi. The school in question is "exurban." Amanda

Lewis makes a similar point, drawing on observations from an earlier "pre-post-racial" period, about schools' minimizing of the racial aspect of incidents between students. Amanda Lewis, *Race in the Schoolyard: Negotiating the Color Line in Classrooms and Communities* (New Brunswick, NJ: Rutgers University Press, 2003), 22. Mica Pollock, *Colormute: Race Talk Dilemmas in an American School* (Princeton, NJ: Princeton University Press, 2005), treats this issue in great depth.

35. Charles W. Mills, "White Ignorance," from *Black Rights/White Wrongs: The Critique of Racial Liberalism* (New York: Oxford University Press, 2017), and elsewhere, and Brandon Buck, "Realizing Wokeness: White Schools, White Ignorance: Toward a Racially Responsive Pedagogy" (PhD diss., Teachers College, Columbia University, 2020), emphasize that white ignorance is produced as part of the system of white supremacy. It is not merely a free-floating, ungrounded failure to learn or know. Other writers have emphasized whites' responsibility to remedy their own ignorance without depending primarily on people of color to help them do so. See Shannon Sullivan, *Revealing Whiteness: The Unconscious Habits of Racial Privilege* (Bloomington: Indiana University Press, 2006). But the integrated classroom is a crucial setting for young people's remedying of this ignorance in a context dedicated to all students learning from all others.

36. "As Students of Color Surpass Whites, a Closer Look at the Numbers," *NBC News*, September 2, 2014, https://www.nbcnews.com/news/asian-america /students-color-surpass-whites-closer-look-numbers-n193811.

37. The number of Blacks at elite colleges who are children of immigrants is 27 percent, compared to 8 percent of the overall Black population at those colleges. Grace Kao, Elizabeth Vaquera, and Kimberly Goyette, *Education and Immigration* (Malden, MA: Polity, 2013), 125.

38. The organization American Descendants of Slavery (https://ados101.com/about -ados) advocates for the perceived distinctive needs and claims of this population, e.g., with respect to reparations. According to our argument in chapter 3, reparations are tied to a specific history and would not apply to recent African or Afro-Caribbean immigrants, at least not to anything like the same extent. Recognizing the historical, cultural, socioeconomic, and experiential differences between ethnically defined groups of Blacks need not lead to tensions among those groups, and many Blacks of all groups, while acknowledging those differences, regard the shared racial identity and race-based experience as central to a solidarity they feel across those ethnic subgroups. Similarly, Puerto Ricans and Mexicans are Latinx ethnic groups with very different histories that are acknowledged by all and need not lead to tension between them (though it sometimes does).

39. Sabrina Zirkel and Tabora Johnson, "Mirror, Mirror on the Wall: A Critical Examination of the Conceptualization of the Study of Black Racial Identity in Education," *Educational Researcher* 45, no. 5 (2016): 301–11. The authors include in their definition of strong Black identity "a racial consciousness of the historical, social, and cultural context of being Black in the United States, including a critical consciousness about race and racism" (302). They recognize that an attachment to being Black does not require this critical consciousness, and they

provide evidence that both forms of Black identity help produce positive educational and well-being outcomes. See also Prudence Carter, *Keepin' It Real: School Success beyond Black and White* (New York: Oxford University Press, 2007), and Angela Valenzuela, *Subtractive Schooling: US-Mexican Youth and the Politics of Caring* (Albany: Sate University of New York Press, 1999).

40. See the Vietnamese student example from chapter 2, 88–89.

41. Angela Valenzuela reports that Mexican American students said that their school disregarded their ties to their home language and culture and devalued Mexican American family life, so that the students felt their teachers did not care about them. Valenzuela, *Subtractive Schooling*, as cited in Kao, Vaquera, and Goyette, *Education and Immigration*, 135.

42. For example, a teacher may refrain from calling on a student from a minority group precisely because he is not sure how to negotiate making neither too much nor too little of the student's racial group membership in the way he calls on her or in how the other students will deal with her. Such "racial ignoring" is obviously not an appropriate solution to the concern. Dorinda Carter insightfully discusses hypervisibility, racial ignoring, and other challenges about Black identity in white-dominant classrooms in "Spotlighting and Ignoring Racial Group Members in the Classroom," in Pollock, *Everyday Antiracism*.

43. The Wells et al. study does suggest that some civic and moral attitudes can be improved in the absence of specific educational initiatives. The study's subjects spoke of improved racial attitudes while (as mentioned) decrying the absence in their schools of any education and discussion about racial matters. Wells et al., *Both Sides Now*. On the other hand, mere copresence, without elements of ideal integration built on it, can sometimes lead to greater, rather than less, hostility. John Diamond and Amanda Lewis, *Despite the Best Intentions: Why Racial Inequality Persists in Good Schools* (New York: Oxford University Press, 2015), 113.

44. Levinson, *No Citizen Left Behind*, describes an impressive program of "action civics" that is particularly suitable to schools with a preponderance of low-income Black and Latinx students.

45. In *Sheff v. O'Neill*, an important integration-related Connecticut Supreme Court case from the 1990s, a white plaintiff (among several plaintiffs, mostly Black) testified that white-predominant schools failed to prepare their (white) students, including him, for life in the multiracial world. Susan J. Eaton, *The Children in Room E4: American Education on Trial* (New York: Algonquin Books, 2009), 111.

46. The distinction between being comfortable sitting in the class and being comfortable challenging the dominant views was made by Chanthyna Chhay, a student in a high school class taught by one of the authors. Blum, *High Schools*, 174.

47. However, being the dominant racial group in society by no means always translates into feeling a sense of ownership, or even comfort, in a class in which the white student is a small minority—when the "critical mass" of white students is absent.

48. The Supreme Court's opinion in *Grutter* did not take an unequivocal stand on this issue, generally implying that the relevant group for critical mass was *all* students of color, but sometimes implying that the critical mass had to be of a specific group. (I am indebted to Adam Hosein for discussion of this point.)

49. An excellent sourcebook for suggestions about dealing productively with race in K–12 classes and schools is Mica Pollock's *Everyday Antiracism*.

50. Note that the forms of "comfort" discussed here do *not* include the comfort that derives from not having one's beliefs challenged in classes. In that particular respect, education should *not* be comfortable. Students across all racial groups need to learn to accept and respond constructively to respectful challenges to their views. This is fundamental to the educational enterprise.

 Note also that the "critical mass" way of thinking about comfort may be historically specific. Over time, students of racial minority groups may grow so accustomed to being in diverse, multiracial environments that they start to be made comfortable not by a critical mass of their own group but by the more general diversity itself. (Nadia Davila, a student in a high school class taught by one of the authors, voiced this view about herself. Blum, *High Schools*, 180.)

51. Note that in integrated classes where whites are a minority, or a small minority, their comfort may well require specific kinds of attention and regard, as discussed earlier with regard to the white girl in the Black literature class (see chap. 3, 126–27).

52. Integration without whites is discussed by Rachel Carver, "Segregation in Segregated Schools," in *School Integration Matters: Research-Based Strategies to Advance Equity*, ed. E. Frankenberg, L. Garces, and M. Hopkins (New York: Teachers College Press, 2016).

53. John Ogbu, *Black American Students in an Affluent Suburb: A Study in Academic Disengagement* (New York: Routledge, 2003); Griffin, *Those Kids, Our Schools*; Diamond and Lewis, *Despite the Best Intentions*.

54. Diamond and Lewis, *Despite the Best Intentions*, 91, 103.

55. Griffin, *Those Kids, Our Schools*, 58–59. The existence of middle-class Black, Latinx, and Native American populations also means that the capital argument—based primarily (though not entirely) on class rather than racial characteristics—could be satisfied by, for example, integrating low-income Blacks with middle-class Blacks and does not require distinctly *racial* integration.

56. Linn Posey-Maddox writes poignantly in her study of gentrifying schools of a smaller number of progressive whites who come to regret how their arrival transformed their local school to a white majority and displaced families of color from a position of strong influence in the school. Linn Posey-Maddox, *When Middle-Class Parents Choose Urban Schools* (Chicago: University of Chicago Press, 2014).

CONCLUSION

1. It is only *almost* always because, as we have seen, sometimes these communities have sought self-determination outside a framework where they are comparing their situation to that of others, especially whites, so equality with whites is not what they are seeking in those contexts.

2. Although *Brown* affirmed both the civic value of public education and the racial integration of schools, it did not specifically affirm the distinctive civic benefits of integrated education itself (e.g., prejudice reduction and cross-racial intellectual engagement and attachments).

INDEX

Page numbers in italics refer to figures.

Made in the USA
Middletown, DE
15 September 2022

10522527R00156